SEIZING JERUSALEM

SEIZING JERUSALEM

The Architectures of Unilateral Unification

ALONA NITZAN-SHIFTAN

A QUADRANT BOOK

University of Minnesota Press
Minneapolis
London

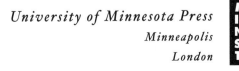

Quadrant, a joint initiative of the University of Minnesota Press and the Institute for Advanced Study at the University of Minnesota, provides support for interdisciplinary scholarship within a new, more collaborative model of research and publication.

Sponsored by the Quadrant Design and Architecture group (advisory board: John Archer, Marilyn Delong, Greg Donofrio, Ritu Bhatt, and Katherine Solomonson) and the University of Minnesota's College of Design.

QUADRANT Quadrant is generously funded by the Andrew W. Mellon Foundation.
http://quadrant.umn.edu.

This book is supported by a grant from the Graham Foundation for Advanced Studies in the Fine Arts.

Chapter 2 was originally published as "Seizing Locality in Jerusalem," in *The End of Tradition?*, ed. Nezar AlSayyad (London: Routledge, 2003), 231–55. Portions of chapters 4 and 5 were published in "Capital City or Spiritual Center? The Politics of Architecture in Post-'67 Jerusalem," *Cities* 22, no. 3 (2005): 229–40; as "Modernisms in Conflict: Architecture and Cultural Politics in Post-'67 Jerusalem," in *Modernism and the Middle East,* ed. Sandy Isenstadt and Kishwar Rizvi (Seattle: University of Washington Press, 2008), 161–82, copyright 2008, reprinted with permission of University of Washington Press; and as "'Frontier Jerusalem': The Holy Land as a Testing Ground for Urban Design," *Journal of Architecture* 16, no. 6 (2011): 915–40, available online at http://www.tandfonline.com. A portion of chapter 6 was published in Hebrew as "'Yesh Avanim im lev adam'—On Monuments, Modernism, and Conservation in the Western Wall," *Theory and Criticism* 38–39 (Winter 2011): 65–100.

The poem "Ecology of Jerusalem," by Yehuda Amichai, translated by Chana Bloch, is from *Poems of Jerusalem and Love Poems* (Riverdale-on-Hudson, N.Y.: Sheep Meadow Press, 1992). Reprinted by permission of Hana Amichai.

Every effort was made to obtain permission to reproduce material in this book. If any proper acknowledgment has not been included here, we encourage copyright holders to notify the publisher.

Published by the University of Minnesota Press
111 Third Avenue South, Suite 290
Minneapolis, MN 55401-2520
http://www.upress.umn.edu

Printed in the United States of America on acid-free paper

The University of Minnesota is an equal-opportunity educator and employer.

24   23   22   21   20   19   18   17   10   9   8   7   6   5   4   3   2   1

Library of Congress Cataloging-in-Publication Data
Names: Nitzan-Shiftan, Alona, author.
Title: Seizing Jerusalem : the architectures of unilateral unification / Alona Nitzan-Shiftan.
Description: Minneapolis : University of Minnesota Press, 2017. | A quadrant book. |
Includes bibliographical references and index. | Identifiers: LCCN 2017008999 (print) |
ISBN 978-0-8166-9427-3 (hc) | ISBN 978-0-8166-9428-0 (pb)
Subjects: LCSH: Architecture, Modern. | Architecture—Jerusalem. | Landscape design—Jerusalem. |
City planning—Jerusalem. | Nationalism and architecture—Jerusalem.
Classification: LCC NA1478.J4 N58 2017 (print) | DDC 720.95694/42—dc23
LC record available at https://lccn.loc.gov/2017008999

For Ruth and Yoav Nitzan

CONTENTS

PREFACE

> The air over Jerusalem is saturated with prayers and dreams
> like the air over industrial cities.
> It's hard to breathe.
>
> And from time to time a new shipment of history arrives
> and the houses and towers are its packing materials.
> Later these are discarded and piled up in dumps.
>
> And sometimes candles arrive instead of people
> and then it's quiet.
> And sometimes people come instead of candles
> and then there's noise.
>
> —*Yehuda Amichai, "Ecology of Jerusalem"*

I GREW UP IN JERUSALEM among the houses, stones, and dumps of several empires, two nation-states, and one nation without a state. As a child I did not recognize the extent to which the urban space around me was implicated in everything we did and thought. Only from afar, as an Israeli overseas, as an architect and scholar, could I begin to understand the crucial role that form and material and spatial configuration play in our lives; only from afar could I begin to see the histories and identities that the urban space of Jerusalem fostered and those it forbade. I learned that in Jerusalem (as in so many places around the world where people fight each other over land and history) this means that architecture inevitably intervenes in the predicament of conflict. Furthermore, as each new shipment of history arrives in Jerusalem, it unsettles the houses and towers that have stored previous deliveries.

In the long years I have spent writing this book, I knew that a critical architectural history of Jerusalem's unilateral unification was necessary—but was it possible? For scholars and journalists around the world Jerusalem is a site of perpetual violence: land confiscation, demolitions, the making and breaking of official treaties. But what is the spatial blueprint of this predicament? How were our conflicts created through the built environment? Our anxiety-ridden climate and its aggressions blur our capacity to historicize Jerusalem as a concrete city, to see its physical form and actual people, its vibrancy and beauty, the myriad tensions and connections embedded in urban space. Instead we are left with a relentless focus on violence, which I fear has turned into a trap more powerful than the instrumental utilization of Jerusalem's histories by its nationalist contenders.

Scholarship is undoubtedly political. Yet I desire a different type of engagement. I don't want to enlist critical tools just to advance one political agenda or another; rather, I want to challenge the dispositions that created, hardened, and weaponized these agendas. As an architect, I wish to study the making of the blueprint on which the current conflict plays out; to look for its logic in the stories of people and professions, of roads and parks, of debates over urban form and experiments in social housing. My aim in this book is therefore both modest and ambitious. I am offering an ethnography of the party in power, that is, of the Israeli architects and planners who shaped, from various positions of dominance, the urban unification they desired. I aspire to understand, through their thought and vocation, how spatial power works in Jerusalem; through them to probe the agency of architecture and urban design in the city's physical and conceptual transformation. The result is a city created and dominated by a huge variety of visions: this book unearths the ongoing competition between numerous architectural agendas and agencies, and thus reveals an entirely overlooked and divergent set of forces working in and over Jerusalem.

This proposition poses its own challenges. The field of architecture has long been held back by an idealized notion of its own autonomy and uncontaminated professionalism. The one architect who refused my request for an interview claimed that architecture is not political, but that in Jerusalem it has lost its integrity to politics. Another architect, left-leaning by Israeli standards, argued against the kind of new history that I was trying to write. "You can tell us," he contended, "that our work was caught in a web of political circumstances we did not account for, but you cannot retrospectively tell us that we *intended* to deprive Palestinians of their land and human rights." I believe that our field must move past these stubborn notions of our own innocence and our own autonomy. *Seizing Jerusalem* is my attempt to do that. I wish to examine how the disciplinary knowledge of architects and planners — their understanding of the ideas and praxis pervading their own domain — assumes agency in the predicament of conflict.

But can my own perspective—as an architect, as an Israeli—set claims for a legitimate historiography of this process? I am constantly asked to account for such questions by my vibrant students, whose political agendas (as secular or Orthodox Jews, as Arab Palestinians, both Muslim and Christian, as global residents of Tel Aviv or ardent settlers of the West Bank) often collide in my classroom. I have learned from them how difficult it is to unsettle national vocabularies but, as a result, how essential that process of unsettling is. This is where critical historiography assumes its own agency. The longer I worked on this book, the more I recognized it is an ethical project. My hope is that we can use history to provoke doubt and curiosity, and this knowledge, in turn, can prevent us from taking our own histories for granted. Throughout the writing of this book, my aim has been to open up—for myself, for my students, and for my readers—a landscape of uncertainties.

Rather than telling a unified story of architectural production, I aim to show how space remains porous despite the meanings imposed on it. Within this porousness, we can learn a great deal. Considering the ordinary issues that affect every city, the conflicts and compromises of urban space, offers us a temporary quiet—an essential moment of reflection. The more we explore, the more we see that histories are numerous and these different histories inevitably, and necessarily, coincide and collide. Studying any, and every, history of the city is useful as long as we remember that these histories exist in a field larger than one perspective can possibly grasp.

In our era of ideological extremes, I wish to argue for the benefits of a pause, for the necessity of listening, for the privilege of being unsure. In order to understand the inner contradictions embedded in the built environment of Jerusalem, we need to pose new questions, and we need to acknowledge—even celebrate—uncertainty. I aspire for less conviction, for smaller and deeper historical accounts, for reducing grand and binding narratives in favor of reckoning with the many dimensions simultaneously at work in the city. My analysis of this particular professional strain within Israel's corridors of power demonstrates, I hope, that the spatial politics of the world's most sacred and most contested city is the consequence of numerous urban engines roaring to life. Fifty years later, it is important to reflect on them and to examine how their efforts to unify led to new urban divisions that today camouflage the deprivation of Palestinians from their right to the holy city. I offer here a careful study of Israeli architecture and planning because it is only by immersing ourselves in the details, it is only by pausing to listen, that we can hear the many voices beneath the cacophony and see the many stories in the landscape all around us.

INTRODUCTION
ARCHITECTURE IN ACTION

The landscape we once regarded as pleasant suddenly became
shocking in its beauty and mysterious qualities . . . what are we
going to do with this magical city that we conquered, which is
not booty, but, rather, our home?

—*Michael Kuhn, "To Jerusalem with Love," November 10, 1967*
(translated from Hebrew)

O N THE SEVENTH OF JUNE 1967, the Israeli army stunned the
world (and itself) by seizing East Jerusalem from Jordan's control. Only three
weeks later, the Israeli government decided to unilaterally unify the eastern and western halves of Jerusalem, yoking together the newly occupied
center of Palestinian life and the capital city of the Israeli state. The result?
An unparalleled scheme to rebuild and relandscape one of the most important cities in the history of the world. Eager to transform the very meaning
of this emotionally charged city, Israeli officials turned Jerusalem—a town
of governmental bureaucracy and religious institutions, as sleepy as it was
divided—into a bustling urban laboratory. A small army of bureaucrats, local
architects, and numerous international luminaries participated in the fierce
competition over what the Holy City could, and should, look like. Over the
next decade, this small army envisioned many futures for the united city;
their beliefs, not only about the proper function of Jerusalem but just as
important about the ideologies of modern architecture and its many discontents, shaped different versions of the built landscape to come. By trac-
ing these competing agendas, we come to deeper understanding of the city
of Jerusalem and of the discipline of architecture, which we explore beyond
the production of built objects and beyond the legacies of individual genius.
In this light architecture and its attendant bodies of knowledge become
nothing less than political action manifested in space.

This is the first architectural history of how Israel created the physical blueprint for contemporary Jerusalem, during a momentous decade that
started in June 1967 and ended with the first political defeat of a Labor government in Israeli history. After the elections in the spring of 1977, Jerusalem's
liberal successors took over a city transformed: new municipal boundaries

encircled vast parcels of confiscated land, on which the neighborhoods, roads, parks, and public institutions of "United Jerusalem" were being feverishly constructed. Since, an ever-widening spectrum of people around the world—residents and pilgrims, terrorists and diplomats—have reckoned with the implications of this spatial transformation. As Jerusalem's built environment was shaped, the politics of these few square miles shaped conflicts around the world. Surprisingly, and in contrast to the overwhelming literature analyzing the results of these negotiations, we know very little about how this transformation came to be. In this charged landscape, steeped in violence, little attention is paid to the professional ideologies that informed the blueprint of United Jerusalem, and very little is known about the architects, planners, and agencies who articulated these ideologies in concrete and stone.[1]

The sources that inform our chronicle—recently released archival documents, alongside a dozen years of interviews with architects, planners, and public servants—shed new light on the compatibility (or lack thereof) between politics and architecture in post-1967 Jerusalem. Decades later, the results are still arresting: the years between 1967 and 1977 represented an overwhelming break with the modern architecture and ideology of urbanism that had dominated the built landscape of Israeli Jerusalem up until the 1960s. Instead, the new United Jerusalem would boast a visual basin of bare landscapes around the Old City (in which the past is either strategically preserved or carefully stripped away), meticulously orchestrated vistas, and a new building style eventually termed "Neo-orientalist." In a mere ten years, the look and feel of the city would be transformed in ways that even the key players did not anticipate.

In these same years, the broader profession of architecture would face some of its most significant challenges since World War II. The discipline itself was mired in the crisis of the modernist city and entangled in the controversial legacy of development; amid these problems, the ruptured evolution of Jerusalem's history posed an awesome, irresistible challenge. Local architects and bureaucrats brainstormed the future of the city together with luminaries from around the world, including Louis Kahn, Lewis Mumford, Buckminster Fuller, Nikolaus Pevsner, and Bruno Zevi. How, they asked, can the city's violent history—including the scars of several wars and nineteen years of division—be turned into an exemplary urban form? How can an ancient city, considered by many to be earth's gateway to heaven, be preserved while at the same time undergoing rapid development?

To prepare the ground for grappling with these questions, this introduction consists of three parts. The first is theoretical: it explains the concept of "architecture in action" and sets forth the compatibility between architectural and political modernist cultures that empowered architects' visions of

Jerusalem. The second is historical: it briefly introduces the ruptured modernity of the Holy City, culminating in the war of 1967 and its immediate aftermath. The third examines the role of architecture in inducing such historical change and how arguments about architectural modernism shape the politics of space in Jerusalem. The turmoil of these years animates the theoretical thrust of this book—how competing ideas come to be articulated in space.

Articulating Ideas in Concrete and Stone

The building of United Jerusalem tells the story of the relationship between architecture and politics—between the daily life of culture and the abstractions of ideology. It may seem odd to think of our built environment as so entangled with the ephemeral world of ideas and beliefs, and yet that tangle is one of the unsettling quandaries of the human condition. Terry Eagleton points to the power that our abstractions can have:

> One can understand well enough how human beings may struggle and murder for good material reasons—reasons connected, for instance, with their physical survival. It is much harder to grasp how they may come to do so in the name of something as apparently abstract as ideas. Yet ideas are what men and women live by, and will occasionally die for.[2]

Eagleton's query reminds us that for people around the world, Jerusalem is both a city and an idea, and for people in the Middle East it is an idea compelling enough to live for and to die for. How was the idea of Jerusalem articulated in concrete and stone? How do thoughts and beliefs manifest as a physical environment, one that bestows on its residents (both actual and virtual) a palpable sense of belonging, identification, and commitment?

The two pervasive approaches to the study of Jerusalem's architecture offer little insight into this perplexity. The standard story frames architects as individuals of great professional merit who eventually surrendered to the outsized political pressures of the Holy City.[3] The more recent, and more critical, depiction frames architects as collaborators with the instrumental politics of territorial dispossession.[4] In the first narrative, architecture poses an autonomous set of values that often clashes with official politics; in the second, architecture provides a physical means to achieve the objectives of official politics. Architects are rendered as either apolitical or pro-occupation, but the professional discipline and its internal dynamics, in both cases, are by and large depoliticized, if not ignored altogether.

This study argues instead for the agency of architecture, which is seen neither as a mere reflection of the agenda of individual architects, nor as a spatial technique representing meaning beyond its confines. Instead, I study architecture as a spatial, visual, and material articulation of ideas. Buildings and urban landscapes, in other words, contain our beliefs. As a result, architecture is both the embodiment of ideas and—especially in areas of national conflicts—participates in framing the way we see nation and faith, ethnicity and history, citizenship and the market. From this perspective, architecture is a verb, a spatial form of action, a mode of operating and politicizing space.

But while architecture is an active form, I do not see it as an instrumental means toward a predetermined political end. Like other aspects of culture, architecture is not driven primarily by shared values or governed only by political interests. As Ann Swidler argues, "a culture is not a unified system that pushes action in a consistent direction. Rather, it is like a 'toolkit' or repertoire from which actors select different pieces for constructing lines of action."[5] Accordingly, if we want to understand how architects act we must consider their professional "toolkit"—the knowledge, skills, and practices architects deem the essence of their professional culture. It is the know-how by which architecture is articulated. With that toolkit, architecture creates both a discursive and spatial reality, which shapes, at times unpredictably, both the actual place and the politics of space in Jerusalem.

But what is the causal link between architecture as it appears in the usual manifestations of any professional culture—school curriculums, professional magazines, seminal texts, and the exhibitions and work of the field's most admired practitioners—and the act of designing and constructing architecture in a particular site within a specific social, political, and economic culture? How does architectural knowledge travel, and how does it interact with different contexts, particularly in contested sites where any architectural action immediately triggers spatial politics?

The key to this query is the proposition to study modernism as parallel phenomena in aesthetic and political cultures. We are used to conceptualizing modernism as an aesthetic response to the challenges of modernity, an encompassing condition of global ramification that stands beyond cultural and geographical specificities. The politics of nation-states seem to offer the opposite: they are place bound, culturally specific, and legitimated by primordial sentiments. But, as Etienne Balibar demonstrates, the culture, territory, and ethnicity of the modern nation-state are also distinct forms responding to the modern condition.[6] We can therefore see in "the nation form" he theorizes an instance of political modernism. If we study the correlation between architectural and political modernisms, we can better understand how architecture assumed its political power in Jerusalem.

In 1967, the discipline of architecture and its modernist practitioners were caught between the age of the grand and binding narratives of interwar modernism and the provocative rebellion of postmodernism that erupted in full force in the mid- to late 1970s. Architects working in the in-between years of the 1950s and 1960s were advocates of modernism but were nevertheless critical of its implications—its complicity in modernization projects that erased cultural specificities and consequently produced alienating environments.

That feeling of being caught in between, and the attendant criticisms that emerged, created a conflict at the heart of the dizzying decade that started in 1967. The challenge of building a united Jerusalem unearthed a theme at the center of this book: a fundamental struggle between what we call developmental modernism, driven toward progress and development,[7] and situated modernism, committed to place and to disciplinary memory and to salvaging the autonomy of architecture and the specificity of its implementation.[8]

Jerusalem became a monumental testing ground for these competing modernisms because the Israeli political culture was undergoing a similar conflict. Politically, its nation-building project—the *mamlachtiyut* (which has typically been translated as "statism")—advocated "progress and development" as a national motto. But culturally, that same *mamlachtiyut* (which is more literally translated as "kingdomism") stressed the ties to the land and its biblically inspired culture and meshed Israeli identity with Jewish tradition and historical continuity.

The making of United Jerusalem is therefore rendered in this book against two corresponding crises: the crisis of the modernist city that provoked a transition from developmental to situated modernism, and the failure of the Israeli legacy of progress and development and its related vision of architecture to address the symbolism of the historical moment of 1967. The many faces of these transitions cemented powerful ties between politics and architecture, allowing different parties to argue their cases through multiple modern forms. By studying them together a new light is shed both on the history of Jerusalem and on architectural development.[9] Before we turn to see how architecture affects historical change, let's get acquainted with the historical predicaments of the Holy City.

Inconsistent Modernization

Jerusalem reluctantly entered modernity under the Ottoman Empire, whose four-century rule over the city lasted until World War I. During the 1830s, the governor of Egypt, Ibrahim Pasha, conquered Jerusalem and allowed the British to establish the first foreign consulate in Jerusalem. After European nations helped the Ottomans to drive the pasha away in 1840, they were rewarded with permission for missionary work in Jerusalem. The Ottomans issued multiple permits to build churches, monasteries, and hospitals, provoking a competition between these nations over the city's most desirable precincts. European and Arab entrepreneurs started building outside the city walls in the mid-nineteenth century. In 1860 Jews constructed their first neighborhood, Mishkenot Sha'ananim, on the edge of the Hinnom Valley.

Although no master plan was issued, an infrastructure of roads and railroads caused commerce to sprawl outside the city walls. In 1898 one section of the wall was broken near the Jaffa Gate to accommodate the visit of Germany's Kaiser Wilhelm II and the promise for progress his trip symbolized. Clock towers, like the one installed near this opening in 1907, signaled the synchronization of the Ottoman Empire with the clicking clock of Western modernization. When the Ottomans peacefully surrendered the city to the British on December 9, 1917, the Mamilla Quarter, which sprawled from the Jaffa Gate along the aqueduct bringing water from the Mamilla pool, was already a thriving commercial quarter, consisting of two- and three-story buildings that extended all the way to the exterior of the city walls.[10]

The British carried with them the promise of modern planning and the Orientalist desire to promote Jerusalem's authentic sanctity. In 1920, the League of Nations granted the British their mandate to rule Jerusalem. Under the British Mandate, ideological brands of modern nationalism—pan-Arabist, Zionist, and Palestinian—enhanced latent divisions among the multicultural population of Palestine, leading, in due course, to one of the world's most persistent and violent national conflicts.[11] Armed clashes between Arabs and Jews during the Mandate foreshadowed numerous wars between Israel and Arab countries.

The British also turned Jerusalem—a rather provincial city during Ottoman rule—into their capital, a symbolic seat of power over the Orient. Modernization took a faster track under their command: the British introduced planning administration, advanced modern industry, developed infrastructure for water, electricity, and transport, issued master plans and building permits, and built numerous governmental institutions. Modern Haifa was the urban frontier of these developments, which the British planned to be the industrial outlet of the Middle East.[12] But they also considered themselves custodians of local traditions, a calling they ardently followed in Jerusalem, which they saw as sacred to all mankind. Charles Robert Ashbee, a renowned leader of the Arts and Crafts movement, shaped Britain's initial plan for Jerusalem as the head of the Pro-Jerusalem Society.[13] Ron Fuchs and Gilbert Herbert term the result "colonial regionalism," hinting at the benevolent imposition of Jerusalem's supposed authenticity on a population wishing to enter modern life.[14] Britain succeeded in marrying the seemingly contradictory poles of modern planning and Orientalist imagery, and thus simultaneously innovated and preserved a desired image of the past.

By inducing modern nationalism alongside Orientalist sensibilities, the

British also provoked, as Daniel Monk convincingly argues, a major shift in the perception of sacred spaces in Jerusalem—instead of just managing their uses, they started managing the claims for these uses. Driven to justify such claims, contending parties constantly invested Jerusalem's sacred monuments with new meanings; these meanings both furthered their claims to the city and also reflected their various modernities. Since their modern identities were animated by emerging nationalisms, each group inscribed its ideal notion of nation on the monuments it claimed. As a result, Arabs and Jews, who would soon become known as Palestinians and Israelis, started rendering the connection between the form of these monuments and the constantly renewed meaning they assumed as primordial and transparent, as if form and meaning had been ontologically one since the dawn of history. Once monuments were appreciated as the "foundation stones" of different national parties, politicians could demand from their constituencies a sense of unconditioned commitment to protect them, a duty to live or die for.[15]

Indeed, in 1948, when the British published their fifth and last master plan for Jerusalem,[16] the bitter war had already erupted. It was triggered by the UN decision, on November 29, 1947, to split Mandate Palestine into two nation-states, one Jewish, the other Arab, and keep Jerusalem under international rule. The ensuing year and a half of violence—known to Israelis as the War of Independence, and to Palestinians as the *Nakba* (disaster)—left Jerusalem divided between Israel and Jordan. On December 5, 1949, David Ben Gurion declared Jerusalem, despite international protest, "the eternal capital" of the State of Israel. His agreement with King Abdullah of Jordan ignored the UN decision to internationalize the heart of this sacred city and consequently marginalized Palestinian claims to the city over the next four decades.

Between 1947 and 1949 the Palestinians living west of the Old City, in Baq'a, Qatamon, Talibiyya, Mamilla, and the German Colony, lost their homes.[17] By July 1948 only thirty-three thousand of the city's sixty-four thousand Palestinian inhabitants remained in the Arab part of Jerusalem.[18] The Jordanian Old City was filled with refugees. In April 1949 Israel and Jordan signed an armistice agreement. When Jordan assumed sovereignty over the West Bank and Jerusalem in 1949, it was wary of its large Palestinian population's affinity with Jerusalem and thus focused attention on Amman, the capital of the Hashemite Kingdom on the East Bank of the Jordan River. Jordan intentionally kept Jerusalem provincial and limited its growth.[19] The entire developed area of East Jerusalem did not exceed six square kilometers (less than 2.5 square miles). The shortage of land created "ribbon development" where suburbs grew without the option of extending the municipal boundary. A new commercial and administrative center was gradually established northwest of the Old City.[20]

Following the course of the 1949 armistice line, the buffer zone wrapped the Old City and its environs. It separated West Jerusalem from the symbolic sites in the East. Israelis could see the Old City across the Hinnom Valley, but Jordanian snipers prevented any physical access. Instead, Israelis developed their semi-isolated West Jerusalem into a modernist capital by building governmental, educational, and memorial precincts away from the Old City.[21] The urban landscape of the two Jerusalems—one ancient and timidly modernized, the other young and symbolically modern—grew more and more divergent.

As the 1960s went on, Israel sunk into an economic recession. By 1967, this fiscal strain was heightened by the anxiety of a possible military confrontation. The Arab states bordering Israel were making alarming and bellicose gestures. There was doubt, both in Israel and overseas, that the country would survive the impending war. In May mutual deterrence between Israel and its neighbors escalated: to military clashes along the northern border with Syria, to an Egyptian evacuation of UN forces, and to a siege of Israel's southern waterways. On June 5, Israel preemptively attacked Egypt and Syria. Jordan, probably misled by Egyptian reports from the battlefield on the southern border, simultaneously launched its own attack on West Jerusalem, ignoring Israeli calls for a cease-fire. By the end of the first day the Israeli government was still considering whether its counterattack should include the Old City, fearing international pressure and damage to sacred sites. But the U.S. and the USSR's plan for cease-fire triggered quick action: Israeli troops entered the Old City on the morning of June 7, and by midday they had already seized the area and its sacred sites (Figure I.1). It was the climax of a war that lasted less than a week but almost immediately became a watershed in the

Figure I.1. An Israeli command car entering the Old City via the Dung Gate during the Six Day War, waving an improvised national flag. Al Aqsa Mosque is in the background. June 7, 1967. Photograph by Micha Bar Am; courtesy of Magnum Photos.

political history of the Arab/Israeli conflict and the international politics of the increasingly chilly Cold War. By the end of the Six Day War, Israel had wrested the Sinai Peninsula from Egypt, the Golan Heights from Syria, and from Jordan, the Palestinian-populated West Bank and, most significantly, East Jerusalem.[22]

Compact Together

To prove their new and unexpected ownership of East Jerusalem, Israelis hurried to create irreversible "facts on the ground."[23] The war's leaders quickly claimed that the right to build was "authorized" by biblical texts, including a verse from Psalm 122, "Jerusalem is built as a city that is compact together" (Figure I.2). Some decisions were insightful, like Moshe Dayan's insistence on leaving the Temple Mount precinct, the Islamic al-Haram al-Sharif, in the hands of the Muslim Waqf. Others were dictated by the desire to preempt international intervention. For more than two weeks, from June 11 to 27, the Israeli government deliberated the most urgent question: Jerusalem's territorial unification. The debate was contentious. Municipal politicians fought for a compact, manageable city; military personnel sought a broad buffer

Figure I.2. Throwing down the partition between the two parts of Jerusalem in June 1967, captioned with the text "Jerusalem is built as a city that is compact together . . . (Psalm 122:3)." Photograph by Photo Ross, Jerusalem. Source: Israel State Archive, TT/57/1.

In June 1967 the partition between the two parts of Jerusalem was thrown down

"...יְרוּשָׁלַיִם הַבְּנוּיָה כְּעִיר אֲשֶׁר חֻבְּרָה לָהּ יַחְדָּו..."
(תְּהִלִּים קכ״ב ג)

zone to ward off further attacks. From this discord arose a radical plan: the 9,000 acres of Israeli West Jerusalem would be combined with the 250 acres of the Old City and the 1,750 acres of Jordanian East Jerusalem, along with 19,000 acres of the still-rural surrounding lands, to make a united city of nearly 30,000 acres.[24] This new Jerusalem, with the stroke of a pen, tripled the size of the prewar city and doubled its population. The roughly two hundred thousand residents of West Jerusalem and sixty-six thousand residents of the East would grow in two decades into a city of over five hundred thousand inhabitants, over a quarter of which were Palestinians.[25]

Legally, Israelis labored to achieve dominion without annexation. Any overt taking of land from Palestinian owners, according to the Ministry of Foreign Affairs, might plant the seed of violence and of future jihad.[26] Municipal procedures provided the solution. On June 28, 1967, the Israeli parliament (the Knesset) approved an adjustment to the country's municipal command: the minister of the interior was now allowed to change the municipal boundaries of any given city. The consequent urban expansion of Jerusalem simply enacted this hours-old Israeli law in the occupied East. Israel would repudiate the ensuing accusation by the UN Security Council against its unilateral unification by claiming that the boundary redrawing was only an administrative procedure, merely a technical effort in the attempt to settle postwar chaos.[27]

The government immediately enshrined the irreversibility of the unification, a tenet that stood sacred for more than three decades, reconsidered only after Prime Minister Ehud Barak agreed (in principle) to split the city in July 2000. Once unification was reached, the government developed a policy based on several goals that would seem feasible during the postwar years, but that eventually proved to be either too ambitious or just misguided.[28] First was enforcing territorial hold over East Jerusalem. This resulted in an industrious building campaign that encircled Jerusalem with housing for Jews. These residential blocs facilitated the second goal: the Judaization of the city, a goal that was undermined by the labor migration of Palestinians who constructed the Jewish settlement of East Jerusalem. The goal of developing an economic infrastructure for this enlarged city met with only limited success.[29]

The Israeli quest to rule the Arab minority was also an unsuccessful goal. In fact, it was a disaster. Unlike Palestinians who stayed in Israel after the 1948 war and became Israeli citizens, residents of East Jerusalem refused to allow Israeli rule to become normal: they rejected compensation for their confiscated land, they objected to Israeli intervention in their civil life, and they declined participation in the political body of Israel.[30] This greatly helped Palestinians to undermine yet another Israeli goal: achieving international legitimacy for their rule. With Israel's official declaration in 1980 that it ruled over East Jerusalem, most foreign embassies departed from Jerusalem to Tel Aviv.[31]

The Symbol and Its Discontents

Israel's initial civil actions, the beginning of its physical blueprint of United Jerusalem, were taken on June 10, 1967, even before the short war ended. Though enormously contentious, and endlessly debated, unity happened fast. By the time Egypt and Syria countered Israel's victory, with their own attack in October 1973, the blueprint of the unified city was already set: new municipal boundaries encircled vast parcels of confiscated land, upon which neighborhoods, roads, parks, and public institutions were being rapidly constructed.

For most Israelis, the conquest of East Jerusalem and the city's reunification became a powerful metaphor for Jews uniting with their past. But perhaps even more significant was the symbolic resolution of the contradiction between a modern territorial state and a primordial Jewish nation. In unifying Jerusalem's two halves, Israelis could simultaneously mesh state power with national heritage, an essential condition for a legitimate nation-state, and a key to fulfill its nation-building project, called *mamlachtiyut* ("statism," or literally, "kingdomism").

That effort at unification required the cooperation of many others around the world. Israelis took seriously the sanctity of Jerusalem to the three monotheistic religions and saw the safeguarding of sacred sites as an essential premise of their unification efforts. However, Israel's political aspirations were painfully at odds with Christians and Muslims, with Palestinians and foreign countries, each rife with its own internal conflicts. Israelis were even split among themselves, between the need to modernize the city, the drive to settle it with Jews in fear of another genocide, the desire to elevate it as a national symbol of the postcolonial state, and the plea to beautify the city as an emblem of universal spirit. These often-conflicting aspirations provoked internal tensions that would shape nearly every decision about the form of this rapidly evolving city.

European and American visitors added their own aspirations: Jerusalem represented not only a grand experiment, a remedy to anxieties about the fate of the modernist city, but also a window of opportunity to reenact the UN resolution—passed in 1947 and mostly ignored in the two decades since—to internationalize Jerusalem. Europeans and Americans hoped they could free this sensual, beloved city from the political claims of contending nation-

Figure I.3. "The sheikh in charge of the mosques on the Haram-al-Sharif (known to Jews as the Temple Mount) watches Israeli soldiers at the Western Wall (the Wailing Wall) which they had captured just a few hours earlier." June 7, 1967. Photograph by Micha Bar Am; courtesy of Magnum Photos.

states, the memory of which as former colonies was still fresh in their imperial memories.[32] At the same time, and conspicuously so, the international contest over the planning of Jerusalem, just like its Israeli counterpart, rarely consulted the Arab world and the Palestinian residents of Jerusalem.

Today, the national struggle between Israel and Palestine over the possession of Jerusalem, both its physical reality and its history, is ongoing. Yet during the first decade after the Six Day War Palestinians had little, if any, influence on the physical shape of Jerusalem. The occupation of Jerusalem in 1967 was a second disaster to the Palestinians, who had already experienced massive dislocation and exile in 1948 (Figure I.3). The trauma was overwhelming, and building up an independent political voice, let alone a planning apparatus, took decades.[33]

During the first decade following the 1967 War, Jordan was the only significant force contesting the Israelization of Jerusalem. Indeed, it only surrendered its claim to sovereignty over the West Bank—to the Palestine Liberation Organization (PLO)—in July 1988. The PLO, in turn, had been established in 1964 and was recognized in 1974 by the Arab League as the sole legitimate representative of the Palestinian people. But the PLO did not consolidate its power in Jerusalem until the 1980s, culminating in the first intifada (1987–93) that eventually won the PLO an international legitimacy in the ongoing negotiations over the Holy City.[34]

Israelis simply refused (and continue refusing) to share municipal power with Palestinian officials. They dispersed the Jordanian municipality of Jerusalem as early as June 28, 1967, aiming to subsume its power within a united municipal government, obviously led by Israelis.[35] In turn, Arab leaders decided that as long as Jerusalem was occupied, a condition they considered temporary, they would reject even the mere evaluation of the city's urban landscape. This policy evolved into a consistent refusal to participate in any planning effort, as in all other areas of municipal governance, that Israelis initiated and might have indicated Arab approval of Israeli occupation. Only in 2001 did the consolidation of Palestinian institutions in Jerusalem mature into a new master plan for the Old City of Jerusalem, which was published in Arabic (followed by an English publication in 2003). According to its authors—the Welfare Association—it was the first Palestinian plan for the city.[36]

The various contenders for Jerusalem express the fierce emotions that persistently animate the competition over the city's symbolic resources. In the monotheistic traditions, Jerusalem is a focus of longing, a formative idea as much as—if not more than—an actual place. As the psalmist decrees, "If I forget thee, O Jerusalem, May my right hand forget her skill. May my tongue cling to the roof of my mouth, If I do not remember you, If I do not exalt Jerusalem, Above my chief joy" (Psalm 137:5–6). According to the biblical text, the idea of Jerusalem eclipses the joys and sorrows of life. The steeper the conflict over Jerusalem gets, the more demanding is the commitment to this idea. Today, the city's stone walls are dotted with posters of Palestinian martyrs and Israeli settlers, the latest in an endless string of reminders that Jerusalem as a city—perhaps *the* city—is worthy of the greatest sacrifices. A popular Israeli song that was written following the occupation of East Jerusalem put this seeming truism in the bluntest terms. Ecstatic Jews chanted to the city: "In our blood, Live! In our blood, Live!"[37] How did architecture respond to such visceral motivations?

Architecture and Historical Change

There is no doubt that the definitive decisions shaping United Jerusalem were made by politicians in the Knesset, in the UN assembly halls, in the American State Department, and in their related legal offices. Yet we do not live in legal documents. The budget allocations of bureaucratic planners are a world away from our hearts and minds; the lines and symbols of a building's blueprint may be of passing interest but do not capture the longings of life.

Instead, we make sense of the world by what we encounter, what we see and feel and consume. But this is precisely why architecture is so important: all of our encounters, all of the seeing and feeling and consuming that we do, is framed by the built environment in which we live. Because architecture is a culture in action, because it is capable of articulating political ideas in matter, space, and form, it is incredibly effective in mediating grand ideas into the practices of our daily lives.[38]

Kim Dovey explains that the efficacy of this mediation lies in its inconspicuousness. He draws on Pierre Bourdieu, for whom "The most successful ideological effects are those that have no words, and ask no more than complicitous silence."[39] Architecture, Dovey argues, operates in this fashion. Its perception is immediate and sensual. It requires no words and asks for no attention. It is consumed in a distracted manner, through sight, touch, and movement. According to Walter Benjamin, its tactile appropriation is established by habit, which governs its optical reception as well. We notice architecture in an incidental fashion; no matter how strong our first impressions, we soon get used to the buildings around us. Our built environment becomes second nature.[40] In fact, as Dovey convincingly argues, "The more that the structures and representations of power can be embedded in the framework of everyday life, the less questionable they become and the more effectively they can work."[41]

This framework is why architecture forms a crucial conduit in historical turning points. Israeli Jews made sense of the 1967 watershed—a victory so astonishing they found it hard to grasp—through daily practices: they moved apartments, integrated into a new neighborhood, created new routine on new streets. The appropriation of East Jerusalem happened first by military might; the far more consequential appropriation, however, happened through the daily habits of everyday Israelis. When they took their kids to school, they moved through new clusters of stone-clad housing, through gates, arched colonnades, and pedestrian alleyways that embedded the Jerusalemite vocabulary into their everyday practices. New houses were built both rapidly and intentionally; their Oriental details were an effort to make new residents feel at home, to pacify the alienation that earlier generations of new immigrants felt toward the mass-produced, plain, reductive housing blocks of the 1950s. These designs *of the place,* however, induced not only greater identification and a significant social mobility, but also, and more important in this context, an effective habituation of political change.

Beyond subtle changes to daily life, the Israeli occupation of East Jerusalem created monumental logistical challenges. After the 1967 war, Israel viewed its victorious acquisition of East Jerusalem with both excitement and bewilderment. Admittedly, Israel held the great Temple Mount and the Jewish Quarter, but the physical fabric of East Jerusalem contrasted so heavily with West Jerusalem that it was unclear what the proper approach for this new Jerusalem should be.[42] The obvious choice was to develop Jerusalem with *sachlich* modernism, the matter-of-fact, bare, and efficient modernism that state agencies had mastered so well in the previous two decades. Yet that style would have deepened the rift between modern West Jerusalem and the ancient city Israel had just seized. East Jerusalem, after all, stood for the idea of Jerusalem because it housed Jerusalem's most precious monuments. The resulting challenge—to revise Israeli architectural practices in order to create a sublime urban landscape, one worthy of Jerusalem itself—became a magnet for numerous architects and numerous methodologies.

Building Narrative

There was no agreement about how to turn the military occupation of East Jerusalem and the political unification of the two Jerusalems into a coherent spatial reality; the structure of this book follows the fierce competition that ensued over the shape and meaning Jerusalem would assume under Israeli rule. The two Israeli parties at the center of this competition were, on the one hand, the state, operating primarily through the Ministry of Housing that was responsible for the new housing built in the outer ring of East Jerusalem, and on the other hand, the city, namely Jerusalem's mayor, Teddy Kollek, and his allies who shaped the open spaces and institutions of the sacred core. Each trusted a different strand of architectural culture to deliver the meaning they wanted their share of the spoil to convey. Our focus on the state and the city thus leads us to an ethnography of the architectural profession itself: to analyzing the rise to power of the sabra circle of architects working with the state and the innovative work of an overlooked group of Anglo architects that Kollek championed.

To understand their architectural agency in Jerusalem, chapter 1 further theorizes the parallels we introduced above between the architectural and political cultures active in Jerusalem and the correlation between their modernist forms. More specifically, it tells the intellectual history of the encounter between architectural and Zionist modernisms and analyzes the simultaneous search of these two modernist movements for a mythical origin as a way to secure their future. Ultimately, the vision of a unified Jerusalem served the desperate circumstances of both ideologies.

Chapter 2 examines the first party: the powerful generation of sabra (Israeli-born) architects, who wished to anchor Israeli architecture in the lives of its citizens by articulating an authentic specificity in their designs. They sought the direct and crude lingua franca of the place instead of the high modernism of early statehood, architecture they considered hygienic and efficient yet cold and alienating. In Israel, the premodern vernacular architecture they sought was, for the most part, Palestinian. This chapter analyzes how architects turned the Palestinian vernacular into a blueprint for Israeli architecture by casting it as biblical, primitive, and Mediterranean. The architecture of the conquered "other" could thus foster Israeli architectural ethics, a vision in which housing became a national home rather than a mere roof over one's head. Such architecture, the sabras hoped, could fulfill the post-1967 mandate of turning confiscated land into a wishfully familiar home and a stronghold of uniquely Israeli architecture.

The home of these sabra architects was the Ministry of Housing, the focus of chapter 3. As a powerful state agency, this ministry was responsible for executing the government's primary policy for the city—a demographic Judaization of Jerusalem. The Zionist goal of building irreversible Jewish facts on the ground was hitherto planned by developmental modernists who advocated rural, working settlements. Israel's sudden victory in 1967 reversed that trend, a shift that required a new understanding of urban architecture—a situated modernism for Jerusalem. This chapter first studies a pivotal project, Ma'alot Dafna, which was built on land confiscated in 1968 and inaugurated a new Jerusalem style inspired by the work of Team 10 and others exploring the place of Man and community in cities worldwide. The subsequent settlement of land confiscated in 1970 resulted in three large housing estates, each the size of a new, middle-class town. Despite their seeming visual similarity, they embody very different architectural ideologies. The zealous yet futile objection of Kollek and his allies to such industrious construction was pivotal in asserting power relations between city and state.

Teddy Kollek, Jerusalem's popular and embattled mayor from 1965 to 1993, realized that he could not halt the ministry's industrious building of East Jerusalem. His retreat is usually attributed to his weakness vis-à-vis the Ministry of Housing, against which the municipality could boast excellent public relations but no resources. In chapter 4 I argue that Kollek developed instead a powerful form of cultural politics, according to which the universal spirituality of Jerusalem is embedded in its urban beauty. He drew inspiration from the British, whose planning practices were informed by the picturesque and Orientalist traditions and were geared toward protecting Jerusalem as a visual idea central to mankind. This chapter examines the institutional and financial apparatus Kollek created in order to advance his cultural politics, and the Anglo-inspired architects he nurtured within the municipality and in allied agencies. The chapter focuses on the design of the Walls of Jerusalem National Park and on the municipal Urban Planning Unit, whose high-rise policy and design-by-planning method help us understand how the political imaginary of Jerusalem's seemingly matter-of-fact landscapes was managed.

Part of the way Kollek circumvented the power of the state was by realizing that Jerusalem's most pressing frontier lay overseas. In order to legitimate Israeli rule over his contested city, Kollek called upon the international community to share custody over Jerusalem. Chapter 5 tells the story of Kollek's Jerusalem Committee, an advisory group of seventy luminaries who agreed to help shepherd Jerusalem into its new identity, but by the same token advanced their own desires and motivations. Lewis Mumford, for example, insisted that Jerusalem was the threshold of a postnationalist world order; Louis Kahn, meanwhile, insisted that Jerusalem was the place to revive the primary notion of human institutions. During its 1970 meeting the committee shredded Jerusalem's modernist master plan, a flagship document painstakingly prepared just two years earlier by all of Israel's major planning agencies. Five years later, architects Lawrence Halprin, Jacob "Jaap" Bakema, and Denys Lasdun turned Jerusalem into a laboratory for the nascent discipline of urban design, arguing against city officials that design, rather than planning, carries the potential of healing the ruptured city and undoing the scars of modernization, division, and occupation.

Such healing was needed at the foot of Temple Mount. Israelis bulldozed the Palestinian Mughrabee Quarter that stood at the foot of the Western Wall before the 1967 war had even ended. Moshe Safdie proposed not only to heal the ensuing urban scar, but arguably to spatialize and concretize the *mamlachtiyut* ideology and its historical narrative. Safdie's sketches, writings, and interviews reveal a systematic search, inspired by the biomorphological studies of D'Arcy Thompson and allied with the pattern language of Christopher Alexander, for the genetic code of the place, for the inner truth and nonarbitrary performance of its structure-form. The last chapter follows in detail Safdie's design process and explains why his unique meshing of archeology, vernacularism, morphology, and prefabricated technology eclipsed proposals by Isamu Noguchi and Louis Kahn, among others. As a proposed embodiment of the *mamlachtiyut* project, however, Safdie's design would ultimately accelerate the dissolution of the unity it symbolized.

In 1987, after twenty years of occupation, Palestinians embarked on an organized battle for independence from Israel. Two Palestinian intifadas (the first uprising lasted from 1987 to 1993, and the second started in 2000, reached its climax in 2002–3, and eventually continued in the Gaza Strip) further shaped Jerusalem and continue to challenge the principles underlying the unilateral unification of Jerusalem during the post-1967 decade. After three decades of suicide bombing, house demolitions, bypass roads, and the eventual construction of a Separation Wall that runs through East Jerusalem, one can no longer identify the professional intentions of architects in the postwar decade.

They wished to protect Jerusalem from aggressive modernization, to focus on Man and his community as the center of architectural production, and to localize and habituate Israeli architecture in its place. Current events render these professional efforts—based on ideas architects shared with their contemporaries overseas—vulnerable. In Jerusalem they are inevitably and inextricably entangled in ideologies that compromise both the residents of Jerusalem and the democratic values to which they are entitled. By way of conclusion we will therefore examine architectural knowledge through the lens of human rights and manifold definitions of democracy.

ENCOUNTERS
MODERN ARCHITECTURE AND
ISRAELI NATIONALISM

> As you approach Jerusalem from the valley, the road ascends
> to a crest overlooking the western hills of the city. Down the
> slopes, a deserted Arab village hugs the hill, small and larger
> cubes made of the stone of the mountain: domes, arches,
> vaults, the mosque's tower, shaded passages, all in harmony
> with the landscape and the sun. At the summit of the hill is a
> series of long four-story apartment structures built in the late
> fifties. They do violence to the mountain. They are foreign, as
> if imported from some rainy, cool European suburb.

> —*Moshe Safdie,* Beyond Habitat

Visitors approaching jerusalem from the west—until June
1967 the only approach under Israeli sovereignty—witnessed an unexpected
sight on the edge of the Holy City: a modernist housing complex (Figure 1.1).
These seemingly incongruous buildings were even promoted in the Ministry
of Housing's publication *Israel Builds* as a flagship government project for Israel's second decade. Known as Upper Lifta (today's Romema), this complex
of free-standing buildings is built on the city's edge, just above the ruins of
the Palestinian village of Lifta, which young architects would come to admire a decade later. The taller H-shaped buildings are built behind two-story
rectangular buildings, the long facade of which stretched along the urban
boundary. The buildings' envelopes reveal the prefabricated method of their
construction and the precise manner in which the identical apartments are
composed and stacked one on top of the other. Built on a platform and raised
on *piloti* (a series of free-standing columns) the new neighborhood is clearly
distinguished from the seemingly arid wilderness underneath; it is, indeed,
its antithesis.

A decade and a half later, the same official publication boasted another
housing complex on the new southern edge of Jerusalem—a city, we should
remember, that after its unilateral unification in 1967, was suddenly three
times larger in territory (Figure 1.2).[1] The project was administered by the
same state agency and addressed the same function of social housing, but its

appearance is strikingly different. The housing units are built into clusters: four-story raw houses surrounding large semipublic patios into which one enters through monumental gateways. Although the basic unit consists of eight apartments served by a singular circulation core, the apartments are different in size and are set back from each other to emulate the indigenous building of the Judean landscape. The plasticity of the composition is enhanced by the rough *tubsa* stone cladding and arched concrete frames of the balconies. Unlike the seemingly floating blocks of Upper Lifta, the houses in East Jerusalem are seated heavily on their foundations. The panoramic photograph of *Israel Builds* intentionally exaggerates the rootedness of the complex, as if it is organically growing out of a Mediterranean bareness—a suddenly desired architectural merit that Israeli architects grew to admire in the topographically astute and authentically local Palestinian vernacular.

How can these two complexes, built in two consecutive decades, be so different from one another? What can we learn from the dramatic shift between them? Does this shift reflect post-1967 political dictates, or alternatively, is it

Figure 1.1. David Anatol Brutzkus, modern housing blocks in Upper Lifta (today's Romema), general view. Source: *Israel Builds, 1964* (Tel Aviv: Ministry of Housing, 1965).

a manifesto of a new generation of Israeli architects? A casual visitor to Jerusalem cannot but wonder about the power of this transformation. I believe the drastic shift in building styles reveals no less than Jerusalem's project of nation building, beautification, and occupation, a project that is especially revealing if examined through the lens of architectural culture. But before we discuss the varied manifestations of this project, we must establish the theoretical platform that enables us to probe the reciprocity between political form and architectural form.

Can ideology take shape within a building? Can architecture advance a political cause? In other words, how do ideas become concrete and stone? In order to inquire into the encounter between Zionism and modern architecture, we have to look at the historical condition in which they emerged and the discourse in which they took shape. Analyzing their shared roots in, and responses to, modernity, we can establish a conceptual framework for understanding their correlated modernisms and the incalculable and not always recognized impact of their modernist dynamics on the politics of space in Jerusalem.

Figure 1.2. Salo Hershman, Giloh, Cluster 11, 1970s. Source: *Israel Builds, 1988* (Tel Aviv: Ministry of Housing, 1988), 112.

The Rise of Modern Architecture and Zionism

Modern architecture is by nature a professional, transnational culture, one that we can define by its "process of intellectual, spiritual and aesthetic development."[2] The things that architecture creates are the result of a particular body of knowledge about the built environment, and its power as a discipline lies in "the way that architecture defines, creates, disseminates, and applies the knowledge within its domain of influence."[3] By contrast, Zionism—a modern, national movement—is a political, place-bound culture that attends to the particularity of Jewish life. Its nationalism creates an exclusive bond between the traditions, occupations, and aspirations of Jews worldwide and the historical territory of biblical Palestine. Its power as a national movement lies in its ability to politically structure the life and identity of Jewish immigrants and to transform the physical landscape of Palestine. Modern architecture occurs everywhere, is used by everyone, and is the product of the pooling of knowledge by a network of educational institutions and professional organizations; in contrast, Zionism can take root only in Israel, for and by the Jewish people, and its cultural practices are administered by the state. On the surface they may seem to have little in common, but upon closer examination we shall see that their intersections are profound.

Our discussion of the encounter between modern architecture and Zionism grows out of the newness of both cultures. Although the former is artistic and the latter political, both emerged from a similar root: out of modernity's often violent encounter with the older traditions that preceded it, and modernity's ensuing rupture of historical practices and modes of production. Modern architecture grew out of the industrialization, urbanization, and technological advances of the nineteenth century, primarily in Europe and the United States. Its modernism emanated from a manifested break with the aesthetic authority of antiquity and with traditional dictates regarding architectural form, composition, structure, and materials.[4] Similarly, Zionism was born through the rise of European nationalism, modern civic movements, the Jewish emancipation movement, and modern anti-Semitism.[5] Its modernism renounced the authority of Jewish law (halachah) and the traditional lifestyle of Diaspora Jews.

An agreement between Zionist and architectural modernisms evolved as early as the 1920s.[6] The successful cooperation of the two movements in Mandate Palestine owes its compatibility to emerging trends within each movement. The consolidation of Labor Zionism in the Yishuv (the Jewish society in Mandate Palestine), and its growing efficacy in European Zionist circles,[7] acquired urgent dimensions with the forced emigration of Jews from Fascist Europe. This rise of Labor Zionism coincided with the development of modern architecture across Europe into a coherent body of ideas and built forms; modern architecture's emergence was the result of a decade of experimentation and collaborations that was strengthened by the establishment of Congrès Internationaux d'Architecture Moderne (CIAM) in 1928—an international organization that promoted the dissemination of modernism and shaped its canonic forms.[8] These correlated developments gave to both movements a revolutionary edge and shared interests.[9]

Both movements began with multiple voices that competed to shape their respective forms. The official narrators of both narrowed the breadth of each modernism and created from a clutter of ideas an official story that propagated a zeitgeist of progress and development.[10] Seminal architectural historiographies, such as Nikolaus Pevsner's *Pioneers of Modern Design,* narrated legends about the evolution of the field, while Siegfried Giedion's *Space, Time and Architecture* intertwined the movements of architecture, art, and technology to cohere a triumphant story. The result of such endeavors was a unified teleological story that rendered modern architecture inevitable and foreshadowed its immense international influence.

The leading histories of the Zionist movement were similarly consolidating and self-promoting. Journalist Theodor Herzl was deemed the movement's father figure, and consequently his articulation of political Zionism—a Zionist strand focusing on providing a political solution for Jews and their deficient civic rights—eclipsed alternate voices, particularly cultural Zionism and its broader, not always political, engagement with Judaism and Jewish identity. The foundation of a state consummated political Zionism's dominant role while incorporating aspects of cultural Zionism into the national ethos. The raison d'etre of the movement was thus constructed around a tight national story: an exiled people return to their homeland after two millennia of absence to revive their national integrity and innovative spirit in the form of a progressive state. Once Israel was established in 1948, and once modern architecture (in Israel and across the world) began to permeate educational institutions, state agencies, popular culture, and capitalist corporations, these histories confirmed and empowered hegemonic practices in both movements.

As the mid-twentieth century wore on, the relentlessly forward-looking perspective of these official voices became less and less satisfying. As colonialism's global grip began to loosen, these official modernisms seemed unable to address the full complexity of the new identities that fought for recognition in postcolonial nations. Nor were these modernisms sufficient for the social requirements of countries that had already undergone massive modernization. The astounding scientific progress that bettered human life via electricity, medicine, and transport also caused the spectacular atomic destruction in Hiroshima and Nagasaki and mass killings in the gas chambers of Auschwitz. The promise of progress seemed more and more dubious. Whether in response to the welfare state or to rampant capitalism, singular progressive modernism in the decades after World War II reached its limits: it lost its capacity to produce meaning for individuals.

After years of racing toward progress, Israeli and modern architectural cultures had both reached an impasse, entangled in the growing controversies of modernization. As the forward progress of these modern movements became increasingly inadequate to the demands of the post–World War II era, modern architects and Zionists alike realized the need to refamiliarize themselves with the foundations of their respective cultures and their historical methods of producing meaning.

Mamlachtiyut: The Future of the Past

For Zionist leaders, the challenge was simple: how to connect the state that they had just established with the Jewish religion and ethnicity that was its raison d'être. The answer, they hoped, could be found in *mamlachtiyut*— typically translated as "statism"—the effort to build a Jewish nation inaugurated in 1948 by Israel's first prime minister, David Ben Gurion.[11] According to Charles S. Liebman and Eliezer Don-Yehya, statism is an affirmation of "the centrality of state interests and the centralization of power at the expense of nongovernmental groups and institutions."[12] They refer to Ben Gurion's forceful dissolution of the Yishuv's social, economic, military, and educational institutions in favor of a centralized state, a course of action whose controversies echo to this day. Ben Gurion's aspirations, however, aimed at something larger than official politics, something instead that could embody his ambitions for Zionism: he wanted to mesh various Zionist strands into a unified national body, one possessing a collective past, present, and future. To this end the project of *mamlachtiyut* was not purely political but had a cultural dimension as well. Moving beyond the official politics of statism, one can appreciate the full expanse of this nation-building effort and the role of architecture in its orbit.

Culture, David Lloyd and Paul Thomas argue, is indispensable for the process of nationalization: "Cultural (or aesthetic) formation comes gradually to play the role of forming citizens for the modern state."[13] If we examine the cultural role of the *mamlachtiyut* project, what we will find is that it secularized Judaism, not only in order to forge the desired national identity, but coincidently also in order to determine Israeli citizenship, which Israeli law granted primarily according to ethnic or religious affiliation.

The cultural perspective reveals the Janus face of the *mamlachtiyut* project, and thus its simultaneous promise and pitfalls. Linguistically, the Hebrew term is a derivative of *mamlacha*, "kingdom." It alludes to the Judean Kingdom, and thus to the ethnic origin of Judaism.[14] So a more literal, and perhaps more accurate, translation is not "statism," as it is typically rendered, but "kingdomism." The grand sweep of this term is fitting, as Ben Gurion's aim was no less than to shape a modern state, both structurally and morally, while also invigorating the primordial essence of the Jewish nation. As such, it targeted the problematic hyphen between the nation's ethnic definition and primordial sentiments, on the one hand, and the state's political-territorial definition and civic sentiments, on the other.[15] The efforts of kingdomism, therefore, were integral to the very making of the nation-state from beginning to end.

But consolidating the hyphenated values of nation and state is not easy; in visual form, the dilemma of consolidation is bluntly illustrated in a celebrated 1950s poster that presents Israel to prospective tourists in an extremely dichotomized iconography (see Plate 1). The scene on the right side of the poster depicts the architectural gist of a Zionist settlement: cubical white buildings, the identical horizontal windows of public institutions, red pitched roofs of residences, and a white water tower that crowns the composition. The built complex is framed with bright green lawns and ordered cypresses in the background and foreground, and above is a blue sky. This view, and its faded contours, dreamily dissipates into a calm whiteness on which the name of the new state, Israel, is printed in bright blue Hebrew letters.

By contrast, a large figure, in transparent browns, covers the left half of the poster. The human shape, of indeterminate gender, creates at once an image and a background and serves as a counterpart to the whiteness on the right. The figure is wrapped in a thin veil (presumably a tallit—a prayer shawl), which marks the figure as feminine even as he/she blows the shofar, a ritualistic instrument typically used by a man. Halfway down its veil, the figure dissolves into a light brown depiction of Jerusalem's walls and the Tower of David, obvious symbols of the ancient nation of Judea. The antiquated edifices form a horizontal continuum with the white buildings on the right. This continuity is interrupted by the figure's veil, which delineates a clear vertical border between the two halves of the poster (and the two halves, implicitly, of Israel): on the right we have the whiteness of the Zionist state, and on the left the brown tonality of the Jewish nation.

The layout of the poster can be read progressively from left to right, the idea of the nation leading to the present reality of the state. The brown figure, with Latin letters spelling "Israel" along the bottom of its veil, would represent the diasporic Judaism. In fact, the figure is exercising the Jewish ritual of the high holidays, blowing the shofar in order to open the gates of heaven, to allow the Jewish people to ask for mercy, that is, redemption. The redemption that Jews have longed for, this reading suggests, is no longer a dream: it has come true in the form of a modernist Zionist state. But its fulfillment simultaneously makes the brown diasporic figure, the diasporic wanderer, obsolete.

There is another way to read the poster, one that stresses the notions of "nation" and "state" as simultaneous. In this view, the brown clad figure with the shofar and the brightly colored Zionist settlement are both inseparably located in "the Land of Israel." This possibility for union—ancient with modern and wanderer with homeland—was the guiding goal of the *mamlachti* ideology. But in Israel's turbulent six decades of existence, the symbols of the ancient nation have never quite managed to fuse with those of the modernist state. The dichotomy within the poster thus bares the impasse of a trapped country, as Adriana Kemp elegantly put it, by illustrating "the incongruity between the political space of the sovereign state and the cultural space of the nation."[16] As we shall see, the architecture developed by the *mamlachtiyut* project was part of an effort to conceal this rift: it was to be modern and progressive, but at the same time local, authentic, and timeless. It sought to cross the white/brown boundary that was not only conceptual but also political and territorial. But before we turn to see how kingdomism was manifested architecturally, let us briefly examine the role of architecture in the process of becoming national.

Building Nationalization

A premise of this study is that architecture is an important ingredient of the broader cultural-aesthetic formation that is by default essential to—in our case—the process of identifying Israeli citizenship and national belonging with Jewish identity. In other words, it is an attempt to marry modern concepts of statehood and citizenship with a traditional sense of belonging and set of beliefs. Tradition is thus the anchor, the fixed and known essence that helps familiarize and legitimize the formation of a novel state. Architecture becomes the most prominent embodiment of that tradition.

This process itself is a modern use of tradition. Nezar AlSayyad reminds us that such modernized tradition cannot be interpreted "simply as the static legacy of the past but rather as a model for the dynamic reinterpretation of the present."[17] In fact, as Lloyd and Thomas argue, precisely because the nation-state is built upon modernity, it has found tradition most useful as "an active form" through which to articulate and legitimate its narrative. Scholars have therefore focused on the methods of manufacturing, transmitting, and consuming tradition.[18] By replacing, as Abu-Lughod suggests, "tradition" as a noun with "traditioning" as a verb, one can divest tradition of its matter-of-factness and fixity, revealing instead the social and political forces that shape it and that it in turn shapes.[19]

These insights are crucial for our efforts; to consider the cultures and traditions of modern architecture and Zionism as verbs, as forms in the making, enables us to probe the inextricably linked processes of nationalizing the people of Israel and building its chosen land. Such inquiry sheds light on the ideological formation of landscapes that we typically accept as a given, as the obvious nature, character, or sense of a place. With this frame of reference we can uncover the agency of the discipline of architecture—the power of its knowledge, debates, influences, and effects—in producing the built landscapes of nationhood.

Architecture is so efficient in producing these desired national landscapes because it is consumed by us every day, immediately, distractedly, and with little focused attention. As such, it possesses a great capacity to frame and embody specific positions of power, which are taken for granted once they take built form.[20] Like the natural landscape, it represents an artificial world as if it was simply inevitable.[21] The power of architecture as a cultural medium, then, lies not only in producing identity—a power it shares with other cultural practices—but also in shaping, often irreversibly, the physical arena in which this identity takes form.

On an obvious level, architecture frames for each of us the private domain of everyday life. On a more foundational but less apparent level, it produces for us symbols and national narratives that we comprehend through the sensations of bodily experience in space. Architecture, as we'll see, is a crucial participant in what Lauren Berlant defines as the "National Symbolic":

> The order of discursive practices whose reign within a national space produces, and also refers to, the "law" in which the accident of birth within a geographical/political boundary transforms individuals into subjects of a collectively-held history. Its traditional icons, its metaphors, its heroes, its rituals, and its narratives provide an alphabet for a collective consciousness or national subjectivity; through the National Symbolic the historical national aspires to achieve the inevitability of the status of natural law, a birthright.[22]

Architecture—from the Egyptian pyramids to France's cathedrals—has historically been a defining ingredient in the stew that makes a nation. Modern nation-states have eagerly appropriated these past monuments as symbols of their modern legacies. It is the purpose of this study to decipher not only how architecture appropriates past edifices—most notably in our case Jerusalem's Western Wall and the visual basin of the Old City—but also, and more poignantly, how architecture renders new traditions and their icons, metaphors, heroes, rituals, and narratives as fixed, obvious, and inevitable.

After its founding, the Israeli government needed to quickly and efficiently nationalize a population and a territory that had been in constant flux for the better part of two millennia. Its self-imposed mandate was thus twofold. First, the people living within the nation's new borders—a majority of whom were recent immigrants from various locales and cultures—had to be transformed into "subjects of a collectively-held history," that is, into a people. Second, a territory that was once Palestinian had to be imagined as Israeli, to be made (in 1948) and remade (in 1967) into a national home that felt like a natural extension of the place. In other words, both the mass immigration and the territorial expansion that characterized the Israeli condition required a laborious process of defusing the line that separated nation from state.

But, if the purpose was to consolidate a national home, or, according to Balibar, to validate a "nation form,"[23] in the secure territory of mythical origins, ethnicity, and history, how could modern architecture be of use? As we have seen, modern architecture by definition manifestly broke away from narrated representations and from historical precedents. During the period between the world wars only a few nation-states expressed their identity, origins, and aspirations by means of the then newly articulated modern architecture. There was an inherent contradiction, it seemed, between the boundaryless international architecture as it was defined in the famous 1923 Bauhaus exhibition and the goals and purposes of national architecture.

Modernism's abstract forms, though shared by different nationalities, could be useful for a particular nationalist purpose: they could accommodate national stories based on negation. In Kemalist Turkey or in modern Iran, for example, modern regimes repudiated recent dynasties in order to depart from their country's Orientalist past in favor of a Western modernization campaign.[24] Alternatively, the clean white forms of modern architecture accorded also with colonial legacies, as seen in the Italian construction of modernism as "Meditterranitta."[25] This concept allowed Italians to spread the image of a resurrected Roman Empire to the northern and southern shores of the Mediterranean, justifying their colonial expedition in North Africa. The Yishuv adopted modern architecture for similar reasons: to negate a malignant past of subordinated Jewish experience and to settle a land whose vernacular forms were identified with another people.

During the 1930s, authoritarian regimes drove modern architecture away from Europe, but the movement's demise under Hitler and Stalin actually expedited its rise into global practice immediately after World War II. On the one hand, modernism's simple form and construction method allowed an efficient use of new building technologies, crucial for the mass-produced housing needed to accommodate the sudden increase in displaced populations. On the other hand, modern architecture easily adapted itself to the modernizing race of Third World countries, particularly after President Truman's Marshall Plan launched a worldwide development project.[26] Since developed, First World countries, particularly the United States, chose modern architecture as their national expression, postcolonial nation-states adopted the style as they aspired to create their own modernized societies and financial stability.

Although many modernisms relied on similar architectural forms, the demands modern architecture had to fulfill in particular geographical and historical contingencies differed greatly, as did the various meanings invested in these seemingly identical modern forms. The last decade's growing body of studies on postwar architectural culture has been dedicated primarily to the First World. Here, the dominant International Style of the United States, for example, differed from the modernism practiced in the welfare countries of devastated Europe. Simultaneously, the rise of postcolonial studies and the fall of the Soviet Bloc have focused attention on the so-called other modernisms of the Second and Third Worlds. The socialist countries of Eastern Europe arguably manifested the most radical form of *sachlich* — or "matter-of-fact" — architecture, denouncing any form of bourgeois culture and cultural possessions. By contrast, new postcolonial nation-states in Africa, Asia, and the Middle East treated modernism as an entry pass to the independent, developed world and placed cultural heritage as high as possible on their priority list. Despite the seeming uniformity of modern forms, and in sharp contradiction to the canonic depiction of the movement as the embodiment of a steadily progressing, unified zeitgeist, modern architecture emerges in these studies as a flexible container of multiple agendas, cultures, and locales, an open-ended practice that can absorb even the pasts it so passionately refuted.

Although Israel always conceived of itself as a Western country, numerous new nation-states shared its modernist dilemma: how to promote an image of progress and development while cohering a sense of a particular community, a unique culture, a shared history, and a collective destiny. In other words: the national elites' (the Labor Zionists, in Israel's case) desire to modernize their country had to be balanced by meaningful cultural legitimization in order to recruit compliance from the people, the subject of their efforts. The question was how to solicit this agreement, or in the words of Etienne Balibar: "How are individuals nationalized, or, in other words, socialized in the dominant form of national belonging?"[27] And, in Israel, how could modern architecture communicate a sense of belonging and familiarity despite its novelty?

The High Modernism of Early Statehood

Let us return to the poster that projects so clearly the Janus-faced image of the *mamlachti* project. The beautifully lit white houses, water tower, and greenery on the right side depict the modern landscape of what we will call "*mamlachtiyut* as statism." Only after we analyze why this kind of architecture—white, cubic, orderly, and plain—suited so well the image of a young progressive state can we understand why *mamlachtiyut* as statism was unable to satisfy the nation's needs.

Charles Liebman and Eliezer Don-Yehya's influential work is a good starting point because they not only position statism under the habitual looking glass of political science, but also innovatively scrutinize the cultural domain. They explain:

> In terms of symbols and style, statism reflects the effort to transform the state and its institutions into the central foci of loyalty and identification. Statism gives rise to values and symbols that point to the state, legitimate it, and mobilize the population to serve its goals. In its more extreme formulation statism cultivates an attitude of sanctity toward the state, affirming it as an ultimate value.[28]

This emphasis on the state, on its institutions and territory, its development and defense, is the notion of *mamlachtiyut* that evolved according to the pretext of the new architecture of the émigré generation. Congruent with the state's slogan of progress and development, this architecture celebrated the newness, unity, and forward thinking of the *mamlachti* project.

Shortly after independence, Israel embarked on an industrious modernization effort. As mentioned earlier, its prime goals were demographic and territorial: to absorb waves of Jewish immigrants, primarily from Europe and the Arab world, and to evenly disperse the growing population over the entire territory of the newly sovereign state.[29] The state's early plans and the resultant modernization of Israel's built landscape have recently attracted considerable scholarly attention.[30] In order to understand the era of this project—starting in the late 1950s, when we can fully see the manifestation of the sabra generation's architectural program—we must first clarify the melding of Labor Zionism and architectural modernisms during the British Mandate, a dowry of the Yishuv that shaped the early landscape of the State of Israel.

The Yishuv's majority of socialist Jews during the British Mandate were attracted to modernism because modernism accorded with the triple negation advanced by Labor Zionism. As a socialist movement, Labor Zionism negated the bourgeoisie. As a revolutionary movement, it negated Jewish life in the Diaspora. And with the advent of the Arab/Jewish conflict in Mandate Palestine, Labor Zionism started also to negate the Middle Eastern and the Orientalist characteristics that had been adopted by the previous generation as an appropriate representation of Jewish revival. This triple negation of bourgeois culture, the Jewish Diaspora, and the Orient structured the work of émigré architects, the group who built the early state. These European Jews, who emigrated to Mandate Palestine and were trained as architects either before or after emigration, would construct the site of the Jewish national home—Mandate Palestine and later Israel—as a tabula rasa, a place "free from past memories."[31]

The (naïve) belief that Israel could be cleansed of its history fit frighteningly well with the notion that modern architecture should offer a new and healthy environment, a clean state, a progressive alternative to the congested, dilapidated, and polluted city of the nineteenth century. Faith in a new kind of urbanism was at the heart of Le Corbusier's influential proposal to build a grid of high-rise buildings, orderly and spacious, on top of the park that was once the center of Paris.[32] Though few of the émigré architects of the Yishuv had trained under or had any professional contact with Le Corbusier, the new architecture they proposed for Mandate Palestine nevertheless followed the modernist vision; as Julius Posener remarked in 1937, the new movement intended to create the "house of the country in which [the Jew] is settling," an island of Western progress in the midst of a backward Orient.[33]

This new architecture—a general term that architects in the Yishuv used to refer to all trends of modern architecture (international, organic, *sachlich*, etc.)—perfectly matched the ideal of the New Jew as defined by the socialist leadership. Both focused on the physiognomy of the body/the building/the town; on health and hygiene, blood and circulation; on the necessity of bodies in the field, houses in the park, and clean and green lungs to cure the body/the city. For socialists, particularly those who identified themselves with the teaching of A. D. Gordon and the invigoration of body and mind through unmediated contact with the land, the new architecture cohered the idea of home.

Émigré architects were trained primarily in German-speaking schools and later at the Technion, the Yishuv's first school for architecture and engineering, later the Israel Institute of Technology. The Bauhaus's influence was significantly important to this group, particularly Hannes Meyer, the left-leaning architect who established the architectural program in the famed school. Meyer, an architectural master of the *neue sachlichkeit* (which translates roughly as "new objectivity" or "matter-of-factness"), considered architecture in its typical guise an obsolete discipline. The modern, socialist subject he envisioned required no more than the simplest, starkest, barest buildings, which would fulfill the primary human need for protection, ventilation, nutrition, and reproduction.

His ambitions were shared across Israel by a host of émigré modernists—Alexander Klein, Julius Posener, Arieh Sharon, and their generation—who designed human environments according to strict scientific criteria. Consider, for example, the work of Alexander Klein. Before immigrating to Palestine in 1933, he had already devised schemes for what he called "existence minimum." He brought modern buildings to scientific perfection, where elemental functional needs are precisely addressed through built form. In this era, even Julius Posener, who would later become famous as a historian of expressionist architecture, was ideologically inclined toward modernist, international architecture. In 1937, during his Palestinian period, Posener claimed that the Zionist village could not rely on the Arab village as a precedent. According to Posener, the Orient had nothing to teach Zionists whose emerging settlements were conducted as an experiment based on scientific hypotheses, a utopian innovation of pure rationality.

Shortly after independence, Ben Gurion appointed Arieh Sharon, a Bauhaus graduate under Hannes Meyer and his project manager thereafter, to orchestrate Israel's first master plan, published in 1951 as *Physical Planning in Israel*.[34] The plan presents local landscapes that naturally adopted the new architecture of the Yishuv and includes images of virgin lands and territories already redeemed by the Zionist project. Overflowing with charts, precedents, and prescriptions, the plan's standpoint was clear: the architectural characteristics of the "new architecture"—rational, functional, technologically updated, and visually cleansed of classical or Oriental symbolism—were appropriate, perhaps even essential, for the project of state building. The ideology of the plan not only maintained but also further perfected Labor Zionism's triple negation.

The *sachlich* modernism of Meyer and others was perfect for such statist and socialist modernization projects, and Israel was far from alone in their eager adoption of its tenets. Regimes around the world saw modern architecture as a vehicle for radical social change—indeed, they found in architecture no less than the means for breeding a new type of man. When Oscar Niemeyer, for example, embarked in 1957 on the ambitious project of building a new, modernist capital for Brazil, he intentionally constructed residential blocks of equal dimensions: "same façade, same height, same facilities, all constructed on pilotis [free-standing columns], all provided with garages and constructed of the same material—which prevents the hateful differentiation of social classes." In Niemeyer's view, the elimination of variation from his "superquadra" would force its residents "to live as if in the sphere of one big family, in perfect social coexistence." Since people cannot change overnight, proper housing was projected to pay off in the next generation: "Children who live, grow up, play, and study in the same environment of sincere camaraderie, friendship and wholesome upbringing . . . will construct the Brazil of tomorrow, since Brasilia," according to Niemeyer, "is the glorious cradle of a new civilization."[35] In Israel, whose leaders entertained a similar aspiration to create a national and modern paragon, the model of this new manhood—

the New Jew—was the sabra, a native of the Israeli state, who became the role model for new immigrants.

As Labor Zionists populated Israel's founding government, the abstract ideals of the new architecture became government policy. The consequences of the triple negation were clear: since the Diaspora had been superseded by the long-awaited reality of a physical homeland, Zionists now had to find a way to house the Jews who came flocking to their new country. In Mandate Palestine, Zionists had spent a lot of time imagining what their new and triumphant home would look like and how they would incorporate modernist ideals that were up until then purely symbolic. But after 1948 these theoretical concerns quickly became concrete, as the new government had to create housing on a massive scale. Within the first eighteen months of Israel's independence its Jewish population soared by 50 percent. It doubled three years later, in 1951, when 700,000 immigrants joined the 650,000 Jews of Mandate Palestine, creating as a result an accelerated rate of migration that was arguably unparalleled even in affluent countries.[36] The powerful complicity of architecture in Israel's similarly unprecedented modernization project created the desired identity between modernism and Israeliness. Simple, white, smooth, and repetitive, the new architecture symbolized health and hygiene, equality and independence.

In the earliest study of Israel's architectural history, written in 1963, Aviah Hashimshoni argues that it was already possible to define an Israeli architectural "tradition." Like Giedion, whose seminal text identified in modernism *The Growth of a New Tradition,* Hashimshoni argued for the maturity of this tradition even if it was just a decade and a half old. The Israeli "tradition," explicates Hashimshoni—who would be one of the authors of Jerusalem's 1968 modernist master plan—"is based on a rational attitude to planning, on the functionalist school, and on new views regarding the organization of urban life and housing."[37] This architecture, he emphasizes, reflects a "matter-of-factness and lack of pretense." It expresses "enthusiasm" and "public responsibility," as well as the Yishuv's spirit of "collaboration and identification with the material needs of building. . . . Despite being un-crystallized and imperfect in form," this tradition "was given with honesty, directness, and vitality."[38] He argues for a moral judgment according to which modern—or more precisely, *neue sachlichkeit*—architecture is progressive and invigorating. It is a nation-building force, unlike early twentieth-century (Jewish) works of Oriental architecture in Ottoman and Mandate Palestine, which Hashimshoni classifies as failed "eclectic experiments" attempting to "create an imposed local 'style.'"[39]

While the veracity of Hashimshoni's grand visions is debatable, the need for this state-building force was undeniable. A matter-of-fact architecture was critical to create the new landscapes that answered Israel's very matter-of-fact needs—namely, to house the waves of immigrants that almost tripled Israel's Jewish population during its first decade of independence. A famed caricature from 1952 portrays the ensuing melting pot as a meat grinder into which people of different ethnicities, occupations, garments, and languages jump en masse. With smiles on their faces, they dive into a processor that eliminates their diversity in favor of a single, ideal product—the sabra, the New Jew whose body is liberated and functionally clothed, and whose spirit is healthy and contagious (Figure 1.3). Architecture and agriculture were the major building stones of this grinder. Modern, hygienic, well-lit, and uniform residential blocks clothed the lives of diverse immigrants, who were expected

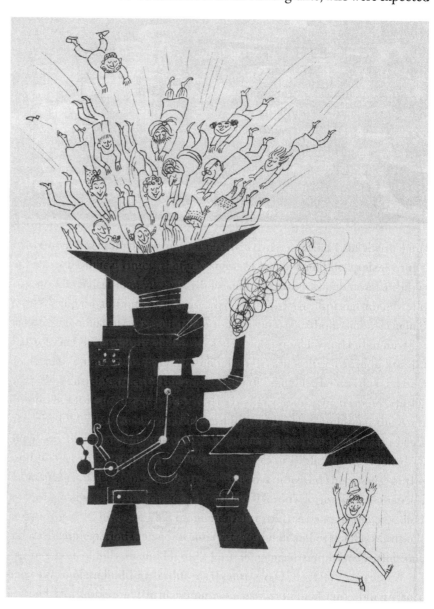

Figure 1.3. Caricaturist Friedel Stern portrays the Israeli melting pot as a huge grinder vacuuming Jewish immigrants from different cultures and molding them into the canonic figure of the sabra, 1950s. Source: *BaMahane,* May 1952. Courtesy of the Israeli Cartoon Museum, Friedel Stern Collection.

Figure 1.4. Amidar Housing for new immigrants in Acre. Courtesy of the Central Zionist Archive, NKH\404616.

to give up their previous identities in favor of a new collective ideal. The bareness of this architecture, its efficient construction methods, and its ban on ornamentation embodied the modesty, practicality, and sobriety of the new regime that turned this hardscrabble of Arab, European, and other diasporic Jews into subjects of industrious social engineering.[40]

For these immigrants the modern architecture of statism often meant erasure. It focused on their bodily needs but neglected their cultural and emotional desires. To paraphrase Slavoj Žižek's analysis, we can extrapolate that *sachlich* modernism primarily communicated "an abstraction of all positive features, a dissolution of all substantial, innate links," or in other words, a nullification of the immigrants' previous identities in favor of the aggressively cooked Israeli melting pot. At the same time this architecture neglected "to offer the subject a positive, substantial identity," to cohere a national character that would grant the new immigrant a place in the Israeli collective.[41] For many, the built landscape of a country, described often as miraculously rising from the ashes of the Jewish genocide, seemed emotionally impoverished (Figure 1.4).

This feeling was shared by many of the sabra generation, who considered the homeland of early statehood empty and bare. Pioneers promised to clothe its nakedness with concrete and cement, while farmers vowed to fertilize its virgin, desert lands until they bloomed. The applicable national home that adorns a 1958 publication of the nascent State of Israel features modern housing served by infrastructures of water, electricity, and sanitation, surrounded by an orderly system of roads, and bordered by perfectly plowed fields. If European modernism evolved in opposition to the packed, dark, and dirty city of the Industrial Revolution, Israeli modernism contrasted itself to the Orientalist city and the Arab village (which appears at the upper left edge of the photograph as a messy primitive cluster). During early statehood this modernized landscape was powerful enough to be accepted as inevitable. But soon even the sabras, lionized by Labor Zionists as the model for the new, destined State of Israel, were not entirely convinced. How, then, did the new architecture lose favor among Israelis as the optimal expression of their national identity? When did modern architecture cease to be considered second nature, a tradition in the sense that Hashimshoni described it in 1963?

Traditioning the New Jew and the New Architecture

Before the 1960s, neither the practitioners of the modern new architecture nor the state bureaucracy that administrated the building effort were much concerned with fostering the cultural and ethnic character of the State of Israel. The new planning bureaucracy did not focus on Judaism as the common denominator of the national community or on the *mamlachti* commitment to territorially anchor this identity by highlighting the return of Jews to their biblical homeland. Their efforts were geared toward the narrower (and more common) definition of the *mamlachtiyut* project as "statism." For the émigré architects who participated in the foundation of the state, the notion of place was built on the negation of the past. As a result, their architecture was geared toward building the state and ignored the broader demands of *mamlachtiyut* as kingdomism—to address the history, ethnicity, and place of the Jewish nation.

The high modernism of statism quickly failed to fulfill the demands of a national program. On the one hand it failed to solidify the desired nativeness of the sabra, and on the other hand it failed to provide new immigrants a national content with which they could identify. Statist modernism thus fell short of convincing individuals, on both ends of the spectrum, to define their social ties and identity "in the dominant form of national belonging."[42]

Slavoj Žižek reminds us that belonging to a democratic state means inclusion within an abstract framework that links people by virtue of what they are not. They are granted citizenship regardless of their race, religion, gender, or profession, the attributes that define their personhood. Rather, they are citizens because they were born in a certain territory and are administrated by its sovereign leadership. As a result, they are subject to "a constitutive lack of any support that would offer the subject a positive, substantial identity."[43] Ben Gurion's kingdomism, in contrast to the statist aspects of his project, offered just that: an identity with "positive features," capable of overriding other identities of the past.

By the late 1940s Ben Gurion already realized that socialism, the ideology on which his party thrived prior to independence, was limited in producing national cohesion. It was foreign to the majority of new immigrants and alienated significant sections of the Yishuv. Like the modernizers of Latin America that Néstor García Canclini analyzes, Ben Gurion and his party legitimated their own hegemony by persuading "their addressees that—at the same time that they are renewing society—they are prolonging shared traditions. Given that they claim to include all sectors of society, modern projects appropriate historical goods and popular traditions."[44] Ben Gurion's "historical goods" and "shared traditions" were based on a golden triangle of people-book-land, or more precisely, on Jews, the Bible, and the Land of Israel. In Ben Gurion's hands, this triad became the blueprint of Israeli culture, the common authoritative narrative of all Jews; but as we shall see, this construction was far from inevitable, just as these categories are not as timeless as they have been depicted.[45]

Projects such as Ben Gurion's kingdomism have preoccupied scholars since the 1980s and have renewed critical interest in the phenomenon of nationalism. Questioning who creates traditions, and for whom, scholars argue that seemingly timeless traditions were in fact invented by different modernizing elites. Despite the agreement on the novelty of national traditions, this top-down analysis fell under harsh criticism. Scholars were looking instead for a nuanced understanding of how national subjects are caught in and identify with the new national order. This was the reason Benedict Anderson's proposal to examine how communities imagine themselves as subjects of cohesive nation-states was so striking. It invested the different national players with agency, recognizing their active role in producing the modern nation. Looking at the mechanisms that enable active imagination, that prompt the capacity of a group to share a language, history, and traditions, Anderson focused on practices such as modern print, cartography, and museology. The cultural turn of the 1980s gave rise to new disciplines such as cultural, gender, and minority studies and furthered our understanding of the cultural practices that adapt, transform, and modernize traditions for new nations.[46] It prepares the ground for a closer look at the realm of architecture, at the cultural practices that shape traditional national landscapes.

These cultural practices reveal the stalwarts of tradition—in our case

Judaism, Jerusalem, and the Bible—as modern resources vulnerable to political power. "The dramatization of the patrimony," Canclini reminds us, "is the effort to simulate that there is an origin, a founding substance, in relation with which we should act today. This is the basis of authoritarian cultural policies."[47] Ben Gurion's kingdomism exemplifies this strength, the capacity to divest primal religious forms of their earlier content and invest them instead with secularized state ideology.

Ben Gurion's biblical-territorial approach, as Anita Shapira describes it, helped him to fulfill the political and cultural requirements of modern nationalism: conceptualizing a national community of Jews ruling a sovereign state, sharing a common past, a concrete (historical) land, and a collective destiny. According to Mitchell Cohen, this attainment completed the reification of the Zionist socialist movement, turning it into a national movement that is unified around common symbols of nationhood.[48] A. B. Yehoshua, the eminent Israeli writer and a distinguished member of the sabra generation, reads in Ben Gurion's identity-making a move "from a New Jew to Complete Jew." In other words, he embodies an attempt to invest in the New Jew the cult of primordial Judaism in order to arrive at a more rounded national identity, reaching beyond its newness. "If asked to summarize the identity of the Generation of the State [i.e., sabras who matured into statehood] as a headline," Yehoshua writes, "it would be: 'The Meaning of Israeliness as Complete Jewishness.'"[49]

It was beneficial for the process of traditioning that the European models of the New Jew had never immigrated to Palestine, as noted by Shlomo Avineri. The second, sabra generation of Zionists was familiar neither with the intellectual origins of the New Jew nor with the memory of a traditional Jewish home in the Diaspora.[50] The sabra—who, according to Moshe Shamir's seminal novel, *Pirke Alik* (Alik's Chapters), "was born out of the sea"[51]—was seen as a clean slate ready to assimilate the values of the new Yishuv without the inner contradictions of the postwar immigrants, and with no preexisting intellectual or religious traditions. Ben Gurion's cultural-biblical Judaism thus equipped the sabra with a history and a territorial rootedness, the very qualities that were hitherto denied by the authority of the triple negation. For the New Jew, who was stripped from the culture, law, and possessions of Jewish diasporic life and was denied the local stereotype of the menacing Orient, the onset of kingdomism provided new coordinates for a fuller national identity.

Living with the Bible, a book written by the quintessential sabra Moshe Dayan, the famed chief of staff and later minister of defense during the Six Day War, demonstrates the extent to which the "sons of the place" considered themselves biblical descendants.[52] They imbued Israeli culture with an enthusiasm for archeology, which legitimized a biblical remapping and re-naming of the land,[53] and they established ritualistic field trips to these newly discovered biblical sites in order to bodily and emotionally experience their heritage. As the national elite, they transmitted these values to new immi-grants, committing themselves to the cultural dimensions of the Israeli social-engineering project.

A risky and rather violent erasure was latent in this project. If "to be cul-tured" as a new immigrant means, according to Canclini, "to grasp a body of knowledge—largely iconographic—about one's own history,"[54] then it also meant that immigrants and refugees, whom Ben Gurion described as "human dust," had to accept a history that eliminated their recent—sometimes trau-matic, other times glorious—past from the Jewish national chronicle.[55] In order to compensate for this rupture, the leap into antiquity, into an origin located two millennia away, had to be performed not only unflinchingly, but also with focused attention on the cultural and religious beliefs of these im-migrants. The task of familiarizing immigrants with a new reality could rely neither on the Israeli landscape of plowed fields, nor on the carpets of white cubical houses that mushroomed all over the nascent state. Rather, it had to engage the cultural and territorial imagination that Jews had always enter-tained in their various Diasporas: the image of Zion, which by default meant the city of Jerusalem. For this reason, Ben Gurion had no choice but to utilize Jerusalem as the major magnet of the gathered exiles. Despite fierce inter-national objection from other governments who wanted a share in the Holy City, in 1949 he declared Jerusalem the capital of the State of Israel. The city he was hitherto willing to compromise, for the sake of independence from British governance, became the spatial core of his kingdomism project, the spatial symbol that unites the triad of people-book-land.

On a 1956 cover of *Time* magazine featuring his story, Ben Gurion's head emerges from the Old City of Jerusalem as the pillar from which a menorah's fingers spread across Jerusalem's sky. The message is clear: if the Roman Titus drove Jews away from their country and Temple, carrying the menorah on their shoulders, it is Ben Gurion who returns Jews to their land. The meno-rah metaphorically returns to its dutiful owners as the official symbol of the State of Israel.

Paradoxically, the city he desired, the one with which American Jewry could identify, was outside Israeli borders for almost the first two decades of the country's life. The Israeli government was located in West Jerusalem, which was severed by the 1949 armistice line from Jordan-ruled East Jeru-salem. The latter contained the city's most symbolic resources, which Ben Gurion needed in order to complete his biblical-territorial vision, and to tra-ditionalize the capital of the modern state. The inaccessibility of the Old City, behind the Ottoman walls and behind Jordan's border, relieved state officials from needing to resolve the inner contradiction between the state's aspiration for progress and development and the nation's narrative of biblical return. The Jerusalem of antiquity could therefore serve as an image and a symbol, without requiring the near impossible tasks of urban planning and architectural design of a site venerated for its sanctity but detested for its backwardness as a built environment.

Kingdomizing Jerusalem with Post–World War II Modernisms

In the context of kingdomism, Jerusalem embodied the cultural heritage of the State of Israel. It therefore had to fulfill "the ultimate purpose of culture[, which] is to be converted into nature. To be natural like a gift."[56] The military delivery of East Jerusalem on a silver platter to the Jewish people—depicted in June 1967 by the caricaturist Kariel Gardos (Dosh)—introduced just such a powerful gift to Israeli and Diaspora Jews (Figure 1.5). It inserted an almost ready-made national symbolic into the Israeli landscape. Yet this gift was also the embodiment of Islamic and Christian culture, and therefore it had to be appropriated in order to also become the natural hub of Israeli and Jewish identity. Culture takes shape in the world around us; it is in the built environment where the "visual and dramatic production of meaning" occurs.[57] Therefore, the conquest of East Jerusalem became a momentous catalyst to architectural processes that were already under way but that couldn't be manifested in their full glory without the most potent territory of the Holy City.

Once Jerusalem was in the hands of the Israeli government, advocates

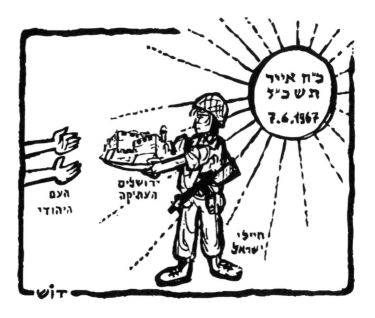

Figure 1.5. Caricature by Dosh (Kariel Gardos) describing "Israeli soldiers" handing a tray with the "Old Jerusalem" to "the Jewish people" under the bright sun of June 7, 1967. Source: *Ma'ariv,* June 8, 1967.

of statist modernism found it difficult to accommodate the demands of the historical moment. In other words, the task of traditioning Jerusalem for national purposes extended beyond the mandate of the new architecture; row after row of plain cubical houses fell short of expressing the fulfillment of a Jewish dream that had been deferred for two millennia. At the same time, members of the sabra generation had already begun their own critique of statist modernism and were already starting to follow and respond to new trends in architecture. They drew their architectural knowledge and support from the post–World War II architectural culture that had put criticism of the modern movement—the bedrock of statist modernism—at the center of contemporary debate.[58] Why did this culture fit so neatly the Israeli demands of the post-1967 historical moment?

Following the devastation of World War II, architects began to contend that in the race to improve the human condition, modern architecture forgot the Man within, that in the grand and seductive swirl of ideology, the modern movement had forgotten Man's sense of place and heritage, and that architecture was a means to associate with fellow men. Many sabra architects identified with this criticism and were thus attracted to some of the leading contemporary trends: the regionalism that was inspired by vernacular environments, the authenticity of the New Brutalism, and the careful preservation of select urban patterns. In order to redeem an impoverished and ugly modernist urbanity, architects turned backward, trying to restore the discipline of architecture's roots and its autonomous values, values that were sought in, through, and before history. Architects gradually lifted the modernist taboo on revisiting past traditions and started looking at history, the vernacular, and the natural world to find authoritative architectural guidelines for situating modernism between people and their places.[59] The passion they felt for the past, however, was neither historicist nor necessarily formal; unlike prevalent postmodernist trends of the 1970s and 1980s, postwar architects did not resort to canonic precedents and remained suspicious of formal conventions regarding the shape and layout of architecture. Their renewed interest in the past primarily emanated from an anxiety about the dissolution of architecture by the very forces that pushed its zeitgeist—the forces of modernity.

It is important to emphasize that these architects were still advocates of modernism and believed in the modernist utopia. However, they felt the latter was caught in the administrative embrace of national and modernization projects and had lost touch with the messy, lived reality of actual people. Team 10 was perhaps the most influential group advocating these views. A group of European architects whose criticism of the modern movement gave birth to the New Brutalism, they resuscitated the latent interest in regionalism, morphology, and the everyday. Aldo van Eyck, for example, a prominent Dutch architect and a member of Team 10, complained that orthodox modernists created "Just mile upon mile of organized nowhere, and nobody feeling he is somebody living somewhere."[60] Van Eyck's generation lamented the loss of such basic notions as hierarchy, community, identity, and place in the well-administered, yet thoroughly alienating, modernist urban environments. They wondered how to forge an identity between people and place through architectural means, that is, how to recapture what builders had been doing for thousands of years. They questioned why modern architecture failed to perform this task that fell within architecture's traditional province—representing and identifying people with their physical environments.

After the discourse surrounding modernist architecture had disparaged the traditional tools of the architectural profession for half a century, architects could finally enjoy, as Denys Lasdun put it, a "physical awakening."[61] Louis Kahn led this return to "architecture as it has always been" by eclipsing formal precedents in favor of timeless architectural principles, by working toward an origin that precedes history, by searching for, as Kahn put it, volume zero of architectural history. "Kahn's search for beginnings," Stanford Anderson explains, "is not merely antiquarian nor merely the identification of sources for imitation, but rather the search for an impulse that may still inform us today."[62] Anderson argues that Kahn's "search was not primarily for physical, built institutions, but rather for what underlies or motivates these associations,"[63] the conditions that precede particular architectural examples yet conceptually enable their performance.

We focus attention on Kahn because he was arguably the most admired architect of his generation. When the European members of Team 10 organized the tenth and last meeting of CIAM, from which they drew their name, they looked for an esteemed figure who would offer an alternative direction from this powerful modernist organization. Although not much younger than the organization's reputed leaders—the omnipotent Le Corbusier or the intellectually astute Siegfried Giedion—Louis Kahn was the perfect keynote speaker of a conference that marked a new generation's rebellion against CIAM's high, authoritarian modernism. The enthusiastic reception of Kahn's work and philosophy in Israel, I believe, emanated not only from a similar generational quest to return to architecture as a timeless discipline, but also, and more forcefully so, from the striking compatibility between Kahn's project and the aims of *mamlachtiyut* as kingdomism. Common to both was the Janus-like construction where one turns to the past in order to face the present and envision the future.

Kingdomism turned to the biblical past not only for an affirmation of the Jewish claim to the contested land of Palestine, but more poignantly, for the original urge that enabled ancient Jews to create their innovative faith, morality, and law in biblical Palestine. Ben Gurion's was a penetrating look through history in search of that fortunate moment of origin, whose place and spirit must be adapted to accommodate the contingencies of Jewish modern life. Like Kahn's voyage into the history of architecture, the Bible served Ben Gurion neither as a repository of authoritative precedents for Jewish political life, nor as a set of rules that could be copied into the present. Rather, he sought the creative impulse that made the writing of the Bible possible, "the intuitive understanding," as he put it, of "the spirit and soul" of creative Judaism, the potential to continue, so to speak, the writing of the Bible in modern Israel.

The first generation of Israeli-born architects, who entered the professional arena just as their homeland became a state, joined this demanding project. Members of this generation found high modernism to lack what the new Israelis most needed: a sense of home in the region and a historical anchor to its heritage. Their discomfort with the architecture of social engineering emanated from its failure to cohere the sense of nativeness they desired. Statist modernism was, for them, a technical but not emotional solution, a shelter rather than a home.

If the founding generation of Labor Zionists carefully heeded the architects of CIAM, the sabras were following members of the European Team 10, particularly Peter and Alison Smithson, Aldo van Eyck, and Candilis-Josic-Woods, the architects who had brought CIAM to an end in 1959.[64] The admiration for Kahn was matched, even eclipsed, only by the veneration of Le Corbusier, whose *Oeuvre Complète* was studied by this new wave of architects with the devotion of Talmudic scholars: they admired its truth to materials, its blunt and honest response to living experience and vernacular traditions.[65] While sabra architects looked primarily to these European sources, the Anglo group of architects was more inclined toward the teachings of Americans such as Lewis Mumford, Kevin Lynch, Jane Jacobs, and Christopher Alexander.[66] Lawrence Halprin helped invigorate new trends in landscape architecture, and Bernard Rudofsky inspired the interest in preserving authentic environments rather than isolated monuments.[67] Common to all approaches was a propensity toward regionalism and historical consciousness, and a focus on people and their urban communities. Overburdened with modernity, architects sought the foundational principle of architecture in the traditional city from which modernism broke away. Through such diverse post–World War II architectural variants, local architects came to define the "Israeliness" of the *mamlachtiyut* project.

Conclusions

National politics, by definition, aim to impose meaning on reality. To succeed in this imposition it must intervene in the beliefs, assumptions, and expectations of its addressees. As we investigate how the nation-state performs this intervention by means of architecture, we must question the agency of the discipline of architecture in this process. We attribute the effectiveness of the joint political-architectural project to its invisibility as a political statement, to the distracted consumption of its results as a matter of fact, a mere set of buildings and streets to live in.

The goal of the *mamlachti* project was to consolidate the people of Israel and devise for it a secular Jewish culture, meshing statism and kingdomism, state and nation. Israeli-born architects, sensing the incompatibility between the two, articulated this predicament in the language of identity and community. In order to devise a concrete and tangible sense of belonging, they sought an unmediated experience of place. We have seen that *mamlachti* architecture emerged from a generation that grew up in the utopian, abstract white houses on the right side of the poster in Plate 1, and who then sought to foster a rooted national identity for themselves by returning to the brown figure on the left. Their descent into the Oriental past was a cautious one, as they negotiated with the brown figure about the proper role of place, history, and nation in creating a more appropriate Israeli architecture. It was a transition from an architecture of negation, and from houses "free of past memories," as Posener put in 1937, to an architecture of "positive features," of wishfully familiar content.[68] Paradoxically, seeking the promised land of native belonging led sabra architects to the Arab village and the Palestinian vernacular, which became a prime paradigm in articulating Israeli architecture—a style that would come into its own just before Israel seized the long-desired East Jerusalem.

Following the Six Day War, Ben Gurion tried to impose his historicized Judaism on the city. No longer in a position of power but still revered by his disciples, he suggested tearing down the Ottoman walls of the Old City, which he considered an obstacle to the meshing of West Jerusalem with its biblical past. Ben Gurion's plan foretold the great challenge that the presence of Al-Quds (the Arabic term for Jerusalem, literally "The Sacred") posed to *mamlachti* architecture. Indeed, after 1967, when the Israeli army took the mysterious veil off of the figure in brown, exposing its edifices to the astounded eyes of Israeli builders, the architecture of *mamlachtiyut*—and indeed, of modernism itself—found its greatest and most problematic moments. In the next decade, the profession of architecture would be glorified and criticized by the many actors who competed for Jerusalem's real estate.

2 PROFESSION
EAST JERUSALEM AND
THE EMERGENCE OF THE
SABRA ARCHITECTS

A culture looks for the symbols of its heroic periods and
assimilates them in its local architecture, as Italy, for example,
relates to the Roman Empire. In Jerusalem, however, the
post-'67 architecture of power absorbed the symbols of the
conquered rather than those of the conqueror.

—*Elinoar Barzaki, head of the Jerusalem Region in the Ministry
of Housing and later city engineer of Jerusalem, interview
with the author, August 20, 1998*

T HE 1967 WAR, and the Israeli army's seizure of East Jerusalem from
Jordan, caught Israel's planning administration unprepared. Immediately
after the war, the newly triumphant Israeli government issued a mandate that
was simple yet would prove nearly impossible to fulfill: it asked Israeli planners to blanket the recently occupied land with built facts on the ground, and
thus to foster a sense of the city's unity under Israeli rule. Jerusalem's unity
became a primary national goal because it symbolized for Israelis the return
of Jews to their mythical biblical origins. But neither Israel's modernist planners nor the politicians who guided them knew how to express such powerful
symbolism through architecture.

   The government's initial efforts reveal the difficulty of this mandate.
On February 12, 1968, eight months after the war, the minister of housing,
Mordechai Bentov, simply advised his planners to give the unified city an
"Oriental character." The "planning principles" he advocated were almost
embarrassingly reductive: "building in stone, relatively low-rise buildings,
within the limits of three stories. . . . Also incorporated are elements of Oriental building such as arches, domes, etc." Speaking to the Knesset (the Israeli parliament), he promised that the architects and planners "are exerting
extra efforts to bestow on these neighborhoods an image that accords with
the landscape and character of Jerusalem."[1] This elusive character, however,
seemed out of reach. Soon after, the design for the first new neighborhood in
East Jerusalem—Eshkol Heights—was completed; fearing that the result was

not Oriental enough, the Ministry of Housing decided to superimpose pre-fabricated concrete arches onto the buildings. This camouflage epitomizes the confused search for a never fully articulated sense of an appropriate look for the new buildings.[2]

In the critical decade following the Six Day War, city politicians, the state government, internationally renowned architects, and urban planners alike all vied to put their mark, and their ideology, on Jerusalem's invaluable landscape. But one group would assume an especially central role in creating (and re-creating) the look of Jerusalem: the first generation of architects who were born and educated in Israel, emerging primarily from the Technion (officially known as the Israel Institute of Technology) in Haifa, until recently the nation's single accredited architecture school. This group of sabra architects would become emblematic of the Generation of the State, the term for the literary and artistic caste of Israelis who came of age under statehood.[3] Though an amorphous group themselves (they never cultivated an organized identity or had a clear leadership), these sabras would, in a few short years, create a coherent architectural image for Jerusalem. Like others before them, they wrestled with the question of inspiration and design ideology. As we shall see, the sabra architects would veer wildly from the modernist ideals of their Israeli forebears, but their way out was equally problematic. The sabra solution to a unifying architecture—fascinatingly out of sync with the Judaization aims of the newly powerful Israeli government—would depend heavily on that readily accessible but seemingly contradictory source: Palestinian vernacular architecture. (See Plate 2 and Figure 2.1.)

Figure 2.1. Ram Karmi, housing in Giloh, Cluster 6, general view. Courtesy of the Azrieli Architecture Archive at the Tel Aviv Museum of Art, Ram Karmi Collection.

The result bewildered many people, including Elinoar Barzaki, the former head of the Jerusalem Region in the Ministry of Housing. Against all precedent, she noted, in Jerusalem, "the post-'67 architecture of power absorbed the symbols of the conquered rather than those of the conqueror."[4] In Barzaki's formulation, the symbols of the conqueror were the cubical and ordered housing blocks of pre-1967 West Jerusalem, as well as the modernist institutional buildings that crowned its government precinct, while the symbols of the conquered were the Oriental stone architecture that composed the picturesque skyline of the Old City and its environment. As we shall see, post-1967 Israeli architecture clearly drifted away from its predominantly modernist practices, emulating instead the architecture of its Arab "other." Why would architects Israelize one of the most contested cities on earth with the architectural forms of its rival nation? And, moreover, how were Israelis able to separate this Palestinian style from the culture that produced it, in order to re-create it as an Israeli architecture?

A distinctive Israeli architecture was already taking shape by 1963, when Aviah Hashimshoni wrote the first history of the country's architecture. This study establishes the architectural modernism that had been adopted by Zionists since the early 1930s as an identifiable Israeli architectural tradition.[5] Its resolution was based on the thoroughly and uniformly modernist landscape that Israelis created during the first two decades of statehood. But problems soon arose with this novel—yet entrenched—modernist architectural tradition, which was replaced by an even newer tradition, but one authenticated by deeper roots: a localist tradition inspired by the tradition of the place. This new practice undergirded the conceptual architectural framework most prevalent in post-1967 Jerusalem. The evolution and force of this localist tradition enabled architects to articulate in space the tenets of David Ben Gurion's nation-building project, the *mamlachtiyut*.

We will find the roots of this architectural tradition in the cultural and professional formation of the new generation of architects, who were entrusted with the national mandate of Israelizing Jerusalem. During the 1960s and 1970s, these architects found themselves inextricably bound up in the crises about modernism that developed simultaneously in their architectural and political cultures. At the same time that architects worldwide were questioning the premises of the architectural modernism advocated by the influential Congrès Internationaux d'Architecture Moderne (CIAM), Israelis were becoming more vocal in challenging the modernization project of Labor Zionism and its decades-long campaign for progress and development. This twofold crisis strongly affected Israeli-born architects, these sabras who were the first natives of the Israeli state. Their emerging critique of both architectural and Zionist modernisms led them to the Palestinian vernacular, particularly to the Arab village that by the time post-1967 construction was under way, had fascinated them for almost a decade.

In order to analyze the journey of these Israeli-born architects, both to Jerusalem itself as well as into the positions of power from which they could shape its physical form, we will examine this architectural generation ethnographically. Such a perspective reveals the links between seemingly discrete elements: the practice of post–World War II architectural trends, the pressing issue of national belonging in a settler society, the appropriation of Palestinian vernacular architecture, and ultimately the ethics of Israeli place-making in art and architecture. In these encounters between architectural and national cultures—the encounter that embodied Ben Gurion's *mamlachtiyut* project within the built landscape—we find that architects were neither autonomous, creative professionals working only within the discipline of architecture, nor simply instruments of official power. I maintain instead that paradoxically, the force of this architectural production is contingent on its seeming political transparency. In other words, although architects created from within the framework of their discipline, their actions were thoroughly politicized at the very point where they were most neutral and professional.

The Sabra Generation

Sabra architects launched their campaign to localize Israeli architecture in the late 1950s. In the territory of the decade-old Israeli state, they saw a homeland fundamentally different from what had been envisioned by the preceding generation, the founders of Labor Zionism. Since the early 1930s, Zionist architects in Mandate Palestine had embraced a modern architecture, which promised a new beginning, a departure from both bourgeois and Oriental life, which they believed had contaminated Jewish life in the Diaspora.[6] These efforts were manifested in projects like Richard Kauffmann's rural settlements, Alexander Klein's minimal standards neighborhoods, and Arieh Sharon's co-op workers' housing, as well as in public buildings ranging from dining halls to cinemas, all joined by their trademark cubical forms: flat roofs, *piloti,* strip windows, and smooth surfaces devoid of decoration. But just a few decades later, sabra architects would claim that the resultant international architecture—by then identified as the architectural tradition of Israel—failed to meet the Zionist promise of a national home (Figure 2.2).

The Generation of the State was a group committed primarily to professional, rather than political, action.[7] Their cultural roots were strikingly uniform—they were native-born, urban, and socialist—and as a result, they tended to internalize a shared set of historical, cultural, and ideological conditions as second nature.[8] The result was multifaceted similarity, consisting of everything from body language to manners, from values to aspirations, as

Figure 2.2. Aerial view of modernist housing blocks in Haifa. Source: *Israel Builds, 1958* (Tel Aviv: Ministry of Housing, 1958), cover.

well as the shared truisms and cultural heroes that granted this group of sabra architects membership in the inner circle of Israeli culture.

The outlook and inclinations sabra architects gained in the Yishuv, and during early statehood, were crucial in helping them navigate through the myriad architectural trends of the time.[9] The social and political elite of the nascent state shared their criticisms of high architectural modernism. As a result, the design choices by the sabra architects were easily, even naturally, accepted by their political peers as sensible and appropriate. They criticized existing practice and promoted critical trends. But their standing was even more powerful because they embraced only the trends they could filter through the cultural dispositions of Israel's inner circle. Their savvy choices would establish these architects as leading professionals capable of mobilizing specialized knowledge into the national arena, a process that yielded not only larger-than-life commissions, but also momentous positions in Israel's national building machine.

Most members of this group were born or grew up in Tel Aviv and attended one of three high schools in the city during the 1940s.[10] These schools were ideological hubs, cultivating "men of European culture in the East" while investing them with the value system of the so-called working settlement, which was considered the elite of Labor Zionism.[11] Later, a program of combined military and agricultural training prepared them to take part in the Judaization of Mandate Palestine and then the War of Independence.[12] The troop of youth sent to Rosh HaNikrah kibbutz in 1947–48, for example, consisted of six future architects, who would have great impact on Israeli building practices, academia, and institutional planning (Figure 2.3).[13] Four would build extensively in post-1967 Jerusalem; one, Avraham Vachman, became an influential professor at the Technion; and another, Ram Karmi, became a prominent architect and educator as well as the first head architect of the Ministry of Housing.

The leading architects of this generation acquired their education almost exclusively at the Technion, either during the War of Independence or in the immediate postwar years. The education they received was highly modernist and bluntly ideological. Their teachers were European émigrés who had been trained primarily in German-speaking schools. Some, like Alexander Klein, had already held a seminal position among modernists in Europe before his immigration to Palestine. Others, like Aviah Hashimshoni, the future author of the *1968 Jerusalem Masterplan,* held prominent military positions. During his long deanship, Yohanan Ratner, who in 1932 inherited the Faculty of Architecture from the founding Orientalist dean, Alexander Baerwald, developed and solidified a strictly modernist curriculum. Revealing of the school's aims, Ratner's career was split in two parallel routes: on the one

Figure 2.3. A combined military and agricultural training in Kibbutz Rosh HaNikrah. Five future architects were in this group; Ram Karmi wears glasses in the center of the first image. The banner states "To the champions of Socialism–Free My People!" Photographs courtesy of the late Avraham Vachman.

hand his architectural practice, scholarship, and deanship; and on the other, his historic role as a general who linked the civil and military leaderships of the Yishuv and developed the structure and hierarchy of the Israel Defense Force. Under his leadership the Technion's architectural education combined a focus on functional needs and built form, thus serving the Yishuv—and later the state—with professional principles similar to those guiding the interwar architecture of *neue sachlichkeit*.[14]

According to Moti Sahar, a powerful institutional architect and a former combat pilot, the sabra generation saw itself as "bound with issues of the nation."[15] This sense of commitment formed their generational identity, but it also sparked their professional revolt. In this context, the 1957 conference in Ohalo, near the Sea of Galilee, was a formative moment.[16] Avraham Yaski, who was a rising young architect at the time and has been, for decades, the powerful head of arguably the largest architectural firm in Israel, remembers his trembling knees and cracking voice when he challenged his revered elders, the founding generation of Zionist architectural modernism and his teachers at the Technion,[17] the architects who had brought the new architecture of European interwar modernism to Mandate Palestine.[18] That conference would be the first of many in which the emerging architects slowly, and painfully, loosened the fierce grip Israel's first generation held over the country and the profession alike.

In the years to come, the divide between the generations would become increasingly apparent. After independence, the older generation of European émigrés had incorporated the modern architecture they had previously practiced into a mass-produced housing industry, which was essential for a country accommodating numerous waves of new immigrants.[19] In the minds of the sabra architects, however, these housing solutions ignored the cultural diversity of the immigrants. Furthermore, they claimed, the architecture of Zionist modernism had failed to create a sense of belonging between people, their community of inhabitants, and the place they share, which in their minds was mandatory for any successful building project. The sabra criticized architects like Alexander Klein for his famous scientific schemes in search of "existence minimum."[20] They appreciated the mass housing Klein and his colleagues created for new immigrants but insisted that in the process Zionist modernist architects treated the inhabitants of the so-called *shikunim* (standard housing blocks) as mere objects. Klein's housing projects, they contended, were certainly efficient but left no room for "culture," which was, according to sabra architects, "what makes human beings into a people and society."[21]

Despite their growing ideological differences, the architectural members of this generation learned a great deal from their elders, particularly about the power of collective effort. By the 1960s they had formed an identity of their own, and leading members among sabra architects even set up a professional group—known as the Tel Aviv circle—that met once a month to brainstorm their projects (Figure 2.4).[22] Although the circle never produced a single written manifesto, it had a very clear agenda that soon filled the pages of *Handasah ve-Adrichalut* (Engineering and Architecture), Israel's lone architectural peri-

Figure 2.4. Meeting of the Tel Aviv circle of architects. From right to left: Moshe Zarhi, Yaakov Yaar, Amnon Alexandroni, Dan Eytan, Ram Karmi, Yitzhak Yashar, Shimon Powsner. Courtesy of Dan Eytan.

odical of the time.[23] The sabra's ideological cohesion also became evident as they gained positions in Israel's Association of Engineers and Architects and began to judge the country's numerous architectural competitions.

The principal focus of their work was housing in new towns, which mushroomed in Israel's territorial periphery after independence. They were commissioned to build such showcase neighborhoods as in Beer Sheva, where both Avraham Yaski and Amnon Alexandroni experimented with a quarter-kilometer-long Corbusian megablock, while their peers Daniel Havkin and Nachum Zolotov designed carpet housing: a low-rise and continuous built fabric with shaded passageways and private patios (Figure 2.5). Similarly, in a neighborhood built in Givat Hamoreh in 1958, Yaakov and Ora Yaar were already inspired by regionalism, a building style that aimed to emulate the authenticity of place-based architecture and was often inspired by the local vernacular of the Mediterranean. White low-rise buildings re-created the space and proportions of traditional streets, an urban form that CIAM abolished, by accommodating the slope of the hill into split-level residential units. Regionalism along with the New Brutalism and morphology formed a triptych of architectural trends that the sabra architects promoted. Across the Israeli landscape, from Dimona to Nazereth, from Arad to the un-built Bsor City, this group of architects conducted bold experiments with the new trends they advocated.[24]

Figure 2.5. Daniel Havkin and Nachum Zolotov, carpet housing in Beer Sheva, early 1960s. Source: Gilead Duvshani and Harry Frank, *"Build Ye Cities": An Exhibition of Israeli Architecture* (London: Institute of Architects and Town Planners in Israel A.E.A.I., 1985), 31.

By 1967 members of the sabra generation were gaining the professional power that would soon be necessary to lead the building of the so-called United Jerusalem. Following the war, their premier position was all but assured. During the 1970s their influence extended from the private sector to the heart of bureaucracy. In 1975 Ram Karmi, arguably the most influential architect of his generation, became head architect for the Ministry of Housing, which centralized the building market in Israel and would, under Karmi, become a hub of sabra activity in Israel. In 1978, Amnon Niv, a younger Tel Aviv architect with related architectural convictions, was appointed as Jerusalem's city engineer. Both appointments provoked a shift in planning and design philosophy as well as professional personnel. Ram Karmi, for example, inaugurated his post by halting all ongoing planning projects, brought three dozen new architects and planners into the ministry, and embarked on a new nation-wide planning program. Again and again, this small but potent sabra group was at the forefront of crucial architecture and planning, a place of influence that continues to this day.[25]

Searching for an Architecture of the Place

Enthusiasm for vernacular architecture typified the new generational strategy, an excitement that sabra architects shared with their colleagues overseas. Instead of the modernist will to re-form society, they sought "the spatial expression of human conduct."[26] They believed an unmediated form of this expression could be found in indigenous architecture, where life, rather than architects, dictated the form of building.[27] As a result, architects shifted their focus to a universal Man, theoretically informed by structural anthropology. In an oft-quoted statement, the influential Dutch architect Aldo van Eyck tells us that

> Man is always and everywhere essentially the same. He has the same mental equipment though he uses it differently according to the particular life pattern of which he happens to be a part. Modern architects have been harping continually on what is different in our time to such an extent that even they have lost touch with what is not different, with what is always essentially the same.[28]

If man is essentially the same everywhere, his environment must be expressed by similar architectural principles. Postwar architectural discourse presented a wealth of mostly primitive examples of this correlation between man and the built places that housed his life. This architecture was believed to be uncontaminated by Western historical conventions or by spurious Western progress. Moreover, unlike regional architecture at (the European) home, it risked no nationalistic interpretation, no painful memory of prewar sentiments. The prototypical inhabitant of these environments was a generic Man, whose specific history, culture, and politics were ignored in favor of a universal truth regarding the instincts of human habitation.

In the United States, architectural critics such as Bernard Rudofsky drew on the Bible and Charles Darwin—the mythical and scientific origins of Western culture—to divest modern architecture of its authority.[29] Rudofsky's *Architecture without Architects* of 1964 emerged as a major sourcebook for architects worldwide (Figure 2.6). It argued that vernacular architecture was "nearly immutable, indeed, unimprovable, since it serves its purpose to perfection."[30] Similarly enthusiastic were followers of Martin Heidegger's phenomenology who wished to understand things as they appear in our experience. They found in vernacular architecture ontological definitions of place, of being at home in the world. The group ATBAT-Afrique in Morocco, whose work combined Arab vernacular with modern architecture, wrote in their statement of principle that "it is impossible for each man to construct his house to himself. It is for the architect to make it possible for the man to make his house a home."[31]

This type of social ethics brought the architectural thinking of Team 10 and of the New Brutalism to bear so effectively on the architectural discourse of sabra architects. Team 10, the group that brought the seminal modernist congresses of CIAM to an end, advocated notions such as urban hierarchy, social reidentification, and a commitment to the discipline of architecture. The existentialist undertones of the Brutalists guided their focus on the now, the as found, and on life as is. Accordingly, they emphasized an aesthetic of crude and exposed local materials, following the late work of Le Corbusier, and utilized the rough, naked, heavy, and elastic qualities of poured concrete.[32]

Sabra architects found in this body of work principles to create new venues for architecture to socialize new immigrants into a national community, and at the same time new means to connect this long-imagined community to a concrete Land of Israel. New immigrants, the sabra generation posited, could not and should not comply with the Zionist vision of a modernist utopia built in white. The sabra generation wanted instead to "transform the Diaspora Jew into a man growing out of the land,"[33] a man whose identity develops as a result of his organic ties to the territory rather than his adherence to an idea foreign to him. Therefore, only an architecture of the place could connect Israelis with a territory to which they wanted to belong, as well as to possess.

The 1960s' use of the term *makom* (Hebrew for "place") referred to the encounter between man and the place where he is. The notion of *makom* is fundamental to sabra art and architectural discourse because, as Zali Gurevitz

Figure 2.6. Bernard Rudofsky, images from *Architecture without Architects: A Short Introduction to Non-pedigreed Architecture* (New York: Museum of Modern Art, 1964). Courtesy of the Bernard Rudofsky Estate Vienna/VBK 2013.

and Gideon Aran have argued, Israeli Jews did not succeed in resolving the ambiguities of their place, namely the tension between the text and the territory. The Land of Israel, according to this argument, has always been an abstract homeland, an idea, an aspiration the Zionist movement inherited from the Jewish religion. At the same time, it was also an actual place, laden with authenticity and sacred history. If the founding generation was devoted to the idea embodied in the State of Israel, the sabra generation embraced the territory itself. The schism between the two constantly disturbed the process of physically inhabiting the land. Because the idea, according to Gurevitz and Aran, preceded the place, the efforts of sabra architects to substantiate the idea in the land were not as spontaneous, or instinctive, or inherent in the vernacular as they imagined. On the contrary, the efforts of the sabras were conscious, determined, and ideologically charged, fundamentally different from the effortlessness of native architecture, which is the product of birthright and direct ancestry.[34]

Sabra architects readily found this nativeness in Arab culture, whose vernacular architecture embodied the rootedness in place they sought. In the cover story on "The Traditional House in the Arab Villages of the Galilee," published in the inaugural issue of the journal *Tvai*, Yoram Segal stressed this unmediated connectedness. The *fellah*, a poor, native farmer who typically uses preindustrial methods, according to Segal also builds and maintains his house, and as a result creates with it "a relationship of belonging, of identification, and of strong emotional attachment" (Figure 2.7).[35] It was precisely this sort of relationship that the sabra architects were seeking.

By the time Segal published his research in 1966, Yitzhak Danziger—a sculptor, environmental artist, charismatic teacher, and conscientious preacher—had already led the basic design studies at the Technion for a decade and was considered by many the forerunner of the sabra's search for

Figure 2.7. Yoram Segal, Arab village in the Galilee. Source: Yoram Segal, "The Traditional House in the Arab Villages in the Galilee," *Tvai* 1 (1966): 19.

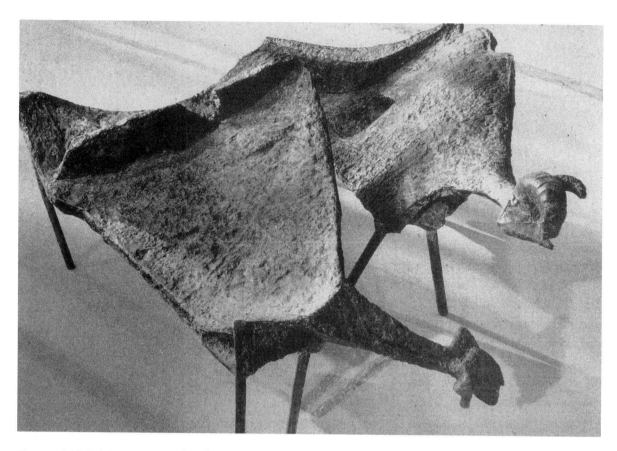

Figure 2.8. Yitzhak Danziger, *Sheep of the Negev,* 1951-64. Bronze. Two units: 109.2 x 195.9 x 82 cm and 83 x 212.2 x 80.8 cm. Collection of the Tel Aviv Museum of Art, 1993. Source: *Makom* (Tel Aviv: Hakibbutz Hameuchad Publishing House, 1982).

local expression. At first, his "will to find local roots" led him to the ancient Orient, and his sandstone sculptures granted him a powerful position among the Canaanites, an influential group of writers and visual artists that aspired to tie Israeli culture to the heritage of the ancient East rather than to diasporic Judaism. After he studied landscape architecture in London, his commitment to finding "the relationship to the place, to the landscape in this country" assumed environmental dimensions.[36] The desert-inspired *Sheep of the Negev* made in 1963—a bronze structure meshing the notions of tent, sculpture, and shelter (Figure 2.8)—reflected this desire.[37] Together with his other works, Danziger's sculpture offered to sabra architects a profound (and rare) example from the older generation of expressing local identity and the essence of the Israeli landscape.

Danziger harshly criticized the Zionist project, not as an idea but as an expression of a typical modernization process. For Danziger, the Orient offered a potential cure to the injury caused by Labor Zionism. Danziger searched for years for his definition of the *makom,* his vision of a perfect place and an appropriate seat for Israeli self-expression; he finally found his answer in Palestinian religious sites, many of which were linked to a Jewish past. Starting in 1973 and until his death in 1977, Danziger dedicated himself to a monumental project he called *makom,* which included photographic documentary and the occasional restoration of places that he believed could function simultaneously as a landscape, a ritual, and an opportunity for Israelis to find a home.[38] These sites could connect Israel to a Palestinian authenticity that had not yet been spoiled by the Zionist project.

Ram Karmi, who worked intimately with Danziger and was trained in the same British school, explicitly distinguishes Danziger's vision from what he terms the "White Architecture" that dominated Israel's first three decades:

> If the White Architecture protested intellectual superiority over the backwardness of "those close to nature," those who do not take part in the universal revolution, then the sabra has already assembled parts of the Arab menu into his unique, new customs. In architecture, it was expressed in the Brutalist building of the 1960s. In those years, an opening was widening for a creative and innovative spirituality that drew from the Israeli way of life.[39]

"The Arab menu" was a modern resource with which the sabras could forge a separate identity from the modernist, "universal revolution" of their émigré parents. They turned instead to the principles of regionalism, morphology and the New Brutalism (localized as Brutalism) that came to rule the day: the principles of native intimacy with the landscape and climate were taken from the region, from the Arab vernacular; the directness and chutzpa of the sabra, in turn, found expression in the gray, crude, and forceful "Brutalist building of the 1960s."

The sabra quest for "unique, new customs," for a quintessential "Israeli way of life," underlies this ambivalence toward Arab culture. Looking back several decades later, Karmi suggests that "emulating the local gave birth to an empathy toward the lifestyle of the Arabs and the Bedouins, and led to a renewed examination of different identity options."[40] Like Arab words in Hebrew slang, Arab attire for Israeli youth, or Arab food in Israeli cuisine, the evocation of the Arab village in Israeli architectural culture was a protest against the dominance of émigré Zionists, a way for sabras to identify themselves as natives.

In 1965, the sabra search for architecture of a place found one of its most profound expressions: Karmi's multifunctional megastructure in Beer Sheva.[41] In the text explaining his award-winning project, Karmi portrayed the Arab village as a set of formal and functional characteristics conducive to a harmonious built environment and a cohesive community. He saw the Arab village as being at home in the region—a sensual place where one could intimately experience space, stone, wind, and light (Figure 2.9). Naturally, the Palestinian inhabitants of these villages play little part in the picture. Their presence is at best generic, and their communal life is rendered as typically Mediterranean.

Karmi's intention was to translate, rather than mimic, regional values and molds. In the Arab village, he claimed, he found typologies that accord with the desert: the cohesiveness of the built material, the shaded, ventilated bazaar, the dissolution of the traditional facade into a volumetric play in which the sun sculpts ever-changing shadows. His attempt to translate Palestinian architecture is subtle. But, Karmi stressed, this typology was not yet part of the Israeli culture that "we" Israelis were so laboriously trying to define.[42]

These examples demonstrate the cultural impasse for Israeli architects. Zionist revolutionary socialism, which attempted to redeem the country through its modernization, did not accord with their generation. This brand of modernism had emerged in Europe, and its sweeping Judaization of Mandate Palestine intentionally ignored indigenous architecture. It also operated from the top down, headed by the Zionist pioneers who salvaged a

Figure 2.9. Ram Karmi, "An Arab Village," drawing. Source: Ram Karmi, "On the Architecture of Shadows," *Kav* 3 (1965): 55–56.

land conceived as tabula rasa. The sabra approach, however, turning to the local vernacular in order to build from the bottom up, was no less confusing. A genuine national architecture required an unmediated expression of the place, but the search for authentic expression yielded perplexing results: native architecture was mostly Arab.

The Israeli search for an alternative to Zionist modernism in the local Palestinian vernacular was thus contradictory: at exactly the time when Arab culture was most denigrated by the Israelis, its intimate code for local connectedness was deeply admired. In the wake of this contradiction, the distinctions between colonizer and colonized, or Western and Oriental, gave way to the ambivalence of colonial subjectivity. Over the last several decades, scholarly analysis of this contradictory condition has emerged in critical response to binary oppositions, such as in Edward Said's seminal *Orientalism,* published in 1978.[43] Such scholarship has habitually focused on the incapacity of the colonized to retrieve an authentic identity not already entangled in colonial subjugation.[44] My interest here is in a similar yet inverted ambivalence: I believe we must examine the dominant professional discourse, rather than the natives, as the object of ethnography.[45] Accordingly, we can see how the colonizer is dependent on the identity of the colonized in order to define an authentic national identity and proclaim one's visceral ties to the place. The Israeli desire to achieve the Arab's nativeness, which was seen as the ultimate expression of locality, sheds new light on a subject seldom frequented by postcolonial scholarship.

The national and professional sentiments of the sabra underlined the Israeli architectural praxis that shaped the urban landscape of post-1967 Jerusalem. This crucial decade brought a fundamental Israeli debate to the fore: between post–World War II architectural culture, the modernist crisis of which echoed in the sabra generation's revolt against Zionist modernism, and a national identity built on a formative lack of substantial rootedness, which provoked a desire for and fantasy about the intimate relationship of the Arab native with the place and its landscape, with stone and light. After the 1967 war, the object of this fantasy—the Arab habitat—was not only suddenly tangible, it was also heavily populated with the Palestinian residents of the occupied territories; as a result, what seemed to be merely an internal debate within the architectural profession was caught up in the heated politics of the Israeli/Palestinian conflict.

Makom in the Making

During the late 1950s and the 1960s, architects of the sabra generation worked for the most part within Israel's geographical periphery. Some of these architects recall repeated requests to the minister of housing for a larger slice of the country's building commissions. According to architect Dan Eytan, the minister typically replied with caution: he would only commission their rather experimental designs when he had to boast about a project in front of international guests and donors. Eytan's memories reveal the self-claimed marginality of this generation vis-à-vis institutional commissions, despite the great admiration they already won in professional circles. This situation radically changed after 1967, a period in which the sabras took on an incredible volume of housing and institutional projects and their architectural convictions matured into a full-scale program, especially remarkable considering their young age.

If Israel's building administration consisted almost exclusively of orthodox modernists, how did younger architects receive the most prestigious commissions of the day? We can examine these dynamics by looking at the excitement around the redesign of the Hebrew University on Mount Scopus, which had been abandoned in 1948, stood empty for two decades as an Israeli enclave in Jordan, and then became the flagship project of the immediate postwar era. The euphoria of the Six Day War and the conquest of East Jerusalem strongly affected American Jewry, whose commitment to Israel was significantly boosted by the victorious Jewish state. Potential donors, whose faith in Zionism had been in doubt, expressed new interest in Israeli institutions. Architect David Reznik recalls such an American donor, who visited the historical site of the Hebrew University—the crown of cultural Zionism—just a few days after the war's end. According to Reznik's account, he was late for the meeting.[46] Dressed in military uniform, he apologized for his inelegance, explaining he had just returned from the war. The donor stepped forward, wrapped his arm around Reznik's shoulders, and according to the architect, ignored the rest of the well-dressed dignitaries while listening to authentic news from the front. A week later, Reznik received an invitation letter to prepare a master plan for the campus.

Reznik, himself an earlier member of the Tel Aviv circle, decided to invite a group of architects he considered to be the most innovative and professional in the country. Their collaborative, and conflict-laden, effort to build the university is beyond the scope of this study.[47] However, it is interesting to note that most of the invitees grew up within the orbit of the Tel Aviv circle.[48] As a result of Reznik's invitation, these young sabra architects got a foot in the door far earlier than they might have otherwise and began their quick ascent into Israel's planning administration.

Concurrently, another group of this generation undertook a different prestigious task: to renovate and rebuild the Jewish Quarter in the Old City. The dense urban fabric, characteristic of traditional Muslim cities, prompted governmental officials to look for qualified architects. Since there was no training in conservation, restoration, or reconstruction in Israel's architectural institutions, the administration looked for precedents, the most recent of which was Old Jaffa. This groundbreaking preservation project, carried out between 1960 and 1967, won its sabra design team—Yaakov and Ora Yaar, Saadia Mendel, and Eliezer Frenkel—large commissions in the quarter. Their projects in particular demonstrate how this generation's critical position toward high modernism and its ensuing new ideas was, after the war, no longer considered peripheral or too complex, as some officials had thought in the 1950s and 1960s.

Apparently, when East Jerusalem fell into Israeli hands, officials discovered that younger architects had already mastered the particular expertise required for the unprecedented task of unifying the city. And what did this expertise look like? What were the ideas of the sabras that the government came to have so much faith in? More poignantly, how did the admiration for the Arab village and for native Palestinian architecture infiltrate the Israeli buildings that started mushrooming on the hitherto Jordanian land?

I suggest that the sabras' sleight of hand, their ability to make the living space of the "other" acceptable—and even desirable—for the new Jewish nation, was made possible in three ways: this native architecture could be read historically, as biblical architecture; scientifically, as one of architecture's primitive, uncontaminated origins; or geographically, as a regional, typically Mediterranean style. To be sure, these were not conscious strategies for cultural dispossession. None of the architects discussed here comprehended the meaning embedded in these choices. While pursuing the best architecture to accommodate the social objectives they believed in, they were following rules already determined by the sabra worldview of the Yishuv.[49] The rules they shared and internalized as second nature emanated from a commitment to the values of the *mamlachtiyut,* the consensual belief in the social ethics of a progressive state seeking to reroot itself in its ancestral land.

History: Biblicizing the Landscape

After the 1967 conquest of Jerusalem's Old City, Israeli Jews rejoiced in a metaphorical return home, especially to the Western Wall and the Jewish Quarter, the symbolic centers of the Jewish people. The consequent increased focus on the vernacular architecture of the Jewish Quarter prompted a national strategy to weaken the authority of Arab architectural forms over Israeli architecture. When Segal wrote about the Arab village in the Galilee in 1966, or when sabra architects simultaneously launched a preservationist approach to the reconstruction of Old Jaffa, they admired the human values and identity embedded in what they saw as generic examples of the region's vernacular architecture. But when architects of this generation started reconstructing the Jewish Quarter immediately after the 1967 war, this vernacular was no longer generic; it was now seen as an embodiment of Jewish history by Israelis.

The cultural groundwork for this approach was prepared by the Canaanites, the group of writers and visual artists with whom the sabra architects often associated. They believed in unmediated cultural connection to the ancient Hebrews, arguing that in the State of Israel Hebrew culture should trump a more generic Jewish culture. The state's education system embraced the Canaanites' desired nativeness and their propensity for archeology, but in contrast to their approach it reinvested these Hebrew cultural forms with Jewish content. Ben Gurion's nationalized version of Judaism, for example, was thoroughly secularized and overlooked rabbinical law (the *halachah*), which he considered diasporic and thus divorced from the authentic connection between Jews and their homeland. Instead, his approach to creating a new-yet-ancient culture connected directly to biblical times, when the primordial impulse of Judaism emerged. In this context the Jewish Quarter and the Western Wall were powerful reminders of the days of Jewish glory. Their tangible presence substantiated Israel's national narrative and anchored its claim over a disputed land. "The Wall," said architect Karmi, "symbolizes the place in which I feel direct roots to King David. I can greet him *shalom*."[50]

Cutting-edge archeological research authenticated this desired feeling of biblical connectedness. While architects were seeking locality on the ground, archeologists sought Jewish history underneath its surface. The two efforts were combined in the reconstructed Jewish Quarter. According to the architect and archeologist Ehud Netzer (formerly Mentchel), and contrary to popular conviction, the quarter was not destroyed by the Jordanians after its military destruction during the 1948 war. Its poor condition, however, meant that by 1967 even piecing together the layout of the streets became a laborious task. In retrospect, Netzer, who headed the survey of the quarter and the preparation of its initial master plan, admits the nostalgic motivation of the team, whose efforts aimed to reconstruct a Jewish presence. Projects such as the recovery and commercialization of the Roman Cardo, or the excavations of the Burnt House underneath a new housing project, would embed, as Nadia Abu El-Haj demonstrates, archeological finds in the physical fabric and spatial experience of the quarter.[51]

Many Israelis were elated by the feeling of Jewish connectedness. Theo Siebenberg, for example, treated the foundation of his new home as a new frontier. Digging into the tangible depths of history, he wished to concretize his ties to ancient Jews and to embody this newly found connectedness in physical form. The gallery the Yaars built in 1972 to accommodate the archeological findings beneath the Siebenberg House—a house they had previously designed for the Company for the Reconstruction and Development of the

Jewish Quarter in the Old City of Jerusalem—exemplifies the architectural sensibility of the time. An open space flows between four levels, creating a section that unifies all the levels and emphasizes the descending depth of the place, as if one was literally sinking into history. The lines of the cut-through floors and the sculptural parapets run along the irregular site and take the visitor through numerous niches, all sculpted in concrete and covered with traditional crude and grainy plaster painted in white, thus creating sharp contrast with the darker excavated limestone. The space, the lighting, and the building technology are all clearly modern, yet the design is crafted, local, and connected (Figure 2.10).

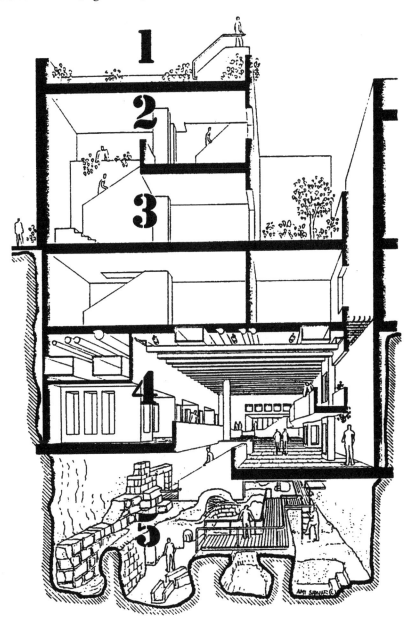

Figure 2.10. Ora and Yaakov Yaar, Siebenberg House in the Jewish Quarter of the Old City, section, early 1970s. Source: Architectural Heritage Research Center, the Technion, Yaar Architects Collection.

Figure 2.11. Sillwan village and Temple Mount. Source: Irit Zaharoni, "Derech Eretz: Man and Nature," in *Israel, Roots and Routes: A Nation Living in Its Landscape* (Tel Aviv: Ministry of Defense Publishing House, 1990), 20–21.

If the architecture of the quarter testified to the continuity of Jewish habitation since biblical times, the new sense of locale could be applied to the surrounding Palestinian villages, whose architecture was perceived as biblical, with the inhabitants as its custodians. Indeed, the "special zone"—the planning administration's term for Jerusalem's most symbolic sites—reached beyond the Old City. It included the Palestinian rural hinterland of East Jerusalem, the planning of which often fell under the rubric of landscape design. The central feature of the national landscape scheme was a green belt around the Old City, previously a British colonial dream, which would visually seize the Old City of Jerusalem. According to one sabra architect, the Arab village of Sillwan was included in this park because "its character gives us a good picture of how the landscapes and villages of Biblical times looked."[52] Publications of the army's educational system compared this village to the archeologically informed open-air model of Herod's Jerusalem, built from 1962 to 1966.[53] This 1:50 scale monumental reconstruction of the so-called Second Temple period (a major tourist attraction in and of itself) confirmed the sameness of Sillwan and Herod's Jerusalem, again emphasizing the continuity of ancient building traditions (Figure 2.11).[54]

Both the sabras and the planning administration made an explicit effort to differentiate the new interest in the vernacular from the romanticism of nineteenth-century Orientalism, pointing to the scientific accuracy of present research as proof.[55] A study of the Palestinian villages in the Hebron hills, for example, enlisted archeology, Talmudic sources, and anthropology to validate the continuity of a residential building tradition from ancient to present times. Contemporary visitors to the region, the study reported, encounter "a lifestyle which seemed familiar from biblical and Talmudic sources."[56] Following a painstaking survey the author concluded that the "houses, which have remained as they were hundreds of years ago, allow us to study and to deduce from the private construction of our time the ancient private building."[57] While this meticulous study contributes greatly to the documentation of endangered Palestinian culture, its scholarly operation at the heart of Israeli academia confirms the role of Palestinians as custodians of biblical culture, the Jewish copyright of which was always taken for granted.

Science: The Noble Savage and the Origin of Architecture

Moshe Safdie, an Israeli-born architect, had immigrated at age fifteen to Canada, where he became internationally known for his groundbreaking Habitat Montreal (first presented at Montreal's Expo 1967). Inspired by the urban landscape of Haifa, his modern Mediterranean hometown, Safdie designed a gigantic megastructure of prefabricated dwelling units, stacked one on top of the other in a manner simulating the look of a typical Mediterranean village. The slogan he marshaled, "for everyone a garden," was achieved by using the roof of each unit as an extended outdoor space, thus offering a suburban lifestyle in the midst of the city (Figure 2.12).

Mordechai Bentov, the minister of housing, went to visit the Montreal Expo shortly after the 1967 war, which put both Safdie's habitat and the

Figure 2.12. Moshe Safdie, Habitat Montreal, Expo 1967. Courtesy of Safdie Architects Archive.

Figure 2.13. Moshe Safdie, comparison between the Arab village (*Mankhat* in Hebrew or *Malkha* in Arabic) and the project it inspired, the Habitat Israel. Courtesy of Safdie Architects Archive.

Israeli pavilion in the international spotlight. Deeply impressed, and keen to develop a prefabricated building industry, Bentov warmly endorsed the promising architect. When Safdie returned home in December 1967, he was already commissioned to design the prefabricated (and not yet realized) Habitat Israel (Figure 2.13). Safdie called the Arab village site of his project by its Hebrew, biblical name, *Mankhat.* "Here," he stated, "was the prototype, the ancient village, with which any modern development would have to co-exist."[58] Realizing the absolute dichotomy between the Arab village and the Israeli superblock, he clearly intended to emulate the former, to contrast abstract intellectual premises with primal instincts of habitation—from life as it is lived. Furthering the roots of these instincts in primary habitation, such as the rudimentary wood structures built by primitive tree people, Safdie advanced a Darwinian logic directly inspired by his acquaintance Bernard Rudofsky's seminal *Architecture without Architects.*

Safdie's architectural philosophy married Rudofsky's vernacularism with the morphology he practiced with Anne Tyng, the partner of Louis Kahn and with whom Safdie spent a year in training. Inspired by D'Arcy Thompson's *On Growth and Form,* morphologists worldwide found in vernacular architecture the key to internal order, to a truth verified by nature itself rather than by the human mind, a truth that had to be discovered rather than invented. Safdie explains:

> Nature makes form; form is a product of evolution. The science of morphology deals with the reasons for the evolution of particular forms. One can study pollen and animal life, rock and crystal formations, and discover the reasons for their particular form. That helps us to understand what man's form-making could and should be.[59]

According to Safdie, the study of "man's form-making," or more precisely, of its evolution, had to emulate the method of morphological research identifying the evolution of animal life and crystal formations.

Referring to Buckminster Fuller's analysis of the need for humanity to utilize its resources, Safdie further explicates:

> The peasants who built a village on a Mediterranean hillside thought of shelter and their community and the relationships between them and the mud and wood they had for building and the sun they lived with and the water they had to collect, from which emerged their environment. They didn't think of it as expression, although it obviously was. They didn't think they were artists, though they obviously were.[60]

The evolution of these peasants' form-making thus depended on their social and material resources in a particular time and place. Safdie insisted that the form of their built environment could take only limited variations and still remain truthful to the specific functional and social demands of a particular group. Otherwise, form-making is arbitrary, that is, a means for individual, even esoteric expression, or outdated artistic conventions, rather than true reflection of a particular community and its unique place.

The Arab village, untouched by Western design, exemplified for Safdie the true origin of architecture and a scientific demonstration of the evolution of the discipline. To his eyes, even the villages of Palestinian refugees after 1948, built with "fairly limited resources" and devoid of historical depth, were "awesome environments."[61] They proved for him that habitation was a result of "the compassionate search for the way people live their private and public life."[62]

Observing post-1967 Jerusalem, Safdie delineated a clear-cut dichotomy between the genuine and noble Palestinian *fellah,* who "takes time out from farming to build himself a house," and the modernized Israeli professor, who "has a house built by a professional architect. The *fellah's* house," says Safdie, "will in all likelihood be the better one."[63] Safdie listed issues such as identity, scale, and public space that is both conducive to social life and complementary to the topography as the human qualities that made the Arab village of Sillwan a better living environment than contemporary Israeli modernist housing. All these merits depended on a long-standing heritage that the Zionist movement either ignored or erased, a heritage that the sabra architects hoped to reclaim with a precise architecture of a place.

In his exposition of the Habitat Israel, Safdie explained his incorporation of advanced methods of construction into this original vernacular model of habitation:

> I wanted to build something that was wholly contemporary, an expression of life today, but that would be as if it had always been there—a kind of fugue with two

instruments, a counterpoint on a remembered melody. Thus evolved the Habitat Israel building system: modular, concrete units, sandblasted to expose the yellow Jerusalem stone aggregate, room sections made out of fiberglass domes, and rotating windows and shutters, all interlocking on the hills.[64]

The "remembered melody" of low, native-looking buildings "interlocking on the hills" could only be an echo of the Palestinian vernacular. By creating a "fugue with two instruments," one vernacular and one technological, Safdie's Habitat Israel could fulfill the Zionist dream of fusing the ancient with the modern. In Jerusalem the origin was biblical, the modern progressive, and the combination of both a validation of a people enduring from a remote past to an unforeseen future. A further integration of this formula with ancient Jewish history brought the Palestinian vernacular to the primary site of the Jewish religion: informed by Josephus, the Roman historian who documented Herod's Jerusalem, Safdie's 1973 authorized design for the Western Wall Plaza followed the description of his Habitat Israel. Likewise, it "was akin to an Arab village in the sense that it followed the hill, each unit had its roof garden, and a series of pathways followed the topography intimately."[65]

The search for an authentic Israeli architecture was ripe with contradictions. Starting in the 1930s, the founders of the state insisted that a home for the New Jew be free of past memories—a modernist new beginning on a clean slate. Yet the stark, rectangular structures that quickly grew seemed to satisfy no one. Nearly four decades later, Safdie's scientific usage of the vernacular and his strict denial of conventional artistic expression was similarly committed to the modernist ethos, but his sources of inspiration characterized a different generation. In his Habitat Israel, Mamilla, and Western Wall projects, among numerous others, his work epitomized the primary trends that sabra architects experimented with: the search for an identifiable place by means of smooth integration of the vernacular (through the use of native structures), the scientific (through the use of morphology), and the technological (through the use of prefabricated bare concrete elements).

Geography: Mediterraneanism

A third way to view architecture of a place came at the tail end of the post-1967 decade, in the publication of Ram Karmi's essay "Human Values in Urban Architecture." Essentially a manifesto, the essay prescribed a list of Mediterranean architectural forms that were to be used as guidelines for future planning. They were intended to help architects resolve the most pressing question of the sabra generation: that of belonging. How could architects establish an architectural language that encouraged personal expression but also defined a vernacular for the national community?

Across Europe between World Wars I and II, the invocation of national architecture typically emphasized the notion of *heimat* ("homeland" in German)—that is, it stressed the particular cultural history of that nation, with a focused attention on aristocratic and bourgeois traditions. The need to possess such a culture, and to show its distinctiveness against all others, caused most European regimes to strongly oppose the architectural avant-garde during the interwar period because it advocated international architecture. How could such placeless architecture, they asked, create a sense of belonging for an ethnic group and a bounded territory? Paradoxically, a famous Fascist postcard that made fun of modern architecture also reveals the regionalist potential inherent in this placeless architecture. The site Nazis ridiculed was Mies van der Rohe's 1927 Weissenhof Ziedlung, an open-air exhibition space and a key monument of the European avant-garde. The cartoon's Orientalist depiction of van der Rohe's space as a Middle Eastern village, replete with camels and Arabs, conveyed the potential decadence of this architecture and the simultaneous laziness it inspired.

This connection was not totally fabricated. The traditional characteristics of Mediterranean building often informed early modernism, as in the cases of Joseph Maria Olbrich, Erich Mendelsohn, and the Mediterranean academy.[66] For Zionist architects, these links, among others, proved that modern architecture was adaptable to their new location in the Middle East.

This interest foreshadowed the expanding fluency of regionalism in the postwar decades. After World War II, and its violent exploitation of nationalist ideologies, *heimat* architecture went out of vogue. The resulting void prepared the ground for the modernist idea of a tabula rasa and its complemented mass-produced building industry. But the desire to belong, to connect to one's place, was not satisfied by high modernism. Instead, regionalism was a natural fit. Far from the universalist, dogmatic vision of high modernism, regionalism instead argued that architecture should express the particularities of any given place, should fit existing means and ways of life, and should be familiar and comprehensible to the people who use it. However, we must acknowledge that regionalism in the post–World War II decades emerged from within modernism and was practiced by modernist architects. Regionalism offered a connection to local built expression without compromising the modernist ban on the historical conventions of architecture. Thus, "architecture without architects" seemed more inspiring than the familiar historical precedents.

Regionalism was introduced to the discipline, along with Brutalism and morphology, as a means to critique high modernism, especially the field's large modernization projects and its anonymous standard housing. Architects working in the 1960s often blurred the boundaries between these three trends. Karmi's own shift, from emphasizing the virtues of Brutalism to praising regionalism, shouldn't come as a surprise, especially when we consider that its precedents go back to his architectural training in Britain. The historian and critic Reyner Banham writes that at the Architectural Association, where in the early 1950s the Smithsons (who initiated the New Brutalism) taught and Karmi was a student, a new generation "saw in Mediterranean peasant buildings an anonymous architecture of simple, rugged, geometrical forms, smooth-walled and small windowed, unaffectedly and immemorially at home in its landscape setting."[67] Hence, Karmi's search for the feeling of home in Mediterranean culture, or earlier in Arab built culture, had strong European roots that associated him with the work of people like Aldo van Eyck, James Stirling, and his friend Kenneth Frampton.[68]

By 1977, regionalism played out in a different geopolitical landscape. The architectural precedents that Karmi looked to were no longer tied to the Arab village, his prime reference during the 1960s, but to the Old City and Greek villages, on the one hand, and to architects such as Le Corbusier and Safdie, on the other. This combined reference to Brutalist, morphologist, and regionalist work led him to closely examine Mediterranean architecture. In "Human Values in Urban Architecture," he invoked the Mediterranean's timeless patterns as a guideline for a hierarchical ordering of the built environment, from the individual house to the street it is on, and then to the square, the bazaar, the quarter, and, finally, to the entire urban fabric. Then he compiled a manual of Mediterranean "structural elements," which he believed should constitute the alphabet of the Hebrew built landscape: the wall, the gate, the balcony and porch, the stairs and threshold, the streets and alleyways. Finally, under the banner of "values," he discussed the application of the lessons learned from Mediterranean architecture to the present day, advocating such popular post–World War II trends as the separation of pedestrians from vehicles and the creation of public spaces in between buildings.[69]

Karmi developed this architectural guide, we must remember, as an administrator. When the government first embarked on the building of East Jerusalem, ten years earlier, he was still considered a rebellious figure in the profession. Many argue that he was responsible for the morphological megastructure of the Hebrew University campus on Mount Scopus. Similarly, among members of the team that designed the housing estate of Giloh in East Jerusalem, he was the bad boy who refused to accept institutional dictates. However, once he became the head architect of the Ministry of Housing in 1975, and had to coordinate a massive slate of new building, his turn to Mediterranean values brought him closer to the architecture of the Shikun u'Pituah team who designed Ma'alot Dafna, to the regionalism of Yaakov and Ora Yaar, who inherited the planning of Ramot from this team, and to the urbanism of David Best who planned East Talpiot. Over the postwar decade, regionalism simply became more and more valuable as a tool to build Jerusalem.

We have discussed the three architectural trends utilized by the sabra generation and how the distinctions between the three were blurred as these architects attempted to create a sense of place. Let us take this analysis a step further: when Karmi fused these trends under a single call to follow Mediterranean urban values, he promoted "Mediterraneanism" as the best umbrella term to describe the architectural developments of the post-1967 decade. The instructions to build low-rise, stone-clad, hierarchical, terraced buildings around common courtyards and along urban streets meant an effort toward the creation of a regionalist, localist, Mediterranean architecture fitting for its place. The term thus pulls together many of the common elements from the disparate but interrelated visions offered by regionalism, Brutalism, and morphology.

The identification of contemporary architectural discourse with Mediterranean architecture is not new. Scholars in several different contexts have used the term "Mediterraneanism" to describe a strategy similar to what Karmi chose for his task in Jerusalem.[70] The concept of *Mediterranita,* for example, was crucial to the architecture and urban development of Italian colonialism in North Africa. Mediterranean tradition stood, in this context, for the heritage of the Roman Empire. The contemporary Italian descendants of the empire took on the mandate of reemploying such architecture in southern Europe and North Africa, the former territories of the ancient empire. Such geopolitical arguments were similarly valid in the Israeli context, where sabra architects integrated the European import of modern architecture with the local Palestinian vernacular in order to create an authentic Israeli architecture.

In the context of a contested land, the idea of Israeli participation in a larger Mediterranean culture divested Palestinian architecture of its authority over the genius loci; instead, the specific architecture of Palestine became subsumed into a larger trend visible around the Mediterranean, and evident both in the ancient world and in our own day.[71] Karmi's turn to Mediterraneanism could thus relieve the Israeli architect of the disturbing hypocrisy of admiring native architecture and disregarding the larger Arab culture that produced it. The association with the European cradle of civilization was pacifying, flexible, and perfectly at home not only in the region but also in contemporary architectural discourse.

Conclusions

As sabra architects developed these three strategies, they aimed neither to dispossess Palestinians nor to gain control over their property. Unlike the institutional planners and policy makers within Israel's government, this group of architects shied away from territorial politics. Rather, they were preoccupied with the national mandate they undertook: to localize the landscape of Israel, and to provide for a diverse population of Jews a wishfully familiar national home. The Tel Aviv circle, the most cohesive group of sabra architects, became a role model for connecting architecture and Zionism. According to Adam Mazor, currently a leading urban designer, the sabra architects of the 1960s and 1970s were regarded as a group that did not work "in order to publish in magazines, but rather, in order to find ways to make Israel wonderful." Mazor and his colleagues saw the sabras as trying "to create the desired image of Israel . . . mainly and mostly Zionism," while also addressing the primary national objectives of the time: "absorbing the gathered exiles and fostering security" in a country surrounded by Arab hostility.[72]

How could architects reconcile their entrenched commitment to the national project with their seemingly impartial professional identities and goals? Apparently, this question never surfaced because the national values of Zionism were taken for granted; for these sabras, the bond between architectural and Zionist modernism was second nature, agreed upon by all legitimate players. Take, for example, Yitzhak Danziger's explication of his vocation in 1964. A sculpture, he said, "should be active and its function multiple—it should unify or divide space, form a part of the landscape, indicate direction . . . it should be alive in an ambiance—in perpetual rapport with its given surroundings."[73] Danziger thus argues for an expanded sculptural field that overcomes the boundaries between object, architecture, and landscape. While the argument itself is integral to the visual arts, the motivation for and the capacity to produce such meaningful interdisciplinary work is contingent, according to Danziger, on factors external to the work of art.

Danziger clarifies: "The inspiration of a sculpture should come from a sense of rootedness in the land, the landscape, and the nation—from thorough knowledge of the topography, the geography, and national values of the land and its people."[74] His powerful claim for the knowledge of the place stipulates several conditions. First, he identifies a core of people who possess this intimate knowledge—the natives of the place; second, he ascribes values to this knowledge and qualifies these values as national; and third, he measures the meaningfulness of a work of art according to the degree to which it forges visceral rootedness, thus its moral contribution to a sense of national commitment. Clearly, Danziger worked toward a language of art that would create social bonds and pronounce local culture, a shared lingua franca for an uprooted people.

For Ram Karmi, who worked closely with Danziger, the reference for such active rerooting was the revival of the ancient Hebrew language. Hebrew, he argued, succeeded to address biblical origin, kinship, and blood. In other words, it translated the national narrative—of a destined Jewish community returning to its biblical past—into contemporary life and culture. Israeli architecture, Karmi contended, should connect those attributes to the land in order to create a spatial arena in which the nation could take its form. This was the mission Karmi undertook when he moved in 1975 from the private sector to the heart of bureaucracy—Israel's Ministry of Housing, which was the most powerful and resourceful player in the Israelization of Jerusalem. The move of Karmi—a successful independent architect and member of one of the country's royal families of architecture—into the state's building head-quarters was thus an ideological claim on behalf of the architectural profession for the right and duty to shape the physical image of the state. As the head architect of the ministry he endeavored to bureaucratically manage the identity of the national home.[75]

In his 1977 manifesto Karmi articulated the credo underlying his architectural leadership. His architectural argument was integrated into a socialist framework. "We must remind ourselves over and again," he insisted, "that architecture is a social art." According to Karmi, "the society . . . builds itself the environment in which it lives"; as a result, its urban structure reflects its priorities: what "the society spends its resources on, what it likes, admires, guards—or does without." His ambition was to work toward "a society that produces in order to live, not one that lives in order to produce." Such society, Karmi held, "will come into existence as a result of planning on the basis of the ideals which built the State."[76]

This utter identification with and commitment to state ideology characterized the sabra generation. Writing on artistic canons and their exclusions, Galia Bar-Or explains:

> The Israeli intelligentsia of the State's first twenty years of existence gave moral-cultural support to the regime in a manner that corresponds to Antonio Gramsci's conception of hegemony—hegemony as "organization of public support," not by coercive means but through identification, the shaping of consciousness, the acquisition of the hearts and the minds of the public, and the crystallization of a "taste" which represents an identification with a collective image.[77]

The collective image was that of the sabra, and among architects, whose careers were dependent on the state's centralized control of the building market, the identification of this collective image with the state lingered well beyond the first two decades. Bar-Or challenges us to examine how, in this context, the sabra rebellion against *sachlich* modernism was tied to "the shaping of consciousness, the acquisition of the hearts and the minds of the public." Arguably, this was the core of the sabra project: how to acquire the hearts, how to instill in new immigrants a sense of collective identity and national belonging.

The Israeli postindependence mission of gathering in the Jewish exiles re-lied on waves of new immigrants. Sabra architects were deeply involved in the pressing question of how to nationalize diverse groups of immigrants. How could they be turned, in Karmi's words, "into a people and society"? More pre-cisely, how could architects instill in new immigrants a sense of belonging—to each other as a national community and to the place as their national home?

Consider Karmi's following exposition:

> We are a people of "new immigrants"; and in the pressure cooker of the State, of continuous meeting and friction, of wanting to assimilate and to belong, it happens that old traditions (which in any case do not take well in a new soil, climate and landscape) gradually dissipate, as does the "Zionist" dream of a people coming to life again in its own country. The vacuum that results cannot be filled with statistics of the typical "public housing project" with the monot-ony of the uniform living pattern that it imposes on the inhabitants, so that they become alienated from all urban social activity.[78]

Karmi's is a crucial point: when people lose their homes, languages, and cul-tures, they experience a troubling void. Labor Zionism, the sabras came to believe, failed to fill this void because it endeavored to nationalize new im-migrants from above: it expected that immigrants would conform with an ideal foreign to them. Moreover, Labor Zionism demanded its new national subjects to subordinate all previous identity to the dictates of the socialist, independent, healthy, and productive New Jew, in whose built environment a rejuvenated, modern nationality should emerge. Sabra architects protested that the resultant modern dwelling units Labor Zionism built for new immi-grants were identical and anonymous and therefore highlighted their uproot-edness without providing for them a new sense of place with which to identify.

Israelis shared this problem with postwar architects overseas. The Smith-sons, for example, manifested that "the task of our generation is plain—we must re-identify man with his house, his community, his city."[79] Similarly, the Israeli architect Dan Eytan told me years later that the kernel of his architec-tural career was the effort

> to make the physical world around us a little more legible for people in the sense that every building tells its story. We must know how to tell this story in a legible way because only then will people befriend the building. Consequently, walking from one place to the other acquires a sense of destination, signifi-cance, and direction. One should build things that make people feel good and comfortable with them.[80]

Eytan explains that people could not adjust to the home that modernist Zionism prepared for them because the story it told them was too abstract—

it was beyond their horizon of meaning. For Eytan, only people who felt comfortable in their environment, people whose habitation corresponded to their existing pattern of life, would accommodate, as new immigrants, to their new society. Eytan articulated an intuitive understanding that Israeli national identity could not be imposed from above; it had to be negotiated through an interaction with the particular way in which people organize their universe of meaning.

In tune with postwar architectural ideas elsewhere, sabra architects tried to understand how people organized their universe. They sought to figure out what held people together and what the essence of a neighborhood was. A good neighborhood, it was understood, creates a community, and a community becomes part of the place if its architecture communicates locality. Subsequently, members of such a community are likely to develop strong ties to the new society. Only then could architecture, as the *Team 10 Primer* strongly advocated, "build toward that society's realization-of-itself."[81]

The social ethics of the New Brutalism—the commitment to real people, their familiar environments, habits, traditions, and vocations—helped architects reach the amorphous clientele of social housing: people of various backgrounds and countries of origin who were imagined by architects but were always an unknown and obscured category before inhabitation. Karmi, who was educated in London at the time the group published its first manifestos there, explained that

> Brutalism wanted to touch people as they are, to talk directly about their associations—to touch the soul, the heart. We wanted to achieve in everything the poetic dimension, the dimension of hitting people's heart, rather than the economic or functionalist dimension of their life. Efficiency was not the sacred goal, but rather human beings . . . as living things holding emotions and dreams.[82]

Karmi learned from Brutalism the means by which he could intervene in the intimate world of the people he built for. His careful study of people's associations, of returning to "the way the city is perceived by the senses of human beings,"[83] was thus the basis for all his significant architectural creations. Karmi wanted to turn alienated immigrants into people with the national identity of the sabra.

But how can one connect new immigrants with a new, foreign place? By providing degrees of freedom that grant immigrants agency. Karmi explains:

> We must seek those solutions that leave room for the new inhabitant to adapt them to his needs and to use them as a vehicle for self-expression; and that can be achieved by creating a number of basic alternatives on which he can imprint

his own variations. The more man can act in and on his environment, the greater his involvement in the place; and the greater . . . his involvement, the longer will his roots grow, and more attention will he pay to his environment, until he at last lovingly makes the strange place his own.[84]

Despite the immense difficulty of implementing this desired method of inhabitation, Karmi did not shy away from a problem that haunts Israeli architects to this day: how to turn occupied land into a familiar home.

To this end, Karmi distinguished between "building" and "architecture," and then between "space" (or "roof") and "place." His claim was that the extant government buildings fell short of being architecture at all; they were merely a system of roofs that failed to create any sense of place. He demanded a complete overhaul of national decision-making. Only then, he argued,

> the creation of a "National Home" and of "place" will achieve its legitimacy as an element that represents and reflects, in physical terms, the cultural aspirations of the community and builds the community in its own land, and expresses its physical and spiritual right to, and ownership over, that land.[85]

This is a momentous statement. Karmi identified the *makom,* the place his Israeli-born generation was seeking, with the national home that Zionism had promised. *Makom,* Karmi argued, is a prerequisite for a national home because only an identifiably Israeli place can provide the moral basis for a people's ownership over the land.

The first generation of Israeli-born architects integrated the global, post–World War II criticism of the modern movement with their country's desire for nativeness. The purpose of this difficult quest was threefold: to make a new territory familiar; to identify new immigrants with this land; and to legitimize the building of an Israeli national home on contested soil. Seeking "the physical and spiritual right to . . . that land," was for Karmi and his fellow sabras, at the heart of Israeli place-making. "Creating a 'place,'" he reminds us, "is a qualitative, symbolic and emotional process," a task that architects—rather than planners or bureaucrats—should undertake. Architecture, as distinguished from mere building, "can reflect and represent the cultural aspiration of a community"[86]—that is, it can create a symbolic place rather than a mere conglomeration of dwelling units. Making the built landscape into a *makom* thus was a way to nationalize their new territory—a way to Israelize Jerusalem.

3 **STATE**
FACTS ON THE GROUND

Do you expect that planners will act more than politicians?
Can an architect voice an opinion more than state-leaders? . . .
I allow myself to say that every act done by a planner—is a
political act. There is no deed of production that does not
have a political meaning.

—*Interview with Yehuda (Idel) Drexler, architect for the*
Ministry of Housing, in "Yehuda Drexler: The Architects Are
Not Active in Shaping the Image and Essence of the State"

IN THE YEARS AFTER 1967, many Israelis, as well as concerned on-lookers around the world, were terrified by the sheer volume and unbeliev-able speed of construction in East Jerusalem. "In the panic that grips the top political echelons," alerted Amos Elon, the leading journalist covering the transformation of Jerusalem, "we are likely to demonstrate our presence in unified Jerusalem through the establishment of a series of slums encircling the city. Is this the Zionist dream?"[1] And yet Elon and his peers were proven wrong. The 106,000 Jews that were housed in Jerusalem by 1985—increasing the city's Jewish population by two-thirds—did not encircle the city with slums but, rather, with a stable belt of middle-class settlements. In the ensu-ing decades, these settlements have become a particularly useful expression of the Zionist dream—an undeniable reality that must be considered in any negotiation over Palestinian claims on this contested city.[2]

The unpredictable success of these residential settlements raises poi-gnant questions: How were remote and desolate sites legitimated as part of a united Jerusalem? How does confiscated land in recently occupied territory turn into a home? How could Jewish residents so quickly inhabit the bare hills of Jordan? The haste, and the newness, of the building project threatened to render East Jerusalem foreign and intimidating. Architecture, and more pre-cisely, the situated modernisms of post–World War II architectural culture, and their attempt to counter the alienating environment of the modernist mass-produced housing with a careful attention to man, community, and place, pacified these anxieties.

This chapter unsettles a well-entrenched truism in the saga of Jerusalem's planning. Architects and historians tend to see architecture and politics in opposition. Teddy Kollek stands for the former: urban values, spiritual beauty, and ethnic pluralism The state advances the latter: territorial sovereignty, building efficiency, and Jewish demography. When the two clash, we are repeatedly told, architectural considerations are submissive to the immense power of official politics. Scholars therefore tend to emphasize the formative power of military occupation and legal confiscation; architecture is seen as mere decoration of existing facts on the ground. What does it matter, political scientists and geographers ask, if the building of East Jerusalem looks like a new modernist town, a mundane suburb of Tel Aviv, or a Mediterranean village? In the standard telling, the relations of power in this contested region are already fixed by the time the architects are called in.

But the closer we look, again and again, the more we see that politics and place are entangled. Politics live alongside us, in the buildings and in the neighborhoods that are deemed as our home. In order for the possession of East Jerusalem to become a fact of everyday life, people (thousands and thousands of people) had to willingly choose to live there. And indeed, those people who became the residents of East Jerusalem were not "settlers" in the sense this term carries today; that is, they did not see themselves as participating in an ideologically driven campaign to control contested land. Rather, they were (and still are today) considered ordinary middle-class Jerusalemites, people who were convinced that the public housing the state provided would not turn into slums but would offer instead an opportunity for social mobility. This chapter offers a different angle of inquiry in order to question the unpredictable success of settling East Jerusalem: instead of demonstrating the weakness of architecture within the grip of official politics, we ask how architecture participated in activating Jerusalem's territorially driven mass housing and question how various groups used architecture to compete for their particular vision of Jerusalem.

Considering architecture as a field of competition, this chapter asks why housing—the most rudimentary and mundane arena of construction in the city—was so crucial in developing the symbolic meaning of Israeli Jerusalem. In the United States, for example, citizens channeled the surge of national pride and confidence following World War II into pleas for a "new monumentality." Their appeal was based on the capacity of monuments to symbolize the rising First World, "their ideals, . . . their aims, and . . . their action."[3] But in Israel, where the combined legacy of gathering the Jewish exiles, settling the land, and embodying its borders relied on housing, the feelings of collective pride and a larger cause were directed to the residential environment. For state officials, home was where identity and belonging were manufactured. This chapter will uncover the methodology of this process.

The definition of home stood at the core of the debate between developmental and situated modernists. The sabra architects we previously reviewed conceptualized the role of the profession and how it should compete for the architectural meaning of the national home that the UN had recently granted the Jews. However, the state that commissioned them was the most powerful constituent in the making of United Jerusalem. We will analyze its agenda via the activity of its most important agency in building a Jewish city: the Ministry of Housing, which was entrusted with a generous budget and the mandate to build the confiscated territories of East Jerusalem (Figure 3.1).

Figure 3.1. President Ephraim Katzir during his visit to the new suburb of Giloh between Jerusalem and Bethlehem, 1973. Photographs by Moshe Milner. Source: Government Press Office, National Photographs Collection, files D61-009, D61-010.

The Ministry of Housing, established as an independent office in 1961, was the primary authority shaping Israel's national landscape. Its efficient building machine was the dominant construction force in the country, the authority against which the new generation of sabra architects initially consolidated their agenda. In charge were architects and bureaucrats who considered the growth of a small department in the prime minister's office into one of the most powerful governmental agencies a miracle. In a few short years they had perfected the art of developmental modernism by specializing in quick design and construction under severe conditions of uncertainty, a knowledge and method they started exporting en masse to the developing world (Figure 3.2).

In the 1950s and early 1960s situated modernists were rarely allowed into the ministry. But the dominance of developmental modernists dramatically changed after 1967, culminating in the 1975 appointment of Ram Karmi to

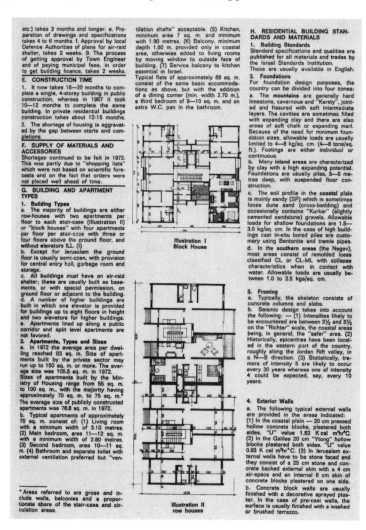

Figure 3.2. Guidelines for the design of standard housing. Source: *Israel Builds, 1973* (Tel Aviv: Ministry of Housing, 1973).

the new position of the ministry's head architect. Prior to Karmi's appointment, the architect in charge was Yehuda (Idel) Drexler, a man whose memory has evaporated from our understanding of Israeli architecture despite his monumental oeuvre, in particular the building of East Jerusalem between 1967 and 1974.

Drexler's success is in large part indebted to the following insight: for most Israelis, the developmental modernism of the Ministry of Housing was unable to express the symbolism of 1967, the unification of the Jews with their mythical past. He articulated this intuitive connection between housing and historical consciousness in a 1976 publication released by the Ministry of Housing. It delineated the essence of the housing in East Jerusalem: "The physical framework of daily life that structures the housing environment enacts the process of socialization for a sizable population. We should therefore posit that during this process a local community assumes a specific form and its public consciousness takes a specific shape."[4] The great appeal of Jerusalem's new housing projects ventured beyond pragmatic considerations and into the symbolic realm: they answered the growing demand for communal life, for character, and for national identity. These houses gave people the feeling they were living in a specific time and place of great historical value.

Constructing the housing projects of United Jerusalem followed two waves of land confiscation. In 1968 Israel confiscated land along the "northern lock" between Mount Scopus and West Jerusalem. The larger confiscation, in August 1970, prepared the ground for settling the Jewish middle class farther out, in three satellite neighborhoods, north, south, and east of the previously bounded city. Architects and planners working in and for the Ministry of Housing took the governmental goals of demographic Judaization and territorial indivisibility as a consensual given. Steeped in the professional discourse of their time, they turned confiscated Jordanian territory—land they considered empty—into an urban testing ground. The result undid the logic of Israel's early national master plan. Instead of urging Jewish migrants to move "From the City to the Village" in order to disperse the Jewish population all over the nascent state,[5] they now wished to consolidate, to structure, to foster a sense of urbanity and character—to concentrate and infuse new housing with a Jerusalemite identity.

These twin goals—consolidating urban space and fostering local identity— were made possible by architectural means. On the one hand, architects labored to harmonize the desired new urbanity with the image of Jerusalem; on the other hand, they turned this urbanity into an irrefutable territorial fact through rapid construction and prefabricated building methods. While reaching a consensus in their goals, this group nevertheless took many different routes, as each architect grappled with different benefits and constraints of official politics, and each was inspired by their specific biography, professional training, and social networks. We will focus our attention on the new Jerusalemite style that Drexler's team articulated in Ma'alot Dafna. Drexler continued to promote its design ideas through his guidelines for the massive satellite neighborhoods of Ramot, Giloh, and East Talpiot, which we review next. A 1976 retrospective document from the Ministry of Housing closes this chapter with further insights into how the home anchored communal and national identity, an integral part of United Jerusalem.

Confiscations

On January 11, 1968, only seven months after the short war ended, the Israeli government confiscated 3,345 dunams (825 acres) of East Jerusalem land, primarily for residential purposes. It included the Jewish Quarter of the Old City and stone-laden hills north of the Green Line (the latter mostly privately owned by Palestinians) that had long been ignored by both countries. The confiscated area was called the "northern lock" because it connected the Israeli enclave on Mount Scopus—including the older campus of the Hebrew University and the Hadassah Hospital—with the northern quarters of West Jerusalem.[6] Although the UN Security Council consequently issued a condemnation against Israel, that did not stop Israelis from launching their ambitious plan: a housing belt encircling Arab Jerusalem. Houses would create more irrefutable facts on the ground, rendering the redivision of Jerusalem impossible.

In December 1969, when William P. Rogers, the U.S. secretary of state, declared support for a Jordanian presence in East Jerusalem, he unintentionally sped up the Israeli settlement process. The initial Israeli response was to add two additional stories on top of the buildings already under construction in the French Hill, part of the northern lock. The monumental response was yet to come: the confiscation of 12,000 additional dunams (2,965 acres) of East Jerusalem. Allocation was crucial: the government again concentrated its confiscations in three empty sites, that is, stretches of stony land claimed by Jordan and owned mostly by Palestinians but never built upon. On each it planned to build a new housing development the size of a small town. The intention was to turn these new settlements into integrated residential neighborhoods for Jews, part and parcel of the city of Jerusalem (Figure 3.3).[7]

The Ministry of Housing, whose mandate was to make this vision a reality, started to plan the new neighborhoods in May 1970.[8] The deadline of April 1971 was set without any certainty regarding the exact boundaries of the proposed confiscation and before having any planners assigned for the task. In a confidential meeting on May 5, the minister and his deputies pre-

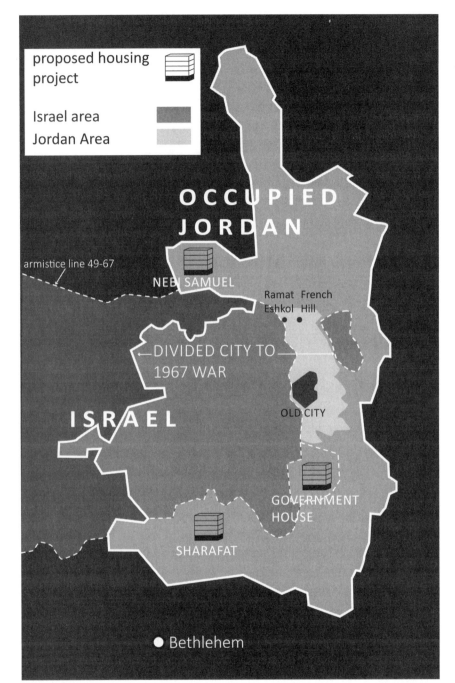

Figure 3.3. Map of Greater Jerusalem (after the August 1970 confiscations), drawn from contemporary press releases.

pared a policy that intended to build "35,000–40,000 residential units and adjunct public institutions" on the proposed land by enlarging "the scale of construction in Jerusalem to 6,000–8,000 residential units per year."[9] Besides numerous tasks such as surveying the land, examining land uses, determining building standards and materials, and establishing planning teams and a special unit in charge of functional programs for Jerusalem, they prepared to negotiate changes in the Israeli Planning and Building Law—a legal maze that was barely five years old—in order to expedite permission to build in East Jerusalem.

Immediately after the government officially announced the confiscation on August 30, 1970, the Planning and Engineering Division of the ministry set a strict building schedule that required many shortcuts. Officials admitted: "It is possible that from a pure urban planning consideration we are entering adventures and procedures that normally we would by no means accept." Under the current circumstances, however, they agreed that they had to "compose the planning guidelines in light of the political decisions according to which we operate."[10] In this meeting, less than a week after the confiscation, they were uncertain about water supply and sewage and about the electricity that the Israeli Electrical Company was not allowed to provide in East Jerusalem, among other worries, but they already had mandated architectural teams to offer a detailed plan for developing the three confiscated sites in just a few months.

Yehuda Drexler, who was to be in charge of all the ministry's activity in East Jerusalem until the elections of 1974, assigned his in-house Housing and Development team (Shikun u'Pituah, abbreviated here as Sho"p) the most hotly debated of the three sites: what would come to be Ramot, situated north of West Jerusalem, next to the tomb of Nebi Samuel. Avraham Yaski, the leading sabra architect, was in charge of planning the lands of Sharafat (now Giloh). David Best, an independent architect of British origin, led the team tasked with designing the site known as High Commissioner Hill (which would soon be renamed East Talpiot). On the surface, the three teams seemingly exhibited a rather unified style. On closer look, however, there was significant variation in their agendas. Common to all was the challenge they posed to the developmental modernism of the older émigré architects. But, as we shall see, it is easier to identify an adversary than an appropriate mode of action. Within the auspicious urban lab provided by the Israeli government, the planners in each of these teams could test their own path and promote their own vision of how to situate home in occupied land.

Years later, Yaski compared their work to that of medieval architects who drew their design in the sand, worked with artisans, and made decisions on site. The idea was to act quickly and professionally. While officials and planners trusted the training, values, and social insights of architects, there was an obvious gap between decision makers and the (often) avant-garde architects who were entrusted with the actual design of the new settlements.[11] The latter succeeded, at times, to draw politicians into their domain. Yaski, for example, described how his team unrolled their blueprints for Giloh on the floor and crawled with the minister of housing in order to capture all the details.[12] The public, however, was kept in the dark. The plans for East Jeru-salem were too contentious. They were devised in secret and would soon be-come the subject of great controversy.[13]

In the coming months, word of the plans for East Jerusalem leaked out. Yet, and despite international uproar and the protest of the East Jerusalem-ites, the vast confiscation in August 1970 hardly registered with the Israeli public. Instead, Israeli Jerusalemites were upset with issues surrounding ur-banism and aesthetics. The public wanted to know how the new neighbor-hoods would look, fearing rapid construction would result in ugly slums. The press was critical of the special committee that would bypass the building law, as well as the emergency bylaws that legitimated these actions. When the Regional Committee approved the building plans, a public debate was inevitable. The impetus behind this protest was the newly founded Council for the Beautiful Land of Israel, a powerful lobby that heightened awareness of Israeli civic society to issues pertaining to planning, aesthetics, and their political impact. But when the council succeeded in calling a press conference to disclose the plans to the public, the planners did not show up.[14] Suspicions grew, as rumors about "eight story standard buildings located on the slopes like 'cigarette packs or waffles,'" as Yehuda Ha'Ezrahi, the powerful head of the Jerusalem branch of the Council for the Beautiful Land of Israel, put it, agitated the anxious crowd.[15]

City officials were similarly reserved, particularly regarding the plans for Nebi Samuel. The political climate was not in their favor. The fear of the American Rogers Plan and its demand for Jordanian presence in Jerusalem cast a patriotic halo around the advocates of mass construction. Sarcastic critics replied that such "patriotism is the last escape of the villain, and is probably also the final justification of the bad planner, who subjugates the aesthetic sensitivity to what he accepts, without sufficient criticism, as a 'su-preme national call.'"[16]

As debate flared, well-known, non-Israeli architects stepped into the breach. These architects included guests of the International Congress of Architects and Engineers, where Buckminster Fuller and Philip Johnson asked Israeli architects to turn Jerusalem into the world's architectural fron-tier. They were joined in December 1970 by over two dozen luminaries who formed the Jerusalem Committee. The harsh criticism of committee mem-bers such as Louis Kahn and Bruno Zevi on institutional planning in Israel took everybody by surprise. The young architects who worked in state and municipal agencies felt they belonged to a broader discipline of architecture, an allegiance greater than the one to their bosses, the older developmental modernists, and their bureaucratic apparatus. The international community encouraged them to treat Jerusalem as the new disciplinary testing ground, a place where architects would cease creating mere problem solutions and commit instead to Architecture with a capital A.

Shortly after the influential architects returned to their home countries, bulldozers began clearing the ground for the three settlements. The press was outraged: "it is possible to ruin Jerusalem with war machine, but also with building machines" (Figures 3.4 and 3.5).[17] They urged Kollek to voice his ob-

בונה ירושלים ברחמים...

Figure 3.4. Adler, "Building Jerusalem in Mercy." Source: *Architon,* June 1973, cover image, Architectural Heritage Research Center, the Technion, Shmuel Yavin Collection.

jections and feared he would become Jerusalem's second Titus.[18] The Council for the Beautiful Land of Israel, meanwhile, continued to alert the public about "the dangers awaiting Jerusalem and the beauty of its landscape. . . . All the balustrades were fired by the Council at the Ministry of Housing and its planners," listing among their "merits" "chaos, confusion and scandals, abandon and public fraud." The perceived irreversibility of the situation caused anxiety, as one newspaper put it:

> And when the peace will come, and the city of Jerusalem—the joy of all the earth, and the sanctuary of the Great King, will return to its former glory— . . . a forest of skyscrapers will run up, made of concrete and cement, and will divide between the yesterday and the tomorrow.[19]

In the light of this debate we can better understand the efficacy of the Israeli building machine. The three settlements that were eventually built reveal the political and professional mechanisms that turned confiscated land not only into a reassuring home, but further, into a stronghold of the Jewish middle class in Jerusalem. Each settlement also exposes a particular aspect of this industrious building: Ramot and the entanglement with official politics, Giloh and architectural design, East Talpiot and urban systems of democratic participation. Together they show architecture's multifaceted agency in shaping Israeli Jerusalem.

Figure 3.5. Demonstration against the government plans in East Jerusalem. Source: *Jerusalem Post,* February 18, 1971.

Drexler, Sho"p, and the New Architecture of United Jerusalem

Shortly after the confiscation, on February 12, 1968, the minister of housing, Mordechai Bentov, explained to members of the Knesset, Israel's parliament, the aforementioned "planning principles" for East Jerusalem. The architecture of Jerusalem, he clarified, would be

> building in stone, relatively low-rise buildings, within the limits of three stories, in accordance with the neighborhoods that border the area under development. Also incorporated are elements of Oriental building such as arches, domes, etc.; building types are especially adjusted to the topographic condition and the slopes of the sites (terraced building). . . . The architects and planners are exerting extra efforts to bestow on these neighborhoods an image that accords with the landscape and character of Jerusalem.[20]

We cannot overestimate the magnitude of the change Bentov suggested; compared to what had been the architectural agenda of the ministry since its inception, issues such as "elements of Oriental building" or "landscape and character" were strikingly novel. In 1948 Bentov was the minister of construction and housing in Israel's temporary government. In this capacity he commissioned the Bauhaus graduate Arieh Sharon, a follower of his own Left-leaning socialist movement, to conduct Israel's highly modernist master plan. The ministry Bentov oversaw for the second time, in 1966, continued to primarily commission the highly regulated housing blocks associated with developmental modernism. How could Bentov, a socialist of the older generation, just two years later advocate such place-based architecture? Why would he offer a manifesto of situated modernism?

The answer is simple: the ideological ground was shifting beneath Bentov's feet, faster than anyone expected. At the forefront of that surprising shift was the Sho"p team of young Technion graduates assembled by architect Yehuda (Idel) Drexler. Their presence was unusual within the Israeli government: instead of commissioning external architects, Drexler's team functioned as a private office inside the ministry. Their professional advantage was profound: meshing the client and the architect in one entity granted the team unusual freedom. Protected by Drexler, a powerful bureaucrat, and relieved from the demands of the market, the team's mandate was experimental and its mission was to engage contemporary architecture's cutting edge. Members of the team were slightly younger than the sabra architects of the Tel Aviv circle yet inspired by similar modernisms. Their head, however, was slightly older than the sabras and even more deeply situated within the profession.

Drexler belongs to a particular breed of architects—professionals working as public servants—who are responsible for shaping the national landscapes of their countries. Drexler is a classic example of this type of servant of the public good, a notion he insisted on evaluating (exclusively) through the Zionist looking glass. His architectural agenda reflected his personal biography: fleeing Fascist Austria in 1939 with the children migration, smuggling into the British deportee camp in Cyprus to train Holocaust survivors, and fighting the bitter battles over Jerusalem during the 1948 war. At the Technion Drexler was drawn to Alfred Neumann, the charismatic advocate of morphological architecture, and favored modern, simple, and functional planning. He started working with the ministry in 1963. To staff his first office, in Upper Nazareth, a developing town in the north, he sought architects among new immigrants. Their team foreshadowed the Sho"p team not only by functioning as an architectural firm within a public agency, but also by seeking to customize mass housing according to the specificity of the place and its diverse immigrants.

According to Drexler, the same agenda guided his work in Nazareth and Jerusalem. When the ministry commissioned its architect to plan "the standard building types," Drexler recalls, "I came with . . . a house in the sun, in stone, in shadow, stepped, connected to the environment, inner courtyards, pedestrians, parking and transportation at the back." In Jerusalem these sensitivities evolved in "stones, extrusions, and sockets." Drexler explained this architectural philosophy in oppositional terms: "we saw in the concept of 'a Jerusalemite building' an excuse to do modern architecture instead of standard types." He deemed this concept was significant because it offered a remedy to the homogenizing malaise of his ministry, "that you don't know if you are in Dimona or in Metula."[21] In other words, he sought the architectural pronunciation of territorial rootedness and regional specificity.

This was exactly the mission he undertook in East Jerusalem. Members of the team he assembled in 1966 perfectly matched this goal because they were steeped in post–World War II situated modernisms. Besides Mediterranean regionalism, Yoseph Kolodny, the reputed intellectual of the team, also cited as influences "Candilis, the Smithsons, van Eyck, the Japanese (Kenzo Tange and the Metabolists), Theo Cosby, van der Brook and Bakema. . . . We were after them," he recalls, "we executed something that was very close to what they envisioned."[22] The members of his Sho"p team were as conversant as their slightly older peers in the sabra circle, fluent in the architectural culture that pervaded Europe, the United States, and Japan in the postwar years, but were arguably quicker to translate these schools of thought into the Jerusalem context. Eventually, their new design methods and evocative free-hand perspective drawings granted the team the superlative "architectural commandos" in architectural circles (Figure 3.6). More important, that budding reputation brought to their drafting tables what might be considered the most important housing project of the first post-1967 confiscation.

Figure 3.6. The Sho"p Team, studies for a hostel in Ramot Sharet, 1967–68. Source: Ministry of Housing, internal publications.

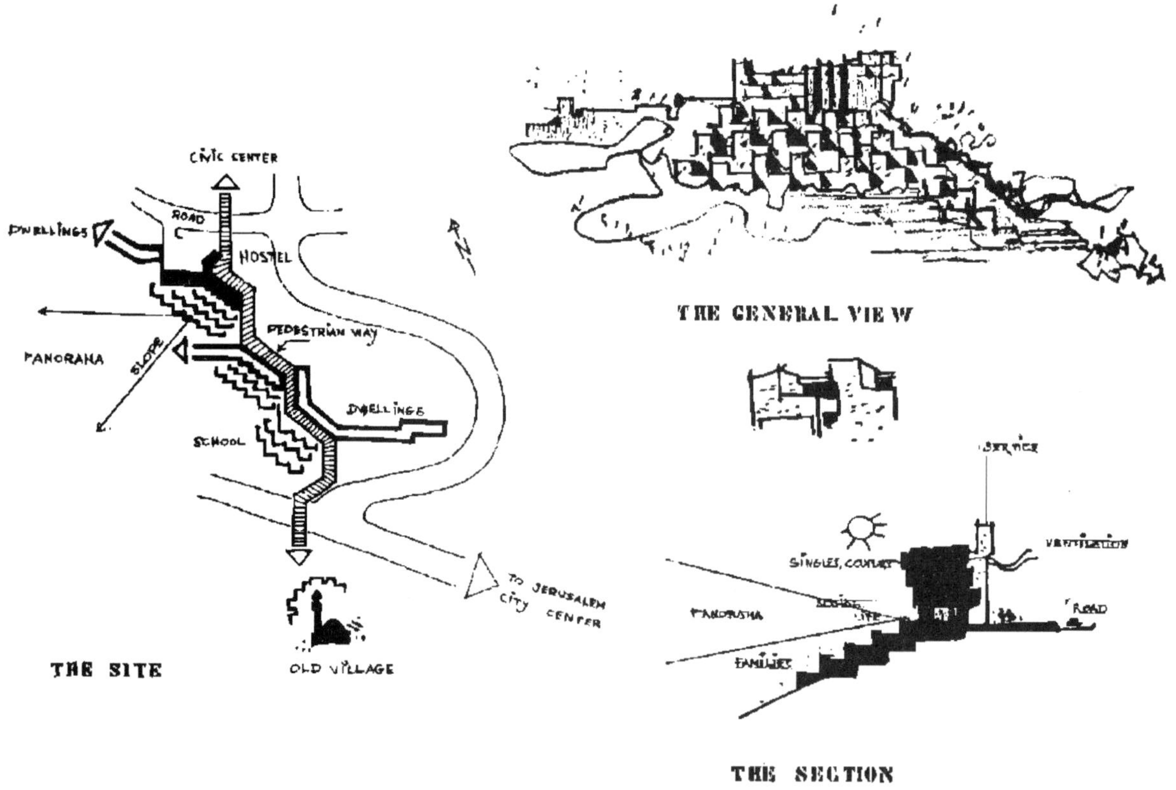

THE GENERAL VIEW

THE SITE

THE SECTION

Immediately after the war, the government was under immense public pressure to rapidly build East Jerusalem. The ministry, quite predictably, entrusted the most important sites to Yitzhak Perlstein, who relocated existing buildings and added prefabricated concrete arches to fulfill the required Oriental flavor. Such efforts suggested that nothing new would emerge from the ministry. But then, in 1968, the Sho"p team undertook the design of Ma'alot Dafna, a residential quarter for 1,400 dwelling units and services for adjunct quarters on an area of 270 dunams (67 acres) spanning the hitherto low-income frontier neighborhood of Shmuel Hanavie and the battlefield of Ammunition Hill.

Amid the desire to imbue housing not only with a sense of community but, more pressingly, with urban vitality, the team's proposition of dense housing along commercial streets was received by both the professional community and the public as a revelation. That proposition, best expressed in their plan for the new neighborhood of Ma'alot Dafna, worked according to principles that were then defined by the new discipline of urban design: instead of laying out an array of efficient building types surrounded by orderly yet unbounded open spaces, attention was focused on communal open spaces, using saturated residential row houses to spatially define streets and public squares.

In the schematic plan the team highlighted in black the residential buildings that define the complex's short spine, and the two crescents that grow away from each of its ends. They marked these pedestrian streets and squares in gray in order to demonstrate how they would form the skeleton of the complex and act as its vivid core. The spine's elongated, slightly curved buildings were designed in the tradition of stone building. The foundations of these buildings are massive; the measure of their basic repetitive unit—the cubical, three-dimensional module of the building—approximates the traditional three-by-three-meter room of stone construction; their structural spans are moderate in size; and their well-proportioned arches, particularly those along the arcades, emulate, through rough stone cladding, traditional methods of stone construction. This traditionally designed core is interiorized and protected, so to speak, from the chaotic city outside (Figure 3.7).

Figure 3.7. The Sho"p Team, Ma'alot Dafna, under construction. Photograph by Ran Erde.

Ma'alot Dafna is therefore a project whose qualities are nearly impossible to grasp from the surrounding streets or parking lots. Emulating traditional Jerusalem neighborhoods, the complex is about urban interiority: it is a sequence of protected, open spaces that prioritize the particular needs of the pedestrian. It is a residential design that allowed individuals to fulfill daily needs while socializing with their community, an environment designed to be experienced in a concrete space and place. In order to exploit this focus on use and sociability, the team implemented a trend prevalent in post–World War II modernism: the car became the modern enemy of a healthy neighborhood. The solution was to separate pedestrians from motor vehicles and create a protected sequence of pedestrian pathways.[23]

(a)

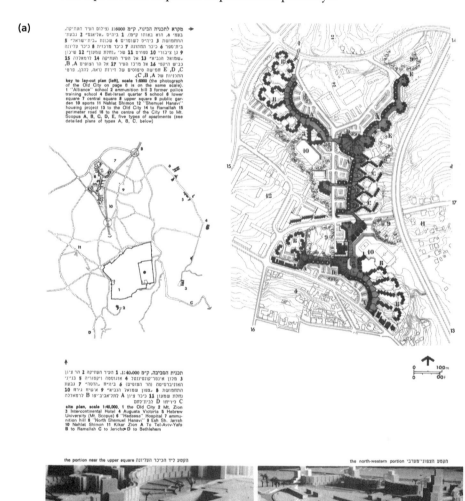

Spatially, the plan echoes the famous dictum of the Dutch architect Aldo van Eyck that "a house must be like a small city if it's to be a real house—a city like a large house if it's to be a real city."[24] Van Eyck articulated a theory according to which the size of an architectural feature can be measured as a human experience only in relation to other components of the built environment. Israeli architects tended to embrace this statement more literally in the contexts of communal planning: when the spatial relationship of a home is rearticulated in the scale of a neighborhood, that is, when a public square is conceptualized as a living room, a playground as a children's room, and a street as a corridor, the neighborhood becomes the container of a big family—a community of shared living style and national values. Accordingly, the apartments showed greater variety with a focus on the separation between private and communal areas, even with split-level duplexes, a recent addition to the state's building vocabulary (Figure 3.8).

(b)

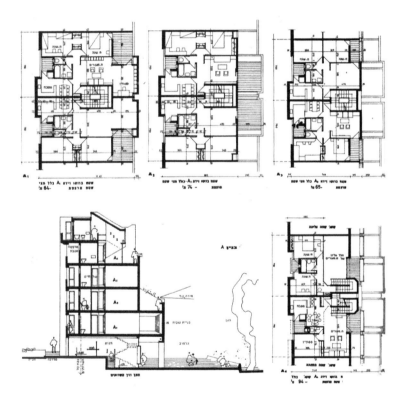

Figure 3.8. The Sho"p Team, Ma'alot Dafna: (a) site plans and model images; (b) section and apartment plans. Source: *Israel Builds, 1973* (Tel Aviv: Ministry of Housing, 1973), 159.

The Ministry of Housing's official publications had almost always promoted the image of unpeopled buildings on empty land. By contrast, the photographs of Ma'alot Dafna depicted pedestrian streets, children, and bikes—images of socialization. These images also fostered the desired sense of urban interiority: an urban womb protected from the city, a quality that became both a major attraction and profound obstacle. On the one hand, it created identifiable residential space and offered innovative urban typologies. On the other hand, its commercial street was disconnected from the urban fabric, and its storefronts were hidden beyond the parking lots that encircled the complex. The result was ambiguous. The design of Ma'alot Dafna succeeded in taming the contemporary inclination toward the megastructure, the ambition of condensing a multifunction urbanity into a single complex. The idea of the megastructure informed the parallel construction of the Hebrew University on Mount Scopus. But this vernacular neighborhood centered around its residents faced the same principal obstacle as the megastructure: the inability to merge into the city, to draw from and enhance the energy of Jerusalem as a whole (Figure 3.9).

In hindsight, the architectural principles of Ma'alot Dafna were forma-

Figure 3.9. The Sho"p Team, Ma'alot Dafna, a view of public spaces. Photograph by Ran Erde.

tive, not only because the same team continued to lay out the initial plan for Ramot. More important, Drexler, who was in charge of the entire project of building East Jerusalem, developed the guidelines for residential settlements that would serve him until he left the office in 1974. As a result, the design principles of Ma'alot Dafna would soon appear in housing estates around the city, the sheer volume of which required even greater land confiscations.

Ramot: Building Blocks of Confrontation

For Drexler, the next confiscation in 1970 was an even greater opportunity. Colleagues describe him herding bulldozers to Ramot as a cowboy herds his cattle (Figure 3.10). He feared neither the international uproar nor the intense criticism at home and was determined to build this settlement at any cost. This sacrifice included a bitter battle that eventually led him to fire the architectural team he had so carefully nurtured. Why was settling Jerusalem, and Ramot in particular, such a mission for him?

Nebi Samuel, the future Ramot, was at the heart of the forceful public debate about building East Jerusalem. The *1968 Jerusalem Masterplan* proposed to build in Nebi Samuel a rural suburb on the outskirts of the bounded city. The Ministry of Housing envisioned instead a comprehensive urban settlement, for which it offered an extended site of 2,750 dunams (680 acres) some four and a half kilometers (2.8 miles) northeast of West Jerusalem. Drexler and his Sho"p team prepared the initial design for the settlement according to the principles that led their design for Ma'alot Dafna. The scale was significantly bigger: a territory ten times larger and an initial framework for eight thousand dwelling units including all related amenities (Figure 3.11).[25]

Figure 3.10. "Bulldozer Constructing a Road to New Ramot near Nebi Samuel," January 10, 1974. Photograph by Moshe Milner. Source: Government Press Office, National Photographs Collection, file D211-008.

Figure 3.11. The Sho"p Team, Ramot. "The Planning Concept"; "Urban Plan"; "Neighborhood Scheme." Source: *Ramot, Jerusalem* (Tel Aviv: Ministry of Housing, 1976). Courtesy of the late Yehuda Drexler.

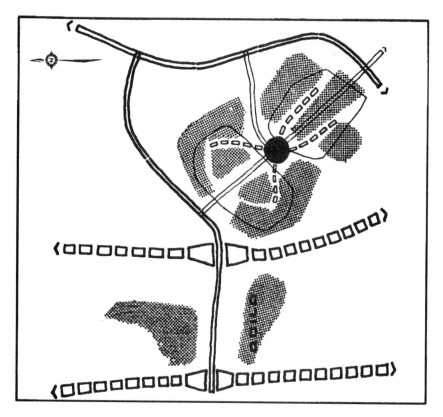

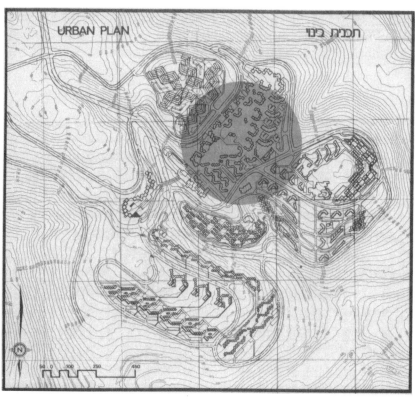

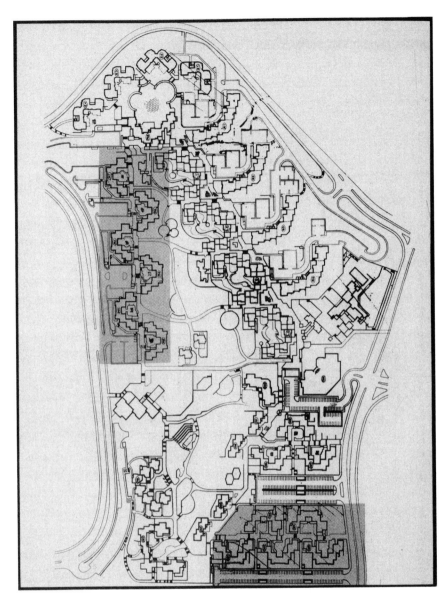

The intention was to create "an urban organism" consisting of residential neighborhoods, each having "individual definition." These self-sufficient neighborhoods had to be connected by a continuous functional system of services and circulation, and accessibility to all units had to be ensured despite the steep topography. As in Ma'alot Dafna, complete separation between vehicular and pedestrian traffic was strictly maintained. The larger scale, however, required the connection of "all the quarter's parts into a unified and consolidated urban environment." This aim was aided by "the formation of a visual unity," yet, and importantly so, without compromising a large variety of buildings that "utilize the site's physical characteristics." Stone cladding was and remained the prevalent unifying feature of these housing estates.[26]

At first it seems as if the team and its head were well coordinated. During the first five months of work, however, a schism grew between the younger team's agenda and the objectives of Drexler, its powerful head. Activist Zionism was Drexler's most important credo. Accordingly, he was not just a talented architect musing with a 6B pencil; he was rather, as Yonathan Golani, the second head architecture of the ministry puts it, "an architectural leader."[27] Nonetheless, his charisma was not enough for the young members of this team, who were emboldened by the overwhelming domestic and international, civic and professional criticism that followed the 1970 confiscation and were consequently eager to push the frontier of architecture in Jerusalem. Accordingly, their protest against their head was cast in professional rather than political terms, accusing Drexler of compromising quality and aesthetics in favor of governmental haste.[28]

By January 1971 the looming dispute was in the open. According to Drexler, it was "to the death."[29] His contenders agreed.[30] Yet, in a letter to the Sho"p team, the arbiter of the dispute insisted that he did not identify any essential matters of disagreement between the contending parties. If so, further questions surface: Why did the Sho"p team insist on bypassing Drexler and discussing their claims directly with the minister and the mayor, and why did the minister of housing, after taking a day to consider their interrogation, conclude they must immediately be fired?

Drexler did not involve the team in the political maneuvers he had to negotiate in order to make Ramot a reality. On February 1, 1971, at the peak of the crisis, he succeeded in convincing the Subcommittee for Principle Planning Issues that Ramot must be built. He offered two arguments. The first married urban and political trends, reversing the famous slogan of early statehood—"from the city to the village"—in favor of urban density. Drexler explains:

> Some claim that in the 1970s there is no meaning to the activism of the 1930s. They say that what we called settlement, hectare after hectare, is no longer meaningful. I personally think that even now, if there is an empty hill, Jews would be told—look, for one hill there is no point in postponing the redemption and undoing peace. If the hill is settled . . . [Jews] would not be deported and will not turn refugees for any fortune on earth. I personally identify with this action, and as long as I am responsible for it I will do it wholeheartedly.[31]

Note the focus on deportation and refugees—from a man who fled as a child from Europe with no family, and thereafter listened to Holocaust survivors in a deportee camp. The team Drexler assembled in Upper Nazareth consisted exclusively of new immigrants. The idea of settling Jews was an unspoken motivation, a consensus shared by all members. The sabra architects did not have the same visceral attachment to these sentiments.

Drexler's second argument was social. During the period Jerusalem was divided, its less-desired neighborhoods were located along the Green Line, where Jordanian snipers constantly threatened everyday life. As a result, these neighborhoods increasingly housed low-income families, mostly Jewish migrants from Arab countries. For Drexler, the newly confiscated land presented an opportunity to move upward the residents of these growing slums and settle them in upgraded social housing. By contrast, the master plan intended to build in Nebi Samuel a low-density suburb of three thousand residents. This plan contradicted every bit of Drexler's activist philosophy of socialist Zionism. He roared,

> To distribute this land to honorary Jerusalemites is a thought one's mind cannot bear. Nobody will build villas there because this is a municipal land and it will assume its market value. Nowhere in the world would one take and split a national land. It serves neither proper planning nor the political objectives we fight for in Jerusalem.[32]

According to Drexler's testimony, these two arguments won him the support of Prime Minister Golda Meir, who decided to approve the industrious building of Ramot.

While Drexler was celebrating his achievement, the press kept alerting the public against the impending prospect of ugly slums. In light of the growing public outrage, the Sho"p team did not hesitate to blame Drexler for overdoing his own activism, claiming that the bulldozers were on the ground before the drawings were completed. The timing of their protest, however, was inspired by external factors: the sudden influx of new architectural ideas that visiting international luminaries had brought to Jerusalem. Like the Anglo group of young Israeli and Anglo architects, who joined local planning teams after their studies in leading British and American schools, they wrote their letter shortly after these architects returned to their home countries.

The gist of their argument was professional. Unlike a private practice, they maintained, a resourceful public agency must invest in research. They wrote that "following the International Congress of Architects and Engineers [in 1970], we have reached the conclusion that we must *immediately* start searching for the appropriate tools for mass production of prefabricated building."[33] Their argument married technological innovation with human values. Traditional construction, they explained, is too expensive and limited in its impact. Thus, in order to be faithful to the human values that underpinned the design already introduced in Ma'alot Dafna to the sheer quantity of housing in the new settlement they had to research and advance prefabricated architecture.

In fact, the ministry was already invested in prefabricated construction. In December 1967 the minister asked Moshe Safdie to develop a prefabricated industry for an Israel Habitat. Drexler himself not only approved prefabricated building in these settlements, he even provided for the radical Israeli avant-garde a generous testing ground for morphological experimentation. Here timing was crucial. At that moment, in the midst of a heated political struggle, he considered the team's demands indulgent. He preferred to cast their protest in economic terms, claiming they forgot their role as public servants and were tempted instead by the great opportunities that fell into the hands of the private sector.

Obviously, Drexler and his team operated on different registers. Drexler's actions were driven by his activist Zionism. The public supported his team's philosophy because it implied aesthetic values that were considered essential to the idea of Jerusalem. The team therefore turned to Mayor Teddy Kollek, the authority on beautifying Jerusalem and the person who had invited to Jerusalem the architectural luminaries they admired. This would be a major mistake, because the two agencies—the ministry and the municipal government—held strikingly different agendas about what Jerusalem ought to be. Public intellectuals, however, rejoiced with the team's protest against their own ministry. The Council for the Beautiful Land of Israel could now conclude that even the planners of East Jerusalem admitted the shortcomings of their enterprise.

On February 26, 1971, Zeev (Ya'akov Farkash), *Ha'aretz*'s caricaturist, dedicated his weekly panoramic cartoon to the unfolding drama's various players (Figure 3.12). "Next Year in (Built) Jerusalem" is a phrase taken from the Passover *haggadah,* denoting Jews' yearning for the sacred city or, in Zeev's version, their conflicting longings for a beautiful and resolutely Jewish city. At the center of the drama, Zeev depicts a ludicrous duel between two European knights. On the right is Zeev Sharef, the minister of housing, holding a trowel, with which he stacks cubical housing units on the hill of Nebi Samuel (the future site of Ramot). Teddy Kollek, his personal friend and political opponent, stands to his left. His eyes, narrow with anger, and his extruding lower lip signal that he is ready to fight over the houses Sharef is stacking. Looming in the background, but central to the composition, is the leitmotif of the fight: the image of Jerusalem, with romanticized domes and minarets nestled in the Judean hills.

The fight is no contest: while the composed Sharef goes about his business, the furious Kollek cannot move. Heavy chains of "party discipline" hold his feet and arm. Robert J. McCloskey, U.S. State Department spokesman, ef-

לשנה הבאה בירושלים הבנויה

Figure 3.12. Zeev, "Next Year in Built Jerusalem," *Ha'aretz,* February 26, 1971. Source: Holon's Comic and Caricature Museum. Courtesy of Naomi Farkash Fink and Dorit Farkash-Shuki.

fortlessly cuts the tip of his sword. Demonstrating the Israeli mind-set that the world stood united against its interests, McCloskey joins King Hussein and UN Secretary U Thant in the upper left corner of the scene. An army of Christian knights, all donning crosses on their helmets to identify them, stands behind the UN building, ready to fight for the city.

Several groups of small figures to Sharef's right carry banners in his support. Prime Minister Golda Meir leads respected Labor ministers on their way to achieve "operation fact," namely, the manufacture of quick, built facts on the East Jerusalem ground. An army of right-wing opposition warriors carries a banner with the slogan "the entire land of Israel," as it follows a concrete mixer. Minute and bitter Palestinian residents, and even tinier astonished new immigrants, watch the massing troops.

On the left, behind Kollek, members of the Council for the Beautiful Land of Israel, spears shaped like flowers in their hands, cry tears over the "Valley of Eternal Crying." Another small group stands directly opposite the houses of Nebi Samuel, shooting numerous arrows at them. Visible T-squares betray their identity: they are the famous architects of the Jerusalem Committee. Just below them stands Moshe Safdie, who carries his newly proposed Habitat Israel housing on a silver plate, turning his head toward the five "architectural commandoes" dismissed from the Ministry of Housing. Stepping down from the "Hill of Evil Council," they load their belongings on their T-squares and compasses while being turned away from the battle by a floating, cartoon finger.

Shortly after the minister dismissed the rebellious Sho"p team, Drexler filled their posts with new Technion graduates who came to Jerusalem en masse, captivated by this hub of action. But it was the original team that broke new ground in Jerusalem and can be credited with the low-rise, topographically bounded counter of Ramot and its communal values. When Drexler left the ministry after the 1974 elections, Ramot was already a fact poured into concrete and stone.[34]

Zeev's cartoon tells a story of top-down planning. If urbanism and politics clash, he suggests, politics will likely win. Civic activism in support of aesthetic values, Zeev concludes, could not allay soldiers combating the demons of historical hostility toward Jews. *Time* agreed in an article on the subject from March 1, 1971, titled "Full Speed Ahead and Damn the Aesthetics."[35] Did official politics indeed succeed in burying aesthetic considerations? Summarizing recent events, Uzi Benziman's headline upheld that "The Battle Was Lost—But Not the War over the Beauty of Jerusalem."[36]

By casting the opposition to Ramot in terms of beauty, public opinion contributed to a schism in the process of making Jerusalem Israeli. This split had territorial implications. The ministry kept building an outer ring of residential settlements around Jerusalem in order to induce its demographic Judaization. Kollek chose to focus instead on the visual basin of the Old City, where he could justifiably turn the beautification of Jerusalem into his life's work. Kollek was burdened by a minute budget, international politics, and party discipline. But as a result, he developed an alternative route that promoted cultural, rather than official, politics.

Arguably, architects became indispensable agents for both the official politics of the state and the cultural politics of the city. Thus, while we keep reviewing the larger plans administered by the dueling knights of Urbanism and Housing personified in Zeev's cartoon, our main focus continues to be the little arrows, the tears and T-squares of the particular groups that translated official politics into the politics of space, identity, and beauty in Jerusalem.

Giloh: A Cluster City

Giloh was the most architecturally conspicuous and the least politically controversial of the three new settlements due to its southern and less symbolic location. It was planned for a confiscated area of 2,700 dunams (667 acres) north of Bethlehem, on the southwestern outskirts of West Jerusalem, from which it was separated by the Palestinian village of Beth Tzafafah. The Ministry of Housing entrusted the site's development to Avraham Yaski, a major player in the sabra architectural circle, who immediately delegated responsibilities to a selected team of peers. In retrospect, Yaski admits that despite his generation's enthusiasm with the forms of the Arab village, none of the planners had noticed the actual (rather than imagined) village of living people and hybrid forms right next door to their own development; the lived reality of those Palestinians was a blind spot.[37]

By commissioning Yaski the ministry reiterated the tradition of "Model Housing," a vanguard of exemplary housing estates that he previously and reputedly led in Beer Sheva. Once commissioned to plan Giloh, Yaski immediately asked the daring and thorny sabra architects Ram Karmi and Eldar Sharon to join the leading team.[38] Karmi studied at the Architectural Association in London during the rise of the New Brutalism of Alison and Peter Smithson and was inspired by James Stirling and Team 10. By the end of the 1960s, he greatly admired the monumentality, plasticity, simplicity, and transcendence of Louis Kahn's architecture. Eldar Sharon belonged to the morphological avant-garde. He married science and design during the years he worked with Zvi Hecker under the mentorship of their teacher and partner, Professor Alfred Neumann, a former CIAM member who introduced the morphological point of view in Israel. Notably, Karmi and Sharon could, according to an Israeli saying, "simultaneously dance in two weddings": on the one hand they led the rebellious sabras; on the other hand, once they joined the practices of their influential parents, Dov Karmi and Arieh Sharon, they were embedded in the state's architectural establishment (Figure 3.13).

Yaski, Ram Karmi, and Eldar Sharon held true to their reputation. Their premise was "no precedent, and definitely nothing sacred. Everything is legitimate." According to Yaski, "every crazy thought was practically developed into axonometric drawings and detailed layouts."[39] To date, none of the early

Figure 3.13. The Giloh planning team. From left to right: (sitting) M. Lofenfeld, G. Ramati, R. Karmi, N. Knoler, Y. Drexler, Y. Gil, Y. Kamon; (standing) I. Levitan, A. Yaski, E. Ferber. Source: "Gilo Quarter, Jerusalem, Interview with the Team," *Alef Alef,* September 1973, 4.

תכנית ירושלים 1969

Figure 3.14. Jerusalem Plan, 1969. Competition panel found in Arieh and Eldar Sharon Office. Courtesy of the Israel Architecture Archive collection.

plans that these architects submitted to the Ministry of Housing has been found. However, two panels of "Jerusalem Plan" dated to 1969, which survived in Eldar Sharon's office, illustrate the contemporary spirit and vision (Figure 3.14). Fearing a sentimental depiction of Jerusalem, the team was drawn to what Reyner Banham termed "the megastructure decade":[40] the 1960s effort to solve the problems of disorganized, inefficient cities with exceptionally large, man-made, self-supporting structures. It was an attempt to do urban planning by means of architecture.

In competition panels for the western entry to Jerusalem that were found in Eldar Sharon's office,[41] miles-long building blocks are juxtaposed with towers that were clearly inspired by the experiments of the Japanese metabolists who infused the 1960s megastructures with metaphors of organic growth to create towers composed of multiple compact cells. People and cars are packed into neat built forms that contain in their multilayered structures every function of daily life. According to Yaski, this concept threaded through Giloh's early plans: instead of a single-handed zoning plan into which other "architects enter and plan a section or a cluster,"[42] an option they considered boring and mundane, architects wished to collectively determine the city plan not by means of policy but, rather, by means of daring architectural design.

Yaski describes the two extreme ends of architectural design they feverishly developed: one was a series of megablocks, which bridged the hills of
the vast site—"buildings that hardly consider the topography . . . creating a
kind of autonomy of their own." The lower part of these blocks was shaped
by the topography underneath, and their top was flattened to provide smooth
surfaces for traffic. Yaski—one of the ardent followers of Le Corbusier, who
studied the *Oeuvre Complete* with Talmudic devotion—borrowed from Le
Corbusier's Plan Obus, the unbuilt 1930s project for Algiers, where extra long
and rather tall housing blocks sensually bent in and around the topography.
In a similar fashion, the team's ideology was to leave the ground intact, vast
and open and free of transportation. "The meaning is," Yaski explains, "de
facto, there are no tall buildings. The height is created by descending rather
than climbing up—the other pole of what one finds in Jerusalem."[43]

Their second option sought the reverse: the highest possible towers.
"From every apartment in this complex," Yaski recalls their aspirations, "one
could see the entire Israel—from the Dead Sea to the Mediterranean shore."
The reason for this rather phallic vision of control was the project's distance
from Jerusalem. The city and its "visual basin, minor character, conventional
building and minimal scale" would stay intact. Far enough from the Holy City,
the team could release the development "from the minute sense of building
in stone," in favor of "a quarter appropriate for the next millennia." Ultimately, both options expressed "a desire to depart from the concepts of Jerusalem."[44] And that was exactly why the result—dwelling units scraping the
sky or hugging the land—did not make it through the planning committees
of East Jerusalem.

Obviously, the radical plans did not accord with the government's wish
to unite Jerusalem through, as Bentov emphasized to the Knesset, a uniform Oriental style. The alternative was found in another avant-garde concept emerging from the architectural hub of the New Brutalists Alison and
Peter Smithson. In 1957 they published "Cluster City: A New Shape for the
Community," which would vibrate through the work of their fellow Team
10 members. "The cluster," they wrote, is "a close knit, complicated, often
moving aggregation, but an aggregation with a distinct structure." Drawing from scientific analysis of ecosystems, they considered the concept the
closest possible "to a description of the new ideal in architecture and planning."[45] But why did they combine scientific analysis of spatial relationship
with social patterns?

For the Smithsons, "the relationship of the country to the town, the
bank and the house, the school and the pub, is conveyed by the form they
take. Each *form is an active force*, it creates community, it is life itself made
manifest."[46] Accordingly, as Hadas Steiner perceptively demonstrates, the

Smithsons believed form should not be an object containing social life but, rather, an embodied action inducing social interaction.[47] According to this method, active aggregates can insert a sense of urbanity into modernist (and rather sterilized) housing environments. The cluster's aggregated "objects generate community, or, in other words, make the underlying principles of an ecosystem visible."[48] Such equilibrium is needed in order for the individual to feel related to, accommodated by, in touch with the life of people around him. The inspiration, like that of morphologists, was scientific, and its model was nature's durable yet active balance between parts, the kind of structure a community needs in order to thrive.

The cluster—a mini universe of sociospatial relationships—became the dominant planning paradigm of Giloh. Yaski decided that Giloh should consist of thirteen clusters, each of which was designed by a different architect and was identified by a serial number as can be seen already in the model of the First Phase (Figure 3.15).[49] The result is a tour de force of sabra architects, who packed the standard units of public housing—the aggregates of the cluster—around skillfully manipulated public spaces. In so doing they gave these residences a legible structure of transitions between intimate and shared spaces. For the Smithsons, Steiner tells us, "meaning was generated at the points where the armature enabled structural legibility, from the scale of the frame to that of society."[50] Accordingly, the meaning of *home*, which was so crucial on this confiscated land, depended on comprehensible movement between different urban scales.

Take, for example, the social meaning of the architecture of Cluster 3 (Figures 3.16 and 3.17). Architects Moshe Lofenfeld and Giora Gamerman took advantage of their steep site and clustered overlapping slabs of dwelling

Figure 3.15. Giloh quarter, model of First Phase, top view. Source: "Gilo Quarter, Jerusalem, Interview with the Team," *Alef Alef,* September 1973, 5.

Ram Karmi

Eldar Sharon

Moshe Lofenfeld
Giora Gamerman

Figure 3.16. Moshe Lofenfeld and Giora Gamerman, housing in Giloh, Cluster 3, 1970s. General perspective and perspectival section. Source: *Israel Builds, 1977* (Tel Aviv: Ministry of Housing, 1977), 198–99.

units around pedestrian streets. In a drawing of a perspectival section cutting through this street, we see a public pathway in the second floor. Its position allows visible access to residential units on three sequential stories. The entry to each unit is designed as a coherent threshold—a space of transition between the intimate space of dwelling and the public scale of the street. This seemingly minor point is crucial in revising the aspects that people disliked in the social housing of developmental modernism. Imagine standing in front of an entry door to an apartment stacked in a modernist block. Next to us, we will see an identical door (or more) located at the edge of a functional landing of stairs. These doors and stairs would look the same in the floor below and above. Our only method of registering the difference between them is by reading the sign on the door. Nothing in our sensual experience of the environment can tell us that we have reached the right place—that we are home.

Lofenfeld and Gamerman's suggested solution to this predicament is a gradual and apparent transition between scales. They distributed the entryways to the residential units directly below, level with, or above the pedestrian street. Residents had to reach them by climbing up or down, through a

Figure 3.17. Moshe Lofenfeld and Giora Gamerman, housing in Giloh, Cluster 3, 1970s. View of a pedestrian passageway. Photograph by Ran Erde.

short or longer flight of stairs, directly from the pathway or over a bridge from which they could look over the street before going home. The differentiated thresholds they created for each unit mark and identify the particular link of every apartment in the cluster to its surroundings. A kid throwing a ball from the bridge would join his peers differently from the one calling "wait" from below. Spatial transitions enabled people to sense their place and how they relate to their community of neighbors.

In order to achieve similar legibility on the larger urban scale, the clusters were shaped according to their role and position in the urban ensemble. Architects were instructed to design each cluster as an urban entry, passage, or edge that would create for Giloh a coherent urban identity—a sense of a neighborhood. Ram Karmi, for example, shaped the cluster he designed at the top of the road climbing to Giloh as a crescent. A curved and arcaded pedestrian street, filled with vegetation, acts as the spine of the complex. An elongated and concaved housing block defines its northern edge, creating a monumental wall toward Giloh, while displaying a playful facade, replete with balconies and concrete arches, toward Jerusalem. Several intimate passageways lead from the upper spine to the garden below; each is structured around an external stairway. On their way the stairs weave multiple private entrances to terraced dwelling units. Karmi composed the units into a spectacular theater facing the entry road from West Jerusalem. Each part of this cluster is distinct and expressive, yet the identity of each is dependent on a legible equilibrium with the others: the arcade, the street, the theater, the housing block that frames the landscape of Jerusalem (Figure 3.18).

Another means of normalizing urban life in new territory was an emphasis on maintaining a multigenerational life cycle in the new housing. Unlike the similarly sized apartments of the typical modernist block, multidisciplinary teams in the ministry insisted on precise mixture (tamhil) of differently sized apartments. Habitually, the ministry designated its public housing to homogeneous groups. Young couples, for example, were housed together in the same compound, and their children grew and left the neighborhood around the same time. As a result, nurseries and schools often closed when those children left the neighborhood, as there was no younger generation there to fill their place. By contrast, a mix of apartments would attract families of different ages and would better simulate the social continuity of mature cities. That social emphasis enabled architectural opportunities: differently sized apartments supplied architects with varied building units with which they could achieve the three dimensional playfulness they desired.

Giloh was a monumental testing ground for the most consistent preoccupations of the sabra generation: Brutalism, regionalism, and morphology. Faithful to the ethos of the New Brutalism, Yaski's team compromised with

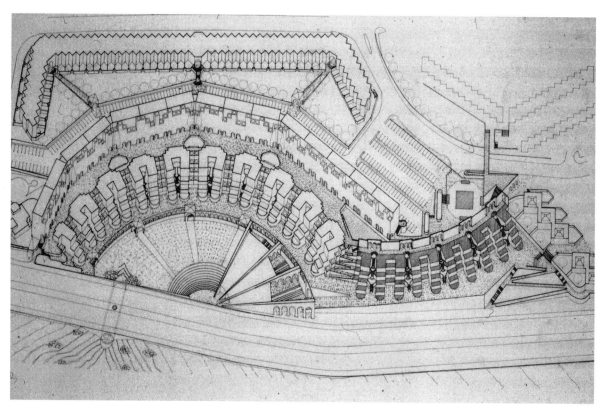

Figure 3.18. Ram Karmi, housing in Giloh, Cluster 6, axonometry, 1970s. Courtesy of the Azrieli Architecture Archive at the Tel Aviv Museum of Art, Ram Karmi Collection.

the ministry's demand for an Oriental feel on the condition of authenticity. If buildings had to be clad with stone, then, they insisted, the surface of the Jerusalem stone had to be roughly treated—a Tubza stone. Arches would not be faked with neatly ordered clad stone but should be true to their means of production. They were therefore poured into a concrete mold and appear unadorned and exposed on the facades of Giloh. When Yaski compares his famous House of the Warrior in Afeka to his Cluster 7 in Giloh, he insists that their architecture is similar despite the difference between the exposed concrete of the former and stone cladding of the latter. In both, every element of the building leaves a distinct expression, the rhythm is similar, circulation protrudes from the main mass, and the section through the building is rich with double-height spaces (Figure 3.19).

Most strikingly, morphologists were given the license to experiment with irregular geometries, space packing, and inventive prefabrication. Amid these experiments, Eldar Sharon's cluster was no doubt the most daring (Figure 3.20). His work interpreted the idea of the cluster by marrying formal analysis with the aspiration for a new vernacular based on communal values. In the plans and cross-section of his cluster we can see how each unit is recessed from the other, creating a diagonal plan of terraced raw houses. Sharon wove flights of external stairs through the open spaces in front of his units, simulating the feel of a Mediterranean village. The forty-five-degree angled walls that protected these spaces vertically enhanced the dynamic layout of the plan. The tallest part of each angled wall reached the lowest part of the angled wall wrapping the next recessed terrace. As a result, not only the stairs, but the entire facade seemed to be climbing to the top of the hill—a site Sharon was asked to enhance.

Sharon and Zvi Hecker, former partners who separately designed two

Figure 3.19. Yaski and coarchitects, housing and retail in Giloh, Cluster 7 under construction, 1980. Photograph by Nati Harnik. Source: Government Press Office, National Photographs Collection, file D210-115.

Figure 3.20. Arieh Sharon, Eldar Sharon and Partners Architects, housing in Giloh, Cluster 4. Courtesy of the Azrieli Architecture Archive at the Tel Aviv Museum of Art, Arieh Sharon Collection.

אריה שרון אלדר שרון ושות' אדריכלים

housing clusters (Cluster 4 in Giloh and the famous beehive cluster in Ramot) sought a morphological understanding of the ideal human habitat and its perfect geometry. The two had studied and collaborated with Alfred Neumann at the Technion, which L. L. Whyte had commended in 1968 for its "teaching [of] basic principles of mathematical, crystallographic, organic, and some man-made forms."[51] The efficient packing of space the professor and his students had consequently developed won considerable international recognition and, more strikingly, institutional commissions. Drexler also admired Neumann as a student at the Technion, and once in charge of building East Jerusalem, he further concretized this legacy through state commissions.

Both clusters testify to the extent the state embraced the most daring postwar avant-garde. But despite this institutional trust, the Jerusalemite middle class refused to purchase apartments in both clusters: Sharon's turned into a landing ground for new immigrants, and Hecker's is now a rather run-down home of low-income ultra-Orthodox Jews. Despite their nuanced

Figure 3.21. Zvi Hecker, Beehive Housing in Ramot, 1970s. Photograph by Ran Erde.

response to the landscape and efficient simulation of spatial relationship characteristic of a traditional *casba* or a Mediterranean village, their avant-garde architecture turned people once again into the guinea pigs of the state monumental housing laboratory. The middle class felt Sharon's cluster violated their privacy, where climbing the (beautifully photographed) external stairs allowed ample views of private terraces, and they refused to accommodate the tilted walls of Hecker's beehives (Figures 3.21 and 3.22). Many residents longed instead to live in a simple Jerusalemite home rather than promote innovation they could not understand.

The current historiographical judgment of Giloh's architecture is as

Figure 3.22. Walkway toward the Beehive Housing in Ramot. Photograph by Ran Erde.

postmodern and Neo-orientalist—a betrayal of the modernist tradition Israel wishes to promote as its true heritage. Critics personify the stone cladding of Giloh as fundamentalist and its arches as nationalist. Such judgment
entangles Giloh's clusters with the protest against the prolonged Israeli occupation of East Jerusalem. The retrospective evaluation of Giloh should
nevertheless ask if, by pushing modernism to its radical ends, Sharon's and
Hecker's clusters did not risk a return to a top-down social engineering. By
the same token, Giloh's focus on social mobility is an important reminder
that stands in stark contrast to the ever-growing gap between the rich and
the poor in contemporary Israel.

East Talpiot: Imageability and Policy

Unlike the sites of Giloh and Ramot, the two residential settlements north
and south of West Jerusalem, which were chosen primarily for their seeming
barrenness and scarce population, High Commissioner Hill had already had a
fraught history and its slopes were long doomed for development. Back in the
1920s, the British chose to locate their headquarters on the top of this ridge
because it bounds the visual basin of the Old City and provided spectacular
views of the Temple Mount. For UN forces, who inherited the impressive
house that architect Clifford Harrison had designed for the British high commissioner, the hill was an ideal location because it straddled the Green Line
that separated Israel and Jordan between 1949 and 1967. Quite symbolically,
this hill was also the primary site that Jordan successfully occupied on June 5,
1967, after it decided to join the war and launch an attack on West Jerusalem.

Israel took back High Commissioner Hill just a few hours later. By August 1967 it returned the precinct to UN forces but demanded Israeli sovereignty. According to journalist Abraham Rabinovich, large development
plans for the ridge visible from the Old City started to emerge soon after
the war, including "hotels, institutions, and villas that only wealthy investors
from abroad were likely to be able to afford."[52] His criticism illustrates the
clash that surfaced between different stakeholders in the city's development
because of the proximity of the site to the visual basin of the Old City. The
Ministry of Housing was in charge of the entire confiscated site and commissioned architect David Best to create a development plan.[53] But Kollek
believed that the northern slopes fell under his jurisdiction as mayor and ignored the ministry's wishes by commissioning the infamous architect Louis
Kahn after "protracted negotiations."[54] The debate over these suddenly valuable ridges overlooking the Old City was further complicated by the tourist
industry, which grew rapidly after the 1967 war.[55]

The vision of a grand development, advocated by a few but despised by many, dissipated as quickly as it emerged. Kollek attributed the plan's demise to Kahn, Best gave credit to himself, and for Rabinovich the person most responsible was no other than the master developer, Minister of Housing Zeev Sharef.[56] He reports that when Sharef surveyed the "superb panorama," he looked at "the entire visual basin of the Old City stretched between the horizons, the walled city itself riding a plateau cupped by the surrounding ridges . . . and said, 'Here we don't build.'"[57] As a result the housing development moved to the southern side of the ridge, where Best planned for the Ministry of Housing a settlement of five thousand dwelling units, which was eventually called East Talpiot.

Best was an Englishman from Manchester who immigrated to Israel in 1951 after he had already completed his architectural training with, among others, the renowned architect of the British Mandate in Palestine, Clifford Holiday. As an immigrant, Best's integration into the top of the profession was unusual. It was helped not only through his relationships with leading architects,[58] but more importantly, through his work under Artur Glikson at the governmental Housing Department in the 1950s, the department that would evolve into the Ministry of Housing. The 1967 war was a significant moment for his integration into Israeli society. His participation in this war fostered his Zionist identity, and he concluded that "I must devote myself in a much more direct way to the building of the state." He prepared for this mission the following year, by leaving Israel and going to MIT.[59]

Lloyd Rodwin had recently established the Special Program for Urban and Regional Studies (SPURS) at MIT and invited practitioners from the developing world to acquire the tools needed to become community leaders in their respective countries. Best thus found himself part of an interdisciplinary group that played a major role in defining urban design, a subdiscipline bridging architecture and planning. The leading urban design figure at MIT was the eminent Kevin Lynch,[60] whose pivotal 1960 book, *The Image of the City,* empirically studies how people perceive the built environment. Lynch observed the experiences of people moving through a city and charted the mental map each of them formed as they encountered urban elements that grabbed their attention. Such a map can reveal "the apparent clarity or 'legibility' of the cityscape," that is, "the ease with which its parts can be recognized and can be organized into a coherent pattern."[61]

According to Lynch, a strong urban image is capable of tying together the components of identity, structure, and meaning that are necessary for the well-being of a city's citizens. Imageability, a term he coined, is therefore

that quality in a physical object which gives it a high probability of evoking a strong image in any given observer. It is the shape, color, or arrangement which facilitates the making of vividly identified, powerfully structured, highly useful mental images of the environment. It might also be called legibility, or perhaps visibility in a heightened sense, where objects are not only able to be seen, but are presented sharply and intensely to the senses.[62]

His description targets the central question of this chapter: What is the impact of design, and more specifically, what is the impact of the urban image, envisioned by architects, on the way people conceptualize a new territory as their home? What are the features that foster a feeling of identity and belonging?

Best listed "the creation of a community" as the first item in his guidelines for East Talpiot, "Criteria for the Planning and Development of a Neighborhood."[63] Notably, such creation must have "both a social identity, a place to belong to, and a physical entity, which will have a visual coherence and be a recognizable sight in harmony with the Jerusalem landscape." Best thus starts with the formative topographical logic of the division between the city and the state. Two sets of crested arrows are drawn back to back on the watershed of the High Commissioner Hill: the darker arrows facing north toward the Old City marked the prime panoramic site Kollek entrusted to Kahn; the lighter arrows facing south, overlooking the Judean desert and the Palestinian villages nestled in its folds, delineated Best's domain. The five thousand dwelling units he was assigned by the Ministry of Housing are again designed topographically "on two major ridges connected together by a great natural amphitheater of land."[64] In his conceptual plan the focal point of this built-up theater is Sur Bahir, a Palestinian village whose picturesque form is well integrated into the bare landscape of the Judean desert (Figure 3.23).

Once the amphitheater was identified, Best exploited his kit of design tools in order to enhance and habituate the natural form. The urban grain he conceptualized (that is, the pattern created by the arrangement and size of

Figure 3.23. David Best, East Talpiot, site analysis. Courtesy of Professor David Best, architect and town planner.

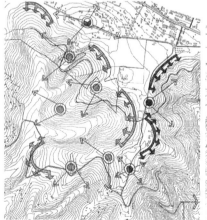

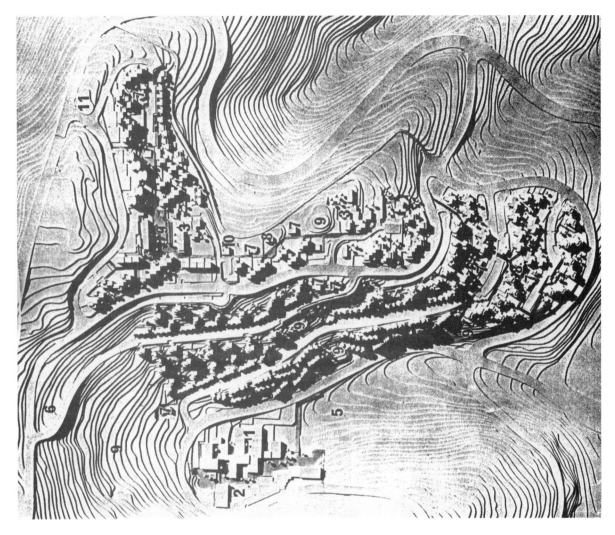

Figure 3.24. David Best, East Talpiot model. Courtesy of Professor David Best, architect and town planner.

buildings) not only emphasized the topographical movement of the natural theater but also amplified its form by raising a dense built mass on the ridges, diffusing it on the slopes, and leaving the valleys that lead to Sur Bahir open and punctuated with public institutions (Figures 3.24, 3.25, and 3.26). His challenge was "to minimize the impact of . . . visual intrusion,"[65] while providing distinct elements of identification for future residents. To that end his design created the clear mental map that Lynch developed by delineating a coherent network of *paths, edges, districts, nodes,* and *landmarks*—the five elements Lynch identified as the primary forms of urban legibility. The main "landmark" was the arid Judean landscape and the village of Sur Bahir, the metaphoric "stage" of the amphitheater.

Best's pursuit at MIT into the "social, economic, and political content" of planning inspired the most important innovation for East Talpiot.[66] Lloyd Rodwin, the SPURS founder, was a firm critic of the Garden City tradition

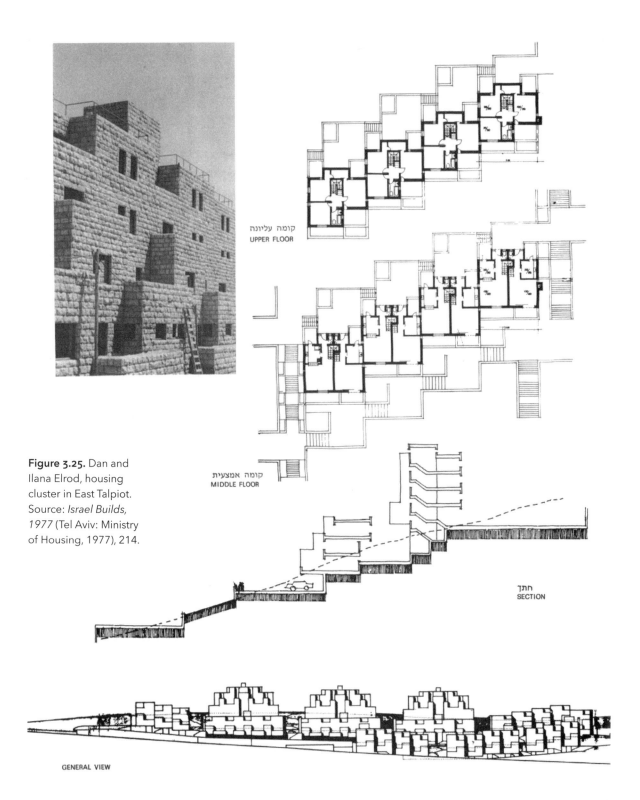

קומה עליונה
UPPER FLOOR

קומה אמצעית
MIDDLE FLOOR

חתך
SECTION

GENERAL VIEW

Figure 3.25. Dan and
Ilana Elrod, housing
cluster in East Talpiot.
Source: *Israel Builds,
1977* (Tel Aviv: Ministry
of Housing, 1977), 214.

Figure 3.26. View of the porous boundary between East Talpiot housing and Palestinian dwellings. Photograph by Ran Erde.

and its regionalist offspring, into which Best had been baptized in the 1950s with Richard Kauffmann and Artur Glikson.[67] Instead of regionalism, Rodwin marshaled the integrated work of multidisciplinary teams—of economists, anthropologists, sociologists, and land-use planners who should, he thought, produce urban policy that focuses planning on people rather than on built forms. He followed this guideline in East Talpiot, where he included in the planning teams not only the architects and engineers assigned by the ministry, but also consultants with backgrounds in social and community work.

The focus of the MIT team on social interaction between "the many different sorts of people who lived, worked, and played in cities, towns, and neighborhoods" was also a product of American politics in the late 1960s. While Best studied at MIT, both Martin Luther King Jr. and Robert F. Kennedy were slain, and his fellow students were often demonstrating in the streets for peace and human rights. This ferment impelled Best to counter "the illusive element [that] has always been the people for which the neighborhood was intended; the future residents." He insisted on "the involvement of residents in the development and maintenance of their neighborhood by creating a direct contact with the planners as the first residents move in, and subsequently the setting up of a neighborhood residents' council."[68]

In these councils *(minhala)* Best implemented the methods of citizen participation he had learned from John Turner, Kevin Lynch, and their peers at MIT. The success of the process depended on the development of leadership among new residents. To that end, Best convinced the ministry to enlarge thirty apartments, out of the six hundred of the first stage, beyond the standard size of social housing. He wanted these apartments to attract families of higher socioeconomic status. "This core of 'involved people,'" Best recollects in his memoir, consisted of, as he puts it, "engineers, university lecturers, and even one of our well-known writers," people with whom he could set up councils of local residents. Members of these councils attended to the welfare of the residents, acted as a go-between with the planning authorities, and were called to participate in the planning process.

But the majority of residents found the professional terminology obscure. The task of the planners was therefore to render the language of planning comprehensible by illustrating abstract "concepts such as: urban form, residential density, movement systems, land use and public open space." The result was "a combination of written and graphic material" through which "the process of planning could be understood, evaluated and subsequently discussed by different categories of participators." In so doing, Best felt he had learned from the social movements of 1960s America and implemented those strategies in 1970s Israel, with even quicker results. His participatory experiments contributed greatly to the initial success of East Talpiot, but Best admits that public interest soon faded.

The public's waning interest should not come as a surprise; Best's memories of "Flower power . . . blooming and the anti-Vietnam campaign . . . growing to a crescendo"[69] were hardly compatible with sentiments back home, where an Israeli euphoria was emerging from the fear of Arab siege that followed the Six Day War. For a brief moment much of the Israeli public seemed eager for participatory planning. Planning opportunities attracted an Anglo-inspired circle of architects and planners, who advocated interdisciplinary approaches that advanced urban design with the tools of urban planning. The various policies that Best delivered from MIT to East Talpiot exemplify this short-lived effort to focus on the resident as an active agent instead of a generic Man, and to treat the residential environment as a multilayered urban system without losing sight of its aesthetic qualities.

The Right to the (Symbols of the Holy) City

In December 1967, a year after the Supreme Planning Committee of Israel was founded in the Ministry of Interior Affairs following the newly approved 1965 Planning and Building Law, its members decided to examine the fruits, and the faults, of Israel's gigantic settlement project during the country's first two decades of independence. They lamented the state's lack of knowledge and experience in "approaching the regional or urban scale." Arieh Sharon, reflecting upon the result of his national master plan, urged planners to change gears, "to give the population that feeling, patriotic I would say, that can be achieved only if the city is architecturally and visually consolidated."[70] Nine years and two wars later, after the Ministry of Housing executed the new tendency for consolidation in Jerusalem, it published an extended essay evaluating the residential settlements the ministry constructed in the interim. By addressing the challenge posed in 1967, the elaborate conclusions of the 1976 document provide a lens to examine the meaning of the building boom we have explored in this chapter.[71]

Notably, the publication is built on a range of contemporary, often radical, schools of architectural and urban thought. Hence, its scholarly nature puts into sharp relief the gap between critical, at times subversive, theories and the ways they are (and are not) implemented by the state in its effort to advance national ideology. The rise of such tensions and inner contradictions in the late 1970s points to the ambivalent boundary between the social housing of the welfare state and the inclination toward postmodern expression in Jerusalem's architecture.

The building boom that followed the 1967 war dramatically transformed the architectural culture of social housing across Israel and particularly in Jerusalem. When this building activity was evaluated in 1976, some seventy thousand Jews were living in the new neighborhoods encircling West Jerusalem. The ministry's report helps us understand how new architectural trends advanced the pivotal demographic, economic, and social change of Jerusalem via housing, which is both an object and an action.

The ministry's analysis drew not just on architectural theory, but also on the theoretical work of the developmental psychologist Abraham Maslow, who proposed to examine human needs in hierarchical order.[72] According to Maslow "we are motivated to fulfill basic needs before striving for higher aspirations" (Figure 3.27). The bottom levels of his celebrated hierarchical pyramid of needs therefore consist of the most basic physical requirements for human survival and then the need for security and comfort. Only after these conditions are met is the individual able to focus his motivations on the more complex needs for love and belonging. The higher need for self-esteem and respect is topped by the highest aspiration of all—the need for self-actualization. The ministry's publication lists an inventory of these needs as embodied in Jerusalem, examines their spatial requirements, and seeks practical conclusions in reference not only to the housing environment but, more poignantly, to the symbolic context of Jerusalem.[73] The title of the ministry's document, *Planning the Residential Environment and Fulfilling of the Human Needs,* indicates its belief in the growing capacity of an already developed state to satisfy needs that eclipse the rudimentary requirements of life.

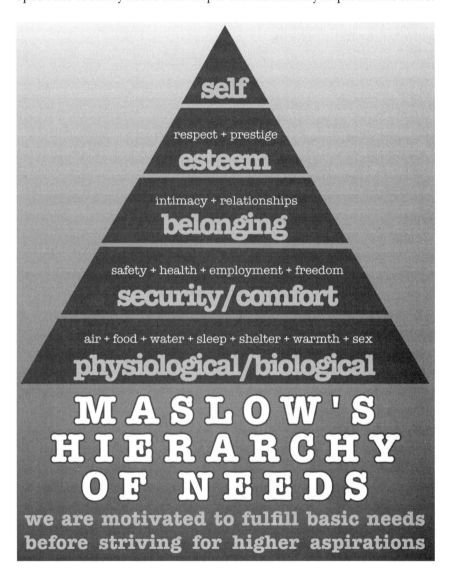

Figure 3.27. Maslow's hierarchy of needs.

It also offers us a startling perspective on the ministry's own understanding of its work, as it considered the last nine years of building United Jerusalem.

In 1963, Aviah Hashimshoni argued that "the functional approach and the aspiration for total organization" were the guiding themes of Israeli architecture, motivated by "enthusiasm, public responsibility, activism and identification with the material needs of building."[74] The ministry's publication acknowledges these values but considers them "zero degree reality," that is, a reality that addresses only the bare necessities of human life. For the socialists who founded the state, the document admits, the sole emphasis on function and utility was necessary in order to inaugurate a new social order. But as Israel's socialist ethos diminishes, and its newly acquired power grows, the developmental modernism that enabled this zero-degree reality provoked a "phenomenon of environmental alienation." Why? Because its *neue sachlichkeit* modernism stops symbolizing for residents "any human meaning that 'touches their hearts' and expresses the basic values of human existence: freedom and respect, trust and responsibility, pride, a sense of continuity and eternity, etc."[75]

These were exactly the values propagated by post–World War II situated modernists, who had often turned to behavioral studies in order to criticize high modernism on its own terrain. The need to "belong," the document accordingly argued, is predominantly sociopsychological rather than functional. Hence, architects of a liberal society must utilize new scientific methodologies in order to fulfill human satisfaction.[76] We focus here on two architectural phenomena that prevailed in the architectural culture of the 1970s: one is the active inhabitation of the street; the other is the role of symbols in the urban landscape. The scientific analysis the document offers for both will help sum up the meaning of housing in East Jerusalem.

In order for residents to identify with their residential environment, the publication argued that they should be actively engaged not just in decorating their house or apartment but in the production of their public spaces. Architects and planners were therefore urged to venture beyond the solution of functional requirements and, instead, to animate "a place that offers a constant 'invitation' for meeting, dialogue, acquaintance, etc."[77] According to another contemporary architect, the meaning of "environment" at the time was "the environment that you create around the user, the children, the group, the system you plan for . . . to plan the open and enclosed spaces in which human action unfolds . . . places to think, to mingle" (Figures 3.28, 3.29, and 3.30).[78]

The ultimate form for such social activity, contemporary critics agreed, is the street, the vivid urban form that CIAM architects eliminated from their vision of the modernist city.[79] As "'the nervous junction' of everyday life," the ministry's document agrees, "the street offers unlimited access to the origin of 'socialization.'"[80] By embracing this perception, the document builds on a nuanced relation between identity, belonging, and urban action. According to Henri Lefebvre, who is cited in the text, to inhabit is to act in and on the urban environment, to mark, model, and shape it, to appropriate it as one's own. Such action goes beyond the developmental exploitation of nature for economic ends. To appropriate time and space means, Lefebvre posits, to transform it into human property. That appropriation is thus the precondition for social development.

According to the ministry's document, the street is the ultimate place for such active inhabitation. Why? It is where children enter social life and where "collective habits" take shape. In the street residents can compare, select, and "'de-codify' identity symbols—outfit, behavior, etc." Its "'urban

Figure 3.28. Moshe Lofenfeld and Giora Gamerman, housing in Giloh, Cluster 3, 1970s. Children playing in a pedestrian passageway. Photograph by Ran Erde.

Figure 3.29. David Best, playground in East Talpiot. Photograph by Ran Erde.

Figure 3.30. Ram Karmi, housing in Giloh, Cluster 6, 1970s. "Fingers" alleys. Photograph by Ran Erde.

supply' of information and experience sharpen observational skills through streaming gazes." Residents thus collaborate "around some consensual and matter-of-fact 'behavioral codes.'" In other words, in the street is where we internalize the many rules of social life.[81]

But when an architect plans a new residential environment, how can one design a public space that would oblige the resident to leave the comfort zone of the apartment and participate in communal life? How can planners convince residents that they will profit from public engagement and that participation will help satisfy their own need to belong? The publication offered a rather surprising answer: by maintaining the residential environment as "a 'reservation' of organic and spontaneous life." Only "non-institutional existence," the document argues, can induce "primary and immediate reactions."[82] This presents an inherent contradiction: How can a centralized state apparatus refrain from institutional planning? This question leads to Kallus and Law Yone's observation about the duality of housing, how it is simultaneously a product of professional labor (i.e., institutional planning) and an ideal of communal (i.e., organic and spontaneous) life. Historical circumstances further amplified the paradox: exactly when Israelis started building their unified city on confiscated land, Europeans and Americans demonstrated their right to the city on both sides of the Atlantic Ocean. During the near-global urban protests of 1968, residents of cities around the world claimed their space against state authorities. Lefebvre is reputed as the philosopher and public intellectual who theorized this "right to the city" and coined its prevailing usage.[83] And yet, the Israeli state cites the writings of Lefebvre in an official document in order to justify its housing on embattled land.

The document addresses the duality between the institutional production of housing and its living ideal by linking science with humanism. According to this logic, if the state updates its planning strategies to accommodate the latest in behavioral sciences, the resultant housing would approximate that living ideal. This logic leads to "the need for symbols [that] belong, genetically and organically, to human sensation, originating in the deepest layers of the biology of man." Moreover, since according to researchers, "the absence of symbols from [the residential] space contributes and creates the state of tension and frustration in which the modern man exists," the right to symbols is a right to healthier life.[84]

The call to revise the ministry's action by adhering to the universality of science eventually turns into a method for justifying its opposite: the scientifically proven psychological need in culturally specific symbols starts approximating postmodern awareness that challenges the universal authority of science. A year after the ministry published its evaluation, Charles Jencks explained in his seminal manifesto of postmodern architecture:

we learn from the beginning of the cultural signs which make any urban place particular to a social group, an economic class and real, historical people; whereas modern architects spend their time unlearning all these particular signs in an attempt to design for universal man, or Mythic Modern Man. This 3-M monster of course does not exist, except as a historical fiction.[85]

The ministry's publication similarly defies the *sachlich* ideology of developmental modernists, whose buildings lacked the cultural references that are meaningful to residents. It similarly criticizes the prevailing economic reasoning. Although "it is difficult to justify the 'economic feasibility' of the symbol based on the customary 'cost-benefit' analysis," it argues, symbols possess "supra-functional significance" and are therefore worthy of the investment they require.[86]

The document thus builds to a logical, though unlikely, conclusion: in order to fulfill the need for "social esteem and self-actualization," urban planning and architectural design would "return to dwellers, in their own residential environment, the 'right' to the values and symbols that express them and contribute to their personality's growth." In other words, residents should identify a value or symbol in the architectural features of the built environment, in the street, the doorstep, or the module of a facade, that they can acknowledge as their own. Through such symbols "man realizes and absorbs the cultural-educational image of the place. The reaction to symbols generates an emotional response that fosters the connection between the man, the place, and the society to which he belongs." That is, the efficacy of symbols is not rational but rather emotional and thus contributes to building social cohesiveness and territorial rootedness (Figures 3.31 and 3.32).[87]

This assessment forms the crux of the ministry's argument: in Jerusalem the connection to the place assumes an "entirely original" dimension; "one cannot overestimate the uniqueness of this case in the human field." Why? Because in this place, "the feeling of belonging is so absolutely identified with such rich and complex superior values: religion, nationalism, culture, diplomacy, etc." These feelings of uplift and belonging are generated by the presence of "unique sites that provide the highest possible level of belongingness"—everything from the Western Wall to the Temple Mount to the governmental precinct of the state. Indeed, these are the sites that attract Israeli citizens to their capital and international pilgrims to their historical and spiritual center. But why should that uniqueness concern a ministry mandated to build the residential environment? Because, this document claims, in Jerusalem "the spirit of the 'Holy City' moves and spreads through the entire space."[88] (See Plate 3.)

This statement takes a clear position in the controversy over the character

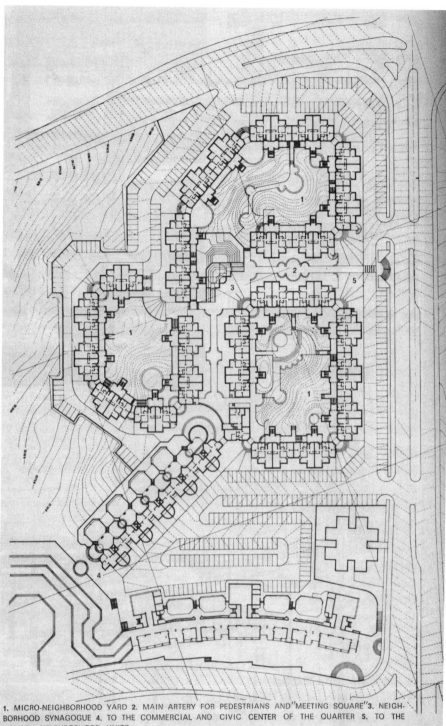

1. MICRO-NEIGHBORHOOD YARD 2. MAIN ARTERY FOR PEDESTRIANS AND "MEETING SQUARE" 3. NEIGH-BORHOOD SYNAGOGUE 4. TO THE COMMERCIAL AND CIVIC CENTER OF THE QUARTER 5. TO THE NEAR-BY NEIGHBORHOOD UNITS

1. חצר של המיקרו שכונה. 2. עורק ראשי להולכי רגל. 3. בית כנסת שכונתי 4. למרכז מסחרי ואזרחי של השכונה. 5. ליחידות השכנות

Figure 3.31. Salo Hershman, housing in Giloh, Cluster 11. Plan. Source: *Israel Builds, 1977* (Tel Aviv: Ministry of Housing, 1977), 200.

of Jerusalem. According to the *1968 Jerusalem Masterplan,* holiness cannot be fashioned in brick and mortar. Jerusalem, its authors determined, should be a modern city in the service of its contemporary citizens. It should respect, rather than impersonate, the holy sites it accommodates. By contrast, just eight years later the ministry's publication begs planners "not to leave the space [of Jerusalem] as a dry and indifferent element which is conceived for the functional living of its residents."[89] It thus implies that in order for residents to feel and identify as Jerusalemites, the city's symbolic presence should be woven into their everyday residential experience.

Figure 3.32. Salo Hershman, housing in Giloh, Cluster 11. Archway leading to semi-private courtyards from which residents enter their homes. Source: *Israel Builds, 1988* (Tel Aviv: Ministry of Housing, 1988), 113.

To better understand the consequence of this new symbolic role in the residential environment we should return to Lefebvre. His *Right to the City* was, according to one of the ministry's planners, "the Bible, the Quran, and the Holy Testimony in one."[90] According to Lefebvre, symbols imbue the act of appropriating space with a concrete character, their performativity saturates inhabitation with social presence. Łukasz Stanek explains the relevance of Lefebvre's insight to the residential environment: "as a site of appropriation, housing becomes 'a substitute for the monumentality of the ancient world' in the conditions of the postwar capitalist society, which 'no longer totalizes its elements, nor seeks to achieve such total integration through monuments.'"[91] This was exactly why Jerusalem as a symbol had to be present in the residential environment: it integrated seemingly disparate parts of life—housing and nationhood—by means of daily experience. Moreover, the ministry suggested that access to symbols as a lived, monumental experience was a civic right: "Far and beyond anywhere else the environment of Jerusalem must symbolize the national-spiritual character of the city, and also, the feeling that this heritage—as an everyday residential given—is the sole right of the residents of this place."[92] In Jerusalem, the right to the city is thus the right to its symbols, and that layer of meaning was best accessed—the ministry argued—not merely in the city's religious sites, but in the residential environment.

Conclusions

In 1971, Yehuda Drexler, the architect in charge of settling East Jerusalem, defended the ministry against its critics, confidently stating that "what we see in Jerusalem . . . is not the planning quality of the Ministry of Housing, but rather, of the architecture in this country."[93] Implied were two assumptions: one, the best Israeli architects were working for the ministry; two, Israeli architects were committed, by definition, to the goals of the centralized state. But such optimistic assumptions grew increasingly complicated in this watershed moment for Israel, as it transitioned from an immigrant society of settlers into an increasingly powerful and significantly larger state. In this context, the housing of East Jerusalem turned into a monumental testing ground for the possible directions of not just Israeli architecture, but also Israeli identity and citizenship.

Immediately after the 1967 war, Drexler set this testing ground in the Ministry of Housing. The bare developmental modernism the ministry had already perfected fell short of fulfilling the aspirations of Drexler's activist Zionism: it did not cohere a sense of home, and its construction was too dispersed to become irreversible facts on the ground. He therefore assembled the in-house Sho"p team, young architects who were well versed in post–

World War II situated modernisms. This knowledge and inspiration underlay their proposition for the housing of Ma'alot Dafna. Although the architectural principles they articulated turned into the prevailing guidelines for residential settlements in East Jerusalem, recognition of their pioneering role has disappeared from our collective memory, not least because of the bitter clashes that ensued between the team and Drexler, its head.

Those conflicts only tell part of the story. More consequential for Jerusalem today are the three massive residential projects that emerged amid the ministry's conflicts. They were built on confiscated land and became, against all expectations, a stronghold of the Jewish middle class in Jerusalem. Of the three, Ramot is the most revealing politically, but its complexities render it less useful for a comparative architectural analysis. Drexler's team had already laid the blueprint for Ramot before it was thrown out of the ministry. Thereafter, the planning of Ramot moved through several hands; new members had filled the Sho"p team, but Drexler, their head, left the ministry after the 1974 elections. Ram Karmi, the new head architect of the ministry, appointed Ora and Yaakov Yaar, prominent members of the sabra circle, as chief planners, and the Yaars, in turn, introduced younger architects to this building lab. The entanglement of Ramot's planning with the turbulent official politics of settlement provoked (rather smooth) transitions that nevertheless obscured its original vision.

By contrast, a comparison between Giloh and East Talpiot—whose early planning stages represented coherent manifestos of their respective teams— helps illuminate the larger struggles at work over the proper shape, and feel, of Jerusalem. The comparison of Giloh and East Talpiot reveals a tension between two schools of situated modernisms: one was inspired primarily by the late work of Le Corbusier and Team 10, the other by Kevin Lynch and the emerging discipline of urban design in the United States. The profound difference between the two epitomizes and foreshadows the difference between the sabra circle and the Anglo circle. Yaski, the leading sabra architect, chose to work with his peers as a team, while Best preferred to be the leader of the design process, communicating that process to his team and to future residents via detailed briefs. Their attitudes fitted their respective sites. The low hills of Giloh provided the appropriate setting for avant-garde experiments—the early design of megastructures, as well as the experimental clusters that were eventually built. By contrast, East Talpiot's proximity to the Old City and its steep topography lent itself to symbolic reading, which connected Best to the British planning tradition in Israel, exemplified by a love of the picturesque and a fascination with the Orient.

One can easily read this difference in the architecture of the two settlements. The planners of Giloh, who were dismissive toward the subtle architectural expression of East Talpiot, sought instead the thrill in architecture, the excitement of its plasticity and form, and the surprising transitions between its sculpted spaces. Their sensual and innovative design provided ample and diverse public spaces for the residents. Not only did they break the monotony of the modernist block, they used the volumes of the residential buildings as building blocks with which they succeeded to mold public interiority.

Like the Giloh team, Best also criticized developmental modernism's indifference to the communal spaces in between houses. But his method was practically opposite to that of the Giloh team: the external landscape determined the three-dimensional design of his housing. He amplified the topography and composed a central pathway replete with hierarchical views. The most conspicuous of these views are directed to the Arab village below, insinuating a sense of benevolent superiority. His houses are simple and explicitly ordinary. Their composition imbues the setting with the narrative of the place. Accordingly, Best articulated the urban design of East Talpiot as a policy, a set of guidelines that he presented to his architects as if conducting an orchestra of different housing types.

In stark contrast, the clusters of Giloh (like the initial megastructures that Yaski's team proposed) testify to its planners' conviction, namely, that architectural design is the appropriate method to shape urban space. Architecture, according to this view, must eclipse the forces of administrative planning and resolve the ruptured modernist city by structuring the relationship between its components by means of three-dimensional design. The clusters of Giloh accordingly contain balanced and exciting domestic spaces. Together, however, they failed to cohere a continuous urban ensemble. Each cluster is an introverted ecosystem, an interiorized landscape that hides behind housing walls and endless parking lots.

Giloh's hierarchy between the infrastructural, the public, the communal, the private, and the intimate is coherent, almost literal, and therefore very easy to identify. At the same time, this prescribed architecture is imposing: its articulate forms are difficult to manipulate and to adjust for personal needs and individual expression. Karmi published a manifesto while serving as the head architect of the ministry, declaring his intention to provide for each family the means to turn its institutional housing into its individual home; yet his architecture is so tightly designed that it leaves little room for multiple readings or modes of habitation. The eventual success of Giloh's first stage of monumental housing suggests that people willingly submitted their own wishes to its proposed narrative.

Just like the internal details, both of these settlements' boundaries are affected by their respective relationship between architecture and landscape. The clusters of Giloh are designed from the inside out, ending with a housing wall that protects its inner courts. Despite the architecture of the place, the existing architecture of the Palestinian village Beth Tzafafah, for example, was invisible to Israeli planners. Again, by contrast, the boundaries of East Talpiot are porous and permissive; they let existing Palestinian structures interfere with the geometric regularity of the neighborhood in order to blend better into the place. The unimposing urbanity of East Talpiot might even have aided the relationship between this settlement and the neighboring Jabel Mukaber, a far more peaceful relationship than most Jewish settlements have had with their Arab neighbors.

These multiple readings of Israel's expansive and centralized efforts to create public housing in East Jerusalem defy any attempt at overarching categorization: the call to house a suddenly expanded nation resulted in a remarkable spectrum of architectural experiments. That spectrum reveals the tension between, on the one hand, the call to cohere domestic belonging in the built environment and in the concrete experiences of its residents, and on the other, the need to infuse suburban residences with the symbolic potency of the Holy City. The first typified situated modernists; the second already incorporated postmodern elements. Yet they all served the grand idea of the modern nation-state and its authority to mobilize resources, to centralize the market, and to cohere a rather unified national identity.

The ministry's evolution of urban thinking throughout the postwar decade eventually ventured beyond the sabra's desire for place making and the contradictory blend of respect for and possession of the land. Planners now aimed to participate in the very creation of the state's mandate. The comprehensive 1976 report, which carefully evaluated the ministry's massive housing expansion of the preceding eight years, reached a firm conclusion: the planner's duty is to assimilate the image of Jerusalem into its housing, because only then can residents benefit from the gravity of Jerusalem; only then can Israelis feel that the national-spiritual heritage of Jerusalem becomes "the sole right of the residents to this place."[94]

The paradox lies in the inspiration to this dictum: the right to the city, the concept Lefebvre developed as a subversive critique, becomes the means by which the state strengthens the possession of its Jewish residents over Jerusalem's heritage, thus fostering and grounding its demographic Judaization—the primary goal of the Israeli state. For Lefebvre, however, the two concepts are not as far apart as they seem: to inhabit a place was to appropriate it, "Not in the sense of possessing it, but as making it an oeuvre, making it one's own, marking it, shaping it."[95] In retrospect, the tension that exists between these two meanings of appropriation—inhabitation and possession—mirrors the tension between the Israeli and Palestinian perceptions of housing in East Jerusalem. For the Jewish population, these neighborhoods were the engine of upward mobility in Jerusalem. They offered residents social housing that cohered a sense of community and social integration. For Palestinians, these settlements were (and are) an active form of occupation amplified by the appropriation of Jerusalem's symbolism. Thus, the architecture of these settlements dispossesses not only the territory, but also the historical meaning it embodies. This dual reading of Israel's centralized social housing frames "housing" with the familiar truth of modernity as a double-edged sword, as simultaneously liberating and oppressing. Even among those who together liberated Jerusalem from foreign rule, it was difficult to find a consensual method for making Jerusalem Israeli.

4 **CITY**
URBAN BEAUTIFICATION

> There is [also] a special beauty about the Old City of
> Jerusalem, the wondrous beauty of a city set amidst the
> timeless terraces and hills of Judea, perched on hillocks,
> surrounded by magnificent stone ramparts, skirted by ravines
> and faced by the gentle slopes of the Mount of Olives and
> Mount Scopus with their commanding view of the plain of
> Jericho, the Jordan River and the Dead Sea.
>
> —*Arieh Sharon in* Planning Jerusalem: The Old City and
> Its Environs

JERUSALEM'S DRAMATIC LANDSCAPES and Oriental beauty are best
experienced within the visual basin of the Old City. The Old City itself, barely
two square miles, crowns Mount Moriah, which rises up from the steep Ben
Hinnom and Kidron valleys and is nestled among higher hills that offer spectacular views over Jerusalem's sacred sites. The key to Jerusalem's beauty lies
in the dramatic play between its stone monuments and these scarcely populated, almost barren slopes. After the 1967 war, this sublime landscape held
little attraction for the nation's Ministry of Housing but was cherished by
Jerusalem's mayor, who realized its strategic potential. The ministry, like
many of Israel's bureaucratic agencies, was concerned primarily with ensuring the demographic Judaization of Jerusalem and its territorial indivisibility. Mayor Teddy Kollek, however, pursued a more abstract goal: the city's
symbolic beautification, which held equal political importance (see Plate 4).

These diverging goals were already evident before Israel seized East Jerusalem from Jordan in June 1967, but tension between the government of
the Israeli state and the government of its capital city blossomed almost as
quickly as the war ended. The first dispute focused on the municipal boundaries of the city Israelis unilaterally unified. Jerusalem's mayor, Teddy Kollek,
and his deputies wanted a bounded, manageable city. Instead they received
a city tripled in size and encompassing vast rural areas lacking urban infrastructure. Then the state started confiscating land in East Jerusalem in 1968
to build more housing within the unified city; the government wished to
speed building by bypassing the recently enacted 1965 Planning and Building

Law. Kollek was asked to head the unified local and district planning committees that aimed to speed up building permits. But when Kollek came to the building sites he was asked to approve, construction was already under way. Following the next major confiscation, in August 1970, Kollek refused to approve housing schemes that were aesthetically controversial and that violated his laboriously prepared *1968 Jerusalem Masterplan*. A couple of weeks later, shortly after the American State Department insisted on a Jordanian presence in East Jerusalem, Kollek changed his mind, reversing to the old Zionist idea of building to enforce rule. Kollek's painful submission—after a stirring public debate—starkly clarified his position: despite being the mayor of one of the most meaningful cities in the entire world, Teddy Kollek commanded very limited power within the engine of official Israeli politics.

The common understanding of the period is rooted in this capitulation: Kollek had excellent public relations skills, the story goes, but little power and no budget to determine the politics of space in Jerusalem. This chapter challenges that notion. We will see that exactly because Israel's state government outmaneuvered Kollek, he chose to operate on a different register: he developed and put into action a powerful form of cultural politics. His politics were based on three premises. First, Jerusalem was a world city, the cradle of the world's monotheistic faiths. It therefore had a global constituency, which was invited to participate in shaping the city. Second, Jerusalem was a city of diverse people, ethnicities, and religions and therefore required enlightened management that only Israelis, Kollek argued, could secure. Third, and most pertinent for this chapter, the cultivation of the city's spiritual beauty was the key to inspiring peaceful coexistence of these three faiths. Since the city's urban beauty was so precious, Kollek concluded, its potential had to be entrusted to the most prominent professionals both in Israel and throughout the world.

Kollek inherited just such a professional team from his predecessor, Mordechai Ish Shalom, who hired in 1964 the finest Israeli planners to prepare a master urban plan for Jerusalem's future. After 1967 it was unclear whether this highly modernist team, and the 1968 master plan it submitted, could fulfill Kollek's aspiration for a spiritual world city. This question provoked two years of zealous controversies, culminating in Kollek's appeal to the international community for help shaping the new, expanded Jerusalem now under his control. Architects such as Louis Kahn, Bruno Zevi, and Buckminster Fuller were among many who voluntarily, and eagerly, participated in the Jerusalem Committee that Kollek created in 1969. In 1970 the committee's outright, almost brutal rejection of the highly modernist Israeli master plan forced Kollek and his advisors to seek new planning directions.

This chapter follows Kollek's itinerary in shaping Jerusalem, starting from his election in 1965 and through the postwar decade. To understand the significance of Kollek's work and his modes of operation we will link three seemingly disparate realms: the political, the historical, and the professional. The first is Kollek's cultural politics, second is the heritage of the British Mandate, and third is the post–World War II shift in the design disciplines — architecture, landscape architecture, and urban design. In the competition to control the planning of Jerusalem's symbolic resources, the intermingling of three realms empowered the cultural agenda of Kollek and his allies.

A closer look at the political realm reveals how Kollek's coalition advanced the geographical division between the city and the state; Kollek invested his political power in shaping and beautifying the topographical basin around the Old City while maintaining a lower profile vis-à-vis the state's industrious building on the outskirts of the city. The logic for this division was rooted in the historical realm. During the British Mandate, from 1920 to 1948, planners focused their efforts on the sacred basin because this place framed Jerusalem most powerfully as a visual idea, a universal constant, over which they took custody in the name of the monotheistic world. Kollek and his coalition argued that for Israelis to assume similar responsibility they had to render this vision in brick and mortar, that they had to culturally, morally, and aesthetically legitimize Israeli rule.

This was a daring proposition for a country whose physical planning was hitherto guided by the legacy of progress and development. Kollek's coalition soon argued its case against the highly modernist 1968 master plan by invoking the third, disciplinary realm of the architecture profession. They were able to deploy influential architectural discourses that criticized the worldwide spread of anonymous post–World War II developmental modernism. Ideas that celebrated the particularities of the place were particularly significant, as was the interest in how people experienced its visual and spatial merits. These trends mark a postwar return to ideas that informed British planners during the Mandate period, most notably a return to Orientalist sensibilities and to the aesthetic philosophy of the picturesque. The invocation of these ideas after 1967, as means for imagining Jerusalem, allowed the newest trends in landscape architecture and urban design to take hold in the city.

These trends included the recent environmental revolution in landscape architecture, particularly the work of Ian McHarg and Lawrence Halprin, the criticism of the modern movement that we already encountered in previous chapters, and the rise of preservation as an environmental discipline. The key players who brought these trends to bear on Jerusalem's built landscape belonged to the situated coalition, namely, Mayor Kollek and his allies, Yaakov Dash and Eliezer Brutzkus from the Ministry of Interior Affairs, and a little known yet highly effective circle of young architects who implemented these ideas in Jerusalem. These architects were educated in or emigrated from English-speaking countries, bringing new perspectives to a country largely planned according to central European models.

We will examine the innovations these players introduced to the disciplines of spatial design, as manifested in two projects: through the *Jerusalem Conceptual Plan* that the Ministry of Interior Affairs submitted in August 1967, which eventually resulted in the "Outline Scheme for the Old City and Its Environs," and through the strikingly rapid authorization of the national park that landscape architect Arye Dvir designed, on behalf of the National Park Authority (NPA), around Jerusalem's city walls.[1] The rapid and enthusiastic international approval of this park convinced Kollek that this architectural direction would win him the desired support of luminaries overseas; it was thus a key to the success of his cultural agenda. We will then follow the structural changes he enacted in the Jerusalem Municipality, yielding, among other things, a successful policy for high-rise buildings.

Common to all these players and projects was the perception of Jerusalem as an urban landscape that required a comprehensive approach, needing the tools of both urban design and landscape architecture to fulfill the aesthetic expectations of a world audience. We usually see design as a blueprint for building construction, but the professionals and the agencies who animate this chapter had neither the budget nor the political power for such massive construction. At their disposal was the institutional power to demolish existing structures and prevent new building by drafting and legislating planning policies. We will conclude this chapter with their efforts to wed design and policy in order to shape the spirit and character of the Holy City.

The Cultural Politics of Teddy Kollek

On June 27, 1967, twenty days after seizing East Jerusalem from Jordan, the Israeli parliament, the Knesset, passed a bill officially unifying Jerusalem. The army relinquished control to Jerusalem's municipal government, and for the first time in nineteen years, the whole city was accessible to everyone. In the *New York Times*'s "Quotation of the Day" Kollek described the crowds crossing into formerly prohibited areas of the city:

> "I think it's the greatest carnival I ever saw. It was an exchange of populations."
> —Mayor Teddy Kollek of Jerusalem as Arabs and Israelis mingled in the city after barriers were removed[2]

Caught up in the postwar euphoria, he rejoiced "the hearts of Jews and Arabs went out to each other despite the difficulties of the immediate past."[3] Kollek rendered the violent past as a historical, time-bound disaster, which had now given way to the true nature of the city. Since, according to Kollek, "Never were the ideas of peace and hopes for peace expressed more profoundly than by Jerusalem's ancient prophets," his city must also inspire contemporary peacemaking. In July 1967 he invited the UN to move its headquarters from New York to Jerusalem.[4]

This was the beginning of a long campaign to internationalize Jerusalem. It was also the opening act in Kollek's masterful performance of cultural politics, which helped make his twenty-eight-year reign as mayor legendary. The mayor's political and aesthetic perspective first took shape in Vienna, a city where one resident coined the term Zionism while another invented the gas chamber. Roger Friedland and Richard Hecht argue that Kollek "tried to make the ideal of a cultured, multiethnic Vienna real in Jerusalem." But, as he was seeking "to make Jerusalem a cosmopolitan jewel, he feared the religious and national hatred that had destroyed the city of his youth."[5] This conflicted heritage turned Kollek into an expert moderator, aided by his charm, respect, and straightforwardness. His spirited belief in his capacity to run Jerusalem as a pluralistic city that benefited all its residents was contagious. Many who objected to Israeli policy were persuaded nevertheless to collaborate with the mayor.

Above all Kollek sought to promote, as the title of his 1968 book puts it, Jerusalem as the *Sacred City of Mankind*. If Jerusalem was the most important place to the three monotheistic religions, then it was not only home to its residents, but also a living presence in the heart of people around the world. Kollek openly declared "the moment Jerusalem became one city it stopped being a Jewish city." For Israelis such a statement was (and is) highly controversial because it challenged the official politics of the Israeli state, whose resolute goal was (and is) to territorially and demographically Judaize Jerusalem. But Kollek was adamant. Despite fierce disagreement from much of the country, Kollek's every effort to address the international constituencies of Jerusalem emanated from this position.

David Ben Gurion, Kollek's political mentor, forcefully articulated Israel's official position. Shortly after the war he described the occupation of East Jerusalem, which "stirred the Jewish people . . . more even than the establishment of the State," as the conclusion of the 1948 War of Independence. "The task of the saviors of Jewish independence of nineteen years ago has been completed, and the capital of Israel of three thousand years ago, the city taken and wholly freed by the heroes . . . of the Six Day War, will remain the capital of Israel forever."[6] Ben Gurion recalls the November 1947 UN decision to split Mandate Palestine between Arabs and Jews and to keep Jerusalem international. But, he argues, "The UN has not succeeded in implementing its decisions," and Israel had to resist, on its own, "the aggressors who rebelled against the UN." Therefore, he explains, "the November resolution on Jerusalem is, in our opinion, null and void."[7]

How could Kollek reconcile the vast gap between his own position and the fervent position of his mentor, not to mention so much of the country? The task is even more astounding when we consider that from 1952 to 1965 Kollek worked directly under Ben Gurion, as the authoritative and competent general manager of the prime minister's office. Apparently the two men, the legendary founder of Israel and his potent right hand, developed a systematic division of labor. Ben Gurion made all decisions on issues dear to him, such as security, immigration, science, education, and relationships with world Jewry. Other issues were the domain of Kollek, who was able to efficiently advance his own initiatives under the irrefutable reputation of the "Old Man."[8] Kollek focused on tourism, and also advanced cultural, intellectual, and aesthetic affairs, such as the annual Israel Festival that hosts leading artists from around the world, or the Israel Museum—his flagship project, and one of Israel's most cherished architectural achievements— which opened its gates shortly after Kollek became mayor.

Kollek's early political career was largely motivated by the desire to establish a distinctively Israeli culture. He lamented Ben Gurion's resignation in 1963 because he felt that "our roots, from many aspects, are still very shallow."[9] He believed that a young settler society had to possess a deep-rooted culture not only to foster nation building, but also to win international recognition. A self-described "messenger of the Zionist cause," he wanted to gather all the agencies dealing with public relations, communication, and tourism under the prime minister's office in order to do what he considered the most important task of all: "to explain Zionism to the world."[10]

But Zionism was not a unified movement. State agencies responsible for shaping the physical and symbolic image of Israel worked in at least two parallel trajectories of nation building. Scholars tend to focus on the first, the more conspicuous project of progress and development, which used natural and territorial resources as well as human labor in order to better the well-being of Jewish citizens. Ben Gurion, his architects, and their brand of Labor Zionism shaped this legacy of progress and development. Despite his affiliation with the Labor Party, Kollek preferred the second, cultural trajectory of nation building, which focused on shared traditions and the establishment of symbolic institutions. He was ambivalent toward socialist agendas and the ethos of a New Jew emerging from the tilled land. For him, a strong Israel would exist only if it could demonstrate a firm cultural nucleus built on visible heritage. This chapter focuses on this more implicit and often cunning project. The production of heritage deployed archeology, architecture, landscape, and historical relics to provide Israel's Jews with a sense of security and stability in a modern world shaken by new forms of violence and new and unsettling mobility.[11] In this less obvious realm, Kollek excelled.

Although the first trajectory is progressive and the second traditional, they are both distinctively modernist projects. And the deep conviction in the need for Jews to return to their biblical home motivated both. Despite this shared ground, Ben Gurion, the prime architect of the Israeli state, operated primarily within the first, developmental venue. Kollek, the highest nonelected official in Israel's public sector, operated within the second—the seemingly apolitical, culturally situated venue.[12] Once Kollek took control of the mayor's office, we argue, his division of labor with Ben Gurion gradually turned into a division between city and state. But with this division, the two projects undergirding the official politics of the state and the cultural politics of the mayor were not necessarily compatible.

Each trajectory used different methods to build the Zionist project. Architects and planners associated with Labor Zionism created the developmental coalition that since independence in 1948 laid out infrastructures and mass housing and was, as Erik Cohen argues, largely hostile to urban life.[13] This chapter focuses on the other coalition of situated modernists, to which Kollek belonged, and on the institutions that enabled the execution of their vision. After the war Kollek turned his far-reaching, but largely unsubstantiated, vision into a proficient bureaucratic machine that substantiated the situated modernists' geographical, ethical, and financial goals.

Competing for Jerusalem's Visual Basin

Israel captured East Jerusalem on June 7, 1967. Two days later, while artillery shells were still exploding in the north, Mayor Teddy Kollek met General Uzi Narkis, the high commander of the Jerusalem forces, along with other military and municipal officials. They walked along the City Walls toward Jaffa Gate and tested a temporary path that led from the Zion Gate to the Western Wall. With these impressions in mind, they set a plan to solve the area's engineering problems by identifying six sites around the City Walls as hazards that had to be demolished. The municipality assumed responsibility and committed to demolish all structures, fences, and blockades in these sites, to clear and prepare them for public use, and to take care of the evacuated residents.[14]

On June 10, a day after Kollek's tour, the association of contractors bulldozed the Mughrabee Quarter that stood in front of the Western Wall. By July 18, six weeks later, all structures in the six aforementioned sites, except the one opposite the Fasat Hotel, had been leveled.[15] Amos Elon, the most prominent journalist covering Jerusalem's unification, commended Kollek for his immediate action. "Jerusalem was lucky" he wrote. "In a crucial moment it had an energetic mayor, gifted with imagination and good taste. He took the bull by the horns and generated in a few weeks' time works of evacuation and clearance which all Jerusalem's lovers and governors have dreamed in vain since 1917,"[16] that is, since the British assumed custody over Jerusalem.

In the course of these six weeks Kollek established his heroic reputation. Documentary films depict the mayor standing on top of the Ottoman walls, pointing to the Old City emerging from the mounting rubble and clouds of dust. Bulldozers were photographed from dramatic angles, ascribing the aura of sublime labor to Kollek's efforts. Accordingly, Elon asserted that "even if Kollek will not be credited with any other achievement, he will be remembered in the historical chronicles of Jerusalem as the man who did the right thing in the right moment and prepared a promising ground for reconstructing a more beautiful Jerusalem."[17] From a contemporary architectural perspective, Kollek's actions are viewed as less heroic and more manipulative: he harnessed wartime violence to reshape his city.

In theory, Kollek only removed the no-man's-land that had divided East and West Jerusalem since the end of the British Mandate in 1948. His ambition seemed clear: to facilitate what he considered "a great day, not only in our history, but in the history of mankind"—the day in which people from East and West Jerusalem could mingle for the first time in nineteen years. On the ground, the reality was more complicated. Kollek knowingly took great risks. "In addition to exploding every wall and every fence that divided Jerusalem," he reports in his memoirs, "we decided to evacuate and clear areas that twisted the image of Jerusalem for very long years."[18] Kollek thus accelerated, amid the postwar jubilation, plans for urban revitalization and

renewal that he had started with the creation, a year earlier, of the East Jerusalem Development Company.

If David Kroyanker, the urban chronicler of Jerusalem, is right in claiming that the national park around the city walls was the most important design decision in Jerusalem since the founding of the Israeli state,[19] then we can credit Kollek and his engineers with the *parti*—the stroke of genius captured in the architect's first conceptual sketch—of this monumental design.[20] According to an editorial in the architectural magazine *Volume,* "much destruction also has an agenda. It has a precision that reminds us of architecture. It has a formal dimension that reminds us of design."[21] The precision of Kollek's explosive charges, the efficiency of his planned bulldozing, and the mandate the city engineer received to expand demolitions as needed exemplify destruction that functions as urban design (Figure 4.1).[22]

For Andrew Herscher, such violence, "like other cultural forms . . . is a kind of inscription, an investment of material with identity and meaning that is irreducible to the intention of the author, the determination of a context, or the explanation of an interpreter."[23] Indeed, beyond the euphoria and the explosives, the contractors who volunteered their services and the mayor who took risks, the destruction of the six sites created a new spatial reality in Jerusalem, one from which we can "register the emergence of power, agency, and identity."[24] A victorious military parade marched through the bulldozed sites the next year (Figure 4.2) and was featured in the inaugural broadcast of the newly established Israeli television, providing just one of many discursive examples of destruction as a constitutive force.

Kollek's demolitions put numerous agencies into a tight competition. His speed granted him a clear advantage; although he could not operate on his

Figure 4.1. Arye Dvir, the Hinnom Valley at the foot of the City Walls, the clearance of the former Green Line that divided Jerusalem, view from West Jerusalem, 1969. Source: *Jerusalem National Park: Preliminary Proposal by the National Park Authority* (Jerusalem: Israel's National Park Authority, 1969), 36.

Figure 4.2. Independence Day parade in Jerusalem, May 2, 1968. Photograph by Moshe Milner. Source: Government Press Office, National Photographs Collection, file D738-002.

own, his rapid and decisive postwar action won him the status of an indispensable partner. Two main coalitions competed for the new municipal land under his control: developmental modernists, clustered in the Ministry of Housing, and situated modernists, mostly in the Ministry of Interior Affairs. Planners in Jerusalem's municipality negotiated between the two, balancing the pros and cons of each group's plan. The fallback was the modernist 1968 developmental master plan that Kollek inherited from Ish Shalom. While Kollek was still faithful to this plan, the Ministry of Interior Affairs was already articulating the opposite position.

In fact, the Ministry of Interior Affairs essentially articulated the cultural agenda Kollek would quickly embrace as his own—the logic of a geographical division between city and state, and the method of urban and landscape design. In due course Kollek would even hire some of their players to his municipal planning machine. Yaakov Dash, the talented head of the ministry's Planning Division, had worked with Henry Kendall on the last British master plan for Jerusalem and was devoted to his ideas. Eliezer Brutzkus, Israel's chief planner, was the most environmentally concerned team member of Israel's 1951 modernist master plan. On June 21, 1967, Brutzkus and Dash declared their ambition to prepare the "Outline Scheme" for Jerusalem and spelled out their desired coalition for the most important task of shaping the Old City: the NPA, the Department of Antiquities, the Ministry of Religious Affairs, and the Jerusalem Municipality.[25] In 1966 this coalition mobilized around environmental and preservation campaigns in Jerusalem. Its members bonded by a common recognition of the past as a prime national and economic resource needing to be integrated into the bureaucratic apparatus of the modern state.

Despite their common interest, the public agencies within this coalition fiercely competed with each other. Dash and Brutzkus got a head start by submitting, in August 1967, the confidential report titled *The Jerusalem Conceptual Plan*. In a complementary document Brutzkus powerfully articulated its argument. The expanded boundaries of "unified Jerusalem," he stated, included twenty-six acres of municipal land. The historical part, that is, "the Old City, Kidron Valley, Shiloakh village [Sillwan], Mount of Olives, Ofel, Mount of Zion and adjunct areas," constituted only 6.6 percent of this new jurisdiction, which nevertheless included "religious, traditional, historical, architectural and landscape values unparalleled in the entire world." According to Brutzkus, this small and symbolically dense portion of land "is not particularly vital for the building and development of greater Jerusalem" because it cannot satisfy the developmental and demographic appetite of the Ministry of Housing. According to this simple strategy, the rich agencies should therefore defer responsibility over this area to situated agencies that would protect it from "hasty 'modernization.' "[26]

Apparently, the situated coalition was less concerned with "sacred sites" and "antiquities" that were protected by faith and science. Brutzkus proposed to focus instead on the architectural integrity of the Old City, including Sillwan, as "a single gigantic and impressive historical monument," and on the "traditional" character of the "unique" enwrapping landscape "that intermingles in the consciousness of the pilgrim and the tourist with the historical sacred concept of 'Jerusalem.'" Brutzkus thus articulated concepts that tied contemporary planning to the city's British heritage, which would in the coming years gain international legitimacy. The key was this aesthetic sense of the sacred. It was why the British Mandate had adamantly protected this

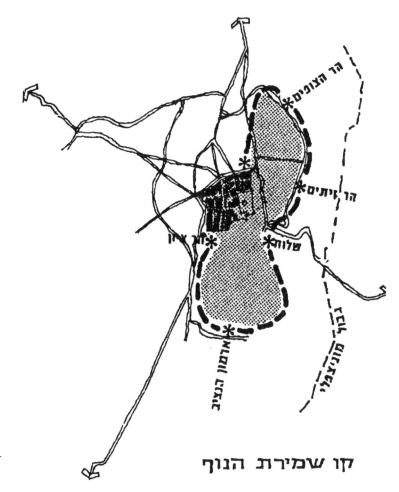

Figure 4.3. "Line of Land-
scape Preservation" and
"Open Space Next to the
Temple Mount." Source: *The
Jerusalem Conceptual Plan*
(Jerusalem: Ministry of Interior
Affairs, 1967).

קו שמירת הנוף

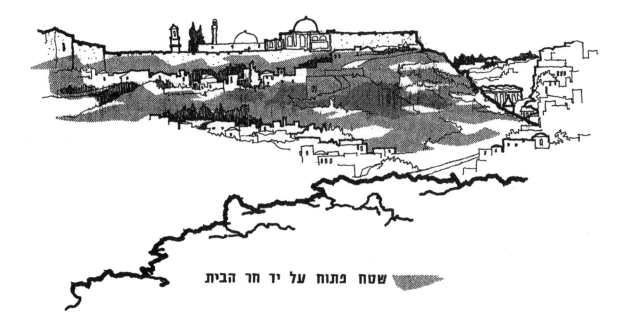

שטח פתוח על יד חר הבית

landscape, and also why the world should condemn Jordan for its bold interventions when the city was divided. It is therefore, Brutzkus concluded, the moral obligation and political debt of Israel to "the UN, the Vatican, and the international press" to protect and rehabilitate the built and open landscape of the historical zone.[27]

What Brutzkus articulated in words, Dash facilitated in plans.[28] The *Conceptual Plan*'s striking proposal for the area around the Old City introduced a new method to the officialdom of Israeli planning—the method of design. One cannot overemphasize the significance of this shift; instead of the familiar two-dimensional colored maps of land uses, infrastructures, and density, the *Conceptual Plan* presented a novel vision in simple diagrams, landscape perspectives, and sectional views of urban areas. These new visual techniques conceptualized the city as a three-dimensional entity and articulated its character in space and form (Figure 4.3). Only two months after the short war ended, the Ministry of Interior Affairs team had already delineated the visual basin of the Old City as a landscape protection zone. They clarified its necessity by drawing an evocative perspective of the valleys that enwrap the Temple Mount, in which the houses of Sillwan, the adjunct Palestinian village, are depicted as part and parcel of the rocky topography, bestowing on the landscape the awe of the sublime.

Their striking new guidelines for the main arteries linking East and West Jerusalem were similarly evocative. As seen in the hypothetical cross section they drew across the former no-man's-land (Figure 4.4), they suggest building the former no-man's-land with connected structures of diverse scale that would best suit this steep urban topography. The inspiration for this visual idea—the complex multilayered section—is clearly the megastructure discourse of the 1960s. Even more so, it appears as a compelling adaption of admired postwar British aesthetics, especially the Greater London Council's influential, unrealized plan for the city of Hook, modeled on the Oriental setting of Jerusalem.[29]

Figure 4.4. "East-West Section near the Former Buffer Zone." Source: *The Jerusalem Conceptual Plan* (Jerusalem: Ministry of Interior Affairs, 1967).

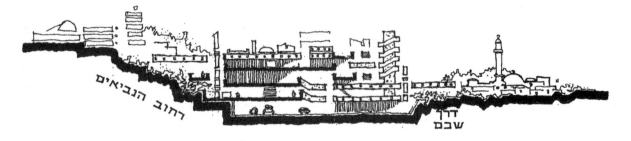

חתך מערב–מזרח
ע׳ שטח ההפקר הקודם

Armed with their concrete vision and design documents, Dash and Brutzkus were determined to gain control over the planning of the historical basin. History proves their great success. Eventually their visionary plan won the Ministry of Interior Affairs control over one of the most powerful tools in shaping Jerusalem: the "Outline Scheme for the Old City and Its Environs," known as *'ayin mem 9,* a binding legal document directing the shape of the holy basin. Dash supervised father and son Arieh and Eldar Sharon who, together with David Anatol Brutzkus (Eliezer's brother), authored the plan. The team worked full-time on the "Outline Scheme" from late 1968 until its submission in 1970. It would take another six years before the scheme was approved by the national government.[30]

A National Park for a World City

Dash and Brutzkus's race to control the planning of East Jerusalem was hampered by the slow-motion pace of committee work set up by their ministry and by which they therefore had to abide. Kollek's bureaucratic apparatus, by contrast, was looser and ready "to turn the bureaucratic machine on its head."[31] The story of the national park around Jerusalem's City Walls is a perfect example. It demonstrates how attuned Kollek was to the opportunities of the moment, and the efficacy of his bureaucratic apparatus.

Shortly after the war ended Arye Dvir, the landscape architect of the NPA who had returned in 1963 after eight years of professional training in the United States, joined crowds of Israelis who flocked to Jerusalem. He was overwhelmed by the magnitude of the occupied territory, its monumentality and symbolic density.

> It hit me: this is a historical opportunity, a one-time moment in the one-thousand-year history of a city . . . to do something, [an opportunity] that within two months or in a short time will not return for a period of one thousand, two thousand years. I had this dialogue with myself, and, within a few days . . . a conceptual plan took shape . . . that said: "Let's take the visual basin around the walls and let's make it a national park."[32]

In July Dvir drew the park he envisioned around the City Walls. His captivating axonometric drawing depicted the visual basin of the Old City from a bird's-eye view, looking from the southwest, that is, from West Jerusalem toward the symbolic treasures of the east (Figure 4.5). Dvir, who believed in the power of the visual image, communicated a clear message: Israel now holds a treasure. Its treatment cannot be limited to a minor promenade by the wall, Dvir's image suggested, but requires instead a holistic approach. Such an approach should divulge the proposed green belt around the city walls as

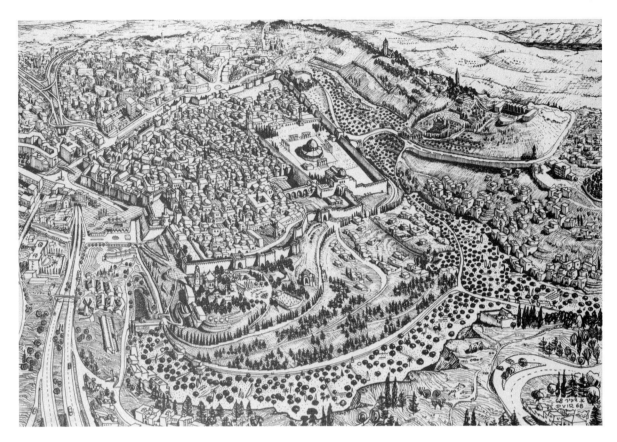

a unified and stratified historical theater, which for Dvir extends to the skyline that encloses the visual basin. Rings of undulated earthwork and planting would highlight the Temple Mount by naturalizing the deep valleys that enwrap it and clearing the views from the encircling mountains. The design of this landscape would be able to enfold modern infrastructure into the topography, thus minimizing modernist interventions that might diminish the area's holistic historicism.

Like the *Conceptual Plan* of the Ministry of Interior Affairs, Dvir's drawing successfully articulated a coherent idea of Jerusalem's spatiality. He revealed its scope to Arieh Sharon and Ian Yanai, head of the NPA, while driving to Jerusalem in August. When "we had about twenty minutes left," he recounts,

> I began describing my idea. Both Sharon and Yanai said: "Since we are on our way to meet with Teddy Kollek, let's present this idea to him." Kollek listened, finished smoking his cigar, and said: "Okay, let's give Prime Minister Eshkol a call." Eshkol was extremely enthusiastic about the idea. He passed it on to the Ministerial Committee for Jerusalem Affairs, which approved it, and within six weeks we had received official approval for this new national park, breaking all [bureaucratic] routines and procedures.[33]

Figure 4.5. Arye Dvir, axonometric drawing of the national park that creates a green belt around the City Walls, 1969. Source: *Jerusalem National Park: Preliminary Proposal by the National Park Authority* (Jerusalem: Israel's National Park Authority, 1969), 1.

The idea of a national park fell to Kollek's hands in a strategic moment. Kollek had already cleared vast areas of the proposed park. Then, all of a sudden, the prospect of clearing the administrative ground took promising shape.

When Kollek moved from the prime minister's office to the Jerusalem Municipality, he brought with him the institutional framework he had created. Most pertinent to Jerusalem was the NPA founded in 1963 under Yanai, who was a close ally from the Ben Gurion circle. Already mayor, in 1966 Kollek pleaded with Levi Eshkol, who had taken over as prime minister on Ben Gurion's retirement, that "Jerusalem has historical sites and special villages . . . with spectacular landscape that must be preserved." Following the contemporary struggles to preserve these sites, he asked Eshkol whether Jerusalem could be recognized as an exception, just "like in the United States, where the National Park Authority handles the parks and gardens of Washington the capital." Envisioning future controversies, Kollek even begged Eshkol to encourage "the head of the NPA to pay special attention to the beauty of the capital,"[34] in other words to allow Yanai, his ally, to prioritize Jerusalem.

Kollek's and Yanai's first attempt to utilize Eshkol's approval of the NPA's authority in East Jerusalem was decisive and quite painful: in July 1967 they lost the competition over the Western Wall Plaza to the Ministry of Religious Affairs. This was a bitter defeat for an agency whose mission was to nationalize historical monuments in order to evince the depth of Jewish roots in the region. The current project, however, was more complicated. Dvir's proposed six-hundred-acre park was intensely urban and included diverse land-uses and a significant number of residential units, an unprecedented setting for a national park. Under these conditions, how was it possible that in September, just six weeks after Dvir presented his idea to Teddy Kollek, the Ministerial Committee for Jerusalem Affairs could already approve his vision for the park?[35] To answer this question we must look beyond the cultural politics of Kollek to the logic of the British precedent and to contemporary methods of urban and landscape design.

The British Heritage

Kollek completed his demolitions in July, Dash and Brutzkus submitted their *Conceptual Plan* in August, and Dvir's initial proposal got the government's blessing in September. Like the authors of the 1968 master plan, they all agreed to revive the British idea of a green belt around Jerusalem's City Walls and suggested methods for its immediate implementation. Why was this idea so important and for whom?

Before the war's end Teddy Kollek had already ordered the bulldozers to clear a large area that would later be included in the national park around the City Walls. In his memoirs, Kollek attributes this vision to the "simplicity and straightforwardness" of the Jerusalem Plan that Henry Kendall drew for the British Mandate.[36] "I was told," he writes, "that the British agreed with the plan wholeheartedly but did not have the money or courage to carry it out."[37] By emphasizing the British ambitions, Kollek infuses the discourse surrounding his demolitions with the highest possible cultural aim: to beautify Jerusalem. He identifies in the British concept an undercurrent of timelessness, a historical constant that he believes must guide contemporary plans as well. By the same token, his writing confirms the compatibility that Andrew Herscher theorized between the seemingly opposite notions of culture and violence.

Indeed, a green belt around the City Walls was a long-standing British objective that appeared in each of the four master plans that the Mandate government prepared for the city of Jerusalem, starting in 1918. The demand for a park started with Jerusalem's first governor, Sir Ronald Storrs, for whom the custody over the Holy City meant caring for "(t)he city of Jerusalem, precious as an emblem of several faiths, a site of spiritual beauty lovingly preserved over the ages by many men's hands." According to Charles Robert Ashbee, an Arts and Crafts leader and Storrs's city planner, the distinct quality of the first British master plan for Jerusalem was "that it isolates the Old City, sets it, so to speak, in the center of a park, thus recognizing the appeal it makes to the world: the City of an *idea* that needs as such to be protected" (Figure 4.6).[38]

Ashbee's dictum echoes entrenched British traditions. One tradition was the eighteenth-century aesthetic theory of the picturesque, which connected the pictorial qualities of the landscape to the vivid feelings it arouses. The other was nineteenth-century Orientalism, which depicted the culture of remote colonies as distant not only in space but also in time, standing for the primitive, sensual origins of the developed, enlightened West. These entrenched traditions meshed in nineteenth-century Orientalist paintings, most notably in David Roberts's (1796–1864) panoramic depictions of the Holy Land (Figure 4.7). Roberts's was a two-dimensional depiction of Jerusalem as it appeared in the Western imagination. Its transformation into a concrete three-dimensional world epitomizes a practice associated with the picturesque tradition, where two-dimensional painting is mimicked within actual three-dimensional settings. A representation, that is, a copy of the natural site, precedes in Western consciousness the original that inspired it.[39]

In Jerusalem, the tools of modern planning mediated the genre of picturesque paintings by Roberts and others onto the real landscape. These gauzy idealized images became a blueprint informing the successive master plans that the British Mandate prepared for Jerusalem. The transition from an imagined Orient informed by nineteenth-century painting to a reconstructed

Figure 4.6. British plans for green belt around Jerusalem's City Walls. Geddes, 1919; Mandatory plan, 1930; Henry Kendall, 1944. Source: Arieh Sharon, *Planning Jerusalem: The Old City and Its Environs* (Jerusalem: Weidenfeld and Nicolson, 1973), 128–29.

The 1919 Scheme

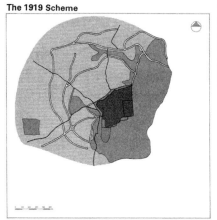

The 1930 Scheme

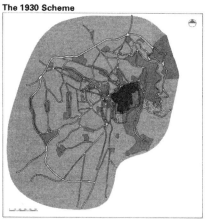

The 1944 Scheme

Figure 4.7. From Teddy Kollek to Louis Kahn, a greeting card with David Roberts's *Jerusalem from the Mount of Olives*, 1839. Source: The Architectural Archives, University of Pennsylvania, Louis I. Kahn Collection.

■ Areas under Special Control
■ Public and Private Open Spaces
■ Residential Areas
■ Commercial Areas
▨ Cemeteries
▤ Proposed Roads

RECEIVED
LOUIS I. KAHN ARCHITECT
JUN 25 1973
1501 WALNUT ST.
PHILADELPHIA, PA. 19102

DAVID ROBERTS — Jerusalem, 1839

Orient instructed by modern planning is crucial. It authenticated contemporary Jerusalem as a true and tangible incarnation of biblical heritage. The documents Ashbee produced for the Pro-Jerusalem Society in 1922 instruct designers how to peel modernity off the Old City and expose, with great precision and accuracy, the details of the original Oriental form—the embodiment of human labor before it was spoiled by modernity. Although created by men, the authenticity of Jerusalem was thus considered firm and truthful as nature itself and was therefore, in British eyes, a trust they had to keep for mankind.[40]

But how could the desired authenticity of Jerusalem's urban form stir an emotional reaction in visitors? Edmund Burke, writing in the eighteenth century, was the first to distinguish between the beautiful and the sublime based on a sensory rather than rational response to aesthetic phenomena. He associated the beautiful with small objects, smooth surfaces, and the clear colors of subject matter, such as a flower or a woman, which stimulate a feeling of positive pleasure. By contrast he identified the sublime with the mighty expanse of the ocean or the steep angularity of mountains, which provoke a sense of danger, power, and awe. The viewer who can look past the anxiety these sites provoke experiences a deep and moving delight.

The key to this impact is the immediacy of sensory perception. Burke writes:

> Whenever the wisdom of our Creator intended that we should be affected with any thing, he did not confide the execution of his design to the languid and precarious operation of our reason; but he endued it with powers and properties . . . which seizing upon the sense and the imagination, captivate the soul before the understanding is ready either to join with them or to oppose them.[41]

Theorists of the picturesque consequently grafted this insight about instinctual sensory perceptions onto the practice of art, harnessing our instincts to create evocative representations of nature. In Jerusalem, where such sensory perception was related not only to religious faith but to fierce political competition, the capacity to provoke irrational emotions was particularly powerful in fostering political consent.

Kollek, cognizant of the power of the picturesque, orchestrated how his guests first encountered the city. He typically avoided the most direct, yet modern, western entrance to Jerusalem, climbing instead from the east up to the Mount of Olives, where guests would face the sublime landscape of the Temple Mount, rising from the steep and barren slopes of the Kidron and Hinnom valleys. This was, of course, the favorite viewpoint of a long line of picturesque painters of Jerusalem.

One of Kollek's guests was the eminent architectural historian Nikolaus Pevsner, an influential participant in the Jerusalem Committee. Pevsner's seminal BBC lecture, "The Englishness of English Art," foreshadowed the return of the picturesque, which he considered the most English of all artistic sensibilities, in postwar British architectural discourse. For Pevsner the picturesque entailed intensive observation of the environment, an empirical study of the landscape that extracts its particular climate, character, and atmosphere. Pevsner applauds artists who criticize the "formal mockery of princely gardens" in France, where the landscape is suppressed by its rulers. By contrast, he argues, the informal, asymmetrical, and varied landscaping of the British picturesque, which leads the viewer into an endless set of surprises, is faithful to nature and coheres its truth. Ultimately, he argues, the picturesque is the fullest expression of British liberty and must therefore be linked to "certain problems of planning which press hard on us today."[42]

As the editor of the authoritative *Architectural Review,* Pevsner took action. He incorporated picturesque sensibilities into his method of visual planning and encouraged the development of the Townscape Movement. His protégé Gordon Cullen published in 1961 *The Concise Townscape,* whose many subsequent editions underscore its influence in configuring built forms and interstitial spaces into irregular and sequential scenery. Even those criticizing in the 1950s the related "New Empiricism" of the London City Council planners that Israelis admired resorted to similar sensibilities. When Reyner Banham challenged architects with the impact of mass culture and environmental technology, he advocated the avant-garde group Archigram and the technological picturesque it beautifully rendered. His colleagues Alison and Peter Smithson's enthusiasm with regionalism and the authentic expression of dwelling in the Mediterranean was projected onto the Palestinian vernacular that Charles Robert Ashbee already admired in the 1920s.

These British traditions—the picturesque and Orientalism in particular—converged again after the 1967 war within the praxis of unifying Jerusalem. They spread in official, professional, and popular circles, among both people and institutions seeking urban beauty. This was, however, a bilateral process: the desire for the picturesque opened a door to the latest ideas in landscape architecture and urban design, allowing a group of young Anglo architects and their new professional methods to quickly impact the Jerusalem landscape.

An Anglo Circle Looks at the Environment

A rising circle of young Anglo architects, who worked in Dash's department on the confidential *Conceptual Plan,* was in charge of reviving British sensibilities in urban design. Most of them were educated in or migrated from English-speaking countries, where they were trained in major universities.

Some were Zionists; some came to take advantage of a transitional moment in architecture and urban planning. Israelis among the group came back home to deliver a new message. American architect Arthur Kutcher, for example, writes that he left the United States because architects there "had lost their stylistic and ideological compass and were foundering." In his account "the old Bauhaus doctrines of corporate, bureaucratic modernism, which had ruled both architectural education and professional practice with an iron fist, were breaking down." But the alternative to "doctrinaire rigidity," he thought, was similarly confusing—"a kind of desperate, irrational, egoistic expressionism." He wished to combat such architectural whims in Jerusalem by installing a think tank of urban planning.[43]

After graduating from Yale University and the University of California at Berkeley, Kutcher joined landscape architect Lawrence Halprin. In his office he met Shlomo Aronson, who continued to pursue his masters at Harvard University and later moved to England to work as a landscape architect in the famed Greater London Council. In 1968 Aronson tempted Kutcher to join the team David Best had assembled to plan Jerusalem's Central Business District (CBD). Best, the eventual planner of East Talpiot, had just returned from a year of advanced studies at MIT. The head of Best's team was Michael Turner, who hitherto worked with Dash on the *Conceptual Plan*. Turner studied architecture at the Bartlett in London between 1958 and 1963, during the exciting transition from a Beaux Arts tradition to the radical modernism of Reyner Banham. Together with others,[44] they introduced strands of postwar Anglo modernism to the Israeli architectural scene, which was firmly grounded in a German modernist heritage, particularly in the Bauhaus ideology.

Unlike members of the sabra generation, who lead Israel's architectural profession to this day, this group of Anglo architects, working primarily in and for public agencies, has passed under the radar of architectural history. There were significant differences between the two groups. The sabra architects studied almost exclusively at the Technion with German-educated teachers. Their generational rebellion was inspired primarily by the late work of Le Corbusier, Team 10, and Louis Kahn, and by the styles of regionalism and Brutalism. Their hub was the Ministry of Housing, and their expertise lay in residential neighborhoods. Although they were passionate about the city, they had little experience in or understanding of urbanism that required an intervention in the existing urban fabric rather than building cities from scratch. By contrast, the slightly younger Anglo circle was steeped in urban practices and experienced in struggles that focused attention on the city as is, or as found, rather than the city as a newly created, pristine set of drawings. Their modernism was therefore participatory and responsive to change. In their eyes the city was a dynamic entity of interrelated systems, and its form was not determined by individual buildings, but rather by their location in, and integration into, the urban landscape.

These Anglo architects were grouped together in 10 Shamai Street, where most of them worked in close proximity to the offices of Amikam Yoffe, Jerusalem's city engineer. It was in Kollek's best interest to keep the external teams working on the different plans for Jerusalem under the watchful eye of his planning bureaucracy. Thanks to their strategic housing at 10 Shamai Street, Yoffe was able to supervise, together with Dash, the team working on the "Outline Scheme for the Old City and Its Environs," for which Dash's ministry held statutory responsibility. To prevent recurring tensions between the overall authority of this team and the design of the national park by the NPA, Yanai offered to move Dvir as well to Shamai Street, further establishing these offices as a planning hub for young designers.[45]

These shared offices also blurred the boundaries between the different planning disciplines. Architects felt at ease crossing between architecture, landscape design, and urban design and did not shy away from the administrative elements of planning policy. Eventually, the interaction between these teams was catalyzed by the criticism of the Jerusalem Committee, resulting in the foundation of the Urban Planning Unit in 1971.

By the 1960s, landscape architecture was already an established discipline in Israel. It was founded by a generation of immigrants, which was largely committed to the high modernist ideals that were developed primarily in German-speaking societies. Spacious green lawns were habitually installed in the early Zionist settlements, despite the arid local climate, embodying the modernist dream of dressing the country with green and letting its deserts bloom. Balanced between national goals and modernist ideals, these landscape architects produced landscapes that were spacious rather than contained—boundless new horizons for the New Jew.[46]

During the 1960s a younger generation of landscape architects started rebelling against the modernist ideal of the founders' generation. Like the sabra architects, this generation of landscape architects pioneered a method that attended closely to conditions of the site, negotiated with its topography, vegetation, materials, and culture, and tried to capture both the spirit and the character of the particular place. Most conspicuous among them were Israeli trainees of the California-based landscape architect Lawrence Halprin. Halprin belonged to an American generation that revolutionized the discipline of landscape architecture after World War II. His interdisciplinary practice set an important precedent. Kutcher, who worked there between 1963 to 1965, reports that fellow employees who were too rigidly trained as architects "needed to be house trained or house broken" in this practice.[47]

For Halprin, the modernist revolution in landscape architecture meant "a whole appreciation of environmental design as a holistic approach to the matter of making space for people to live."[48] He choreographed built and open landscapes and studied the way people move through them in order to address the human experiences of individuals and social groups for whom he facilitated rooted and sensual public spaces. Particularly innovative were his interventions in dense urban fabric that evinced not only his training among and collaboration with architects, but his contribution to the new discipline of urban design.

Halprin's contribution to and impact on the architectural debate in Israel may be less surprising in light of his training with non–landscape architects in the Graduate School of Design at Harvard while under the tenure of the legendary founder of the Bauhaus, Walter Gropius, and his colleagues.[49] Several of Halprin's classmates at Harvard—Philip Johnson, I. M. Pei, and Paul Rudolph—had significant projects in Israel. For Halprin, however, Israel was more than an opportunity for commission. His mother, Rose Halprin, was the president of Hadassah, a major philanthropy organization for Zionist women. Following her creed, in 1933 he spent three years working on a kibbutz. His return visit in 1955 was well prepared: his mother reassured him that "Ben Gurion; Golda Myerson, Teddy Kollek (director general of the Prime Minister's office)," and "Mr. Eshkol Minister of Finance" were all waiting to meet him.[50] Years later his role as a quasi insider would ease his way into commissions for Jerusalem. As a close advisor to Kollek, he would help advance the projects of architects he mentored in California, most notably, Arye Dvir, Shlomo Aronson, Arthur Kutcher, and Gideon Sarig, all of whom would dramatically alter the local practice.

Dvir was the first of Halprin's lineage. He was trained as a landscape architect in the fortuitous period between 1955 and 1963, just when his revolutionary mentors, first Halprin and later Ian McHarg, broke out with their innovative design work. Although their influences were thoroughly infused into his work, one must analyze the impact of each designer on Dvir's most important work—the national park surrounding Jerusalem's City Walls—in order to fully appreciate the multiple methodological innovations within this project.

Orientalism: Animating the "As Found"

As noted, Dvir's proposal for the national park was already approved in principle in September 1967. The copyright for this idea belongs to Eliezer Brutzkus, who, a year earlier, assembled the situated coalition in order to save Lifta, the Palestinian village admired by architects. The Israel Land Authority planned to bulldoze the remains of the deserted village in order to develop Jerusalem's western entrance. To stop them, Brutzkus proposed the simple yet effective strategy that Kollek would adopt a year later: declaring the village a national park and developing it in collaboration with the NPA and the Jerusalem Municipality.

Brutzkus repeatedly argued for the formative role of such Orientalist landscapes to the consolidation of an Israeli built heritage: the occupier needed the material culture of the occupied in order to define its own patrimony. Yet there is a major difference between the Orientalism that was practiced within developmental agencies aiming to devise a local character for Israeli housing estates, and the Orientalism that aimed to recover Jerusalem's past by accentuating the tangibility of its authentic remains. The latter meant distancing oneself from Jerusalem's modern actuality and isolating its primal form. Thus, whereas sabra architects sought in the Arab village the primitive form of human habitation, the Mediterranean way of life, and the custody over Jewish origins in the land, the Orientalism of Halprin and Dvir was particular to Jerusalem, to its unique presence and its pictorial image. As such, it was much closer to the British rather than the Israeli Orientalist praxis.

When Dvir envisioned the experience of his proposed park, he returned to Brutzkus's ideas: "The visitor, the pilgrim and the tourist wish not only to see the Old City, but to also receive some of this special historical feeling, to try and describe in their imagination 'now, here lived David and Solomon thousands of years ago, here they graze their flocks.'"[51] Scholars of tourism have demonstrated how sites are designed to accommodate the expected image that visitors bring with them.[52] Here tourism was only one ingredient in a much more complex equation of religious and national sentiments. The British were the first to restrict building around the City Walls in order to accommodate what Patrick Geddes called "the most sacred park in the world."[53] If the park was to evoke the emotional terrain associated with the original birthplace of the three monotheistic religions, it must be kept in its original, authentic form. Its universal meaning is thus contingent on its perceived authenticity, which should come across in an effortless encounter with bare forms untouched since biblical times. The question was, How can one physically fulfill this expectation?

No professional was more influential in addressing imagined Jerusalem than Lawrence Halprin. In a letter he wrote to Kollek in 1971, following the deliberation of the Jerusalem Subcommittee for Town Planning, he warned,

> I am concerned about the "gardeny" approach to the Parks in the valley & around the city walls. . . . Jerusalem's "quality" depends heavily on its landscape—which is silvery gray not green—which is strong & rocky not grassy & soft. I resent all

the topsoil & grass & fancy paths & cute shapes that seem to be cropping up in the Jerusalem Landscape.[54]

Halprin does not hesitate to educate Kollek: if you want to deliver an as-found quality, the landscape of the visual basin around the Old City should appear untouched by modern embellishment, revealing the strength of the silvery rock on which the eternal city was built (see Figure 4.13, below).

Halprin's concerns had already been considered by his devoted student, whose plan for the national park aimed to extract the hidden, innermost qualities from this land. In 1969 Dvir presented his ideas in an impressive design document—a large-format, meticulously illustrated, and visually evocative publication. This unprecedented landscape document contained systematic colored maps, drawings, photographs, and sketches with design guidelines. This was not a comprehensive plan, and in fact, smaller portions of the park would later be commissioned to other landscape architects. Instead, the goal of this document was to render the different fractions of the landscape into an inseparable whole, one that deserved legal protection in the form of a binding law.

Consider, for example, Dvir's instructions for planting vegetation. His premise was clear: the City Walls had to be the focal point of the visual basin in order to render its biblical character. He therefore proposed planting belts of lower shrubs near the wall; taller, strictly Mediterranean trees on the slopes; and groves in the valleys. As a general rule he outlawed "standard, rigid and uniform planting," asking instead to accommodate the folds of the topography. "Forest should be loose, unregimented with plenty of variety," he wrote in his plan for the park; in other words, it should possess an as-found quality.[55]

Dvir's sketches are systematic—a series of spatial episodes that together composed the desired idea of Jerusalem as a lived experience (Figure 4.8). He requests in his plan that the city remove all evidence of modern infrastructure, including high-rise buildings, electricity lines, and of course, arterial roads. The landscape he envisions is shaped through large gestures, sculpting the slopes with wide terraces. Into the rises of these terraces, he suggests embedding the small functional structures that he would no longer allow to stand freely on the surface. A spatial portion of the plan is devoted to the City Walls, avoiding any landscape design in their immediate vicinity, as if to give the impression that the walls emerge out of the rock. It is an act of modernist minimalism that eliminates details in favor of a single major visual movement.

Dvir is particularly outspoken about the qualities of the Palestinian residences, what he terms "picturesque ensembles," and which he seeks to

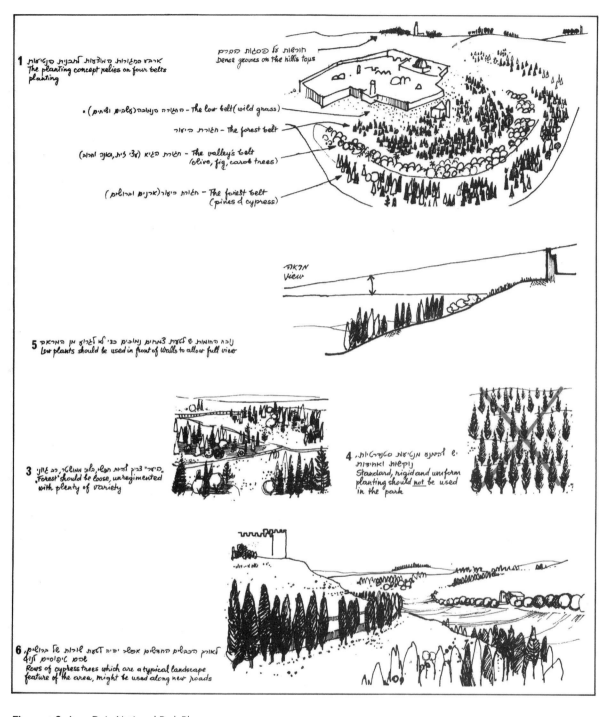

Figure 4.8. Arye Dvir, National Park Plan, 1969. Design instructions: (left) planting and (right) construction, terraces, and skyline. Source: *Jerusalem National Park: Preliminary Proposal by the National Park Authority* (Jerusalem: Israel's National Park Authority, 1969), 28–29.

10

10

9 בניים גדולים על הרכסים יקלקלו את קו-הרקיע
Large buildings on ridges would spoil the skyline

9 קו-הרקיע הקיים מאופיין ע"י מבנים קטני-ממדים המודגשים ע"י מגדלים
Existing skyline is characterized by small scale structures, accented by towers

7 בניים מט-לרודים ביתין הגבול המערבי של הפארק יש להסיר
Existing run down buildings which form the western boundary of the park should be removed.

11 הצעה לבניים חדשים לשיפור חזית הגבול המערבי. בחזית: כביש מוגבה
Suggested new buildings to improve facade on western boundary. In foreground: elevated highway

preserve because "the visitor, the pilgrim and the tourist wish to see not only the Old City but also to get something of the special historical feel [of the setting], to try to conjure up in his imagination: 'right here, King David and King Solomon dwelt thousands of years ago, here the herds grazed, etc.'"[56] His images of Sillwan strikingly resemble those of Yoram Segal's Arab village. The grainy photographs, like those of ancient trees and walls, have an artistic feel and a documentary quality. When reproducing such images in line drawings, Dvir omits architectural features, such as the triptych window common in nineteenth-century Arab vernacular housing, in favor of small carved windows. Unlike other sketches in the proposal, the images of Sillwan are empty of people and their belongings—only simple volumes asymmetrically cluttered under the blazing sun. These images instruct the viewer how to look, how to undo modernity and poverty, and instead let the beautiful simplicity of the ancient architecture shine through (Figure 4.9).

Dvir's dream was to plan Sillwan like Yemin Moshe, a Jewish neighborhood across the Hinnom Valley, where low-income families were removed, buildings were carefully restored, and artists—carefully vetted by an admission committee—settled in. "In theory," Dvir reminiscences, "it was a nice thought." In reality, Meron Benvenisti, the deputy mayor for East Jerusalem, refused to include Sillwan in the national park and, as a result, restrict the life of its residents to the status of biblical specimens. The NPA, aware of what they considered a growing bureaucratic obstacle, decided to compromise as long as they could achieve their design goals for the park. Once their plan was principally approved by the Israeli government, Dvir produced many policy papers that succeeded in securing the interests of the rather weak NPA against other stakeholders. The eventual declaration of the Walls of Jerusalem National Park on March 31, 1974, was a mere rubber stamp to an already established fact on the ground. In order to understand how such a powerful statement succeeded within the complex spatial politics of Jerusalem we now turn to examine the impact of McHarg's methodology on Dvir's plan.

Ecological Planning and the Picturesque

Halprin's presence in Jerusalem was crucial, as was the impact of his many trainees. According to Dvir, however, the contribution of his second mentor, Ian McHarg, was equally important yet seriously overlooked.[57] This influence is most evident in the compatibility between the scientific method of McHarg's ecological planning and the picturesque sensibilities of the British precedent found in Dvir's proposal. Elizabeth Meyer convincingly argues that modern landscape architecture understands "design as site interpretation, and site as program, not surface for program."[58] In other words, it intervenes in the way we grasp the landscape and make sense of what we see. She

הצד הדרומי:
כפר־השילוח

THE SOUTH SIDE :
The Village of Silwan (Siloam)

למטה : על אפיו של כפר־השילוח, הצומח כביכול מתוך הסלע,
יש לשמור בשל יופיו העוזרי ; הוא גם נושא עמו את אווירת
הנוף של ימי קדם.

below : The character of Silwan village which seems
to grow out of the rock should be preserved for its
picturesque beauty; it also suggests the landscape
of ancient times.

מימין : כמה קבוצות של בניינים
בשטח עיר דוד הן מטרד אשר יש לסלקן.

right : Some of the buildings on the site of the City
of David are an eyesore and should be removed.

Figure 4.9. Arye Dvir, National Park Plan, 1969. Photograph of Sillwan Village and instructions to preserve the picturesque ensembles. Source: *Jerusalem National Park: Preliminary Proposal by the National Park Authority* (Jerusalem: Israel's National Park Authority, 1969), 24, 33.

therefore poignantly asks: "How did landscape architecture reveal the site? Which site was revealed: the one at hand, or the ideal one?"[59] We address this challenge by analyzing the ways in which Dvir harnessed McHarg's scientific method to substantiate picturesque sensibilities, as a result producing a landscape that evokes a particular state of mind.

McHarg pioneered the subdiscipline of ecological planning in Philadelphia. His seminal book, *Design with Nature* (1969), grew out of his legendary University of Pennsylvania course Man and Environment, which Dvir attended in 1952. Dvir recalls the leading scholars McHarg invited to discuss

"Zen and Buddhism, physics and the quantum theory . . . and Judaism and Christianity . . . and Western attitudes and Eastern attitudes,"[60] aiming to integrate philosophy and science in order to explore the role of values in planning. McHarg's conviction that people would enjoy the healing power of nature only through a humble recognition of environmental values, according to Dvir, stems at least in part from his mentor's military service during World War II.

McHarg was a lieutenant in the Scottish Second Independent Parachute Brigade Group. Dvir believes that the invitation McHarg extended to him to come study in Philadelphia might have been related to this war experience. When McHarg was assigned to duty in Mandate Palestine toward the end of the war, he refused to follow the British policy of closed borders because he "was not going to throw the bloody Jews to the sea."[61] At that time Dvir's father was hiding members of the Jewish armed struggle in their modernist apartment in Tel Aviv; these fighters called McHarg's parachuters "anemones" and tried to assassinate them because they prevented Holocaust refugees from reaching the shores of Palestine.

This coincidence is the first detail Dvir reveals about a mentor he admired.[62] It may be less incidental than it seems. We tend to overlook the formative impact of these military experiences on the design professions. But Halprin, McHarg, and many of their generation, who personally experienced the violent results of utopian regimes, lethal technological innovations, and sweeping ideologies of the World War II era, lost the appetite to change the world and to bend nature to human whim. For them, the only stable reference that survived the war was the individual. Man as is. The family of man therefore became the focus of postwar architectural culture. Instead of the developmental desire to overcome nature, nature was now valued as refuge.

Harnessing these values, McHarg carefully read the environment, analyzed his collected data, and extracted from it guidelines for site planning and design strategies. He started with a systematic breakdown of given landscapes to their constituent physical and social values, including factors such as history, hydrology, vegetation, wildlife, scenery, recreation, and institutional and land values. Then he registered each layer of data on a single transparency. Once the transparencies were layered one on top of the other, he could analyze the multifaceted data and devise several alternatives for sustainable planning.[63]

McHarg's method of design alternatives thus challenged developmental practices; he is considered the forerunner of a sustainable sensibility, protecting the equilibrium between natural and human environments. Unlike his nineteenth-century predecessors, however, he did not rely on artistic intuition but instead trusted the validity of empirical facts. He claimed "anyone who employs the data and the method would reach the same conclusions" and believed that his design principles were imperative because "any engineer, architect, landscape architect, developer and the client himself were bound by the data and the method."[64] Yet, despite McHarg's strict commitment to science and ecological determinism, Peter Walker and Melanie Louise Simo remind us that he was initially trained as an artist, preferred the picturesque British garden, and was recognized as the successor of Frederick Law Olmsted's tradition.

This connection between picturesque sensibilities and the empirical foundation of ecological planning was the strength of Dvir's proposal. The proposal's efficacy lies in its capacity to translate the character and spirit of Jerusalem into concrete physical guidelines. Dvir's plan was three dimensional, easy to grasp, visually suggestive, and scientifically informed. Kollek identified a potential engine of urban politics within it.

The axonometric view of the park that we reviewed earlier was an effective start (Figure 4.5). This bird's-eye-view drawing evokes the sensuous character of Jerusalem's built topography. But unlike the famed picturesque paintings of Jerusalem, Dvir based his drawing from a precise map, simulating future computational methods. The resulting axonometry functions as both a communicative and descriptive tool. On the one hand the high angle captured the vastness of the valleys that surround the Temple Mount, allowing a holistic image that was impossible to see from the ground. On the other hand it already suggests specific solutions for integrating modern infrastructure into the undulating contours of this scenic landscape. The relatively precise and moderately emotive drawing was not only a working plan but also a blueprint for design and legal praxis. Clearly, much of his effort was spent not only on envisioning the park but, more poignantly, on verifying its applicability and legitimizing its costs—namely, the confiscation of a vast, highly symbolic territory from the eager claims of developmental modernists and real estate developers.

When Dvir applied the systematic, scientifically oriented method of McHarg to Jerusalem, he had to adjust his mentor's focus. "In Jerusalem the problem was not primarily ecological, but was a much more complicated problem of historical, visual, touristic, archeological, and ethical dimensions, all those things together."[65] Dvir analyzed these values and created for them different informative maps (see Plate 5). The full version of his submitted 1969 preliminary report for the national park starts with historical maps of "the Walls of Jerusalem from the Jebusites to today" and continues by positioning the lines of "the ancient water system" in the contemporary landscape. Other maps register a vast variety of environmental information such as land uses, scenery, green areas, and architectural qualities.

This systematic method of layered information allowed Dvir to unpack, analyze, and recompose the entire visual basin of the Old City as one comprehensive system, and to adjust its design according to the values he attributed to its diverse components. Once these values were documented on a map, he could construe appropriate design proposals about everything from circulation to vegetation, leveling to infrastructures. Dvir applied McHarg's famous method of alternatives on only one area: the multilane highways he objected to so vehemently. The ability to decide between alternatives coopted his audience against the traffic arteries that the master plan team prescribed next to the City Walls.

The significance of his method lay in its scientific determinism. Although he argued for a preservationist approach, he avoided the emotional rhetoric about Jerusalem as a sacred landscape. His arguments were supported instead by empirical, scientifically proven data. As a result, decision makers no longer perceived the tension between development and sustainability as an opposition between, on the one hand, efficiency and economics and, on the other, beauty and emotions. Officials were asked instead to judge between two alternative sets of values that were equally validated by modern research methods.

Dvir demonstrated the conclusions of his layered data in a series of sections that he cut across the topography and used as an effective design tool. These sections not only animated the topography, but more importantly, they allowed Dvir to pierce through the different analytical layers of the survey maps and design the park according to the stratified information of their combined data. Consider, for example, how the section through the steepest part of the Kidron Valley, just below the Temple Mount, synthesizes the information Dvir previously mapped (Figure 4.10). The steep V section is mostly bare, curved by terraces leading to archeological findings—portions of the old city walls and water conduits—and punctuated by sparse groups of trees. Sewage would run beneath landfill covered by a planting of olive groves.

Figure 4.10. Arye Dvir, National Park Plan, 1969. Section: across the Kidron Valley. Source: *Jerusalem National Park: Preliminary Proposal by the National Park Authority* (Jerusalem: Israel's National Park Authority, 1969), 58.

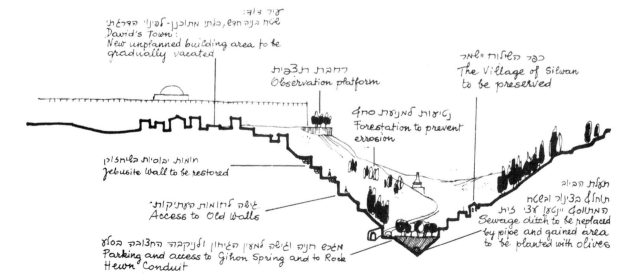

The section prescribes a different treatment for each slope. On the eastern slope the houses of Sillwan have been deemed worthy of preservation; on the western slope, an open access to archeological digs is reserved. Yet above the slope, in the closest area to Temple Mount, the less attractive contemporary residences of "David's Town" are destined to gradual removal in favor of new, yet unplanned construction (see Plate 6).

His systematic method also helped resolve the western side of the park, which had troubled Kollek, Yanai, and Dvir alike, because it included the seam between East and West Jerusalem that ran along the western edge of the Old City. This stretch was where most of Kollek's demolitions took place, along with the attendant evacuation of low-income Jewish families, mostly of Arab origin. This area is also where urban renewal gave way to pictorial serenity and, by the same token, to the financial market. In Dvir's sectional drawing, the western and more modernized part of the city is reunited with its ancient core by authenticating the seam between East and West Jerusalem, making it part and parcel of the more authentic landscape in the East, with which it was now integrated as part of one organic system. These two sections detailed by Dvir demonstrate his greatest success: they instruct planners to turn what was planned as part of a modern city into an authentic, as-found landscape. Consider, for example, the Wolfson Park that landscape architects Lipa Yahalom and Dan Zur designed in the Hinnom Valley following Dvir's guidelines (Figure 4.11). According to Ariel Hirschfeld, an influential literary critic, their design is "so attentive to the place and its spirit, that it seems as

Figure 4.11. Yahalom-Zur Landscape Architects, General Plan for Wolfson Park in the Hinnom Valley, which forms a part of the National Park, 1971. Source: *Arcadia: The Gardens of Lipa Yahalom and Dan Zur* [in Hebrew], ed. Nurit Lissovsky and Diana Dolev (Tel Aviv: Babel [Architecture], 2012). Copyright Yahalom-Zur and Babel.

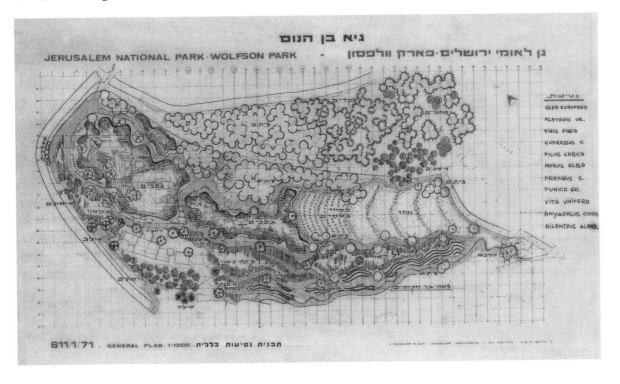

Figure 4.12. Yahalom-Zur Landscape Architects, Wolfson Park in the Hinnom Valley, 1970s. Paths, walkways, and retaining walls. Photograph by Dan Zur. Source: *Arcadia: The Gardens of Lipa Yahalom and Dan Zur* [in Hebrew], ed. Nurit Lissovsky and Diana Dolev (Tel Aviv: Babel [Architecture], 2012). Copyright Yahalom-Zur and Babel.

Figure 4.13. Arye Dvir, National Park Plan, 1969. "The North Side–Notre Dame." Source: *Jerusalem National Park: Preliminary Proposal by the National Park Authority* (Jerusalem: Israel's National Park Authority, 1969), 38.

if it is its everlasting form, as if the place is not at all a park, but rather, the green valley that has resided since antiquity next to Mt. Zion, with its roaring cliffs, trees and ancient pathways" (Figure 4.12).[66]

The use of photography similarly helped to fuse the parts of the city and conveyed precise emotions. Dvir's report includes thirteen high-quality, black-and-white, artistically grained, and playfully shaded images, which serve several purposes. Close-ups of stones and trees encourage the viewer to have a sensory engagement with the landscape. Various sites are pictured without any modern obstacles and are orchestrated to give the impression of an uninterrupted, flowing space. In the foreground of one such image (Figure 4.13), looking toward Notre Dame, we see elegant curved stone paths, fences, and terraces; what we don't realize is that this artful composition blurs the huge urban scar of the triangle between East and West Jerusalem that de-

spite numerous city efforts, had never healed. A set of four panoramic images are similarly systematic in their representation, capturing a 180-degree
view of the proposed locations of the park adjacent to different parts of the
city walls. The frontal, wide-angle composition of each image transpires as
documentary, therefore serving as a blueprint for design. Together with the
sections, these facades helped to project a precise image onto the landscape,
whose construction was a meticulous negotiation between the Jerusalem on
the ground and the pictorial Jerusalem of imagination.

The plan was eventually presented in June 1969 at the first plenary meeting of the Jerusalem Committee, where it was applauded. On July 6 the *New
York Times* featured on its front page the park's approval by a "World Panel"
(Figure 4.14). The newspaper reported: "After almost a week of study, the 42
advisers from 19 countries declared a projected Jerusalem park 'satisfactory'
and said that it would serve to reinforce unity of the city." This unity, however, had a price:

> Under the plan, vast alterations would be made in the landscaping around the
> 16th-century walls and in pedestrian and traffic patterns. Many Arab practices
> would be changed. The significance of the committee's endorsement lies in its
> timing and in the neutralizing effect it may have on some critics of Israeli plans
> for the former Jordanian sector of the city.[67]

The piece was correct: Kollek, Yanai, and Dvir succeeded in neutralizing any
opposition to major shifts in the landscape of Jerusalem through a systematic, modernist interpretation of the British ideals of Orientalism and the
picturesque.

Design by Planning

After the Jerusalem Committee's warm embrace of the national park in June
1969, Kollek looked forward to their next meeting. In December 1970 an influential segment of his committee of international luminaries formed the
Subcommittee for Town Planning. During a stormy meeting, the committee harshly criticized the Israeli *1968 Jerusalem Masterplan*. Kollek took the
opinions of these international luminaries very seriously. In the aftermath
of the committee's judgments, the Ministry of Interior Affairs, which had
initially been excluded from the master plan team, joined the prestigious
coalition. Their earlier political defeat turned victorious. Dr. Yoseph Burg,
then minister of interior affairs, was happy to announce in the Knesset that,
"The Ministry of Interior Affairs will not hesitate to exercise all its *moral* and
legal prerogatives in order to secure a new and different *ideological foundation,*

World Panel on Jerusalem Supporting Plan for a Park

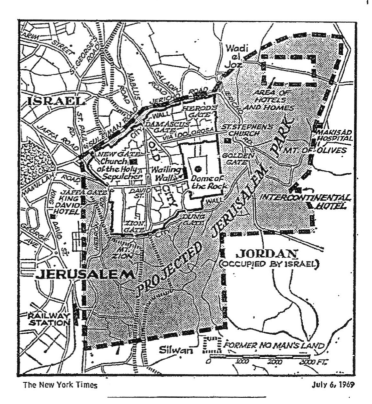

The New York Times   July 6, 1969

BY JAMES FERON
Special to The New York Times

JERUSALEM, July 5 — The Jerusalem Committee, an international panel including town planners, historians and art scholars, has endorsed a vast rehabilitation plan drawn up by Israeli authorities for the area outside the Old City walls.

After almost a week of study, the 42 advisers from 19 countries declared a projected Jerusalem park "satisfactory" and said that it would serve to reinforce the unity of the city.

The 600-acre park would surround the historic walls of the Old City—including a thin strip on the north—and introduce far-reaching changes in the western and southern approaches, almost all of it within the sector annexed by Israel after the 1967 war with the Arabs.

Under the plan, vast alterations would be made in the landscaping around the 16th-century walls and in pedestrian and traffic patterns. Many Arab practices would be changed.

The significance of the committee's endorsement lies in its timing and in the neutralizing effect it may have on some critics of Israeli plans for the former Jordanian sector of the city.

Mayor Teddy Kollek began organizing the committee last year and planned its first meeting months ago. The experts'

Continued on Page 12, Column 3

Figure 4.14. "World Panel on Jerusalem Supporting Plan for a Park," *New York Times*, July 6, 1969.

worthy of *the concept of Jerusalem* as a capital, with all its historic, religious and geographical implications."[68] After clarifying that his ministry was in defiance of the premises of the master plan, which he claimed that the ministry had been shown too late to change, "Dr. Burg stated with evident satisfaction that the specific regional plan for the Old City, in which the Ministry of Interior Affairs had participated, had drawn wide praise."[69] This was also a message to Kollek. Apparently, his partnership with the situated coalition garnered more approval with the international community than with his own people.

The quickest professional response came from the aforementioned Anglo group of young architects who worked on the projects the committee reviewed. "Stimulated and disturbed" by what they had heard, they created a manifesto and distributed it to Kollek, all the teams involved with the master plan, and the Jerusalem Committee members. The manifesto stated: "Planning is an integral part of the functioning of the City and is as much concerned with PROCESS as with PLAN." This distinction was important because what Jerusalem needed, they argued, "is a new planning process, not a new plan." They asked Kollek and state authorities to look at other cities in order to devise a means of communication between the disciplines, a process that "must take place at all levels from policy to implementation and must allow for feedback and review." They demanded transparency, public participation, and "means for the information and education of the public," using media and the public school system. By requesting an experienced leader, they ultimately reiterated one of the central demands of the Jerusalem Committee, which eventually volunteered to serve as just such a liaison.[70]

Kollek's response was fast and decisive. He nominated his most trusted deputy, Meron Benvenisti, to restructure the city's planning bureaucracy. The result was the aforementioned 1971 founding of the Urban Planning Unit, composed of architects and planners of the Anglo circle, and the immediate recruitment of Nathaniel Lichfield, a renowned player in the British New Towns scene, who joined the municipality as Jerusalem's chief planner in August 1972.[71] Michael Turner explains why the activism of the Anglo architects prompted Kollek to hire its members.[72] The manifesto they composed after the 1970 meeting argued for planning directions that could have saved Kollek from the malignant modernization of the 1968 master plan and offer instead a propensity for the design procedures that made the national park such a stunning success.

The unit, located in the already bustling offices at 10 Shamai Street, became a hub of interdisciplinary planning. Their key word was process, which entailed full architectural responsibility for every step of planning. We cannot overstate the importance of their position. It required the direct intervention of architects in the decision making of a national government, a role that was only possible by understanding the bureaucracy involved in Israel's public planning, the intricacies of policy making, and the power of public opinion. As designers, this group of architects understood that to shape the city is not only to build it, but also to manage its appearance, to direct and orchestrate its image. Their method included the use of cognitive maps, visual analysis that helped them articulate the Jerusalem they desired and then manifest it through urban policy.

The various tools at their disposal embodied alternative modernisms that revived British traditions. This circle of architects was well acquainted with the principle of visual planning and with the townscape movement promoted by Pevsner and Cullen. They were similarly familiar with Kevin Lynch's analysis of urban perception through cognitive maps from their work with Best on the CBD plan. They found inspiration in Lewis Mumford, who considered Patrick Geddes, the successor of Ashbee as the British Mandate's planner of Jerusalem, his ultimate mentor. They were so excited by Mumford's prominent presence in the Jerusalem Committee because the regionalism he advocated was geared toward communal values; similarly, his plea to restrict dense high-rise construction that benefited developers at the expense of the public good further inspired their agenda in Jerusalem. The strength of Lichfield, the unit's new British head, lay in translating this agenda into policy. The picturesque sensibility, focusing on the connection between visual properties and sensual experience, had gradually turned into an operative tool.

The path from this sensibility to operational utility is crucial to understand. Design is habitually considered as a tool for shaping new construction. The challenge of the unit was to control the building boom of Jerusalem using the tools of the city's aesthetic merits. The vision of the unit was architectural: it addressed, in three dimensions, the topography, the built fabric, the proportions, and the relationship between the city's various components. But implementing this vision required legal, financial, and territorial means. The result was a significant expansion of design thinking; instead of directing new, specific construction projects, their plans grew to shape and regulate the image of the entire city. The Anglo circle of architects, under Lichfield's guidance, with Kollek's strong support, and despite opposition from developmental agencies, became involved in the minutiae of public policy like no architects before them.

Besides the costly appropriation of land and its development, the architects consulted on measures of legal management, such as building permits, reparcellation, regulating temporary uses, and setting relocation requirements. Other measures were financial, including questions of taxation, joined dwelling grants, and relaxing rent control. Perhaps the group's greatest innovation was utilizing what Lichfield deemed "indirect influence," namely, "public opinion and pressure" as well as "party political pressure."[73] Toward these ends they relied on civic organizations such as the Council for the Beautiful Land of Israel, founded in 1968, whose journalists and academics exerted considerable pressure over decision makers.

Other members of the situated coalition were in charge of legal reinforcement. Moti Sahar, the district planner in the Ministry of Interior Affairs, was most committed to this method. Sahar returned to Israel in 1967 from training in the United States in order to participate in the war as a combat pilot. His choice to serve as a public architect expressed, in his mind, a similar commitment to "issues of the nation." As a civil servant his power emanated from full command over Israel's Planning and Building Law, which he memorized by heart, and he established the exclusive mandate of architecture to shape spaces. According to Sahar "every field must speak in its own language, and architecture should be understood through notions of space."

Sahar insisted that one "must know the tool," that is, the building law, in order to advance public interest in the city. No matter how strong a developer would be or how famous architects are, they cannot bend the law. According to Sahar "the only things that succeed in this world are things that you approach with a prejudice," with a fixed and determined idea of what you want to achieve as a professional. The profession's authority was the key. In his arguments with politicians he compared an architect to a surgeon, asserting that no public committee would decide for the latter when and how to use his scalpel. Architects, he argued, should hold similar authority over issues of space. Accordingly, he was alarmed by the idea that planning is merely a set of vague policies. "A policy," he posited, "is an Outline Scheme," that is, a binding legal document.

After a careful study of Jerusalem, Sahar's firm position was familiar: keeping the livelihood of the Old City by protecting it from urban transformation, enforcing the stone-clad rule, and fostering the "visual lucidity" of Jerusalem. This is why he enthusiastically participated in "one of the most stirring planning affairs in Jerusalem,"[74] the battle over high-rise buildings in the visual vicinity of the Old City. The forerunners of this battle gathered in the Urban Planning Unit, where they developed a policy paper to counter the pressure for tall and dense construction. We focus on this document because it demonstrates the situated coalition's skills in turning the desire for beauty into obligatory policy.

"High-Rise Walls of Greed"

After the 1970 meeting of the Subcommittee for Town Planning, Halprin wrote Kollek a passionate letter with guidelines for landscaping Jerusalem. One recommendation stood out: "In the bowl surrounding the Old City I make a plea for an architecture which symbolically does not stand up like a clenched fist facing & threatening the landscape of Jerusalem but lies like an open palm embracing it."[75] Halprin's plea was not directed at a particular project but, rather, suggested a comprehensive policy. He asked to maintain a mild, horizontal urban landscape in order to highlight, rather than compete with, the central drama of the historical core. The panoramic perspectival view he would propose for the Mamilla project demonstrates how wide terraces with low or no plantation, punctuated by a few cypresses, pines, and palm trees, could turn the former buffer zone between Israel and Jordan into a spacious stage on which the City Walls and the David Citadel powerfully perform in front of the modest terraced houses of Moshe Safdie's habitat.[76] The restrained park he suggested not only framed the sites it bordered, but more importantly, echoed the desired horizontality of Jerusalem's skyline (Figure 4.15).

This was the skyline that Arye Dvir, Halprin's trainee, envisioned. He articulated Halprin's outlook by rendering the distant urban landscape as part of his design for the national park around the City Walls. His plan asked to protect the "existing skyline characterized by small scale structures accented by towers," instead of "large buildings on ridges" that would "spoil the skyline."[77] In other words, Dvir argued that the values of a circumscribed project are contingent on the larger urban context. The latter, he maintained, should be explicitly planned in order to animate the spirit of Jerusalem (Figure 4.16).

Figure 4.15. Lawrence Halprin, proposal for the landscape architecture of the Mamilla project, perspectival view from the south, 1973–74. The Architectural Archives, University of Pennsylvania, Lawrence Halprin Collection, 014.box.38.

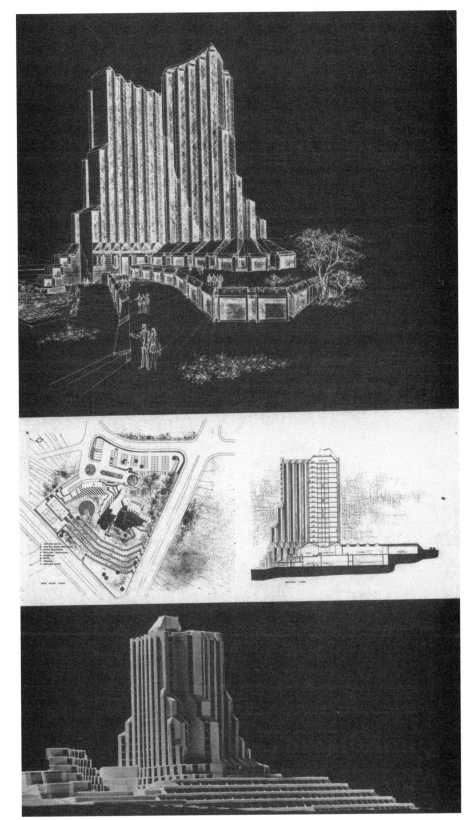

Figure 4.16. Yarmitzky-Azmanof Architects, Hyatt Hotel, perspectives, 1972. Source: *Tvai* 10 (1972): 52.

Halprin and Dvir's anxieties were warranted. While for Dvir "towers" meant the minarets and bell towers that traditionally adorned Jerusalem's skyline, by 1972 the municipality reported on no less than twenty-eight buildings in approval and construction phases whose height exceeded twelve stories, and on a considerable number of additional buildings rising above the eight-story limit established by the 1959 master plan.[78] This was an unprecedented vertical shift in what had been primarily a horizontal landscape for thousands of years.

This shift alarmed the Jerusalem Committee. "The future of the Jerusalem skyline" particularly agitated its members during their plenary meeting in 1973. The *New York Times* reported on the committee's anxiety over breaking "the graceful contour of the surrounding hills . . . by a proliferation of modern high-rise hotels, office and apartment buildings that have sprung up as part of the extraordinary building boom in Jerusalem." The story focused particularly on Louis Kahn, "the most vociferous critic of the high buildings," who thought these high-rise encroachments were "as ominous as invasion. . . . They loom over the Old City like a band of Indians on the hilltop, ready to charge."[79]

For international critics the threat was imminent: ruthless capitalism's invasion into the spiritual core they envisioned as a refuge from the global dominance of wealthy financiers. "I wouldn't feel this way about Pittsburgh," Kahn admitted, "But Jerusalem is something special—a kind of trust from all mankind." For Buckminster Fuller these "high-rise walls of greed" threatened to ruin "the whole mystery of Jerusalem," which is "wrapped up in the vistas out to the Judean wilderness. . . . Nothing should block them." Isamu Noguchi was milder. For him these high-rise towers were "all right . . . so long as they are kept well away from the Old City."[80]

Among the various types of tall buildings, hotels provoked the most pressing internal conflict. The sudden interest of major hotel chains in Jerusalem signaled prosperity and prestige and was therefore supported by the Ministries of Finance, Commerce, and Industry. Moreover, the building of foreign hotels in East Jerusalem legitimized, de facto, the controversial Israeli rule over this territory. At the same time, prestigious hotels insisted on prime locations on the ridge overlooking the Old City. The imminent tourist boom thus provoked yet another clash between the developmental and the situated coalitions in Jerusalem. On the one hand, the hundreds of guest rooms in the new high-rise hotels would boost the tourist industry and the country's economy; on the other hand, these towers would ruin the primary amenity the industry relied on—the spiritual potency of Jerusalem's urban beauty. For the future architects of the Urban Planning Unit, the right to this beauty was a civic privilege in danger.

Apparently, the situated coalition's flagship project was launched before the unit was even established. It was a campaign to lower the height of a proposed tower for a new Hyatt Hotel on Mount Scopus. The government offered the confiscated site to investors in 1969 and was delighted to sign a contract with the luxurious Hyatt chain in 1970, a chain hotel building whose construction would enhance Israeli sovereignty over East Jerusalem. By the end of the year the architecture team of Yarmitzky-Azmanof submitted their design for the Hyatt Hotel: a twenty-one-story tower of three hundred rooms,[81] which later increased to 414 to ensure profitability. The designers emphasized the vertical rise of the tower from its terraced lower floors by grouping together narrow vertical modules, separated from each other by narrow window strips. The gradual trimming of the tower's peripheral modules allowed the main volume to soar along alternating vertical strips of glass and stone.

While the design moved in and out of Israel's planning committees, the young group of Anglo architects stirred the debate by deploying their most evocative tool: the rendered image. Arthur Kutcher rendered an image of the new tower as it would appear from the Hill of Evil Counsel south of the Old City. Kutcher recalls:

> It was Esther Niv who encouraged, I think the word is demanded, of me, that I draw the hotel as it would appear from that viewpoint, rising above and behind the Dome of the Rock, dominating and dwarfing it. At Esther's insistence I gave the drawing to Yuval Elizur of *Ma'ariv* and to Abe Abramovitch of the *Jerusalem Post*. Leaking the drawings was unauthorized and quite irregular, particularly for a low-level municipal employee such as myself. Abe Abramovitch described the effect of the publication of the sketch in *Ma'ariv*, "There was an almost audible public gasp," he wrote. That was the end of the high-rise Hyatt Hotel.[82]

In reality, the hotel's end required a few additional steps. The drawing that was published in May 1971 prompted the professors of the Hebrew University to act against the "high-rise monstrosity" that threatened to rise next to their campus. In June 1972 the government appointed Al Mansfeld, the architect of the Israel Museum, whose horizontal spread simulated the layout of an Arab village; Moshe Safdie, who was similarly inspired in his design of the seminal Habitat; and Yaakov Rechter, the architect of the then-groundbreaking Tel Aviv Hilton. Together with Dash and Yoffe, they were asked to submit a professional evaluation. Their adversaries criticized their quick recommendation (to limit the height of the hotel to four stories and spread its mass across the entire site, similar to the Israel Museum or Habitat) as biased. Nevertheless, the 1973 meeting of the Jerusalem Committee reactivated the debate and eventually convinced the local committee for planning and building of the municipality to not pursue the tower.

The alternative design that Paul Rudolph proposed in 1974, together with Itzhak Efroni and Zeev Scheinberg, followed the recommendation of Kollek's international luminaries. It consisted of modular vaulted units, set in a low-rise, high-density complex that was neatly arranged around inner courts. Although it was never built, it probably inspired David Reznik, who presided over yet another design of the Hyatt in 1978.[83] Reznik succeeded in maintaining the Hyatt requirement for a multistory open-space atrium despite the four-story restriction by manipulating that section of the building. Instead of rising up, Reznik's design monumentalized the space by letting the central atrium descend from the entry level along the steep topography, toward a series of open public courtyards around which he clustered guest rooms in a dense horizontal layout rather than a towering pattern.

Meanwhile, the struggle over the Hyatt hastened the preparation of Jerusalem's "Building Height Policy." In 1972 Shlomo (Solly) Angel joined the unit after a consulting period in England while finishing his doctoral studies at Berkeley with Christopher Alexander, whose seminal *Pattern Language* he would coauthor. Angel worked with Turner and Kutcher on the guidelines for height restrictive policies, which "related on the whole to visual appearance" (Figure 4.17). According to Lichfield, by 1974 the guidelines were approved by the Jerusalem Municipality. Although they were strictly followed, they never assumed a statutory status. As a result, the enforcement of the unit's high-rise policy was contingent on Kollek's guardianship and evaporated soon after he left the mayor's office.[84]

These policy guidelines did not focus on buildings or projects but rather on the array of spaces that were created between them, that is, on a field of spatial relationships in the city. The purpose was not only to identify a holistic landscape in the sum of urban components, but more importantly, to carefully analyze the spatial, formal, and experiential relationship between these components. For the Anglo circle, the key to producing Jerusalem's particular urbanism was articulating the relationships between these many components of urban space and infusing these relationships into design guidelines. Their work, as we'll see at the end of our narrative, foreshadows current practices of landscape urbanism. In a particularly telling map, the entire CBD is rendered according to the number of permitted building floors. The graphic result effectively creates a dynamic urban topography that animates the Anglo circle's desired character of Jerusalem. The success of these guidelines and their attendant policies in halting or terminating numerous towers in the name of the public, that is, in setting firm limits to capitalist growth, represents one of the most powerful public advocacy projects in the history of

Plate 1. "Israel," 1950s poster published by the State of Israel Tourism Department. Courtesy of Central Zionist Archive (KRA\324).

Plate 2. Aerial view of the reconstructed Jewish Quarter with the remains of the Hurva Synagogue, Jerusalem. Courtesy of Albatross Aerial Perspective.

Plate 3. "Jerusalem, a City of Atmosphere." Studio Vishoff for the Jerusalem Municipality, "Dahaf" advertising. Courtesy of Central Zionist Archive (KRA\1322).

Plate 4. Teddy Kollek in front of Jerusalem city walls. Photograph by Bern Schwartz; copyright Bern Schwartz. Courtesy of the Bern Schwartz Family Foundation.

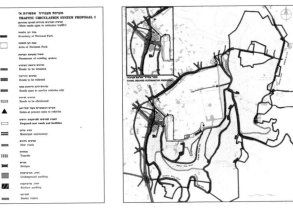
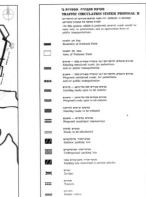
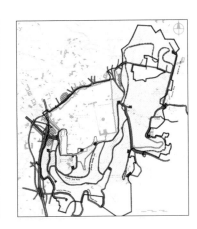
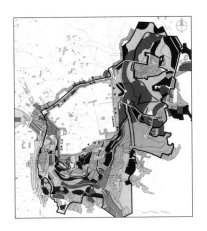

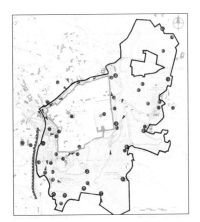

Plate 5. Arye Dvir, planning proposal for the National Park. Two alternative proposals for traffic circulation system (above); proposed green spaces (lower left); pedestrian circulation system (lower center); observation points (lower right). Source: *Jerusalem National Park: Preliminary Proposal by the National Park Authority* (Jerusalem: Israel's National Park Authority, 1969), 49–50, 54, 56–57.

Plate 6. Yahalom–Zur Landscape Architects, view from Hinnom Valley toward the southeast, 1970s. Photograph by Dan Zur. Source: *Arcadia: The Gardens of Lipa Yahalom and Dan Zur* [in Hebrew], ed. Nurit Lissovsky and Diana Dolev (Tel Aviv: Babel [Architecture], 2012). Copyright Yahalom–Zur and Babel.

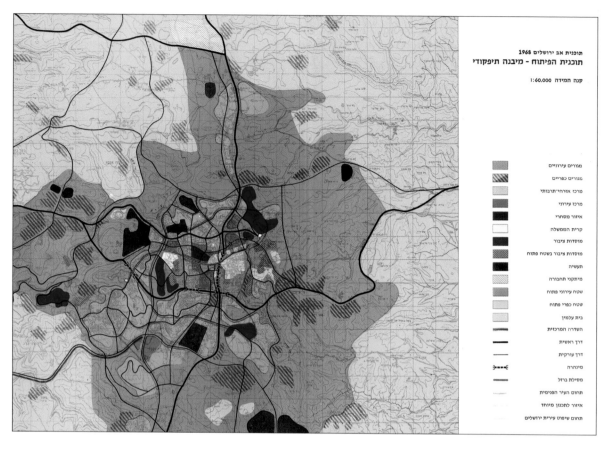

תוכנית אב ירושלים 1968
תוכנית הפיתוח - מיבנה תיפקודי

קנה המידה 1:60.000

ממורים עירוניים
מנורים כפריים
מרכז אזרחי-תרבותי
מרכז עירוני
איזור מסחרי
קרית הממשלה
מוסדות ציבור
מוסדות ציבור בשטח פתוח
תעשיה
מיתקני תחבורה
שטח עירוני פתוח
שטח כפרי פתוח
בית עלמין
השדרה המרכזית
דרך ראשית
דרך עורקית
מינהרה
מסילת ברזל
תחום העיר הפנימית
איזור לתכנון מיוחד
תחום שיפוט עיריית ירושלים

Plate 7. Jerusalem master plan for 2010. Source: Aviah Hashimshoni et al., *1968 Jerusalem Masterplan*, volume 1 (Jerusalem: Jerusalem Municipality, 1972), 102–3.

Plate 8. Arthur Kutcher for Shlomo Aronson Architects, proposal for the Western Wall Plaza. Courtesy of Shlomo Aronson Architects Archive.

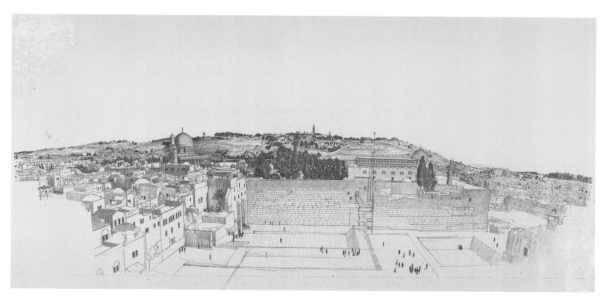

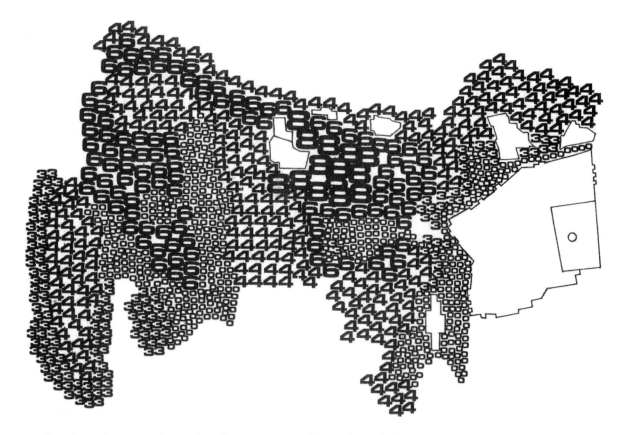

modern Jerusalem, one that enjoyed a momentous boost from the international architectural community.

In 1974, toward the end of his short term as Jerusalem's chief planner, Lichfield summarized the planning efforts around the Old City as "aiming at preservation of the open landscape, creation of parks around the Walls, restoration of villages near the Walls (e.g., Sillwan and Yemin Moshe), protection of the skyline and slopes framing the city."[85] Lichfield described the force of the restored urban landscape as a matter-of-fact experience—or rather, as its obviousness, the feeling that it was always already there. It is exactly the landscape that W. J. T. Mitchell describes as verb rather than noun: the lay of the land is not just geography but is literally "a process by which social and subjective identities are formed."[86] Mitchell further suggests:

> Landscape as a cultural medium has a double role with respect to something like ideology: it naturalizes a cultural and social construction, representing an artificial world as if it were simply given and inevitable, and it also makes that representation operational by interpellating its beholder in some more or less determinate relation to its givenness as sight and site. Thus landscape . . . always greets us as space, as environment, as that within which "we" (figured as "the figure" in the landscape) find—or lose—ourselves.[87]

Figure 4.17. David Best et al. for the Jerusalem Planning Department, city center building height recommendations, 1973. Source: *Building Height* (Jerusalem: Jerusalem Municipality, 1973).

The Jerusalem Committee sought a landscape for the city that not only would enable Israelis to find themselves as a nation but would allow Westerners to find their imagined geography of the Holy Land. It was thus a physical space whose beauty was shaped by the British heritage, animating for Europeans and Americans, as well as a growing body of local enthusiasts, "the greatest collective landscape mirage the human imagination has ever projected for itself."[88]

Conclusions

Having explored the cultural politics of Mayor Teddy Kollek, one must question how his negotiation between local, national, and international demands affected the urban landscape of Jerusalem. For Kollek, Jerusalem was a *Sacred City of Mankind*. He believed that Jerusalem is not a Jewish city, but rather, a Jewish deed. It is an urban endowment that Jews established for the world; it is therefore their moral responsibility to protect that offering. The idea of Jerusalem as a Jewish custody rather than possession was a radical proposition for most Israeli Jews, for whom the unification of Jerusalem was a metaphor for the union of the Jewish people with their original homeland. Kollek knew that for them a unified city "meant everything that Israel means." And yet, he insisted, a unified city is not solely a Jewish city, and since 1967 "we have been going through the process of absorbing this fact, not only intellectually but with all our being."[89]

This cultural policy has had far-reaching consequences. Jerusalem differed from other cities in Israel because it addressed a global constituency. Kollek accordingly decided that "the outside world has a right of opinion, and we have an obligation of considering this opinion."[90] Such obligation required a measure of municipal autonomy from the official politics of the state. Unlike most studies of Jerusalem, we have seen that Kollek succeeded in achieving the latter not only because he was, as claimed by the *Washington Post,* "Israel's number one salesman—on a first-name basis with hundreds of world leaders, with access to the pocketbooks of the Western world."[91] More significant but less obvious, Kollek established a bureaucratic apparatus that was shared with state agencies but was led by his own people. The combination allowed him to bypass the strict limits of his municipal budget and his relative powerlessness in the official politics of the state.

The global network that Kollek created for the world-city he envisioned was rooted in the philosophy of British colonial rule, in which the sanctity of Jerusalem was embodied in its beauty. Accordingly, the urban image of Jerusalem was a precious resource that the British had promised to protect for the monotheistic world. By addressing the same global constituency, and taking custody over Jerusalem's aesthetic merits, Kollek legitimized Israeli rule internationally, at the same time that he justified his economic and professional outsourcing domestically. His vision drove him to recruit architects with compatible design agendas, whose work at times even explicitly continued the British planning traditions. Kollek found this compatibility among young Anglo architects who formed an effective professional circle in Jerusalem. Eventually, they helped him to address the demands of his foreign advisors, many of whom had been their mentors overseas.

But what was the gist of the British tradition? Why did it serve Kollek's cultural politics so effectively? And how did new trends in spatial design match its cause? We have suggested that, for the British, Jerusalem's prime asset was its Orientalist authenticity, that the city's emotional appeal was contingent on its picturesque qualities, and that urban planning provided the methods for managing Jerusalem as a modern city while fostering the picturesque quality of its urban landscape. In other words, British Orientalism and the aesthetic philosophy of the picturesque assumed its modern incarnation through urban planning. This modern discipline eventually authenticated the gist of the British Mandate: protecting Jerusalem as a visual idea.

Kollek not only adopted, but also updated this cultural policy to address the desire for peace in the Cold War era. The key was, again, the authenticity of Jerusalem, which was stressed as the thing itself—not a representation of an idea, but rather, the inspiration, the real biblical origin. Accordingly, Jerusalem's spirituality was layered into its physical form throughout its history, and therefore its landscape is a testimony to its multiple histories, and as such a precious resource for peaceful coexistence. Kollek invited the globe's architectural luminaries to join his Jerusalem Committee by arguing that Jerusalem's urban landscape promised to unify ethics and aesthetics, between the heritage of Jerusalem and the physical space where that heritage was made manifest.

Like the British, Kollek's commitment to this heritage imbued his planning apparatus with Orientalist attitudes, aiming to keep the look and character of Jerusalem as faithful as possible to the imagined biblical Orient. Since the Old City epitomized this look, Kollek quickly bulldozed the area around the Old City, making room for the green belt that the British had envisioned around its walls. The national park that Arye Dvir planned shortly after the war on behalf of the NPA resurrected and advanced this British idea. It halted modernity from damaging the serenity of ancient Jerusalem, while highlighting its commanding presence in the sacred visual basin. International critics applauded the plan because it projected the Orientalist authenticity of Jerusalem onto the landscape. In their eyes Dvir's design for the park embodied the awe-inspiring interaction between nature and man in its primal form, thus creating a respectful, unfettered physical setting for the spirituality of Jerusalem.

Unlike the British, Dvir's greatest success was the rapid declaration of the green belt as a statutory national park. This success can be attributed to his professional training in the United States, particularly with Lawrence Halprin and Ian McHarg. The new methodologies he acquired in America helped him advance the essence of his project—an environmental experience of biblical Jerusalem—far beyond what the British had ever been able to do. The plan thus animated British Orientalism with the latest concepts in landscape architecture. In turn, it also made this experience emotionally evocative by designing according to picturesque sensibilities. But how could one turn this sensibility into a design method? Dvir addressed this challenge with new methods of ecological planning that rendered the picturesque scientifically correct, and with experiential landscaping that made it sensually effective.

For Kollek, the contrast between the successful reception of the plan for the national park and the harsh criticism of the modernist *1968 Jerusalem Masterplan* clearly determined the design direction that would best advance his cultural politics. The new direction required a fundamental restructuring of the municipal planning bureaucracy, resulting in a new Urban Planning Unit, headed by a newly recruited British chief planner and populated by members of the young and innovative Anglo circle. Although the unit was rather short-lived and the turnover of its members was high, its interdisciplinary approach and its method of design by planning had far-reaching consequences.

We have focused on the unit's interdisciplinary method for preparing a high-rise building policy because it reveals the British underpinnings of the Anglo circle's urban and landscape design. The guiding logic of this document is architectural design. It relies on a three-dimensional interpretation of the city and boasts a careful analysis of space, proportions, and urban form. Its mode of operation, however, derives from the realm of urban planning and is articulated by the language of urban policy. The result is an unexpected conjuncture: the use of economic and legal measures to enhance the picturesque qualities of Jerusalem, thus transforming British ideas into building praxis. In this fashion, a host of factors converged: ideas emanating from Geddes's organicism and Mumford's regionalism; the picturesque that undergirded Pevsner's visual planning and Cullen's townscape; the focus on urban experience in Halprin's experiential landscape; and the scientific analysis of ecology and everyday patterns in McHarg and Alexander's treaties, all in various ways participated in reviving the British idea of Jerusalem.

Among the situated coalition's most ardent advocates of the autonomy of architecture, of its exclusive mandate to deal with built and open spaces, were those who expanded the architectural toolbox in order to achieve the urban design they desired. According to Moti Sahar, architects can endlessly argue about the merits of their design in order to advance an alternative.[92] To counter their argument, he argued, the civil servant must protect the best interest of the city and its residents through the legal means at his disposal. The result was design by policy, even by legal rules, that eventually ensured the projection of Jerusalem's authenticity not only onto the immediate vicinity of the Old City but, more significantly, onto the urban geography that Kollek succeeded in withholding from the state, namely, the visual basin of the Old City.

Reflecting on his years as Kollek's deputy mayor for planning, Meron Benvenisti, the charismatic official in charge of the Urban Planning Unit, regretfully noted that "the Safdies and the Karmis," that is, charismatic architects rather than public servants, had greater impact on Jerusalem than those who were elected to serve its best interests.[93] The reason, he thought, was rooted in Kollek's propensity for the arts and the compelling language that architects used and politicians found too obscure to rationally object to. Benvenisti, however, principally sided with the architects of the unit under his authority. He prepared with them an alternative to Safdie's controversial urban development of Mamilla, a neighborhood linking East and West Jerusalem. A bitter conflict erupted between Benvenisti and Kollek, who took this project under his wing. This example sheds light on a fundamental difference between "the Safdies and the Karmis" and the Anglo circle, and the reason Kollek embraced this circle but at the same time often put its recommendations on the back burner.

Despite his propensity for beauty, and his firm alignment with the situated coalition, Kollek was a steadfast Zionist of the Ben Gurion school at heart. This form of Zionism required immediate and resolute action. Kollek insisted on the aesthetic implication of this action and opened it to global intervention, but he did not compromise the national ambition to quickly create facts on the East Jerusalem ground. According to Kollek, the shape and meaning of Jerusalem could not be left to the contingencies of life, habit, or human whim. It had to be firmly directed from above.

The architects Kollek favored were those who sought to understand the genetic code of Jerusalem, the key to its unique balance of beauty and spirituality. By contrast, the Anglo circle insisted on the process of negotiating city form with the public, the use of media and education, and securing democratic values in physical planning. This approach intimidated Kollek because it could have led to unexpected results. It left too many open ends. For Pevsner and his followers, the idea of the picturesque stood for democratic values and a sense of liberty because it was based on the dynamic registration of the city with the public. But for Kollek and his circle of architects, the translation of these values to design praxis was threatening because it involved too many actors and was vulnerable to public opinion, and could thus impede his urgent and resolute plans to stir the transformation of Jerusalem. Kollek was so eager to maintain control over the image of Jerusalem that he would recruit the world to help him.

5 **FRONTIER**
A HOLY TESTING GROUND
FOR A DISCIPLINE IN CRISIS

> I feel that in Jerusalem not merely the fate of Israel, but the
> destiny of the world in the centuries to come may actually be
> at stake.
>
> —*Lewis Mumford*

T HE PREEMINENT PUBLIC INTELLECTUAL Lewis Mumford described Israel's seizure of East Jerusalem from Jordan as "one of those singular moments of which the great physicist Clerk Maxwell once wrote: when an insignificant force, exerted at a propitious moment, may effect an enormous change which would otherwise be beyond human possibility." Mumford wasn't particularly concerned with the military's role in this "enormous change"; he was enthralled instead with the possibilities for architectural, urban, and political change at this "propitious moment." Mumford was far from alone in declaring the unification of Jerusalem in June 1967 as a potential turning point in human history.

Three years after the war, in a letter Mumford wrote to Mayor Teddy Kollek, he explained why "so many people of all faiths and philosophies" had enthusiastically accepted the mayor's invitation to participate in the advisory body of the Jerusalem Committee and to evaluate the plans for the city's future.

> It is surely because the very nature of Jerusalem transcends all narrow local
> and partisan interests. Instinctively, everyone realizes that if Jerusalem could
> be unified by acts of good will and free consent, without military or economic
> coercion, that spirit of unity might spread in time to the rest of the world.

Mumford, in other words, roots the appeal of the moment in political *and* disciplinary cultures. He compellingly suggests that Jerusalem's spirituality not only made evident the impasse of modernist urbanism, but more powerfully, it foreshadowed "the destiny of the world in the centuries to come." In the new era, he wrote, "world-cities" and a "world-government" might eclipse the power of modern nationalism and its structure of sovereign nation-states.[1]

Lewis Mumford and Buckminster Fuller were the most far-reaching utopians among Kollek's invitees, but just two of the many who flocked to Jerusalem, eager for the opportunity to shape this historical moment (Figure 5.1). According to *Architectural Design,* in 1967 Jerusalem was "belatedly thrust into the twentieth century, after being dormant for a few hundred years."[2] This account, like many both inside and outside the Holy City, portrays Jerusalem as undeveloped yet beautiful, stagnant yet laden with history—an archetypal Orientalist locale pregnant with opportunities.[3] To Mumford, Jerusalem presented, "despite all present divisions and antagonisms . . . a potential source of unity," which could be found in its spatial, material, and historical attributes.[4] For Louis Kahn, Bruno Zevi, Christopher Alexander, and Lawrence Halprin—to mention only a few of the people recruited by Kollek—the city offered an irresistible testing ground. That ground was desperately needed, for theirs was a discipline in crisis. Jerusalem after the Six Day War, and thanks to Kollek's salesmanship, became a tantalizing beacon, a new frontier for the era marked by timid modernization. Here was a city bursting with historical significance, yet with virtually no traffic lights. And here was a group of foreign architects and planners desperate to escape from contemporary Euro-American urban renewal, inner-city highways, and sprawling suburbia. In Jerusalem's Orientalist authenticity, these men and women sought salvation from the ubiquitous modernity at home. The result would be a painful clash over the very meanings of development and modernization.

According to Philip Johnson, "Jerusalem await[ed] its twentieth century, its Israeli shape." This shape assumed international importance because it would test the possibility of an alternative modernist urbanism. Johnson advises Kollek:

Figure 5.1. Teddy Kollek (right) with Louis Kahn (center) and Buckminster Fuller during the Jerusalem Committee visit in Jerusalem, December 1970. Photograph by Isamu Noguchi. Courtesy of the Isamu Noguchi Archive.

You have to dream big. Once, when our country was young and energetic like Israel, we had crackpots who dreamed. We used to be giants in our own land. Now maybe it's your turn. This is the Israeli century . . . you can still plan a new Jerusalem. Too late New York, Tokyo, Moscow; our future is behind us. Yours is still ahead. . . .

Your plan will be . . . the first twentieth-century urban place, and the only one in the world with a history like Jerusalem.

But what, we must ask, were the measures according to which Johnson and company could judge if Jerusalem would "be either great or trivial"?[5] And for whom?

Mumford's 1970 letter dampened the postwar enthusiasm with a reminder: "For it is only in terms of the immediate moment, that is, the last three years, that the conditions essential to [a unified plan's] execution even partly exist. Those conditions unfortunately are as closely tied to military events as was the previous dismemberment of Jerusalem."[6] Mumford was alone in suggesting the impact of violence on urban planning. He challenged the capacity of a worldly committee to simultaneously address Zionist aspirations and Jordanian loss.

But addressing both was exactly the goal of Kollek's cultural politics, which aimed to shift the focus on Jerusalem from political antagonism to shared values. Kollek's extraordinary effort to involve the international community in shaping Jerusalem had an immediate, though unanticipated, effect: it brought the contemporary crisis of the architectural discipline and its modernist praxis to dramatically bear on the shape and meaning of Jerusalem. At the same time it also created a disciplinary think tank—a rare opportunity for professional brainstorming of the highest caliber, and a powerful engine of contemporary disciplinary critique.

This chapter examines the Jerusalem Committee and questions how its conceptualization of Jerusalem as the frontier of a rapidly changing architectural discipline affected its planning. The committee was founded in 1969, and the subcommittee it created to consider Jerusalem's urban planning met the following year. Two additional plenary meetings, in 1973 and 1975, took place during the first postwar decade.

We first focus our attention on that single, yet consequential, meeting of the Subcommittee for Town Planning. In December 1970, architectural luminaries and local politicians fought over the highly modernist Jerusalem Masterplan the leading planning agencies of Israel submitted two years earlier, as well as its complementing plans for urban transportation, the Central Business District (CBD), and the Old City and its environs. The subcommittee's debate over the plans turned the confrontation between the developmental and situated modernisms into a colossal clash.

The subcommittee, and thus the Jerusalem Committee as a whole, was adamant in insisting on situated modernism, which in turned spurred major changes in the city's municipal planning administration. The shofar of this change was the newly recruited chief planner, the British Nathaniel Lichfield. He spearheaded the 1973 plenary meeting of the Jerusalem Committee, during which two of Moshe Safdie's megaprojects were approved. After Lichfield's retirement in 1974, the promise to design for spirit and character, which the committee enthusiastically endorsed, was put again on the negotiating table.

As the 1975 plenary meeting approached, the developmental modernists were increasingly associated with urban planning, the modern discipline based on spatial management and policy making, while situated modernists tended to identify with the premises of urban design. The rise of the latter, as an official discipline lodged between architecture and urban planning, coincided with Israel's industrious (re)building of the Holy City, keeping the city at the frontier of architectural experimentation. During the committee's 1975 plenary meeting, these disciplinary tensions unfolded between architects Denys Lasdun, Jaap Bakema, and Lawrence Halprin, and their opponent, Meron Benvenisti, the deputy mayor of Jerusalem, over the proper tools and ethical right to coordinate the city's built fabric. This chapter ends by returning to Mumford's letter to Kollek in 1970, in order to examine the mayor's desire to remake Jerusalem as a world-city in the context of Mumford's plea to move beyond the pitfalls of nationalism.

The Jerusalem Committee

From the outset, the Jerusalem Committee was a political act. It was an international initiative of Kollek, who attempted to transcend the limitations of his political power by inviting, in the summer of 1969, seventy luminaries from around the world to supervise the Israeli unification of Jerusalem. He assured these men and women that "the problem is not ours alone, as residents of the city; it belongs, in a sense, to the entire world, to all those people who are Jerusalemites in their hearts and minds."[7] Kollek happily reported that only one invitee refused to join the committee as long as East Jerusalem was occupied,[8] an impressive validation of his effort to make cultural affairs autonomous from the conspicuously controversial politics of the state.

Kollek stressed the advantages of his cultural policy when reporting to the minister of foreign affairs, Golda Meir, about the anticipated discussions of "projects that we plan in the city."

> It seems to me that the mere fact that such luminaries agreed to participate in this kind of committee, and are even willing to come to Jerusalem especially

today, when in the UN and especially in UNESCO, they feel apprehensive about our right to act in the city—is extremely important.[9]

Meir asked in return to "publicize the discussions of the conference and its constructive results," because these prestigious discussions "in greater Jerusalem . . . provide a definitive answer" to the challenges Israel faced "far away in New York."[10]

The inaugural plenary meeting of the Jerusalem Committee, convened on June 30, 1969, was well represented by architects and visual artists, alongside numerous Nobel laureates and dignitaries of the arts, letters, and religion. As we have seen, Kollek considered the beautification of Jerusalem the centerpiece of his cultural policy and therefore turned architects into indispensable agents toward this goal (Figure 5.2). Their enthusiastic support of the national park around the city walls confirmed the importance of contemporary architectural and landscape design in tailoring the planning of Jerusalem to a Western audience and its preferences. The park, however, was only a small part of Jerusalem's ongoing physical transformation. The committee concluded that a more focused attention was needed on issues pertaining to urban planning, and a subcommittee was formed for this purpose. The subcommittee's lone meeting the following year was a momentous architectural event.[11]

During the next three years the municipality reorganized its planning

Figure 5.2. Lawrence Halprin, drawings of the Jerusalem Committee members, 1973. Source: Halprin's sketchbooks. Courtesy of the Architectural Archives, University of Pennsylvania, Lawrence Halprin Collection.

apparatus, presenting it to the Jerusalem Committee during its second plenary meeting in June 1973. In this meeting Safdie already showed, for the first time, his design schemes for the Mamilla Quarter and for the Western Wall Plaza. The meeting's success was due to the leadership of the British planner Nathaniel Lichfield, who acted as Jerusalem's chief planner. Lichfield was the kind of international leader the committee had sought. But after his unexpected retirement in 1974, the absence of a leading international planner from the third plenary meeting in December 1975 provoked heated debates, particularly on issues pertaining to the new discipline of urban design.[12]

Some of Kollek's invitees were already familiar with Israel through previous architectural commissions, competitions, or criticism. Kollek most admired Louis Kahn, whom he had commissioned to design the Hurva Synagogue and to whom he would commission the Northern Slopes of the High Commissioner Hill. Among other involved architects, Johnson had already built a nuclear power plant, Safdie was developing Habitat Israel, Halprin had recently designed the landscape of the Hadassah Hospital campus in West Jerusalem, Isamu Noguchi had just completed the sculpture garden of the Israel Museum, Zevi repeatedly judged international competitions in Israel and was deeply involved in local architectural circles, and Mumford was engaged in an extensive correspondence with Artur Glikson, a leading institutional architect in Israel. Together with Israeli consultants, they helped Kollek weave together an unparalleled network of architects, planners, and critics around the world, all dealing with the challenge of planning Jerusalem. Kollek boasted that when *Newsweek* magazine listed the leading architects of the time, almost all of them were members of the Jerusalem Committee.[13]

It is difficult to overstate the importance of this team to post–World War II architectural culture. The modern movement in architecture had started in the interwar period as an avant-garde movement with social underpinnings, advocating rational planning, technological innovation, and bare aesthetics. The movement's emphasis on functionalism, mass production, and proper infrastructure, as well as its famous call for separating the city into secluded zones of work, habitation, recreation, and transportation, was intended to redeem the nineteenth-century city from the deleterious effects of industrialization, intense density, and dilapidated infrastructure. But during the interwar period, the abstract and internationalist discourse of modernists came under attack from many nationalist regimes.[14] After World War II, the already established modern movement gained enormous power. As advocates of order, efficiency, and mass production, modernists led the architectural reconstruction of a devastated Europe.

The Congrès Internationaux d'Architecture Moderne (CIAM)—founded in 1928 and led by, among others, Le Corbusier and Walter Gropius—was the main organ of this evolution.[15] It is unclear whether any postwar profession had a modernist organization that was as powerful, and therefore as difficult, to contend with. And yet just three decades after its founding, the younger architects of Team 10 brought CIAM to an end. Their tenth congress in 1959 rendered CIAM outdated and consequently pushed forward a momentous shift in the history of modern architecture from the ethos of development to situated modernisms attentive to the values of the European welfare state.[16]

A decade later, Kollek would solicit the major advocates of this upheaval to his Jerusalem Committee. Jaap Bakema, who would soon shape the course of the 1975 plenary meeting, was an instrumental actor in this group of rebels. The keynote speaker he and his colleagues invited to the tenth congress, in order to mark the new era, was Louis Kahn, who was known as the philosopher of architects and who advocated a return to the timeless dimensions of Architecture with a capital A. Bruno Zevi also challenged CIAM by preaching for the organic architecture of Frank Lloyd Wright. Denys Lasdun led the revolt of the Brutalist group in London. Fuller was the admired father figure of the 1960s radical avant-garde, and Christopher Alexander harnessed computation to systemize the virtues of vernacular architecture into his influential "pattern language." Philip Johnson, who had put CIAM's leaders on a pedestal in his seminal 1932 MoMA exhibition *The International Style,* actively contributed to the critique of the movement.[17]

Academics and journalists were also present on the committee. Nikolaus Pevsner, whose *Pioneers of Modern Design* complemented Giedion's *Space, Time and Architecture* as an alternative history for modern architecture, promoted "the cityscape movement" and the notion of "the picturesque" in visual planning in his role as the influential editor of the British *Architectural Review.*[18] The rival magazine to Pevsner's, *Architectural Design,* attracted the younger generation of architects, including British members of Team 10. Theo Cosby, who launched the magazine's radical phase, was succeeded by Monica Pidgeon. She was one of three women attending the 1970 subcommittee meeting. Other journalists, editors, and museum directors sat side by side with such influential artists as Isamu Noguchi and Max Bill as well as planners such as Charles Haar, a Harvard professor who helped create in 1966 the Model Cities Program for President Lyndon Johnson, and landscape architects Halprin and Robert Zion, who were instrumental in revolutionizing the field during the 1960s. One can only imagine the influence of such a group on the architectural culture of a tiny country struggling to enter the developed world.

The committee's international influence emanated from its professional autonomy: in the realm of aesthetics and humanism, the committee members had a mandate to speak in the name of universal values. There was nevertheless a generational difference within the committee between older architects, whose lives spanned the violence of two world wars and their aftermath, and therefore wished to find in Jerusalem the threshold to an era transcending global violence, and younger architects who were more focused on starting a disciplinary revolution. When Buckminster Fuller suggested that Jerusalem would become "de-sovereignized" and a "world-man-territory" of world citizens, because it "is at the still center of the revolving forces of history," Kollek remained outside the fray.[19] The power of his agenda lay in the strict separation of official politics and planning: "This city has to live regardless of politics," he insisted. "What we want are competent opinions on town planning."[20]

His adamant stance set the tone for the committee's inaugural meeting. *Architectural Design,* for example, reported that "all too conscious of the politically explosive background to their deliberations, the Committee had endeavored to keep to basic planning issues common to all cities and people irrespective of race or creed."[21] The seeming neutrality of this highly professional debate, empowered as it was by the inner dynamics of the architectural discipline, was arguably its greatest strength. It allowed for Jerusalem's beautification process to conceal its political apparatus—to normalize a particular narrative of Jerusalem under the umbrella of universal aesthetic value.

The Subcommittee Meets the Zionist Blueprint

Convened eighteen months after Kollek's initial gathering, the December 1970 meeting of the Subcommittee for Town Planning was a rather unusual occasion. Mayor Kollek convinced the five chief planning agencies of Israel to voluntarily submit their coordinated *1968 Jerusalem Masterplan* and its three complements—plans for the CBD of West Jerusalem, for transportation, and for the Old City and its environs[22]—for the scrutiny of the subcommittee's thirty-one reviewers, who hailed from nine countries.[23] The subcommittee would later convey to Kollek how "much impressed" they were "by your staff's readiness to present the plan candidly and openly, and to subject their intellectual children to the onslaught of strangers."[24]

On Saturday, December 19, these thirty-one members convened in Jerusalem for a three-day meeting. The invitees received a comprehensive package prior to their arrival, including a full list of Israeli and foreign participants, reports on the four plans under review, a program of the conference and the tour, and background materials. Before the meeting they also received a long memorandum from Mumford, which might have affected the tone of the upcoming deliberations. Kollek opened the meeting, urging the guests to consider three trends: "pilgrimage, increasing immigration, and the movement of Israelis to Jerusalem." Buckminster Fuller continued with a keynote address, in which he "described Jerusalem as 'the place where man first began to use his mind,' a place which 'belongs to all of us.' "[25] Revealing his radical vision of the future, he hypothesized that "property will shortly become obsolete," that "man will become *world man*," and that soon, "ownership becomes onerous." Like Mumford, he believed that only in Jerusalem could such global de-capitalization start. This is the point where, he mused with close eyes, "we may *just* save the world for man."[26] His address was followed by a large team of Israeli planners, who presented the 1968 master plan and its supplemental plans.

The next morning began with a revelatory experience: the invitees boarded a flight that provided a bird's-eye view of Jerusalem's imposing landscape, and they listened to planners about its proposed transformation. From the airport in North Jerusalem, the guests were bussed through the new Israeli construction in East Jerusalem. Despite the international uproar and local turmoil around the controversial settlement on confiscated land, the new dwellings drew little if any of the guests' attention. Similarly overlooked, to judge by the lack of commentary, was the speedy construction of a new campus for the Hebrew University on the formerly besieged Israeli enclave on Mount Scopus.

This mountain was the dignitaries' first stop in their carefully choreographed itinerary around the visual basin of the Old City (Figure 5.3). The Old City of Jerusalem tops Mount Moriah, which is nestled among a ring of higher ridges. Arieh Sharon and Eliezer Brutzkus, the authors of the "Outline Scheme for the Old City and Its Environs," took the guests along the eastern ridge to the Mount of Olives, explaining en route the principles of their plan. Arye Dvir described the plans for the nascent national park that lay around the city walls as the bus descended down the scarcely populated Kidron Valley to visit the Absalom and Hezekiah Tombs, before climbing up again to the southern ridge, the former seat of the British high commissioner who governed Mandate Palestine and was replaced by the UN forces. This circular route around the Temple Mount, from east to west, up and down the steep topography, followed the path of the sun. It allowed the guests to experience the morning light softening the golden glow of the Dome of the Rock, the jewel of al-Haram al-Sharif (the Muslim Noble Sanctuary), then the bright light falling on the southeastern corner of the Old City—the tallest section of the Ottoman-era city walls—and eventually, during a late lunch in the Kotel Yeshiva, the sunlight washing the Western Wall, the holiest site for Jews.

The subcommittee then drove from the High Commissioner Hill in the south, through Abu Tur, and north toward Mount Zion, crossing the recently removed no-man's-land that had split East and West Jerusalem for the previous nineteen years. The controversy around the availability of open land for the tourist industry would eventually generate design commissions for two committee members—Louis Kahn and, later, Lawrence Halprin. When they reached the Zion Gate, Yehuda Tamir, who led the reconstruction of the Jewish Quarter by the Ministry of Housing, took the group on a walking tour through the quarter. Noguchi's photographs of the occasion reveal the

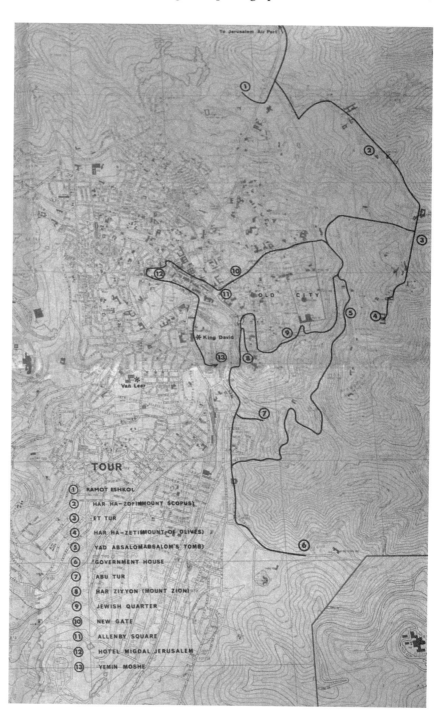

Figure 5.3. Jerusalem Committee Meeting Program, itinerary of the Jerusalem tour, December 18, 1970. 030.II.A.39.9 LIK. Courtesy of the Architectural Archives, University of Pennsylvania, Louis Kahn Collection.

sense of Orientalist enthusiasm that this sensual experience provoked in the foreign dignitaries (Figure 5.4).

After lunch they crossed through the New Gate to West Jerusalem. They climbed the City Tower where David Best discussed the plan he authored for the CBD and then headed back to Yemin Moshe (a low-income, picturesque slum turned into an artist colony) overlooking the proposed national park, where the steep Hinnom Valley descended to the Judean desert. Kollek's bulldozers had cleared this part of West Jerusalem immediately after the war,

Figure 5.4. Louis Kahn and Buckminster Fuller on the Old City tour, December 1970. Photographs by Isamu Noguchi. Courtesy of the Isamu Noguchi Archive.

and its bare surface was awaiting what Johnson called "its Israeli shape." The guests' home away from home at the King David Hotel, where they could enjoy similar views, was now only minutes away.

The subcommittee's expansive tour of the Holy City was both the culmination of several years of work and a great frustration for Israel's building administration. When Kollek started sending the invitations to the potential members of the Jerusalem Committee, a large Israeli team had already completed its interim master plan for the Holy City. The plan, which was quickly adjusted after June 1967 to accommodate the unified city, had begun three years prior, when Kollek's predecessor, Mordechai Ish Shalom, established an interdisciplinary professional team to coordinate different agencies and their budgets in order to modernize the city.[27] The greatest achievement of Ish Shalom was to solicit powerful state agencies as partners while maintaining coordination under municipal hands. Thus, the Ministries of Housing and Transportation and the Israel Land Authority, all with considerable budgets, empowered the relatively weak municipality, and in the process upset the officials at the Ministry of Interior Affairs, whose national focus rendered them (temporarily) powerless in these crucial local negotiations.[28]

Ish Shalom chose his principal planners, Yoseph Schweid and the brothers Zion and Aviah Hashimshoni, from the professional and academic establishment of Zionist modernist planning. Zion had already had a leading role in Israel's first ultramodernist master plan in 1951.[29] Aviah, the team head (and the author of Israel's first architectural history), was a professor of architecture at the Technion, where by the mid-1960s he represented the modernist-functionalist camp in Israel's single architectural school. He was an advocate of the *neue sachlichkeit* (matter-of-factness) modernism, of bare and functional building devoid of sentimentality and aimed at serving the well-being of individuals and their social organizations. Among younger collaborators we find Avraham Vachman, a sabra of the Rosh HaNikrah group (who still maintains that the 1968 plan was the best ever made in Israel); Yishayahu Ilan, a rare institutional architect among Orthodox Jews; and Israel Kimhi, who would later become a major municipal planner.

The 1968 master plan inherited from its Zionist predecessors the logic of an ordered environment, but in opposition to earlier attempts to draw Israelis from the city to the village, the plan stressed the benefits of urban form and welcomed its potential density.[30] The goals of the plan were threefold: national, municipal, and universal. It first established the civic importance of the presumed national capital, then provided for the well-being of its inhabitants, and finally reinforced the global significance of Jerusalem's religious sites. These goals were translated into a set of objectives for which the plan provided detailed physical "solutions."[31] Numerous diagrams described the desired relationship between built and natural landscape, specifying a plain architecture and conveying a distrust of visual expressiveness (Figure 5.5). The plan specified a contained city geared toward the everyday needs of its residents, with a modernist infrastructure, extensive road systems, and convenient distribution of urban activities.[32]

The logo of the plan reveals its primary concept: an inner city that was nestled in a larger, clearly bounded city. The inner loop consisted of two clearly distinguished centers (one religious, the other civic) that were paired rather than fused together. The former contained historical and religious sites and was centered on the newly seized Old City; the latter was comprised of state institutions and was located within the Government Precinct of West Jerusalem (Figure 5.6). In total, this "inner city" consisted of approximately seven square miles. (The larger bounded city, made primarily of residential neighborhoods, then spread to the north, south, and west for another twenty-seven square miles.) According to this plan, the two clearly circumscribed cores were symbolically and aesthetically self-contained. Implicitly, these two core structures spatially articulated the authors' political understanding of Jerusalem as the nation's capital: a geographic split between civic

Figure 5.5. Diagrams of the city and the Metropole. Source: Aviah Hashimshoni et al., *1968 Jerusalem Masterplan,* volume 1 (Jerusalem: Jerusalem Municipality, 1972), 63.

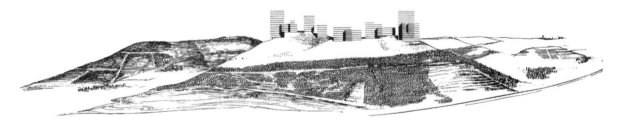

Figure 5.6. The *1968 Jerusalem Masterplan* scheme for the city structure. Source: Aviah Hashimshoni et al., *1968 Jerusalem Masterplan,* volume 1 (Jerusalem: Jerusalem Municipality, 1972), 62.

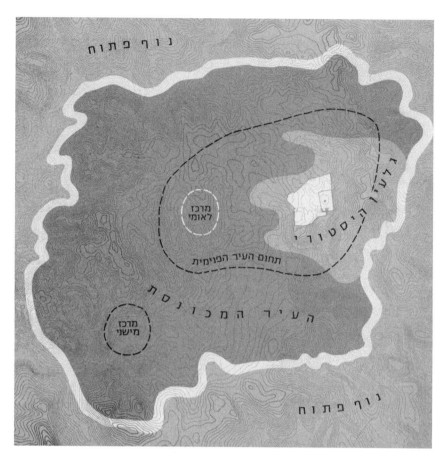

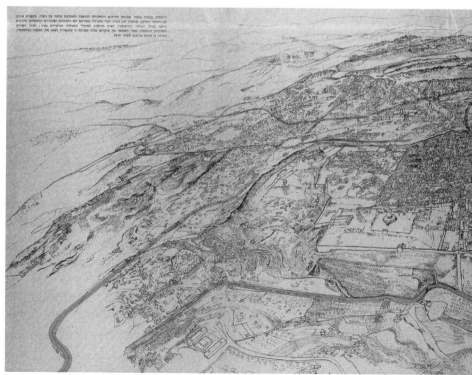

and sacred monuments offered a resolute separation between the state and religious faith.

The main challenge of unification following the 1967 war was to tie the hitherto isolated West Jerusalem to its new metropolitan context. The planners tested three layouts: the first concentric, centering around the historical core; the second linear, connecting Jerusalem to the Palestinian hinterland by stretching the urban structure from Bethlehem in the south to Ramallah in the north; and the third, a dispersed layout that wove the linear north–south scheme with a similar east–west connection to the Israeli shore (Figure 5.7 and Plate 7). The result was a grid-like structure that, according to the plan's authors, combined the virtues of both directional schemes. The plan protected the Old City as a profound historical monument but implied that this precinct should not halt the modern evolution of urban function. For the advocates of situated modernism this gesture to modernization was a bright red flag.

Despite the proposed transportation arteries that would cut through the city, the authors wished to maintain the built pattern of Mandate Jerusalem along major commercial and residential streets. They also adopted the British principles of open valleys free from construction, and stone-clad architecture. In opposition to colleagues from the Ministry of Interior Affairs, they insisted on keeping the CBD close to the Old City and asked to integrate some governmental agencies into the downtown area to encourage better

Figure 5.7. Perspective of Jerusalem with proposed road scheme map for 2010. Source: Aviah Hashimshoni et al., *1968 Jerusalem Masterplan,* volume 1 (Jerusalem: Jerusalem Municipality, 1972), 84–85.

interface between citizens and their state. It was a plan inherently designed for users: efficient, convenient, stressing urban flow, and resisting overt symbolism. It prioritized the residents of the city over its pilgrims, without specifying the ethnicity or faith of either. Nevertheless, the most symbolic act this plan proposed, a monumental boulevard running from Mount Scopus to the national cemetery of Israel on Mount Herzl, clearly empowered the Israeli state.

The other symbolic act was to specify distinct gateways to the bounded city that would celebrate its coherent urban boundary. Again, these gates were conceptualized in motion, designed as scenery that the modern driver encounters as she climbs toward Jerusalem (Figure 5.8). The image of a bounded city was favored by the mayor because it allowed for efficient municipal management. There was no intention, however, to halt the city's growth. On the contrary, the plan was geared toward urban density and even acknowledged the option—taboo until now—of high-rise buildings.

The Israeli plan was lauded for its empirical precision. The two volumes that would document the work of the master plan team consist of numerous measures of demographic growth and housing units, transportation requirements and land uses. The meticulous research and careful statistics of the plan gave it a scientific aura. It graphically delivered accurate data, the result of extensive research that was packed into diagrams and colored maps. Its precision and systematic logic, as well as its methodological rigor, won the master plan near-unanimous support throughout city and state authorities.

Figure 5.8. Proposed entryways to Jerusalem. Source: Aviah Hashimshoni et al., *1968 Jerusalem Masterplan,* volume 1 (Jerusalem: Jerusalem Municipality, 1972), 70–71.

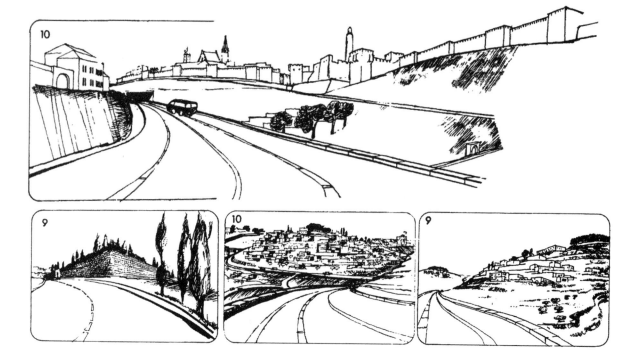

In August 1970, the professional reputation of the 1968 plan was subject to public debate. The plan championed a definition of a clearly bounded city, but that month the Israeli government violated this guideline by confiscating more than four thousand acres of East Jerusalem land. Its goal was simple: the government wanted to build residential neighborhoods that would ensure Israeli rule over the recently occupied land. The ramifications, however, were grave: the confiscation resulted in a local and international uproar. Kollek sided with the critics who protested that politicians abused the professional integrity of the master plan in the name of settlements and compromised aesthetics in favor of occupation. In this heated atmosphere, scrutinized by news media worldwide, expectations for the December subcommittee meeting were high.

Two Modernisms Clash

Arthur Kutcher came to Jerusalem in 1969 to work on the CBD plan. At Yale he studied with the renowned architectural historian Vincent Scully, who would write an enthusiastic foreword to his magnificently illustrated 1973 book, *The New Jerusalem*. After graduating from the University of California at Berkeley, he was hired by Halprin to practice in his landscape architecture studio. In Jerusalem he was known as a gifted draftsman and the relentless bad boy of the junior Anglo circle. On the second day of the subcommittee's meeting, it was probably Halprin who invited Kutcher to the private meeting he was to convene that Saturday night to discuss the plans that had just been presented to the committee. Kutcher reported:

> At a hastily called special session, closed to the public, the members of the Committee expressed their feelings about the plans to the Israeli authorities. Most of them were enraged by what they had seen. Some of them wept, others were nearly hysterical, and at least one was taken ill. The officials, who had expected the usual pat on the back given by such convocations of visiting firemen, were completely amazed. It had apparently never occurred to them that anyone would take a town plan so to heart.[33]

To judge by Halprin's comments of that meeting, Pevsner had to calm Zevi, who lost his temper searching the 1968 master plan for some "basic idea" to hold to. Alexander could see "no understanding of how 500,000 to 900,000 people are to live" in United Jerusalem, while Lasdun protested that "there is no approach to change." Sandberg was worried that "the old city has no spiritual base anymore," that its heart "has not been beating for five hundred years," and that building the Jewish Quarter as a slum would fail to bind "spirit . . . to its environment." Luigi Piccinato reminded his peers that

"Roads don't serve a city. They *structure* the city." Kahn aimed for the transcendental, searching for "background which understands spiritual institutions." Invoking Zevi's point he concluded, "What the [?] plan is serving is NOT apparent." Kollek tried to withstand this attack by defending the needs of Jerusalem's inhabitants, advocating tolerance, and desperately focusing on the city's image and spirit. Obviously, this unequivocal rejection of the plan devastated and confused him and his fellow Israeli hosts.[34]

According to the *Jerusalem Post* in the following days, "The foreign critics were not wielding a scalpel on the master plan, but a guillotine."[35] Surprisingly, their criticism addressed neither the internationally contested designation of Jerusalem as a unified Israeli capital nor the public's frustration with the implications of the government's land confiscation. Identifying the malaise of modernist urbanism in the plan, the critique turned into a trial against the imposition of the Zionist modernist blueprint on the city of Jerusalem and its ancient, universal image.

The international committee's unanimous assessment was that the master plan had "no vision, spirit, theme, or character." "We were not given a clue to an aspiration," Louis Kahn protested. "We were given a problem analysis."[36] The plan's method of solving Jerusalem's physical problems evoked the subcommittee's worst fears: the demise of architecture in the face of scientific and administrative operations. Discussions were saturated with anxiety over the prospect of turning Jerusalem "into a modern, International Style *ville radieuse*—skyscrapers, massive housing projects, freeway spaghetti, and all."[37] Journalist Amos Elon suggested that the proposed road system would turn ancient Jerusalem into a "gas station sacred to the three religions."[38]

In retrospect, the conflict seems inevitable: the international committee, acting on behalf of world cultures, took upon itself the mandate of protecting the city from the specter of modernization, which threatened Jerusalem in particular because of its political importance.[39] Israelis, for their part, were not thrilled to live like cultural relics.[40] Kollek's protest, not surprisingly, was blunt: "You would like to drive up in big cars but you want us in Jerusalem riding on donkeys. No matter how charming and picturesque that might be, the rest of the world forges ahead into the twenty-first century."[41] Given these contradictory pressures, how was such a city to develop?

The debate went far beyond the search for a correct planning procedure. The subcommittee's deliberations brought to a head the divisions between the developmental and situated modernisms at the heart of this study, together with the cultural and political baggage they carried. On the one hand were modernizers, primarily architects and bureaucrats and planners who worked for municipal and state agencies, who followed the logic of progress and development, the famed bedrock of Zionist planning.[42] Their position demanded comfort and efficiency for every resident who lived within the bounded city (as defined by the 1968 master plan), without dealing with the complicated issues of national divisions. On the other hand were a diverse group of modernists who were the vocal center of the Jerusalem Committee and united around their criticism of the modern movement in architecture and the ways that "modernization projects" co-opted their discipline.[43] Their call for monumental, regionally appropriate architecture would be aimed to spatially realize the idea of Jerusalem as a spiritual center. The competition between these developmental and situated modernisms affected everything from democracy to religion, from Orientalism to nation-building ideologies.[44] Laid bare in these debates was one of the era's most pressing questions: Whose history, religion, and nationality would the built landscape of modern Jerusalem materialize?

Like many postcolonial states, Israel endorsed the high modernism that prevailed after World War II. Its planning agencies extended the rather crafted modernism of the Mandate period into a larger, infrastructural, and mass-produced scale that accorded with the national aspiration for progress and development. The *1968 Jerusalem Masterplan* remained faithful to this developmental logic; by contrast, this modernist logic was gradually losing its appeal over the course of this decade and across much of the world. Consider, for example, the criticism that Mumford included in his letter to Kollek on the master plan's most precious merit—its rational, scientific method.

> Let me point to a basic fallacy which this plan shared with too many other contemporary plans: the fallacy of extrapolation. This pseudo-scientific practice consists of taking accurate statistical evidence based on past events as a rational guide to the future. Except in dealing with the briefest time span, say five or ten years, that practice cannot be justified: the future so defined is not the real future at all, but an accelerated and amplified past.[45]

This was a serious accusation. Mumford rendered the progressive, scientific promise to better the lives of people as a mere rehearsal of existing modern procedures.

In all likelihood, the only thing that Mumford and the other critics fully shared was a common enemy: institutional, modernist urban planning, as embodied in the urban renewal schemes spreading from Sweden to Brazil. Just as the now-dominant Team 10 had crucified the ideals of the older CIAM, so too did the subcommittee's architects identify the *1968 Jerusalem Masterplan* as an institutional enemy and excoriated its ideology and methodology. In order to redeem the alienating and dull modernist urbanity that such planning produced, architects turned their back to the discipline of architecture, trying to restore its autonomous values. They gradually lifted the modernist ban on revisiting past traditions and started looking at history, the vernacular, and nature to find authoritative architectural guidelines for situating modernism between people and their places.[46]

After advocates of modernist architecture had so vehemently disparaged the traditional design practices of the profession, architects could finally enjoy, as Denys Lasdun put it, a "physical awakening." Louis Kahn led the return to "Architecture as it has always been" by eclipsing formal precedents in favor of timeless architectural principles, such as "our relations to earth, sky, fire and water; the myriad ways of defining space and controlling light, of relating materials and structure to all these elements, of establishing systems of order (including disorder)."[47] Architects sought similarly timeless rules in vernacular traditions that were dictated primarily by instincts regarding habitation rather than by rational planning.[48] Instead of creating rational, artificial urban areas, Christopher Alexander, for example, suggested emulating the stratification and inconsistent built patterns of older cities.[49]

The committee therefore contended that since it was impossible to deny the weight of the aesthetic and spiritual qualities of Jerusalem, the knowledge for its growth had to be sought within the discipline of architecture. The architectural critic Wolf von Eckardt stressed that architects working in Jerusalem required unique skills for translating "poetic-subjective experiences such as sacredness, charm and mystery into architectural design terminology of stone, concrete and asphalt."[50] Christopher Alexander insisted that the "answer to how one makes this a religious city should be present in the morphology of the existing plan."[51]

In his summary of the December meeting, Kollek highlighted the panel Louis Kahn had chaired on the theme of Jerusalem: "The participants insisted that there must be a 'rapport' between building materials and design, between streets and houses, between mountains and valleys and the buildings on them. They called for an integrated concept of planning which would include the buildings, roads, sound, visual aspect and quality of the city."[52] It was a very clear call to move from two-dimensional planning to three-dimensional architecture, from rational management of the city to integrated design. Khan, who led the discussion, thought it was the only possible way to touch the very core of the controversy. "Jerusalem," he adamantly concluded, "deserved the aura of the unmeasurable."[53]

Orientalism and Spirituality in Brick and Mortar

Statements such as Kahn's reveal the cultural and ideological convictions that churned beneath the professional concerns of the Jerusalem Committee. When Israel turned to the West's international elite—and thus to the dominance of Christian cultures—for legitimization, the ramifications were significant. Recruiting international architects also meant recruiting their values, though Mayor Kollek may not have intended such a domino effect. Just as committee members brought to Jerusalem their own ideological battles around architectural modernism, they also brought their own religious and cultural preconceptions about what Jerusalem should look like.

The beliefs of the committee members, as vehement as they were professionally disguised, complicated the mayor's decision to hold the values of all three monotheistic faiths equal. Jewish tradition was known for its distrust in visual expression, a trait that played to the hand of Fascists who identified its inclination toward abstract form with degenerate art, often considering various practices of the interwar avant-garde a Jewish conspiracy. This entrenched Jewish tradition guided the political leaders of orthodox Zionism at the time. But Judaism's encounter with modern nationalism, and moreover, with the newly occupied territories, provoked significant modification of Jewish traditions that are passionately debated today.[54]

The committee's deliberation of the Islamic practices in Jerusalem was obviously much more complicated. Muslims declined to participate in the Jerusalem Committee in order to avoid legitimizing Israeli rule over Jerusalem. In their absence, Kollek solicited other experts on the subject of Islam. During the 1975 plenary session of the Jerusalem Committee, for example, Bernard Lewis, the renowned Orientalist scholar, conducted the session on Jerusalem as a center for three religions. After scholars presented Judaism and Christianity, Lewis explained that circumstances had prevented the desired presentation of Islam by a Muslim. Turning instead to Jewish scholars of Islam, he concluded: "It is therefore a great tradition of detached, objective, and sympathetic scholarship that the school of Islamic Studies in the [Hebrew] university in this city builds, and it is from this university that we draw our pseudo- or crypto-Mufti for this evening."[55] To suggest that an academic Orientalist can articulate an authorized Islamic position implies a view of Islam as a religious abstraction, which ignores its inextricable links to the political force of the Arab states and the Palestinian residents who claimed Jerusalem.

In his seminal work *Orientalism*, published just three years after this plenary meeting, Edward Said attacked this kind of "detached, objective" scholarship of "crypto-Mufti[s]." That Lewis, Said's most eminent scholarly rival, was one of the consultants protecting the interest of Islam attests to the shortcomings of this endeavor.[56] The result was a monotheistic world, minus its Muslim contingent. It consisted of Jews and Christians, whose respective international power was grossly disproportionate to each other and to that of Muslims. As a result of this arrangement, Israel was expected to accept the West's centuries-old idea of Jerusalem as a spiritual site of (Christian) pilgrimage, while the daily needs of the country's Muslims (and Palestinians in general) were largely brushed aside.

The marriage of the West's centuries-old image of Jerusalem with the new field of urban planning had begun with the British Mandate. For the British, Jerusalem was a sacred trust, "the City of an *idea* that needs as such to be protected" (Figure 5.9).[57] This idea of Jerusalem rested on a long tradition of Orientalist depictions of Jerusalem, the essence of which, according to Daniel Monk, is "an *imaginary* realm of archaic plentitude."[58] What the British intended to restore was not the Jerusalem they encountered—an Ottoman city coming to grips with modernity—but rather the Jerusalem they anticipated: the authentic, biblical city that featured in the Orientalist texts and visual representations they had mastered in Europe. British plans were therefore a means toward stabilizing the Orientalist image of Jerusalem, and tools of modern planning were used to highlight the urban features that fit this image while halting any development that risked the city's wishful authenticity.

The British approach extended from landscapes and vistas to the last masonry detail of what Ron Fuchs has termed "colonial regionalism."[59] As a result, their style relied heavily on the Palestinian vernacular, which they documented, preserved, and carefully guarded. Aiming to preserve and sustain, rather than to radically reform, this colonial regionalism was obviously incompatible with the Zionist movement. With Israeli independence in 1948, the country's first wave of Zionist architects sought to reform the British approach, insisting that any Palestinian architectural heritage was only a shabby background against which efficient and hygienic Zionist building could be shown to its greatest advantage.[60]

The architectural team that authored the master plan inherited this Zionist position. Geared toward convenience and efficiency, they prioritized the symbolic function of Jerusalem as the capital of Israel and its operation as a contemporary city.[61] The Israeli team compared the Jerusalem Committee's criticism with the old British colonial attitudes. In particular, they dismissed what they considered to be an irrelevant enthusiasm with the exotic Orient.[62] How, they wondered, could Israelis prefer insignificant Ottoman edifices over the civic symbols of the unified capital? Identifying edifices such as the city walls as "Ottoman"—a four-hundred-year-old ruling culture that Zionists considered decadent—divested the powerful image of "the walled city" of its potency.

Advocating a vibrant CBD, a massive transportation infrastructure, and a dense modernist city with identifiable urban boundaries, the drafters of the plan prioritized Jerusalem's civic values over its religious overtones. They viewed criticism of the plan and its values as emanating from the cultural disposition of their international critics: the latter represented the Christian

Figure 5.9. Henry Kendall, "The Approaches to Jerusalem." Source: Henry Kendall, *Jerusalem, the City Plan: Preservation and Development during the British Mandate, 1918-1948* (London: His Majesty's Stationery Office, 1948), 9.

aspiration for Jerusalem, a heavenly Jerusalem on Earth.[63] The Israeli planners dismissed such an ideal as emotional naïveté, an untenable aspiration that prevented foreign critics from recognizing Jerusalem's needs as a contemporary city. Thus, they argued in favor of an option that recognized the spiritual value of everyday life, which has to exist by moral vow. This value overcomes the value of the naive urge to tie spiritual life with external material expressions.[64]

Intriguingly, by defending their master plan with "the spirit of the Torah which emanated from Jerusalem,"[65] they married their choice of modernist planning to the Jewish mistrust of visual monumentality and its emphasis on the sacredness of the everyday. In doing so, they also articulated a particular connection between the Jewish religion and the Israeli state. Israeli nationalism, they argued, did not require visual symbols or material representation. Its raison d'être and legitimization was rooted instead in the significance of ordinary people and their human deeds.

Israeli developmental planners thus mobilized a powerful strategy: they divested the committee's criticism of a desirable universality by locating its arguments in a specifically Western, and inherently colonial, cultural context. They presented the critics' desire to design a townscape of Oriental beauty as idolatry, a naive approach that would undermine the tenets of the Jewish religion.

In hindsight their criticism accords with the writings of W. J. T. Mitchell, who warns us that the overburdened landscape they refused to sanctify risks becoming "a magical object, an idol that demands human sacrifices, a place where symbolic, imaginary, and real violence implode on an actual social space."[66] Both Mitchell and Daniel Monk have demonstrated the immense power of aesthetics to escalate political conflicts, particularly in Jerusalem.[67] Their criticism points to the danger in solidifying nationalism and imperialism alike in both sanctified landscapes and poetic geographies. The Jerusalem Committee's investment in this aesthetic power helped transform the urban landscape of post-1967 Jerusalem. By objecting to its premise, the master plan's authors aligned themselves instead not only with the values of Judaism but, more urgently, with those of the Israeli state.

Civic Rule versus Religious Faith

The proper balance between religious and civic authority is, of course, always a weighty question. Urban planning is no exception. In an earlier forum Yoseph Schweid, one of the 1968 plan's principal authors, stated that he and his colleagues were following the values upon which the Israeli state was founded.[68] By contrast, the Italian Bruno Zevi, an influential proponent of Organic Architecture, a politician, and a zealous Zionist, insisted during the 1970 meeting that the "present plan [is] an instrument against Israel. Jerusalem is something more than people living there."[69] He thundered, "This is collective hara-kiri. Everybody has abdicated. There has been no effort to have a new vision of life."[70] At the end of the session Louis Kahn chaired during the 1970 meeting, its participants, in front of the entire subcommittee, their Israeli hosts, and the press, declared the necessity of having a theme for the city, a theme that should concentrate (in this order) on Jerusalem as religious center, learning center, national capital, and regional center.[71] In one sentence Kahn reversed the entire value system of the Israeli master plan: the national capital was no longer the prime objective, only the third in a list of four, with the religious center clearly at the top.

Kahn's reversal of the master plan's contested priorities highlights the tension between the different parties claiming Jerusalem. The international invitees, as well as their Israeli hosts, constantly referred to the city's religious groups—Christians, Muslims, and Jews—rather than to the political actors involved: the international community, Jordanians (to be later replaced by Palestinians), and Israelis. In so doing they subsumed the national conflict over sovereignty within a pacifying spiritual realm of shared monotheism. Limiting themselves to their architectural and urban expertise, which would help embody such spirituality, the invitees felt greater urgency to criticize their own discipline, architecture and urban planning, rather than challenging the greater political complexities of the place in which they wished to implement their revised modernism. As a result they ignored political tensions in favor of the architectural and aesthetic implications of beautification.

This architectural bias was particularly conspicuous in the subcommittee's criticism of the master plan's dual core proposition. The master plan proposed to focus the inner city on two cores: a civic center in West Jerusalem and historical-religious center around the Old City in East Jerusalem. The international committee objected to this split. A modernist capital could exist anywhere, the visiting architects thought, and the significance of Jerusalem, as Zevi protested, eclipsed the mere well-being of its residents. A spiritual center of such magnitude and beauty, they argued, had to emanate from the core of the Old City outward in order to achieve a unified image of civil and spiritual coherence. In their fervor they ignored the political difficulties of such a proposition. Religious sites were overburdened with the symbolic power of the state, thus imposing on an already contested site a problematic mesh of religious and state power.

For example, the proposed plan for a Central Boulevard was one of the committee's favorite targets for criticism. The boulevard ran from Mount Scopus to the national cemetery and memorial on Mount Herzl, threading through two academic campuses, the city center, and the Government Precinct. Since the boulevard connected the most important civil institutions and national monuments of Israel, Israeli planners envisioned the road as an urban statement expressing the role of Jerusalem as the capital of their state. For Lewis Mumford, the boulevard, wide enough to hold military parades, indicated that "the municipal authorities have been faithfully carrying out their assigned duties in the spirit of Baron Haussmann, without realizing that it is to Isaiah that they must look for guidance."[72] Isaiah, the biblical prophet whose loving vision of Jerusalem Mumford contrasted to Haussmann's Paris, suddenly emerged within the committee as the great hero of Jerusalem in its post-1967 incarnation.[73] Yet the plan's authors specifically shied away from this kind of ethno-religious symbolism. By proposing the Central Boulevard as a thread linking the civil centers of the state, they created a potential dialogue between the symbolism of the Israeli state and their understanding of Jewish faith as an abstract religion based on human deed.

The representational demands of the international committee caused it to overlook this important democratic distinction between religion and state. In 1970 the other nation claiming Jerusalem was Jordan, whose capital of Amman was forty-three miles away. Once Jordan withdrew its claims to Jerusalem in 1988, the international community could no longer ignore the Palestinians' demand to make Jerusalem their national capital. A separation between state and faith would confine Jerusalem's symbolic core to religious practices, thus encouraging both the Israeli and Palestinian states to develop their national institutions separately in East and West Jerusalem while sharing the same symbolic nucleus. Instead, the present reality is far more problematic.

According to the committee, a unified religious and civil nucleus was needed in order to secure a timeless vision for the city. This vision should be based, the committee argued, on Jerusalem's spiritual and educational qualities — that is, on religious and historical motifs. The demand to thematize Jerusalem, of course, was rife with complexities. Residents, tourists, and pilgrims had to grasp such a theme, or narrative, by means of spatial configurations and visual imagery. But whose narrative should Jerusalem's image represent? For committee members the correct answer was the universal narrative of the three monotheistic religions. Only an international audience could determine that universal narrative; this was exactly the reason they undertook the responsibility of participating in this specialized advisory committee. But as we explore the committee's work, does its pure professionalism start to look more and more like a distinct form of international — that is, Euro-American — cultural politics?

"Planning for the Spirit and Character of Jerusalem"

The subcommittee's resolutions in 1970 were far-reaching, anticipating a paragon of urban planning:

> What the plan calls for are principles of physical order, a set of planning guidelines so firm that they will directly generate the plan of a great city as it evolves, and so well grounded in functional, social, economic, emotional and symbolic issues that agreement of them may gradually be reached.[74]

Could Jerusalem's urban laboratory develop according to such ambitious guidelines? Apparently, Professor Haar and architects Halprin and Fuller, who reported in 1971 from Jerusalem to committee members worldwide, were thrilled with the municipal response to the committee's demands. The Urban Planning Unit had already been created shortly after the committee meeting. Kollek also solicited advice from the Greater London Council, whose chief planner came to help set planning procedures in Jerusalem. In August 1971, Meron Benvenisti, the most influential official in Kollek's administration, was on his way to London to find a chief planner for Jerusalem. As a result, Nathaniel Lichfield was hired a few months later.

Lichfield was a pivotal urban and environmental planner in Britain, and played a key role in the development of the 1960s New Towns, long admired in Israel. He was exactly what the committee, and the Anglo circle, had wished for: renowned and accomplished, well versed in contemporary discourse, and speaking an architectural language the committee wished to hear. Although he was not an architect by training, his leadership made the 1973 second plenary meeting of the Jerusalem Committee a smooth ride in comparison to the dramatic subcommittee meeting in 1970 and the plenary meeting that would follow in 1975.

Lichfield believed that "to people around the world Jerusalem *is* the Old City," and that it is not only the "900 metre square abounded by magnificent walls" that spark "the historical associations of 3000 years," but "the huge natural bowl within which it lies on twin hills."[75] In the documents he circulated to the Jerusalem Committee in preparation for its second plenary meeting in 1973, he therefore sided with the position of his addressees. He tried to mediate between the idea of Jerusalem and its modern urban context, a challenge that drove him to articulate the evasive yet central concept that he termed the "spirit and character" of Jerusalem. In his view this spirit and character "must be respected, treasured and protected if the development of the city is to live up to the expectations that the world has of it."[76]

In order to address this momentous mandate, Lichfield challenged architects to link emotional urban experience to brick and mortar, the very same pairing that had enraged the developmental modernists who authored the 1968 master plan. To counter their opposition, Lichfield carefully and methodically tied form, space, and materials on the one hand with living patterns and spiritual practices on the other. Jerusalem's spirit and character, he argued, was a combination of four interrelated ingredients: first was "the endowment of nature," from topography and "peering stone" to "cloudlessly blue sky" and "special light"; second, the relationship between the "built environment" of succeeding occupying cultures and nature, the scale, layout, and materials of historical monuments and settlements; third, the spirituality of Jerusalem, symbolizing "a way of life which transcends the ordinary";

and finally, the division of the city between Israel and Jordan as independent countries.[77]

It was this final aspect that seemed to compel Lichfield the most:

> Since 1967 the unity of Jerusalem in a hostile world has thrown on it both the focus of dissent and also the hopes for a peaceful co-existence of formerly and presently divided people. The spiritual yearning which Jerusalem has offered in the past has now been transformed into a spiritual yearning for a peaceful future for mankind.[78]

Such statements played on the most pertinent ethno-religious concerns of many committee members, and even grappled with the potential violence of urban planning alluded to by Mumford. Like committee members, Lichfield believed that the city was a potential "meeting place for Jews and Arabs," and that as such it could foreshadow a different era in world politics.

The question was how to project these vast and diffuse goals onto the urban landscape and integrate them into its physical planning. The answer, Lichfield suggested, lay in the city's topography and spatial form. He was convinced that it was not only the central location that "drew King David to found his City there, but also the magic natural qualities." He therefore qualified his former definitions with another list of physical merits. First, he asserted, "Zion could hardly have existed on a flat featureless plain in a poor climate." Second, the city's geographical and built diversity leads to "strong contrasts . . . within minutes driving time": standing nearly side by side are human history and the bare desert, primitive quarters and modern residences, open mountains and forests. Third are the city's "strong boundary definitions, strong edges" of rather separated neighborhoods and discontinuous built patterns. When approaching the city, "within a matter of meters a different picture is seen from a moving windscreen."

Lichfield argued that these "special qualities and the people to whom they matter" must be taken into account when "Planning for the Spirit and Character of Jerusalem."[79] The committee members could not have accepted his observations with greater enthusiasm. At least one of them, Nikolaus Pevsner, must have been delighted to find a faithful depiction of, and commitment to, the picturesque sensibilities in the documents prepared by Lichfield. According to Pevsner these qualities betray, as the title of his seminal BBC lecture indicates, "The Englishness of English Art."[80] Lichfield's document thus secured the persistence of the British colonial legacy in Jerusalem.

During the following year, Lichfield developed his observations into planning principles for the city, which accommodated the diverse trends of contemporary situated modernism. New approaches in preservation, landscape architecture, and the townscape sensibilities that guided the method of "design by planning" were most conspicuous. Lichfield called for "a large measure of preservation and protection," even rehabilitation of entire quarters and "occupation of the structures which is needed in order to maintain them." He treated landscape design as a functional necessity, including not only parks, but such open spaces as "a new setting for the Western Wall" or "the setting for exposed archeological digs." He demanded that contemporary planning respect the appeal of the terrain's "bareness from vegetation" and suggested carefully designing the limited number of approaches to the city in order to induce the feeling of "going up to Jerusalem."[81] Eventually he implied that such an approach may be conducive for a new extensive development away from the Old City.

Crucial to Lichfield's success was his restraint and delicacy; he advanced his situated modernism, and countered the developmental practices of the Israeli planners, with British manners.[82] The ongoing conflict with developmental modernists assumed a different tone in the writings of Arthur Kutcher, one of the Anglo circle rebels who founded the Urban Planning Unit in the Jerusalem Municipality. Kutcher adamantly ties developmental modernism to the crisis of the modernist city, arguing that under "the blazing and merciless light of the Jerusalem sun, one sees with stabbing clarity what in other places is still blurred: the moral and stylistic bankruptcy of modern architecture, and the suicidal impulses of contemporary town planning, 'trend planning,' 'accommodating pressures,' like a physician accommodating disease."[83] Significantly, Kutcher's text ties "modern architecture" to contemporary "city planning," in what turns out to be a partnership with dire consequences. In so doing, he points to a tension between architecture and planning that had been growing for over a decade.[84]

Critics of planning anchored their demands by focusing their attention on the urban place. Instead of planning the city for the sake of efficiency, order, hygiene, and profit, it should be a locus of formal, spatial, and social identity that was believed to induce a feeling of belonging and social connectedness between different people and their urban environment. This new focus called for new skills, which were rooted in design methodology.[85]

Architects understood why developers found architecture wanting in the postwar quest to revise and improve urban forms, but they insisted that its methodologies still possess the authority needed to better urban life. Leading professionals increasingly marshaled urban design rather than policy as a means to heal cities. Institutional recognition followed: in 1956, José-Louis Sert convened the first urban design conference at Harvard's Graduate School of Design (GSD).[86] A couple of years later Paul Rudolph, then the dean of Yale School of Architecture and during the 1970s one of the designers of the

Hyatt Jerusalem, explained the reasons for such innovation: "The public is confused as never before about the exact function of an architect, for we have gone through a long period where the specialists talked only of social responsibility, techniques, economy and the architect as a coordinator. We have even apologized for being concerned with visual design."[87] This situation prompted Sert to establish in 1960 the first North American urban design program, where students could examine the impact of design methodologies on cities.[88] Teaching at neighboring MIT, Kevin Lynch understood cities as the social units of civilization, possessing size, density, grant, outline, pattern, insisting that people shape them and are shaped by them.[89] Denys Lasdun, who would play a major role in the next plenary meeting of the Jerusalem Committee, invoked Lynch in order to distinguish between the tangible and organizational modes of urban planning, clarifying that "planners and architects need to understand each other's disciplines and not try to do each other's work."[90] If, as Safdie would claim, city planners were not comfortable with "the architects' world of visual and aesthetic determinants for the manipulations of space, land and their organization,"[91] a new professional then had to assume responsibility not just for creating buildings but for conceiving whole cities as well. The necessity of merging site and city, of the specificity of architectural design within the expanse of the urban landscape, demanded a new subdiscipline. The field of urban design answered that need.

In light of planning's growing power, architects wished to institutionalize this distinction. In 1970, the Royal Institute of British Architects proclaimed urban design as a specialized field. In 1973, the American Institute of Architects followed suit.[92] Clearly, these institutions intended to counter the developmental modernism of post–World War II planners and developers who, according to Safdie, had spent billions of dollars on "urban renewal in one of the most ambitious face-lifting efforts in history." When Safdie became the director of the GSD urban design program in 1978, he not surprisingly returned to Jerusalem, calling it "one of the most fascinating laboratories of urban development,"[93] reiterating the reason architects so willingly came there to debate the future of urban design.

Form and Beauty: Debating Urban Design in Jerusalem

Preparations for the third plenary meeting in December 1975 were tense. The 1973 war erupted just four months after the previous plenary meeting of the Jerusalem Committee, clouding the euphoria around United Jerusalem. Even the cultural mandate of the Jerusalem Committee was undermined: shortly before Kollek's invitees gathered in Jerusalem, UNESCO condemned Israel "for its attitude . . . in altering the historical features of the City of Jerusalem and by undertaking excavations which constitute a danger to its monument, subsequent to its illegal occupation of this city."[94] Now, the committee had to prove that its mandate was more professional, universal, and culturally attuned than the UN.

Kollek was also troubled by changes in the municipal planning administration: Nathaniel Lichfield promised that he would address the committee's demand to complement "the more analytic studies of land-use" with "proposals for architecture and urban design," and to avoid any planning decision that does not take into account "this visual creativity" and "sense of form."[95] But when the committee next returned to Jerusalem, Lichfield was no longer there. The attempt to impose an external authority—a familiar international figure the committee could trust—created tension with officials in the existing administration. Lichfield's marriage to an Israeli helped to get him hired but was not enough to keep him in his post. After two years in office, and clashes with the city engineer who was not happy to partially relinquish his authority, Lichfield returned to England.

In his absence Meron Benvenisti, Jerusalem's deputy mayor for planning, assumed leadership over the third plenary meeting.[96] This change cast the ongoing controversy between architects and politicians in the most explicit terms possible: a contest to see whether architects or administrators would ultimately determine the physical image of Jerusalem. During this third plenary meeting, three members (architects Denys Lasdun, Lawrence Halprin, and Jacob Bakema) met with Benvenisti's city officials in what turned out to be a very telling moment in the history of urban design.

Benvenisti began the meeting by presenting the municipality's planning philosophy. As a native Jerusalemite, a student of history, and the son of a legendary Israeli geographer, Benvenisti believed he had all the qualities needed to transform Jerusalem—this, in fact, was why he had been elected. Architects, he contended, might define aesthetic values but were incapable of balancing the urban elements necessary to ensure the inhabitants' quality of life. Committee member Sixto Durán Ballén, who was the mayor of Quito and an architect by profession, supported this cause. "We architects," he confessed, "are forgetting that we are only tools, as [are] doctors in regard to sickness or as lawyers in regard to lawsuits."[97] Benvenisti insisted it was the task of the politician, rather than the professional, to achieve compromises among the various loci of city planning, such as transportation, sanitation, or design. "The way I see the city of Jerusalem in the future," he asserted, "is based on *my personal values.* . . . I don't think that you study that in the university or in a technical institute."[98]

The problems began almost immediately after his presentation. Planning is political, admitted the architects, and is indeed the politician's domain.

Lasdun, Halprin, and Bakema presented a united front against Benvenisti and urged him and the other politicians at the meeting not to confuse planning with urban design. "As I understand it," Lawrence Halprin complained, "there is no guidance on an aesthetic, three-dimensional basis of what should be happening in the town of Jerusalem. Now that is . . . what I would call 'urban design,' the gluing of things together."[99] Thus a conflict developed: Benvenisti cast himself in the role of urban coordinator, seeing in it the authority to impose a value system on the built environment; the architects wanted that same role in order to control the gluing together of different aspects of the city. To win their case, the architects distinguished between administrative and spatial coordination, the latter representing their domain, their set of values, and their hard-won knowledge from "the university or [the] technical institute."

The architects clarified their demand: to control urban connectedness via specifications they each prescribed for their preferred models. They relied on the Jerusalem Committee's verdict that a three-dimensional vision for the city could be developed only by replacing the main operative tool from the conventional two-dimensional, schematically colored, land-use plans to a three-dimensional scale model of the city.[100] In an essay Halprin wrote that year on "The Use and Misuse of Plans," he clarifies the underlying logic of his demand:

> The tyranny of the two-dimensional form imposes the medium of one art form on another. The essential qualities of environments, whether they are urban or natural, have to do with three-dimensional qualities, undefined spaces, hardness and softness, changing qualities of light, translucent color, forms lacking definition, change over time. What is perhaps most important is that we perceive them from inside, not from outside (except on the limited occasions when we are flying). We walk in and through them. They have sequence, and change is an essential ingredient.[101]

Only through models, they argued, could they study the relationship within these environments between buildings, streets, built fabrics, and fragments of the urban landscape in order to glue them together. For Lasdun, the in-between glue was infrastructure; for Bakema, the in-betweenness was primarily social. It confirmed the process of growth and communication between people and communities.

Bakema, a senior member of Team 10, focused on cities and the ways architecture could restructure commercial and residential quarters. His neighborhood units were conceived as visual groups, enhancing a sense of belonging among residents (Figure 5.10). In existing and prospective neighborhoods, Bakema focused on urban connectors. He stressed their importance in Jeru-

Figure 5.10. Jaap Bakema, "Transitional Elements," sketch, 1961. Source: Collection Het Nieuwe Instituut; archive code BAKE, inventory number 42.

salem, where planners had to better understand Jerusalem's unique communal mosaic of social backgrounds and lifestyles.[102] Clearly, the visions of Lasdun, Halprin, and Bakema were quite different from Benvenisti's.

Lasdun wanted a guarantee that municipal authorities would not confuse the production of particular architectural projects with the overall urban spatial coordination he advocated. He pointed out an important methodological change: architects' traditional models, prepared to design or supervise buildings, were missing the point. He therefore cautioned, "If you set about making a model which shows the plastic nature of the building, the windows, the stone work, the shape of the building, then you are wasting money and wasting time."[103] An urban model was needed instead, one that captured the spatial relationships among buildings in their urban setting. He insisted that "what we are talking about . . . are the spaces in between—and space is a language of architecture; it is trans-national and stands outside time."[104] In other words, Lasdun demanded that Israel's politicians accept the fact that a professional principle could overrule a political or administrative one because of its indisputable universality.

In hindsight, Halprin wrote Kollek a few days after the meeting, the concerted focus on the model might have been too narrow. The meeting as a whole, he felt, was less satisfying than before, maybe, he suggested, because the UNESCO cloud was too heavy. He complained about too many projects and too little coordination, and directed his outrage at the politicians, writing:

we were told that the "politicians are planning Jerusalem, *NOT* a professional" & that the politicians who are planning Jerusalem "can face you with a clear conscience & we are not ashamed of what we are doing." This left me (& I think others as well) uneasy & confused as to how to make any positive input.

Halprin felt they "were there simply to be informed" and that their "input was both useless & not desired."[105] He therefore asked Kollek to expose the committee to the larger planning community in Israel, suggesting the Ministries of Interior Affairs and Housing as a powerhouse of decision making and therefore as appropriate addressees.

The official resolution of the meeting did not shy away from promoting the discipline's set of values against those of national and municipal agencies, explaining:

> While recognizing that final responsibility for municipal planning decisions must appropriately lie in the hands of those concerned with the totality of facets involved, namely the Jerusalem administrative authority, the Committee stresses the immense importance of the aesthetic and technical contribution of a Chief City Planner, without whom the planning process can be seriously impaired.

Kollek took this criticism to heart. Two years after the meeting he hired Amnon Niv to serve as the city engineer. Niv was a designer with a 6B lead pencil at the tip of his fingers, the charismatic architect Kollek sought. In 1978 he launched his tenure with the fourth plenary meeting of the Jerusalem Committee. At the same time he started building the Jerusalem Model the committee demanded with students at the Technion.

Niv was a situated modernist of the Israeli school. He was trained at the Technion and was the chief architect of Israel's nuclear plant in Dimona. Although not a member of the sabra circle, he was closer to their agenda than he was to the planning ideology of the Anglo circle. In the twilight of his life Niv lamented two people he admired but lost as the result of his role as city engineer. One was Safdie, who never forgave Niv his criticism of Safdie's Mamilla project. Niv attributed the second, more complicated loss to Kollek's personalized working relationship: once he turned into Kollek's closest advisor instead of Meron Benvenisti, both Niv and Jerusalem lost one of their most daring and sharp-minded public servants.[106] After eleven years in office, Niv was succeeded by Ehud Tayar and Elinoar Barzaki, both of whom had previously directed the Jerusalem Region in the Ministry of Housing. Kollek learned his lesson: instead of fighting the ministry, he recruited those who knew its praxis.

According to historian Michael Dumper, the Jerusalem Committee continued to exist after Kollek lost the 1993 election, but its power diminished.[107] Israel Kimhi, a sabra member of the unit and the future head of the Policy Planning Department at the Jerusalem Municipality, argues that eventually, and particularly after the outburst of the Palestinian intifada in 1987, major guidelines of the rejected 1968 master plan resurfaced and shaped a different city. In the early 1970s, however, the subcommittee's demands almost buried the plan before it even got off the ground.

The City against Nationalism

The extraordinary commitment of numerous luminaries to volunteer for Kollek's Jerusalem Committee exemplifies their belief in Jerusalem as a pivotal agent of global change in both political and architectural cultures.[108] Mumford, Fuller, and Kahn were probably the most ardent believers in this potential. Fuller envisioned Jerusalem as the site in which private property would be abolished in anticipation of a postcapitalist era, Kahn aimed to recover in Jerusalem the essence of spiritual institutions common to all people, and Mumford articulated a full-fledged program to launch a postnationalist world order in Jerusalem.

Common to all was a fundamental premise: they believed that only in Jerusalem could one crack open the West's imposing, yet fossilized, cultural and social structures and release the living impulse that enables and sustains human association—the fundamental "inspiration to live," in Kahn's words. Mumford considered modern nationalism the most imposing of these structures, and therefore argued that with all due respect the monumental task of actively operating the "cultural and religious forces" that this city required went far beyond "the province of the municipal authorities." In fact, it "demands for its fulfillment the activation of ideas, institutions, and forces capable of overcoming the irrational factors which make it extremely difficult for both pan-Arab and Orthodox Zionist ideologies to come to terms with existing realities."[109] In other words, for the unification of Jerusalem to overcome the irrationality of national aspirations, it must involve transnational and transtemporal factors.

Mumford therefore drew a single, unequivocal conclusion: "To denationalize and de-politicize Jerusalem is, I submit, the first practical step toward preparing a long-term plan for Jerusalem's future—and the world's." No less. Most striking is Mumford's choice of the adjective "practical" to describe a vision that aims to irreversibly change the current world order. He determinedly proposed:

Jerusalem must become, not a national capital, but a world capital, whose extra-territorial status will be protected and cherished, not by this or that self-appointed military guardian, but by all the peoples of the world—peoples who are sick with longing for the peace and security that the present power structures of national states and expanding empires do not even remotely promise.[110]

Mumford pushed the tension between the city and the state—Jerusalem and Israel—to its radical conclusion: if any city is identified as a holy place by virtue of the "arcane forces and human impulses" that create it, then the transtemporal "religious office" of the city transcends, by definition, the rather recent structure of the nation-state.[111] Accordingly, the city of Jerusalem, the holiest city on earth, must inspire the world to exceed this seemingly entrenched world order—one that has already transgressed its limited historical span. Only in Jerusalem, Mumford concludes, can modern nationalism finally meet its expiration date.

Why should the unification of Jerusalem activate this historical pivot? Because it initially inspired the sacred act of expressing human association in built form. Mumford warned that every city is in constant danger of "erosion, defacement and corruption." The remains of a city's "original vision" are hardly visible "unless each fresh generation renews it." The task of a contemporary plan for Jerusalem is therefore to expose "the very nature of Jerusalem" because in it one can find the potential of transcending "all narrow local and partisan interests." This nature appears in "the structure of the city, its topography, its soil, its ancient walls, its historic sites." He insisted that the very concrete attributes of landscape, architecture, and urban form can "make Jerusalem in its presence and person, a potential source of unity."[112] This is why Mumford considered the act of unifying Jerusalem so crucial: it may prove that a physical space can inspire a society built on shared institutions rather than divisive nationalisms.

For Mumford and Kahn in Jerusalem the institutions of faith and learning must eclipse those of government. Kahn designed the Hurva Synagogue, where people could meet to share their faith, and treated the Northern Slopes of the High Commissioner Hill as a spatial sanctuary from which he proposed to launch a "cultural mile," interlacing institutions of culture and leisure. Mumford's most specific proposition for Jerusalem was a "World University, whose special task would be to offset deep-rooted national and religious particularism by emphasizing the universalism of the scientific method and the fresh outlook of the modern world."[113] Mumford sought to establish this university next to the Hebrew University. Did he know of the similar aspirations that guided its founders? Thirty years earlier Erich Mendelsohn, for example, pleaded to design the campus of the Hebrew University because he believed, like his fellow cultural Zionists, that the cultivation of knowledge in Jerusalem would stimulate the development of a new postnational era in world history.[114]

Mumford's wish to remove Jerusalem from national claims did not take into account the lives and aspirations of the people who actually lived there. These residents' religious and national sentiments were a means of surviving the hardships of the modern era, including the Jewish Holocaust and the Palestinian *Nakba* (disaster). The expectation that Jews would give up the nation's most powerful symbol was far-reaching in its implications. Ignorance of Palestinian residents' particular nationalism, endemic to both the Jerusalem Committee and the Israeli planners and architects, was equally problematic; Palestinian aspirations were discussed instead in the context of an all-embracing and therefore vague pan-Arab nationalism.

Paradoxically, the plan that contained an embryonic concept of national and religious cultures was none other than the *1968 Jerusalem Masterplan* that Mumford so vehemently criticized. The authors of the plan, unlike their situated modernist opponents, wanted to strictly separate state institutions from those of religious faith. They rejected the demand to integrate the image of the Old City onto modern Jerusalem, asking to secure it instead as a site for religious practice, pilgrimage, and tourism, thus aesthetically and functionally distinct from the everyday life and governmental activity of the modern capital. The master plan could have been deployed to relieve religious sites from the burden of possessive nationalism,[115] the kind we see today in military ceremonies by the Western Wall or in national assemblies within al-Haram al-Sharif. Recognizing the national competition over Jerusalem could have advanced the simultaneous growth of an Israeli center in the Government Precinct in West Jerusalem, and a Palestinian one in the institutional compound of Abu Dis in East Jerusalem, both away from the holy sites. But instead, the Jerusalem Committee's fear of excessive modernization, and its desire to impose Jerusalem's sanctity over the city's entire residential area, instigated a wholesale rejection of the plan, thus throwing the baby (the civic features of the plan) out with the bathwater of scientific extrapolation for population growth.

Conclusions

For the renowned invitees of the Jerusalem Committee, particularly the subcommittee of architects and planners that Mayor Teddy Kollek convened in 1970, Jerusalem was an intriguing frontier for a discipline trying to cope with the postwar surge of urban development. Architects worldwide, who struggled in their respective countries with the contemporary crisis of the modernist city, found a new frontier in Jerusalem to counteract timid modernization. Nearly overnight, one of the holiest cities of the world submitted itself to urban renewal, and architects leaped at the opportunity. Jerusalem was laden with contradictions and possibilities. It was ancient and new at the same time — steeped in history yet transformed daily by an industrious project of modernization. The ramifications were clear: Jerusalem was an ideal testing ground, the perfect place to decide the fate of modernist planning and the urban capacity of architectural design. Kollek sent out international invitations to his urban laboratory in order to make Jerusalem a city of mankind, a status that was contingent, he realized, on the appeal of Jerusalem's aesthetic merits to the monotheistic world.

But to whom did Jerusalem belong? Whom should the new plans address? Was it primarily the city of its residents, the capital city of Israel, or the most important spiritual center for the monotheistic world? This debate revealed a tension that is woven throughout this study between developmental and situated modernists.

For the developmental modernists who authored the 1968 master plan, Jerusalem was first and foremost the capital of Israel. As such it should be a modern and efficient city that respects its heritage but is not halted by its past. The plan aimed to establish a connection between the Israeli state and the Jewish religion that was not contingent on visual symbols or material representation. On the contrary, the authors of the plan argued that according to the Jewish tradition these ties are rooted in the significance of the ordinary human deed, amounting to a greater focus on the residents of Jerusalem and the citizens of the state. This position, they insisted, stands in stark contrast to the Christian investment in the visual image and its embodiment in material and form. This argument helped them counter the Jerusalem Committee's harsh criticism: instead of succumbing to the committee's demand to build for "spirit and character," they interpreted the foreign dictate in the context of British colonialism, arguing that the State of Israel rendered such Orientalist attitudes obsolete.

For situated modernists on the international committee, Jerusalem was far more than the people living there, as Bruno Zevi made clear. Lewis Mumford, Louis Kahn, and Buckminster Fuller characterized the opportune moment of Jerusalem's unification as no less than a threshold in world history, in which modern nation-states, Israel included, composed only a thin contemporary layer. They sought in Jerusalem the original inspiration for individuals to form a society, to create cultural and social institutions, or as they put it, the "arcane forces and human impulses" that make a city a holy place. If the foundational impulses that urge people to live together could be channeled, they believed, a new sense of unity would emanate from Jerusalem onto the world. This aspiration figures so strongly in the deliberations of the Subcommittee for Town Planning because its members found this impulse or inspiration in the physical attributes of Jerusalem. Nathaniel Lichfield, the British planner that was hired to lead Jerusalem planning in response to the committee's request, managed to articulate and outline the physical merits that made up Jerusalem's spirituality and thus pacified the committee in its 1973 plenary meeting. Once his short tenure expired, the debate rekindled with a slight shift to the new province of urban design.

The younger generation of the Jerusalem Committee was more modest in its aspirations, aiming at a disciplinary revolution rather than a global one. For them, the 1968 master plan was a prime example of obsolete two-dimensional planning that fails to see the city in its concrete presence, for its space and volume, through its form and material. Their quest to situate planning in the full concreteness of the place required a transition to design methodology on an urban scale, which had just been officially recognized as the subdiscipline of urban design. In this context, Jerusalem became an optimal urban laboratory to test the role of design in defining the relationship between the different components of the city. Only such treatment, they argued, had the capacity to extract from the urban ensemble that desired and evasive character, the intangible dimension that distinguishes one city from another.

During the 1975 meeting of the Jerusalem Committee Jaap Bakema, Denys Lasdun, and Lawrence Halprin argued with Deputy Mayor Meron Benvenisti, stating that the spatial management of the city required professional training and that the values of urban design should guide Benvenisti's administrative urban management. They focused their demands on the construction of a three-dimensional model of the city, which started in 1978 and continues to this day with every proposed project in the Old City precinct and in the city's CBD.

The model is only a small indication of the committee's far-reaching influence. In 1974 Lichfield left Jerusalem, and Ulrik Plesner, a Danish architect, a former partner of the renowned Sri Lanka architect Geoffrey Bawa, and a committee member, was asked to become Jerusalem's chief architect. In a letter to Monica Pidgeon, editor of *Architectural Design* magazine, he reveals how far the municipality was willing to go to accommodate the demands of the Jerusalem Committee.

> In 1970 the Municipality did not plan. It hired a private group of planners who prepared the master plan, which was presented and rejected in 1970. Only after this, in 1971 did the Municipality start its own planning department. . . . Nearly all the energies and emotions of the first two or three years went into reversing the old plan, fighting the big roads and the big buildings, and [then]

determining the problems, starting to solve the most serious ones, etc. — all in less than six years. Most towns I know of have been planning for thirty years or more. And if London and Paris and many other nice towns could have made the same 180 degree turnabout in so few years, then they might have remained the better towns they used to be.[116]

Plesner establishes Jerusalem as a paragon of responsive planning. In hindsight he has a point: the transition from developmental to situated modernism in Jerusalem was strikingly quick.

Assembled by Kollek in response to the criticism of the 1970 meeting, the Urban Planning Unit was instrumental in changing planning priorities in Jerusalem. The high-rise policy it articulated was strictly followed throughout Kollek's tenure as mayor, preservation measures were installed, and highways were rejected. Kollek steadfastly maintained the integrity of the Green Belt around the City Walls, and the Jerusalem Foundation he founded in 1966 financed its chain of gardens (Figure 5.11). A cultural mile was installed, including parks and institutions such as the Sherover Promenade along the ridge of the High Commissioner Hill, a theater in the old Khan building next to the railway station, an artist colony that replaced the evacuated low-income residents of Yemin Moshe, the Cinematheque on the slope of the Hinnom Valley, whose biblical austerity was recovered from underneath a bulldozed rundown neighborhood, and an acoustic shell in the Sultan Pool farther up the valley, overlooking the Tower of David. These and other projects are meticulously integrated into the picturesque landscape of the ridges and valleys enwrapping the Old City.

Kollek's apparatus was central in the patronage over most landscape and cultural projects in this vicinity — from his municipal planning units, to the governmental organization he controlled, to the professionals he favored. Louis Kahn, whom he considered "the Dean of American Architects,"[117] was at the top of this list. The design of the Hurva Synagogue and the Northern Slopes of the High Commissioner Hill with which Kahn was entrusted exemplify this trust. Moshe Safdie and Lawrence Halprin mutually collaborated to garner similar attention from the mayor. Their success is well documented, not only in letters, but more concretely in realized commissions and a prolonged influence on Jerusalem's physical form. At the same time their formidable position in the American profession and academia extended the global impact of the Jerusalem urban lab. Moshe Safdie's decision to turn Jerusalem into the signature city of his tenure as the head of Harvard's Urban Design Department testifies to the pedagogic lesson he believed the city held for international students, who would then return to protect the original character of their home cities.

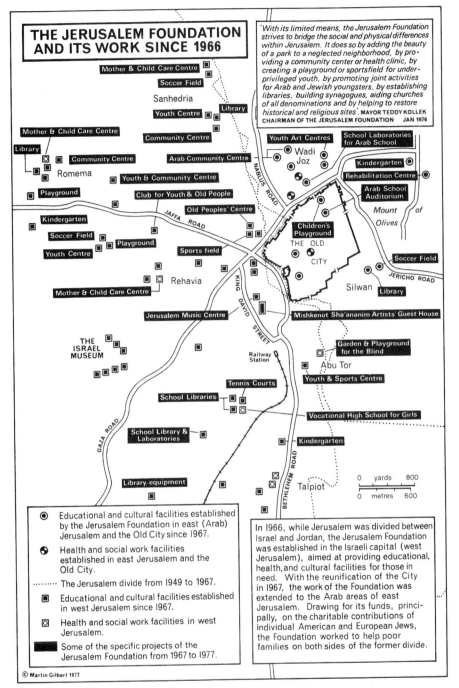

THE JERUSALEM FOUNDATION AND ITS WORK SINCE 1966

'With its limited means, the Jerusalem Foundation strives to bridge the social and physical differences within Jerusalem. It does so by adding the beauty of a park to a neglected neighborhood, by providing a community center or health clinic, by creating a playground or sportsfield for underprivileged youth, by promoting joint activities for Arab and Jewish youngsters, by establishing libraries, building synagogues, aiding churches of all denominations and by helping to restore historical and religious sites'. MAYOR TEDDY KOLLEK CHAIRMAN OF THE JERUSALEM FOUNDATION   JAN 1976

Mother & Child Care Centre
Soccer Field
Sanhedria
Youth Centre
Library
Community Centre
Mother & Child Care Centre
Library
Community Centre
Arab Community Centre
Romema
Youth & Community Centre
Playground
Club for Youth & Old People
Kindergarten
Old Peoples' Centre
Soccer Field
Playground
Youth Centre
Sports field
Rehavia
Mother & Child Care Centre
Jerusalem Music Centre
THE ISRAEL MUSEUM

Youth Art Centres
Wadi Joz
School Laboratories for Arab School
Kindergarten
Rehabilitation Centre
Arab School Auditorium
Mount of Olives
NABLUS ROAD
JAFFA ROAD
Children's Playground
THE OLD CITY
Soccer Field
JERICHO ROAD
Silwan
Library
KING DAVID STREET
Mishkenot Sha'ananim Artists' Guest House
Garden & Playground for the Blind
Railway Station
Abu Tor
Youth & Sports Centre
Tennis Courts
School Libraries
Vocational High School for Girls
GAZA ROAD
School Library & Laboratories
Kindergarten
Library equipment
BETHLEHEM ROAD
Talpiot

0   yards   800
0   metres   600

- ◉ Educational and cultural facilities established by the Jerusalem Foundation in east (Arab) Jerusalem and the Old City since 1967.
- ◕ Health and social work facilities established in east Jerusalem and the Old City.
- ⋯⋯⋯ The Jerusalem divide from 1949 to 1967.
- ▣ Educational and cultural facilities established in west Jerusalem since 1967.
- ◩ Health and social work facilities in west Jerusalem.
- ▬ Some of the specific projects of the Jerusalem Foundation from 1967 to 1977.

In 1966, while Jerusalem was divided between Israel and Jordan, the Jerusalem Foundation was established in the Israeli capital (west Jerusalem), aimed at providing educational, health, and cultural facilities for those in need. With the reunification of the City in 1967, the work of the Foundation was extended to the Arab areas of east Jerusalem. Drawing for its funds, principally, on the charitable contributions of individual American and European Jews, the Foundation worked to help poor families on both sides of the former divide.

© Martin Gilbert 1977

Figure 5.11. Sir Martin Gilbert, "The Jerusalem Foundation and Its Work since 1966." Source: Sir Martin Gilbert, *The Routledge Historical Atlas of Jerusalem* (London: Routledge, 2008); copyright 2008; reprinted by permission of Taylor and Francis Books UK. www.martingilbert.com.

Although the planning community in Jerusalem was split in evaluating the impact of the Jerusalem Committee on Kollek's monumental beautification of Jerusalem, the historical record reveals the extent to which Kollek followed the committee's recommendations and the far-reaching structural changes he was willing to undertake in order to accommodate its demands for situated modernism in Jerusalem. Why was Kollek so attentive to the committee's demands? In retrospect, the new subdiscipline of urban design became a major tool in Jerusalem for articulating spatially an urban meaning that politicians could not achieve politically. By tailoring the visual idea of Jerusalem to the Western world via contemporary urban design and successfully competing with the state for Jerusalem's symbolic resources, Teddy Kollek preserved a measure of autonomy in his municipal politics. Consequently, architectural knowledge became an engine in negotiating the politics of space in Jerusalem, and architects, empowered by the perceived neutrality of their professional knowledge, became important cultural agents separate from official politics.

All the participating parties in our story agreed about the unparalleled importance of Jerusalem, but they differed on two crucial matters: its ultimate purpose, and its rightful owner. The gist of Kollek's cultural politics argued for the renewed status of Jews as the forerunners of monotheistic cultures. His desired custody over Jerusalem was therefore articulated not necessarily in the language of a Jewish "right," but more readily in that of a Jewish "duty." Although he considered Jerusalem a world city, he believed that Israeli Jews should watch over the city and that leaders of his stature would protect it best. This understanding restored to Jews their status as a chosen people, responsible for guarding the very treasure they initially contributed to world culture.

This is exactly why Mumford's letter came as a shock. In his view the centuries-old Jerusalem was too big of an enterprise for the Israeli state alone, one that ventured beyond the historical horizon of Zionism. Its nature, the character it developed over the ages,

> transcends the desperate hopes for re-establishing Zion there that helped Jewry to keep alive during the darkest moments of the Diaspora. Judaism has given Jerusalem to the whole world, and the moment has come to realize this gift must now be validated and sanctified by a plan that will set Jerusalem apart from all the other cities of Israel.[118]

Jews, he implied, have completed their task. They are entitled and encouraged to settle in new modernist towns around the country, but not in Jerusalem, where a world government must take the lead. Mumford was fully aware that his proposal to make Jerusalem into "a new kind of world metropolis" might seem "an attempt to cheat Jewry of its ancient hopes," and admitted that he "felt obliged to remain silent as long as the very existence of Israel was threatened," for fear of justifying the "disruptive aims" of Israel's enemies. His new and firm conviction that "the time for silence has gone by" apparently foreshadowed the more recent advocacy for a post-Zionist state, arguing that once Zionism has completed its historical mission of building a shelter for persecuted Jews, its ideology should be replaced by a commitment to a conventional state belonging to all its citizens.[119]

But, whereas contemporary post-Zionists shied away from religious symbolism, clinging to the abstract definition of democracy, Mumford and other committee members insisted that Jerusalem's planners must enhance its symbolic features. To situate modernism was thus a universal message, as was the beauty of Jerusalem. It belonged to world citizenry rather than to a state that won sovereignty over the city through violence.

But why, according to Mumford, should Israelis agree to retreat from the city they desire? The option should appeal to Israelis because

> once ready to entertain the possibility of such a departure, the leaders of Israel and the planners of Jerusalem would find as their allies and collaborators the best minds in every country—including, it seems reasonable to hope, the genuine leaders of through [sic] in Arab and other Moslem countries.[120]

Mumford left the main question open: Who is in charge and how can one reach this desirable consent of Arab leaders? What is the nature of this alliance, and where does power reside?

Paradoxically, it was Archbishop George Appleton who addressed this question in a spirit much closer to Kollek's strategic goals. His plenary address to the Jerusalem Committee in 1973 was a challenge to Jews:

> the treatment of Jerusalem will decide, I believe, whether the Jewish people are faithful to their divine calling. . . . To be a chosen nation with a particularity of vocation is a tremendous calling. It's a tremendous burden and there are many of us in the Christian Church and, I'm sure, among devout Mouslems, who would like to be their friends and partners in this great task. . . . God grant that later generations may not weep over the city which we pass over to them.[121]

This strong statement of support on behalf of the Christian clergy lent credence to the cultural politics of Mayor Kollek: to have the Christian world recognize the role of Israel, and at the same time to undermine Muslim authority by naturalizing its consent.

The result, however, was different than expected. The appeal to the international community, to the religious office of any city, and to the spirituality of Jerusalem in particular, ran the risk of overlooking the particular ways in which people organize meaning in their lives, an incredibly complex process that is always so explosive in Jerusalem. Eventually, this benevolent imposition on local residents created a beautiful urban zone that cut through the city and provides spectacular views for tourists and foreign residents. The most precious areas of Jerusalem are now shared not only by the monotheistic faiths, but also by the twenty-first century's more inclusive faith in the global market.

PROJECT

THE WESTERN WALL PLAZA

> We are asking, why are we here? The Palestinian problem,
> et cetera. The most obvious place in the country in which we
> do not have to explain ourselves at all is this place [i.e., the
> Western Wall]. Therefore this place awaits a great act.
>
> —*Ram Karmi in David Cassuto, ed.,* The Western Wall:
> A Collection of Essays Concerning the Design of the Western
> Wall Plaza and Its Surroundings

O<small>N JUNE 7, 1967,</small> the third day of the Six Day War, Israeli troops broke through the Lions Gate into the Old City of Jerusalem. Conscious of their own place in history, they hurried to the Western Wall of Temple Mount, the remainder of Herod's Temple and the holiest site for Jews in the whole world. The following day Jerusalem's mayor, Teddy Kollek, gathered representatives from the national, municipal, and military authorities in order to determine the immediate future of the Western Wall precinct.[1] Surprised to discover how narrow the corridor was between the wall and the Mughrabee Quarter in front of it, the invitees were adamant that the corridor should be expanded, to allow the nation to gather and meet its past (Figures 6.1, 6.2, and 6.3).

Figure 6.1. Israel Defense Force Chief Rabbi Shlomo Goren carrying the Torah during the IDF breakthrough to the Old City of Jerusalem, June 7, 1967. Photographer unspecified. Source: Jerusalem Historical City Archive.

231

Figure 6.2. Residents of Moshav Zkenim Meuhad nursing home praying at the Western Wall, Jerusalem, 1912. Source: Jerusalem Historical City Archive.

Figure 6.3. The Western Wall precinct before the demolition. Source: Israel State Archive, TS/3027/45.

Arieh Sharon, the architect of the group, quickly drew boundaries for a new plaza, which necessitated vast demolition of the Mughrabee Quarter.[2] The required machinery arrived before the war was over. On the night of June 10,

> bulldozers pounded with a deafening roar upon the Mughrabee neighborhood . . . , their fangs extended and their steel teeth taking bites of the small, meager, densely packed houses and the fences of courtyards and alleys. . . . As houses, domes, arches, and the vaults of alleyways collapsed and crashed to the ground, disappearing into piles of rubble, a wide, ever-expanding plaza running the length of the valley appeared through the clouds of dust that covered the area.[3]

But the vast rubble plateau that was once the Mughrabee Quarter took Israelis by surprise. The Jewish anchor in the Old City, right in the heart of Islamic and Christian Jerusalem, had become an amorphous field of debris and giant stones (Figures 6.4, 6.5, and 6.6).

Figure 6.4. Mughrabee Quarter, general view, 1934. Photographer unspecified. Source: Moshe Akiva Druk, *The Western Wall Album* (Jerusalem: Ministry of Religious Affairs, 1969).

Figure 6.5. Demolition of the Mughrabee Quarter, June 1967. Photographer unspecified. Source: Moshe Akiva Druk, *The Western Wall Album* (Jerusalem: Ministry of Religious Affairs, 1969).

The tearing down of the Mughrabee neighborhood was the first step in a contentious project to reconfigure the area around the Western Wall of the Temple Mount. Half a century later, authorities are still debating what to do with this perpetually incomplete and emotionally sore site. In 1977, and after two years of intense deliberations, the government approved the plan that Moshe Safdie had proposed for the site in 1973. But a rabbinical ban over its commercial and tourist facilities impeded its execution. The plan proposed a huge metaphorical theater, which would overlook the Western Wall, composed of descending cubes and terraced plazas. The height of the Wall itself would gain an additional nine meters by digging up the current plaza, exposing twelve layers of stone until reaching the Herodian street beneath. The ancient passageway, just thirteen meters wide, would then be turned into a praying plaza, slightly lower than the ample spaces for national assembly. Farther to the west, also overlooking the Wall, a double-height public ar-

Figure 6.6. The Western Wall and the Mughrabee Gate to Temple Mount. Photographer unspecified. Source: Jerusalem Historical City Archive.

cade would host the required public institutions and tourist amenities into the theatrical setting (Figures 6.7, 6.8, and 6.9).

The plan still haunts the imaginations of many in Jerusalem. According to the journalist Nadav Shragai, "each time that anyone sneezes too loudly around the Western Wall precinct, the Ministry [of Religious Affairs]'s bureaucrats jump and scream, 'This is a Safdie plan being sneaked in through the back door!'"[4] In the twenty-first century, as in the twentieth, ultraorthodox media saw in any proposed change for the plaza "the rejuvenation of the 'Safdie Plan,' which, through considerable work, and the help of god, had been removed from the agenda, preventing the disgrace of the People of Israel."[5] For some, it seems, the plan's phantom presence holds the power to change reality. Such fear—of a mere architectural proposal—prompts us to explore the immense appeal of Safdie's plan in the light of its contemporary architectural culture, as well as the conflicted national demands it negotiated.

Here we will see how Safdie, and the architectural culture to which he belonged, offered the Israeli authorities a spatial articulation of the state's official narrative—the return of Jews to their biblical homeland after two thousand years of diasporic life. The strength of this proposition lay in its

Figure 6.7. Moshe Safdie, plan for the Western Wall Precinct, 1974, model. Courtesy of Safdie Architects Archive.

Figure 6.8. Western Wall Precinct after demolition, 1968. Photograph by Shmuel Joseph Schweig. Courtesy of National Library of Israel, Shmuel Joseph Schweig Collection.

architectural and urban dimensions—its proposed urban form made this history feel natural and inevitable, as if it was always there. What Safdie offered, in other words, was a concrete manifesto of the Israeli national building project—the *mamlachtiyut* (a concept that literally translates to "kingdomism")—a task so portentous that even the people of the book could not articulate it in words. The pressing question—whether a conceptual program should precede architectural design, or rather, whether architecture could contain such a concept within its disciplinary domain—was firmly debated by world-renowned architects and two ministerial committees. The proceedings of their deliberations shed light on the ways in which architecture embodies and advances ideas about history, religion, and nation, and their internal conflicts.

This chapter will first discuss the meaning of the Western Wall, and then the initial plans for its plaza. In order to understand the premises of Safdie's authorized plan, we examine the architectural philosophy that guided his design process, which we then study through the early sketches of this project. Safdie presented the complete design for the first time to members of the Jerusalem Committee in 1973. The sharpest criticism in this session came from Louis Kahn and Isamu Noguchi, whose previous designs for the same site we briefly explore. The eventual presentation of the plan to the public in 1975 provoked national debate that not only divided secular and religious Jews, but also architects with different modernist convictions: the sabra circle of architects who aligned with Safdie's vision; and on the other

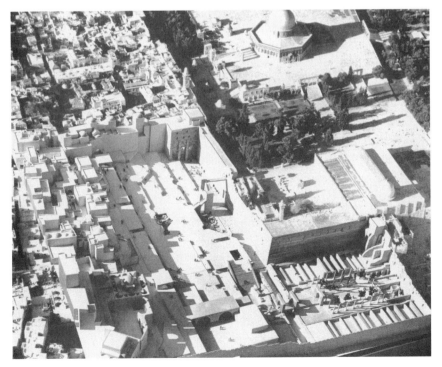

Figure 6.9. Moshe Safdie, revised plan for the Western Wall Precinct, 1982, model. Courtesy of Safdie Architects Archive.

side, members of the Anglo circle, who joined forces with Orthodox Jews in objecting to the project.

The chapter follows the public response to the open exhibition of Safdie's project, the correspondence between the authorities who continued to negotiate the section of the plan that Safdie designed for the Supreme Rabbinical Court, and the proceedings of a 1975 conference in the Van Leer Institute that explored the theology of the Wall and evaluated the proposed architectural plan. Particularly valuable are the proceedings of two ministerial committees that deliberated over the project between 1975 and 1977. These investigations reveal not only the reasons for both Kollek's and the state's enthusiastic embrace of the plan, but also, and equally important, why it was never built.

The Western Wall

The Western, or Wailing, Wall, *ha-kotel* in Hebrew and *al-buraq* in Arabic, is a retaining wall that supports the platform of what Jews refer to as the Temple Mount, and what in Islam is al-Haram al-Sharif, "the Noble Sanctuary." According to Jewish tradition, the holy of holies of the Jewish Temple was built on this platform, around the Foundation Rock from which the creation of the world had begun. Jews believe that it is on the same rock that the binding of Isaac took place, when Abraham was asked to sacrifice his son as an offering to God. For most Jews, the Western Wall is thus not sacred in and of itself; it is instead a reminder of their destroyed Temple. In addition, Jews believe that the Shechinah, God's presence, which hovered over the Temple, has never left the site. In the thirteenth century this conviction was made official by rabbinic authorities, who declared this segment of the western retaining wall the primary site of Jewish worship and a symbol of yearning for Jews worldwide.[6]

During the four centuries of Ottoman rule (1517–1917), Jews were allowed to pray by the Wall despite its sanctity for Muslims, who themselves believe that the Wall is where Muhammad tethered his winged steed when he came to Jerusalem on his "Night Journey" from Mecca.[7] Under the British Mandate, however, the Wall turned into a primary site of national conflict between Jews and Arabs. After the tumult of World War I, and with the prospect of national sovereignty in their respective grasp, both groups began to invest this key religious site (and its surroundings) with political ideologies that they construed as integral to the sanctity of the site and thus to its meaning for their respective constituencies.[8] The two decades of Jordanian rule (1948–67) only enhanced the symbolic importance of the Wall and its accompanying ideological fervor, as the government minimized Jewish presence in the Old City by destroying the synagogues of the Jewish Quarter and banning Jewish ritual by the Western Wall. At the same time the emerging nation-building ideology of *mamlachtiyut* further invested the now inaccessible site with explicit state ideology. For Israelis, whose nationality was defined as Jewish regardless of whether they were secular or devout, the *kotel* was not only a religious site, but more significantly, a prime symbol of Israeli identity, a concrete proof of Jewish sovereignty in antiquity, and a legitimization of the historical right of Jews to Jerusalem.

Paradoxically, as long as the Wall was in Jordanian hands, the yearning of Israeli Jews for the Wall suspended the immanent clash between their opposing perceptions of its meaning—as Judaism's religious site or, alternatively, as Zionism's historical monument. The minute the Old City fell into Israeli hands, Orthodox Jews started realizing how incompatible the secular *mamlachti* ideology was with their religious practice and faith.

Yitzhak Rabin, then the famed chief of staff of the Six Day War (who as prime minister would be assassinated in 1995), epitomized the *mamlachti* position. For him the Wall was the ultimate symbol of national unity. When honored by the Hebrew University for his military achievement, he told his exultant audience: "the paratroopers, who conquered the Wailing Wall, leaned on its stones and wept, and as a symbol this was a rare occasion, almost unparalleled in human history."[9] Rabin's troops, however, were representatives of a state fulfilling its historical call. According to this national view, the Israeli nation-state brought Jerusalem back to the Jewish people, ending their misery. The symbol of this secular salvation was naturally, for Rabin and so many others, the Western Wall, the central assembly place of the State of Israel. Thus, for *mamlachti* Israelis the Wall was and is the most sacred place in Israel due to its national importance.

For Orthodox Jews, including the Zionist strands within it, the Wall is first and foremost a particular kind of religious site. The architects who worked for the Ministry of Religious Affairs agreed in 1971 that the Wall is the dearest, "most memory-laden structure for Jews." However, they stressed, "it is not the holiest place for Jews," a category that is reserved for the site of the Temple.[10] They believed that making the Wall—the stones themselves—into the site par excellence of Jewish nationhood violated the fundamental objection to the worship of material objects in Judaism. This is because the Wall, as Ariel Hirschfeld put it, is a "place whose entirety, whose full depth, is made of what is beyond it"; it is thus a "supra-place and no-place."[11] At the Western Wall, in other words, Orthodox Jews protected their religious faith from national secularization.

The tension between the religious and national uses of this site immediately assumed territorial dimensions. According to Deputy Mayor Meron Benvenisti, the authorities that competed over the Western Wall Plaza came to resemble two enemy countries caught in a long-term dispute.[12] The most plausible solution was to redefine the site itself. The western retaining wall of the Temple Mount is 490 meters long. Only the seventy meters of the Wall north of the Mughrabee Gate have been traditionally allocated to Jewish prayer. The Ministry of Religious Affairs argued that defining those seventy meters as a sacred site meant that they had jurisdiction over the praying plaza.

Since independence, the state had developed its own forms of sanctity. The new faith that sociologists called "civil religion"[13] granted archeologists new authority; with each new excavation of relics, they scientifically legitimated the historical claim of Israel to biblical heritage by means of concrete and tangible findings. With an accompanying sense of entitlement, Professor Benjamin Mazar, the head of the newly established Archeological Commission, started excavating south of the Temple Mount before the government had formally approved the dig.[14] All parties claiming the site accepted, as a fait accompli, the dig's gradual expansion north along the Western Wall. The eventual limit of this dig—the bridge to the Mughrabee Gate of the Temple Mount—established the boundary between the two conflicted authorities.

A year before the war erupted Kollek already obtained permission from Prime Minister Levi Eshkol for the National Park Authority (NPA) to manage such archeological sites in Israel's capital. The NPA was one of few agencies under his influence that allowed him to expand his reach beyond municipal limits. Following the military mandate to manage all occupied archeological sites during the immediate postwar weeks, the NPA considered itself the natural candidate to win jurisdiction over the state's prime historical monument. When David Ben Gurion shed a tear by the newly seized Wall and protested against a nearby toilet that violated its sanctity, Ian Yanai, the head of the NPA, promised his mentor that he would personally clean and shape the site. Kollek, in turn, promised to help.[15]

But in the next couple of weeks, Prime Minister Levi Eshkol was continually reminded of an earlier promise to the Ministry of Religious Affairs.[16] On July 13, and over the strong objections of the NPA, Eshkol awarded the Department of Holy Places, a subset of the ministry, jurisdiction over the Western Wall. The secular leadership, imbued with the euphoria of historical fulfillment, was not happy to fully relegate the primary symbol of Jewish nationalism to religious hands. Since *dat* in Hebrew is "religion," the caricaturist Zeev suggested naming the events unfolding around the Wall "The Datican" (Figure 6.10). On July 28, Zeev depicted the minister of religious affairs celebrating his newfound status. Before 1967 the ministry managed a single ancient site of Jewish sanctity in West Jerusalem. Now, at the upper left corner of the caricature, the legendary general director of the ministry dances next to "the factory for the production of holy sites," while further below the minister himself returns, gratified, from "an acquisition tour in the West Bank," loaded with holy sites such as Rachel's Tomb and the Cave of the Patriarchs in Hebron.

At the center Zeev features the minister hovering over his prime asset, the Western Wall, like the Shechinah herself. He thus authorizes the "Wall Guard," another version of himself, this time in a knight uniform, to protect the Wall from other national agencies that want a share. A couple of tourists

Figure 6.10. Zeev (Yaakov Farkash), "The Datican," a caricature featuring the minister of religious affairs and his general manager imposing Orthodox Jewish law on the Western Wall Plaza and other holy sites in the West Bank, *Ha'aretz,* July 28, 1967. Source: Holon's Comic and Caricature Museum. Courtesy of Naomi Farkash Fink and Dorit Farkash-Shuki.

at the bottom of the caricature articulate the cartoonist's message (while an Orthodox Jew seemingly covers his eyes to the sight of the sleeveless woman). Staring at multiple signs declaring rules of holiness and gender separation, the tourists wonder: "Where is the Wall?" The more pressing question, however, was left open: Which party, the clerks of the Ministry of Religious Affairs or the secular archeologists and architects that opposed them, would untie the rope that held together the two figures in the minister's hands—one named "religion," the other, "state."

The Ministry of Religious Affairs's proposal of a surprisingly modern architectural plan in 1971 hinted that the answer was anything but obvious. After winning jurisdiction over the Wall, the ministry immediately asked its usual suspects, particularly Yosheph Schonenberg, an orthodox architect, to prepare the bulldozed site to accommodate mass pilgrimage and gender separation. In 1971, Schonenberg joined forces with landscape architect Shlomo Aronson and members of the cutting edge Anglo group. Aronson and Arthur Kutcher, the former employees of Lawrence Halprin, led the Planning Survey commissioned by the ministry.[17] They conducted a thorough visual and functional analysis of the site (Figure 6.11), and consequently offered several planning alternatives to be considered according to the way uses and rituals might develop by the Wall in the near future (Figure 6.12 and Plate 8). In light of the huge success of the Israel Museum's recently completed sculpture garden, the ministry invited the famed Japanese American sculptor Isamu Noguchi to strengthen the team. His design proposal remained in nascent form.

Despite the ministry's use of contemporary, international architects, Jerusalem's secular agencies worried that the Wall's new design would be made to suit orthodox demands. Kollek joined the Archeological Commission and the newly created Company for the Reconstruction and Development of the Jewish Quarter in the Old City of Jerusalem (JQDC) in order to overcome the defeat he and Yanai experienced. The Archeological Commission was the first to bring Moshe Safdie to the national precinct. Safdie had been commissioned a couple of years earlier to design the privately owned Porat Yoseph Yeshiva on the southwestern corner of the site. In 1970 Safdie agreed to design their archeological dig with no compensation and promised to fund-raise and extend the archeological project's area in collaboration with the Jerusalem Municipality and the JQDC. The latter two agencies commissioned Safdie to design the entire plaza in 1972. In order to appease the minister of religious affairs, Safdie had to collaborate with his orthodox architect Schonenberg. By the time of this appointment, however, Safdie's design was already well under way.

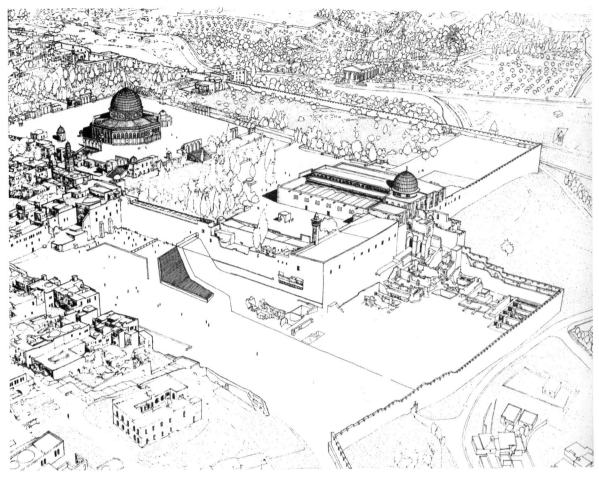

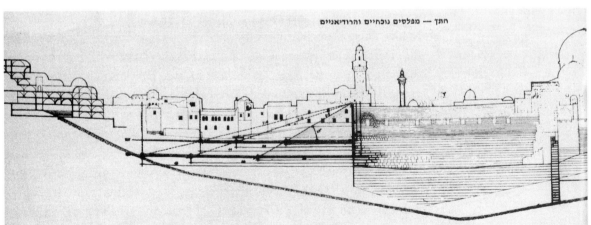

Figure 6.11. Arthur Kutcher, the Western Wall Plaza, Herodian and contemporary levels, 1970, general and section views. Source: Arthur Kutcher and Shlomo Aronson, *The Western Wall Planning Survey* (Jerusalem: Ministry of Religious Affairs, 1970–71).

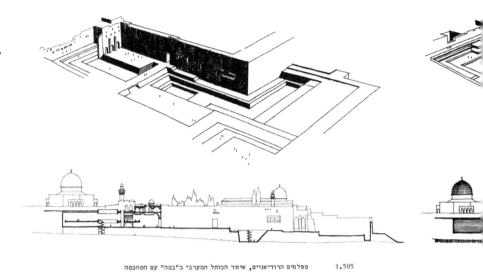

Figure 6.12. Arthur Kutcher, the Western Wall Plaza, Herodian and contemporary levels, 1970. Source: Arthur Kutcher and Shlomo Aronson, *The Western Wall Planning Survey* (Jerusalem: Ministry of Religious Affairs, 1970–71).

מפלסים הרודיאניים, איזור הכותל המערבי כ"במה" עם המחכמה   1.505

In Search of the DNA of the City

The determined secular coalition wished the design of the Western Wall Plaza to reflect the values of the *mamlachti* project. They believed the young architect Moshe Safdie was the right person to erect their desired national symbol. A former Israeli, an emerging architectural celebrity, and a forceful critic of the modern movement, he embodied both the national and architectural ambitions for a concrete Israeli place.

Safdie's family emigrated from Israel in 1953 when he was a fifteen-year-old idealist thoroughly identified with the state's socialist leadership. At McGill University he developed his passion for large-scale architectural systems whose components are structured according to scientific logic. In Louis Kahn's office, where he trained for a year, he bonded with Ann Tyng, for whom the environment was "molecules and crystals that make it up and the systems that structure them."[18] Her "bible" was D'Arcy Thompson's *On Growth and Form*. This canon of morphological research, Safdie stated, was "more important than any work on architecture I had read."[19]

His ensuing collaboration with Christopher Alexander, an architect and mathematician who brought computer-inspired "pattern language" to bear on city form, was based on a mutual "faith in a rational process" and "interest in the environment that was the product of evolution."[20] Both admired Bernard Rudofsky's *Architecture without Architects,* which described "large-scale environment made by men for themselves."[21] Just as nature perfected the correlation between form and function, they believed indigenous cultures optimized form to fit their social, psychic, and economic needs.

According to Stanford Anderson, vernacular architecture's appeal lay in its scientific credibility—its ability to compete with the modern movement

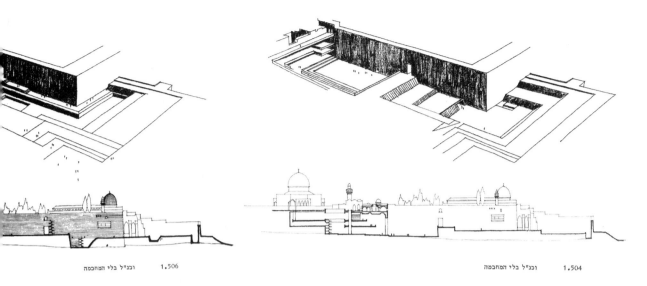

וכנ"ל בלי המחכמה 1.506 וכנ"ל בלי המחכמה 1.504

on its own terms.[22] Research, according to this logic, could discover, measure, and quantify the merits of both natural and man-made forms. For Safdie, deciphering the morphological code of the vernacular could release the environment from the arbitrary whims of expressive architects.[23] He protested against Philip Johnson's indulgence in "the feeling of wonderful freedom," looking instead for a responsible "solution" that "is a process moving toward the *truth*."[24] In other words, the science of morphology and the anthropology of vernacular form could prove that there was a universal logic—exact, quantifiable, and thoroughly rational. Architectural design thus had the "moral obligation" to emulate this logic in order to responsively structure the built environment.

If the environment was made up of a multitude of structures, and if "structure" in the morphological sense was "organization, complex and arrangement," it followed that

> Each aspect of form is an aspect of structure. The structure of a building is not just what holds it up; it is also the structure of light, the structure of air, the structure of distribution of services through it, the structure of movement, the psychic structure of human response to location, identity and privacy.[25]

Safdie was engaging a fundamental postwar argument, as architects starting in the 1950s criticized the style of functionalism that ruled the day and articulated their own alternative desire for a "rich environment" that could embrace "delight." This criticism "occurred not because the basis of functionalism was wrong but because it didn't go far enough." Functionalism, according to Safdie, failed because it isolated and exaggerated a particular aspect of architecture. By contrast, he suggested a structural exploration of "the fundamental nature of living form."[26] The work of the architect was thus to synthesize the different facets of structures—shapes, spaces, materials, identities, activities, and emotions.

This focus on structure constituted a momentous ideological shift in both architectural and Zionist culture. Architecturally, structure was not "that which holds the building up,"[27] but rather, the "fitness to form" of different aspects of a given environment. As such, structure could not be conceptually (and thus technically) separated from the enveloping skin of the built space, or operationally distinct from its function and use, as was often the case in high modernism. For both Safdie and Alexander, structures were neither "parameters nor requirements; what is significant about them is that they are statements of the generic qualities of a particular environment."[28] Once these qualities were identified, a building that works as a system could embody them. A building system was consequently not a technical assembly of repetitive parts, but rather, a spatial arrangement of "elements which are *space-makers,* elements which have inherent in them the environmental characteristics synthesized from generic requirements."[29]

Note the momentous difference Safdie delineated between *space-makers* and *program,* the bedrock of the *sachlich*—literally matter-of-fact, or objective—modernism prevalent in early Israeli statehood. "Words can only be a program," he said, and as such they can rationalize and project requirements and uses. By contrast, "design process is one of synthesis and integration" based on the identification of requirements and qualities *in* a given environment.[30] This also explains the repetitive use of the term "environment" whose rules must be found, as opposed to "building," which is a product of rational or whimsical human deed. Safdie's conclusions were a far-reaching statement: if the generative qualities of the site were successfully translated into space-makers, many of those "can then be related to each other by an overall structure—a kind of DNA of the city."[31] This biological metaphor served to anchor Safdie's firm conviction: only by following the encoded rules dictated by the environment can man-made creations reach the fulfillment and truth of a natural form and thus satisfy, like nature itself, our functional and emotional needs.

The national implications of this agenda were similarly provocative. Previously, socialist architects had used the correlation between physical form and rudimentary human needs to devise a brand of architectural modernism that responded to particular conditions but, more importantly, aimed to change them. Scholars have argued that early Israeli modernism actively helped erase the former identities of new immigrants and molded them in the form of the new state.[32] This role served a society bound by a strong collective cause that considered individual preoccupations irrelevant. Safdie grew up in this culture, which drew him to architectures of collective use, like housing and public institutions, that perform in social rather than individual terms.

In Safdie's reading of the Indian pueblo, for example, we find one of many instances where his architectural and national convictions merge. Architecture, he admitted, must cater to individual needs,

> But there are certain societies where the identification isn't to the individual but more to the immediate group, such as the Indian pueblo. The individual felt so much part of his tribe that he was satisfied with that kind of identity, and so the physical environment expressed it. The pueblo was the identity of the tribe.[33]

Notice the last line: the building does not only accommodate the tribe, it *was* its identity. In other words, architecture does not represent meaning or identity that exists outside of its domain. Individuals who identify themselves as a group can articulate their identity in architecture. The question was how to articulate the physical environment in a way that expresses the unity of the Israeli tribe.

Safdie sought inspiration for this unity between postwar architectural culture and ancient Jerusalem in two primary sources: first, the traditional vernacular architecture of Jerusalem, and second, the ancient palatial architecture of King Herod. The first would anchor the "Israeli place," the other, the history of that place.[34] When he worked on the housing of Habitat Israel in 1970, he sought in native vernacular architecture an alternative to the Israeli modernist housing blocks that he considered alienating. But his consistent search for the authentic Jerusalem vernacular yielded perplexing results: the preferred models were, for the most part, Arab (Figure 6.13).

Safdie was mesmerized by the allure of Arab culture: "they build so much better than we do and their towns are so much more wholesome than ours. Their art, their poetry, their clothes, their jewelry, their music is the soul of this land; there is so much we can learn from them."[35] And he did. The Habitat community he envisioned in Jerusalem was "akin to an Arab village in the sense that it followed the hill, each unit had its roof garden, and a series of pathways followed the topography intimately."[36] Safdie found a similar description in the reports of the historian Josephus, himself a Roman Jewish convert, who documented Jewish Jerusalem before the destruction of the Temple in 70 AD.

Josephus's writing had also informed Professor Michael Avi-Yona, who in the mid-1960s directed the building of a 1:50 scale public model of Second Temple Jerusalem, which depicted Herod's architecture in detail. Safdie often referred to this model, which provided him "inspiration in designing Jewish institutions" (Figure 6.14).[37] It was part of a search for precedents similar in power and quality to the Roman architecture that had inspired his mentor, Louis Kahn. While conceiving his monumental designs for the plaza, King Herod's architecture became a great revelation and the thorough revival of his achievement an explicit aim. Safdie's remarkable synthesizing skills

Figure 6.13. Moshe Safdie, slide comparing Israeli modernist housing (Kiryat Yovel) to an Arab village (Sillwan). Source: "Safdie in Jerusalem," Royal Institute of British Architects lecture.

would bring this and all other inspirations to bear on the design process of the Western Wall Plaza.

Design Process

Together, Teddy Kollek, Yehuda Tamir, the head of the JQDC, and Meir Ben-Dov, the deputy head of the Archeological Commission, agreed with Safdie on a number of premises that preceded the initial design of the plaza. As a national enterprise, it should embrace Jewish ritual, archeological digs, state institutions, and the tourist industry, each of which would inhabit the area. The project would encompass the entire area around the southwest corner of Temple Mount within the Ottoman walls—a thirty-acre L-shaped area that encompassed jurisdictions of both the Archeological Commission and the

Figure 6.14. Professor Michael Avi-Yona, model of Jerusalem during the Second Temple period, 1966. Scale 1:50. Source: "Safdie in Jerusalem," Royal Institute of British Architects lecture.

Department of Holy Places, two agencies that were hostile to each other. Instead of just the seventy meters of the existing praying plaza, the dimensions of the new Israeli plaza would stretch along a continuous two hundred meters of the ancient wall.[38] In the wake of the 1967 war, the intention of Safdie together with Kollek et al. was to quickly execute the projected plan to plant irreversible facts on the ground in this contested site.

The multiple sketches that Safdie drew between 1971 and 1973 reveal the central dilemmas underlying the design process. First, how to invest the site with a sense of monumentality after the bulldozers that leveled the Mughrabee residences irreversibly changed the spatial relationship between the visitor and the Western Wall. That is, how to restore the sense of sublimity that the physical proximity to the tall Wall once inspired while catering to the expected crowds and their diverse public, religious, and touristic requirements. Second, how to bridge between the monumental scale of the Wall and Temple Mount that form the eastern facade of the plaza, and the vernacular scale of the Jewish Quarter that sits atop the western slope. Third, how to heal the conflicted site through a cohesive and efficient ordering system. And finally, how to integrate ancient monuments and contemporary architecture.

Safdie started to plan the plaza after already completing his design for Porat Yoseph Yeshiva. According to architects who worked on the project in his office, one cannot underestimate the yeshiva's influence on the plaza's design process.[39] The yeshiva was a single building, while the entire plaza was an entity that required the tools of urban design. Accordingly, in a sketch from September 23, 1971, Safdie suggested a space for a slow, ritualized entry to the precinct. A visitor coming to the Old City through the Dung Gate (the closest Ottoman gate to the Western Wall) would first enter an urban "interlude," a spacious gateway building. Safdie borrowed its typology—a square building around an internal court—from the Umayyad palaces that had just been dug up east of the proposed structure (Figure 6.15). The gateway filled the gap between the excavated palace and the Yeshiva farther to the west. Behind the gate lay the great drama of the plan: Safdie suggested digging a monumental urban square, leveled with the Herodian street adjacent to the ancient wall, some nine meters below the present ground level. Its length was determined by the extent of the exposed wall, and its width by the distance between the Wall and the cliff of the Jewish Quarter.

The square posed a geometrical challenge that the Planning Survey team of Schonenberg and the Anglo group had already explored. The team compared the San Marco Square in Venice (a square of similar dimensions) to the amorphous new square in Jerusalem. The former features a historical monument, San Marco Church. The uniformity of the surrounding facades highlights the monumental Byzantine church, which dominates the square

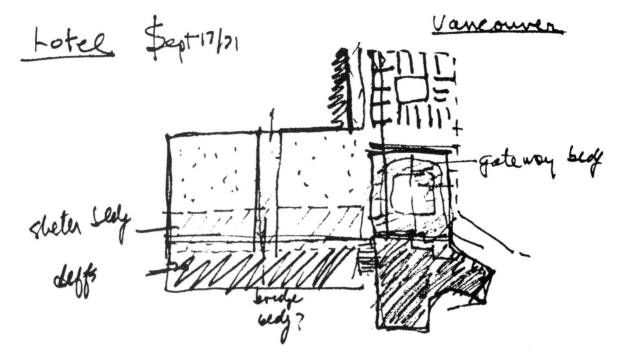

hotel $ept 17/71   Vancouver

shelter sdy

deff?

gateway bldg

bridge
sdy?

and functions as a pivot between the two arms of an L-shaped urban space. In Jerusalem, by contrast, the most impressive monuments in the vicinity of the Wall (the Al-Aqsa Mosque and the Dome of the Rock) were above and away from the urban square. More poignantly, once the site was broadened to include the entire L-shaped space surrounding the southwest corner of the Temple Mount, the holy Wall appeared as merely one side of the longer, squared arm of the L-shaped space.

Under these spatial conditions, Safdie's proposed design for the square (Figure 6.16a) was dramatically imbalanced: it was bounded by a continuous monolithic wall to the east and by a cliff supporting fragmented housing to the west. Safdie was fixated on this cliff and explored two alternative building systems to address the challenge it posed, one a space-frame megastructure, the other service piers made of hollow stones (Figure 6.16b). Both systems were based on Kahn and Tyng's 1950s revisionist approach to architecture through the use of new technologies. "In Gothic times," they write:

> architects built in solid stones. Now we can build with hollow stones. The spaces defined by the members of a structure are as important as the members. These spaces range in scale from the voids of an insulation panel, voids of air, lighting and heat to circulate, to space big enough to walk through or live in.[40]

Kahn and Tyng argued that thanks to new technologies, the structural skeleton of a building should no longer be considered a distinct entity made of

Figure 6.15. Moshe Safdie, plan sketch of the Western Wall Plaza with a gateway building and the Porat Yoseph Yeshiva, September 17, 1971. Source: Moshe Safdie's sketchbook. Courtesy Safdie Architects Archive.

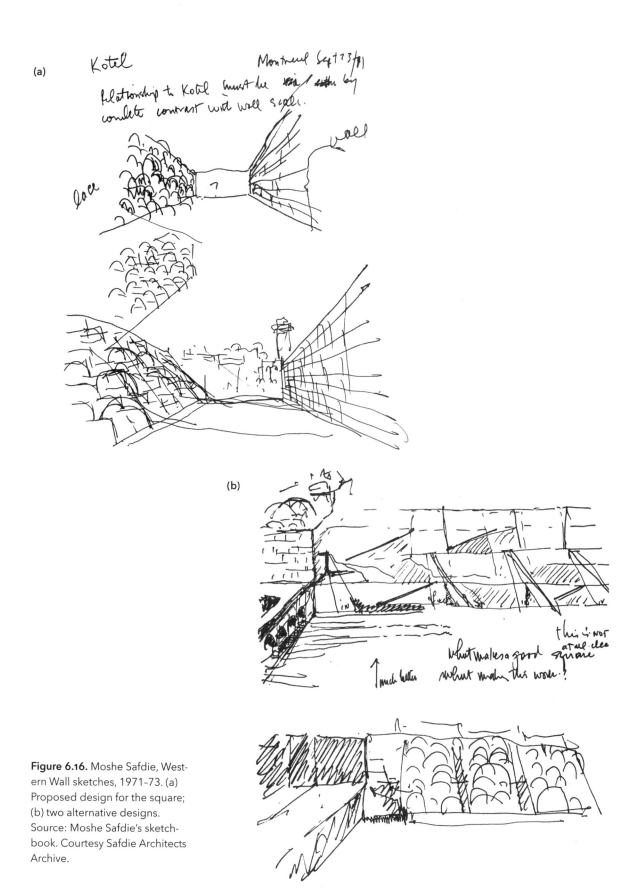

Figure 6.16. Moshe Safdie, Western Wall sketches, 1971–73. (a) Proposed design for the square; (b) two alternative designs. Source: Moshe Safdie's sketchbook. Courtesy Safdie Architects Archive.

solid matter. Alternatively, it can be hollowed out by building a space frame, that is, a "three-dimensional framework of struts and braces which defines a structure and distributes its weight evenly in all directions." Though lightweight, "a space frame forms a very strong, thick, flexible structural fabric that can be used horizontally or bent to a variety of shapes."[41] An open latticework web of lightweight tubular diagonals contains spaces big enough to accommodate all the systems that serve the buildings: ducts and wires, machines and circulation. The idea that the structure can better a building's performance gained huge currency in the 1950s and 1960s architectural culture.

Safdie's idea of the square as a space-frame megastructure grew out of the formal contrast between the solid Western Wall and a leveled slope facing it. The neat square between them is bisected by a bridge leading from the plane that covers the cliff of the quarter to the Mughrabee Gate at the opposite end. The result is a monumental portal to the Temple Mount (Figure 6.17).

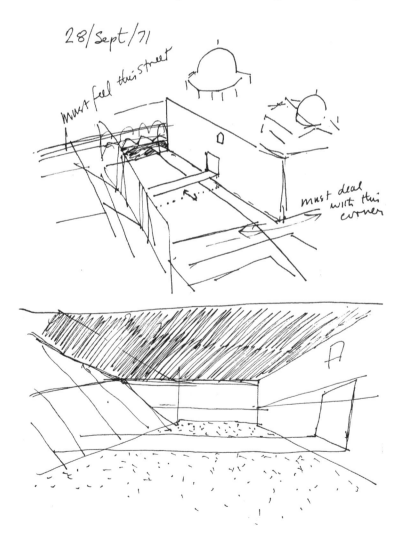

Figure 6.17. Moshe Safdie, Western Wall sketches, September 1971. Source: Moshe Safdie's sketchbook. Courtesy Safdie Architects Archive.

As in the best morphological architecture of the time, a school to which Safdie was thoroughly committed, he designed the slope as a huge space frame, whose structural members also delineated interior and outdoor space. The space frame developed Kahn and Tyng's concept of "hollow stones" into a comprehensive building system that was economic in built material, generous in the angles it allowed, and addressed the complex directionality of the site. The contemporary entry that Safdie submitted to the Centre Pompidou competition provides a more complete articulation of this system. The proposal demonstrated how the forty-five-degree structural frame creates a building that functions as an urban environment while offering an artificial slope covering a theatrical space—two urban conditions that coalesce in the Jerusalem plaza (Figure 6.18).

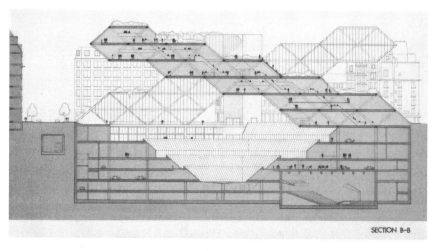

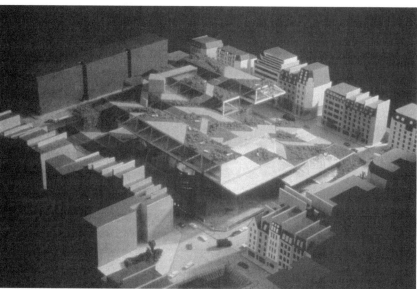

Figure 6.18. Moshe Safdie, Pompidou Center Competition, Paris, 1971. Section and model. Courtesy of Safdie Architects Archive.

Safdie's second alternative addressed the notion of descending volumes down the cliff of the Jewish Quarter as they appeared in Professor Avi-Yona's reconstruction of the site. Safdie systemized these volumes by following a similar structure to the one he designed for the Yeshiva: a series of piers that function as hollowed structural walls. Institutional and public spaces were composed into a built tissue that was stretched between them. In September 1971 Safdie suggested situating the piers perpendicular to the Wall, and three months later he rotated them ninety degrees, turning them instead into retaining service walls parallel to the solid Western Wall (Figure 6.19). By integrating all the complex's services into the hollowed piers, Safdie adopted yet another principle of Louis Kahn—the separation between serving and served spaces—an influential formulation that freed the main, served spaces from structural and infrastructural constraints.

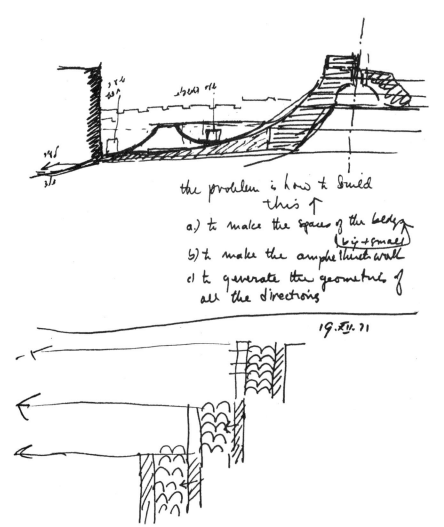

Figure 6.19. Moshe Safdie, Western Wall sketch, December 19, 1971. Source: Moshe Safdie's sketchbook. Courtesy Safdie Architects Archive.

Both alternatives led Safdie to abandon the scheme of the flat square in favor of a metaphorical amphitheater descending to the Wall. He gradually realized that the efforts to accommodate the different spaces of entry, archeology, prayer, and bureaucracy in one traditional square were incompatible with the morphological structure of the Old City. Instead, he decided to stress the formative contrasts of the site. The Temple Mount was a singular structure but had been intentionally built as such—a pivotal urban statement. Safdie's intention for the Western Wall Plaza was the opposite: to immerse rather than foreshow, to assume strong presence without breaking the morphological structure of the Old City, to create a place that would look as if it had always been there without compromising its novelty.

On December 18, 1971, Safdie started a process that would lead to the final form of the project. He drew the entire site as a set of terraces that overrode the remnants from the initial proposal of the Dung Gate entry building. A day later he summarized the major problems this idea posed:

a) to make the spaces of the building (?) big + small
b) to make the amphitheater wall
c) to generate the geometries of all the directions [see Figure 6.19]

In January 1972 he introduced a new dimension to the scheme. Although the strict pier-walls are still there, the overall image is different. "This scheme instead of emphasizing the terraces & amphitheater," Safdie writes, "is a scene of 'fortresses folding over.'"[42] As we shall see, the understanding of the project as morphological scenery would gain enormous importance.

Simultaneously, Safdie sought a geometrical resolution to the requirements of scale, form, and directionality in his theater-like building system. He turned to D'Arcy Thompson, his preferred researcher, for inspiration. Thompson explored the "fitness to form" of natural phenomena, looking at the way the form of a wing provides a perfect solution to aviation, the form of a bone to stability, or the form of a soap bubble to weightless enclosure. Safdie was particularly attracted to Thompson's study of "infinite variety within repetitive systems," which allowed him to "to create variation and permutation of dissimilar objects" within such systems.[43] This was exactly what Safdie needed in order to systematically mediate between the Herodian, religious, institutional, and vernacular scales of the site.

In the search for formal and mathematical laws of expansion, Safdie looked at Thompson's geometrical analysis of shells and marked what Thompson considered the essence of "the equiangular spiral":

In the growth of a shell, we can conceive no simpler law than this, namely, that it shall widen and lengthen in the same unvarying proportions: and this sim-

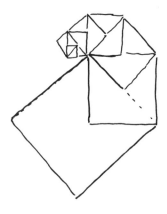

Figure 6.20. Moshe Safdie, proportion study for the Western Wall project. Source: *Plan for the Western Wall Precinct* (Jerusalem: Ministry of Religious Affairs, 1974).

plest of laws is that which Nature tends to follow. The shell, like the creature within it, grows in size *but does not change its shape.*[44]

According to this logic, Safdie drew a spiral proportional system made of perfect squares. The diagonal of each square in this spiral system is the base of the next size square. This system of gradual growth helped Safdie calculate the prefabricated elements that would become the building blocks of the entire site (Figures 6.20 and 6.21).

In the yeshiva Safdie had already experimented with such prefabricated systems, which he developed for the new project as a system "flexible enough to relate to different programs."[45] Take, for example, the creating of domed interior spaces from such concrete elements, each in the form of a square sheet, from which a quarter of a circle is cut out. By joining four elements along the imaginary bisecting lines of half a cube, the circular cutouts take the shape of a voided dome. To create a chain of domes each base is supported by three additional elements. The repetition of this system can simulate in space, rather than material, the pendentives of classical buildings.

Figure 6.21. Moshe Safdie, plan for the Western Wall Precinct, diagrams of transitional scale and the architectural vocabulary of prefabricated elements, 1974. Courtesy of Safdie Architects Archive.

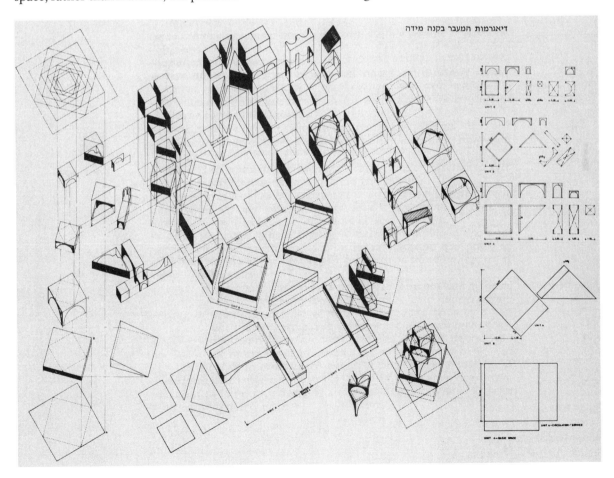

דיאגרמות המעבר בקנה מידה

The method of generating these elements was crucial for efficient construction. Since their form and size were generated from the same morphological system, their dimensions could be calculated into systematically succeeding sizes. As a result, their interrelatedness ensured efficient prefabrication. In other words, Thompson's scientific logic led to a system of unified yet diverse prefabricated elements that would allow, according to Safdie, the construction of the entire complex in only six years.

A few years later, in 1975, Safdie would report that these systems helped him resolve "a very principle point in my approach to the plan, that the institutions and the plaza would be one thing—not buildings that define a plaza, but part of the plaza."[46] Safdie thus envisioned a total, structural building system, an urban environment whose impact surpassed the individual buildings. Sketches dating to January 1972 reveal the ongoing struggle to resolve the conflict between the different perceived uses of the site. The sketch features an early implementation of the proportional system, which allows Safdie to achieve the flexible directionality he desired—to create the spin of an amphitheater curling around the southwest corner of Temple Mount while also accommodating the flow of visitors from the Dung Gate and their movement toward the archeological garden that would lie south of Temple Mount (Figure 6.22).

In 1973 Safdie would develop this resolution into a complete design package. The final submission articulated a full set of prefabricated elements that would create a theater of descending volumes, smaller near the Jewish Quarter and larger nearing the excavated Herodian street. This theater conceals a service street that runs underneath the complex, feeding the commercial and

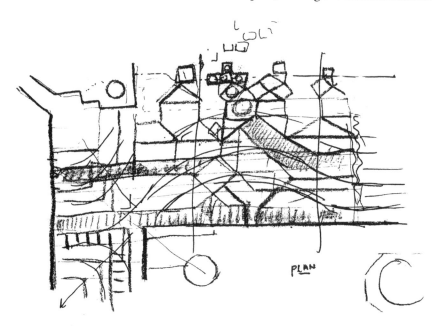

Figure 6.22. Moshe Safdie, sketch, January 1972. Source: Moshe Safdie's sketchbook. Courtesy of Safdie Architects Archive.

(a)

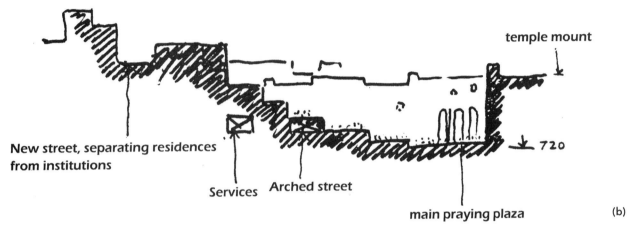

temple mount

New street, separating residences
from institutions

Services   Arched street

720

main praying plaza

(b)

institutional facilities of the complex. Wide arcades of serial voided domes allow panoramic overviews over the praying plaza and the archeological garden designed according to Islamic precedents (Figure 6.23a). A cross section perpendicular to the Wall establishes the historicity of this project; it entirely eliminates the current level of the plaza by physically removing the debris that accumulated after Jews were expelled from Jerusalem in 70 AD. By clearing diasporic memories the project reinstates the biblical layer of Herod's Jerusalem, the authentic birthplace of Judaism (Figure 6.23b).

Safdie's system induced an urban and national reality devoid of ruptures, one that despite its novelty could be experienced as a matter of fact, as if the DNA of the place had finally been discovered. In one instance Safdie developed a detailed design for the Supreme Rabbinical Court according to this framework of building-as-systemized-environment. He conceived the court as a piece in a larger puzzle, whose formal language was first developed at the yeshiva and later spread in a revised form over the entire precinct. The effort to reach the morphological code of the place, its cipher for space-makers, meant that such DNA was inherent to the site and structured the precinct's built form since antiquity; Israelis, in turn, could now approximate its truth.

Figure 6.23. Moshe Safdie, plan for the Western Wall Precinct, 1975. (a) section; (b) schematic section: public terraces to main plaza. Source: David Cassuto, ed., *The Western Wall: A Collection of Essays Concerning the Design of the Western Wall Plaza and Its Surroundings* (Jerusalem: Jerusalem Post Press, 1975), 68–69.

Such seeming inevitability makes Safdie's design particularly fitting for *mamlachtiyut,* the conceptual bedrock of Israeli statehood that brings Jews back to their place, the same place over which divinity hovers.

International Criticism

Safdie first presented his project to the Jerusalem Committee just before the outbreak of the 1973 war. This international committee of luminaries was gathered by Jerusalem's mayor, Teddy Kollek, to supervise and consult the Israeli unification of Jerusalem. Two of the participants, Louis Kahn and Isamu Noguchi, had previously proposed designs for the same site and through their intimate familiarity provoked the most poignant criticism of Safdie's work.

Louis Kahn, during his 1973 review of Safdie's project, called for a greater restraint in approaching the Wall. He conceded that Safdie's arches had "a living quality to it," yet they belonged, he argued, "to a different scale." He explained to his former apprentice that

> It is so very intimate, and you may tire, you see, of the interplay of the arches and finally get very much exhausted. . . . I think it can be done in just a few strokes, and be equally contained in spirit. I think it must be done with the greatest restraint, and not with such exuberance.[47]

Kahn also criticized the modular transitional system that Safdie used to mediate the monumental scale of the Wall and the residential scale of the Jewish Quarter. He argued that such an attempt to subordinate the entire precinct to a unified ordering system would produce an artificial homogeneity. "There is a greater force," Kahn insisted, "greater, actually, distinction of the transitional, along lines which don't try to homogenize one theme with another."[48] Kahn's criticism targeted the greatest achievement as well as the most controversial aspect of Safdie's design. Kahn argued that Safdie's comprehensive synthesis of different periods and themes divested this ruptured site of its power. He preferred to exploit these historical ruptures, while Safdie laboriously tried to heal them.

Kahn had been invited to design the Hurva Synagogue in the Jewish Quarter immediately after the 1967 war.[49] The significance of the Hurva, he suggested, was inseparable from that of the Western Wall. According to Ram Karmi, Kahn treated the Hurva and the Wall as a single urban complex, in which he reconstructed the primal notion of a synagogue. The Western Wall was the ark while the Hurva was the bimah (platform) from which the prayer is conducted. The design Khan submitted for the Hurva also delineated a pilgrim route connecting these two focal points that was named the "Prophets' Way." That the bottom of the excavated Wall was the lowest point in the Old City and the Hurva rose above both the Dome of the Rock and the Holy Sepulcher accentuated this relationship (Figure 6.24).[50]

Other scholars recently viewed Kahn's remaking of the Jewish Quarter as an attempt to predate the notion of a temple through an architectonic inquiry into the primal form of faith and worship.[51] In spite of Kahn's bold, oversized Hurva, he approached the Western Wall with great restraint: at the end of the prophets' path that connected the Hurva and the Wall, he kept a large flat plaza. At its northeast corner, between the Wall and the building perpendicular to it, Kahn delineated a roughly sixty-by-sixty-meter square for excavations. The southern and western edges of the square would moderately slope down until they reached the Herodian street below, revealing the full depth of the Wall. Safdie, who considered Kahn his only mentor, catered to a greater drama.

Figure 6.24. Louis Kahn, proposal for the Hurva Synagogue, the "Prophets' Way," and the Western Wall Precinct, 1967. Section and plan. Source: David Cassuto, ed., *The Western Wall: A Collection of Essays Concerning the Design of the Western Wall Plaza and Its Surroundings* (Jerusalem: Jerusalem Post Press, 1975).

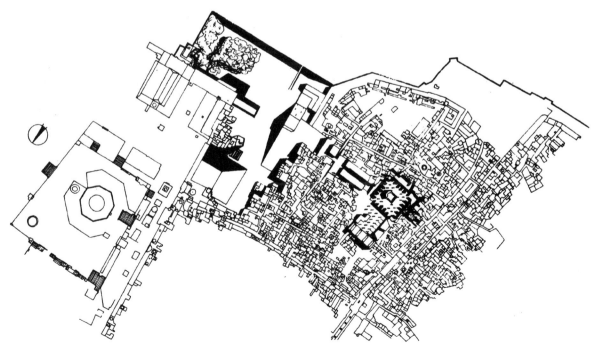

Isamu Noguchi also found Safdie's reference to a single ancient history dubious. The will to "connect" with the past, he thought, subsumes the present. Noguchi abhorred the "archaistic attempt to make . . . a fake area of the past when what we are today is not to be denied."[52] In his own proposal from 1970, Noguchi instead suggested a symbolic conception that prioritized the historical memory of exile. The memory was embedded in the existing praying plaza, the seventy-meter-long boundaries of which, under Noguchi's plan, were left intact. Accordingly, he constructed the present ground level of the plaza as a ceiling that hovered over the archeological excavations and created two plazas, one on top of the other; the lower level, consisting of items from the site's excavated past, was meant to coexist with the Ottoman level of exile—the present level. Each level was to occupy a different physical and symbolic terrain. The Wall would, therefore, mediate between the two modalities. A stele of stone would define an intimate praying area separated from the larger plaza, giving worshipers protection from the visiting public's gaze. The stele, which symbolized the Jewish people praying in front of the Wall, rises out of its anchor in the bedrock, symbolizing how the Jewish people rose out of their past up to the present and beyond. Noguchi argued this arrangement would be the ultimate expression of Jewish endurance throughout the ages (Figures 6.25 and 6.26).[53]

Designers who wished to dispute the singular conceptualization of history would repeatedly refer to Noguchi's conceptual drawing of a section cutting through the praying plaza parallel to the Wall. But many interpreted this section, which cut through the gigantic stele of stone, as a reminder of the Holocaust.[54] Others felt that the stele of stone was a poor invocation of the

Figure 6.25. Isamu Noguchi, proposal for the Western Wall Plaza, 1970, model. Source: Arthur Kutcher and Shlomo Aronson, *The Western Wall Planning Survey* (Jerusalem: Ministry of Religious Affairs, 1970-71).

Qa'ba in Mecca, a connotation that maligned Noguchi in Israeli culture. In his memoirs Safdie passionately emphasized Noguchi's non-Jewishness and incapability to understand monotheism:

> As he spoke . . . I saw the image of his model—that great black block of his, rising through the platform in front of the Wall. He spoke of worship and I thought of his pagan altar. I felt my blood boiling. I wanted to scream out, "Your difficulty is in understanding the worship of a god who is not an object, and needs no object by which to be represented. . . . You do not understand the fundamentals of Judaism!"[55]

Safdie dismissed Noguchi's proposal as the work of a gentile incapable of understanding Jewish faith.[56] Paradoxically, the Orthodox Jews who commissioned his work for the Ministry of Religious Affairs considered Noguchi's rather modest proposal as a worthy setting for Jewish ritual and

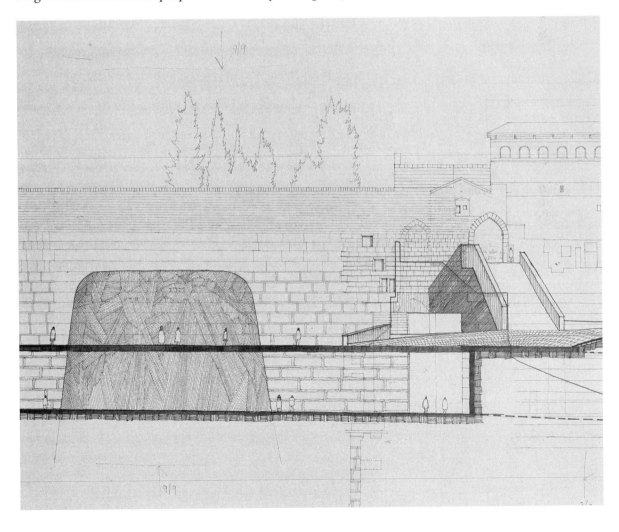

Figure 6.26. Isamu Noguchi, proposal for the Western Wall Plaza, 1973, detail. Courtesy of Shlomo Aronson Archive.

a proper interpretation of the meaning of the Wall that Safdie, they protested, violated.

Kollek placed the issue of the designer's ethnicity high on his agenda. This was the reason he objected, despite many requests, to conducting an open competition. He later admitted that he feared a German might win the project,[57] as was the case a decade earlier when a German team won the prestigious Manshiya competition for Tel Aviv's Central Business District. Thus, when Kollek succeeded in eventually soliciting the approval of the Jerusalem Committee, he could present to the government an architect who was simultaneously an international star, a worldly Jew, and an Israeli citizen. Paradoxically, the Jewishness of the architect was far more important to the secular authorities than to the Ministry of Religious Affairs that commissioned Noguchi in the first place.

Kollek overlooked his and the JQDC's agreement with the minister of religious affairs, who had already, in 1972, insisted on a joint appointment of Safdie and Schonenberg, an observant Jew who previously directed the ministry's Planning Survey, to work on the Western Wall Plaza. Apparently, Schonenberg learned about Safdie's presentation to the Jerusalem Committee from the newspapers.[58] This oversight alienated the religious community, which was deeply offended and anxious about being marginalized during the plaza's design. In retrospect, Kollek's eagerness to gain international support and legitimacy might have caused him irreversible damage at home.[59] The minister of religious affairs, Zerakh Verhaftig, who had previously and willingly negotiated with the secular authorities the plan Safdie and Schonenberg seemingly coauthored, retracted his consent,[60] while both Kollek and Safdie laboriously tried to fix the insult. This fragile collaboration between very different conceptions of both architecture and Judaism came to an end.

Israeli Reception

On August 22, 1974, Kollek asked the government to advance a plan for "the emotional focal point of the Jewish people."[61] His official request reflected the ideas already embedded in Safdie's conceptual design for the plaza. Although the war had subdued the national appetite for grandiose projects, the government decided to consider the plan. On September 2 the Ministerial Committee for Jerusalem Affairs went on a tour of the site. Two weeks later, the committee officially requested to open an exhibition of the project, to solicit public response, and to appoint a professional committee to deliberate the project.[62] On July 1, 1975, Safdie exhibited the model of his project to the public in a meticulously prepared presentation. A magnifying optical device allowed viewers to overcome the abstract nature of the model by imagining the spatial experience of moving through the proposed space (Figure 6.27).

The unprecedented quality of the exhibition overwhelmed the Israeli public. Perhaps the greatest appeal of Safdie's project was its capacity to overcome the issue of a program, for which no agreement was in sight. In most commissions, the architect receives an architectural program that specifies the requirements of the client: the functions of and uses for the space, square footage, the relationship between different segments, necessary facilities. Programs, however, are not limited to quantitative data, but also engage the qualities and character of any given project, as different pedagogic philosophies, for example, would yield different schools of thought. The more complex the concept of the project, the more complicated the articulation of its anticipated merits. A basic question emerges in such proposals: Can the client specify these needs and merits in advance or should they be the mandate of the architect?

Safdie was a firm believer in the latter. He did not believe that the rationale of a written program could determine design. The program did not generate the resultant image; rather, it was contained in it. According to Safdie's position, the project's raison d'être could not stem from an authority external to the discipline of architecture. Instead, architecture had to use its own disciplinary knowledge—its memory of architectural precedents and principals—in order to articulate an architectural form, which in this case was the idea of the Wall. Accordingly, the minister of justice, who supported

Figure 6.27. Presentation of the Western Wall Precinct to the president of Israel, Ephraim Katzir, 1975. From left to right: Moshe Safdie, President Ephraim Katzir, unidentified, Mayor Teddy Kollek. Source: Moshe Safdie, *Jerusalem: The Future of the Past* (Boston: Houghton Mifflin, 1989), 132. Courtesy of Safdie Architects Archive.

Safdie's project, explained on Israel's single television channel that the evaluation of this entirely architectural project required experts trained in the discipline of architecture.[63]

In preparation for this professional committee, the Ministries of Education and Religious Affairs convened a public conference at the Van Leer Institute in the spring of 1975. Its first panel deliberated the historical and theological status of the Wall. In the second panel architects evaluated the pros and cons of Safdie's scheme. Ram Karmi, arguably Safdie's most influential contemporary among Israeli architects, best expressed the meaning of the Wall to the secular proponents of the *mamlachtiyut* project. As the representative sabra and the charismatic chief architect of the Ministry of Housing, he declared, "the Wall symbolizes the place in which I feel direct roots to King David. I can greet him *shalom*." As such, he added, "it is the most obvious place" in Jerusalem where Jews do not have to justify their existence against Palestinian claims.

According to Karmi, every ruling nation in Jerusalem's history had imprinted its message onto the city's landscape. It followed that since "the Six Day War was a great act" of people who came "to Jerusalem with great spirit and full hearts," it deserved an architectural expression of no lesser magnitude than people "who thought the message they had for Jerusalem was the most important message in its history."[64] This symbolic mandate, he argued, could not be fulfilled by the high modernism of early statehood. The latter could provide necessary housing solutions for Jewish refugees or modernist master plans for the state, but it failed to impart a national home, a place of native Israeliness, the perfect example of which should be the Western Wall Plaza.

For both modernist and Jewish orthodoxies, the monumental scale of Safdie's design seemed to be a timely—rather than timeless—expression for a site that exists beyond temporal bounds. As a former member in the survey team, Michael Turner was alarmed by Safdie's Zionist articulation of Jewish history. He lamented that Safdie's design loses the particularly Jerusalemite trait "in which you walk through history and you feel the entire lineage of Judaism. . . . The six hundred years of the Wall as the Wailing Wall are also an inseparable part of our history," he professed, and they "should receive a microcosmic expression in this site."[65] He was afraid that the biblical Wall, stripped of its two millennia of Jewish worship, might become a single archeological edifice rather than a multilayered, living, Jewish core.[66]

State officials did not evaluate the project's architectural merits, but they could easily identify the virtues of Safdie's conception. Safdie's project monumentalized the Wall; it was interwoven into the archeological sites and incorporated their architecture; it was rich in biblical imagery; and, finally, it was designed to take advantage of prefabricated technology. It was, therefore, the ultimate expression of the *mamlachtiyut*—it united the biblical past with technological progress and created concrete, fast, and beautiful facts on the ground.

As was the case with the national park surrounding the city walls, work continued while deliberations took place. The design of the first project in the descending plaza, the Supreme Rabbinical Court, was already developed under the supervision of the contractor (Israel's Department of Public Works) and the user (the Ministry of Religious Affairs), a pairing that promised to battle each other over every step of the design process. Although orthodox Zionists shared the national appetite for archeological excavation because they wanted to affirm Jewish reign in the region, they firmly refused a secular substitute for the Temple Mount. Orthodox Jews thus found an extroverted Israeliness in Safdie's design and resisted the incorporation of their institutions into this statist, secular worldview. Riffing off the word *dos,* a derogatory name for an ultra-Orthodox Jew, an orthodox architect went so far as to claim that Safdie proposed to construct "dosneyland" (Figure 6.28).[67]

In his correspondence with the Ministry of Religious Affairs, Mordechai Shoshani, the head architect of the Department of Public Works, supported

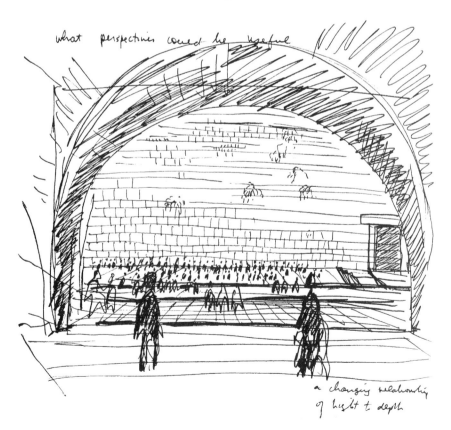

Figure 6.28. Moshe Safdie, Western Wall sketch, 1972. Source: Moshe Safdie's sketchbook. Courtesy of Safdie Architects Archive.

Safdie's grand design against criticism seeking restraint. "Herod's wall" he said, "is a monumental structure, as the size of its stones makes it worthy of being a 'city of a great king.' [This stands] in contrast to the ridiculously small stones of Suleiman the Magnificent [of the sixteenth century], who regarded Jerusalem as just another city in his kingdom."[68] In order to return Jerusalem to its former glory, his message went, one should avoid the minute Orientalism of the Turks, and evoke instead Jerusalem's greatest builder: Herod.

For Shoshani, Safdie's design looked not only to the past, but to the future: "old and ultra new—stone and glass, a stylization of typical Mediterranean architecture in modern garb." Safdie's approach, he stressed, "employs the best [of today's] technical and artistic innovations, with no need for kitschy, saccharine elements of eclecticism or imitation."[69] Shoshani celebrated Safdie's project because he thought it could bridge the present and the past without disregarding modernism. But if it was modern at heart, why did the project attract such heated opposition from architects of the modern persuasion?

The public exhibition of Safdie's project and the solicited responses prepared the ground for the aforementioned committee of seemingly unbiased professionals. The Shimron Committee included independent architects and representatives of the municipality, the Archeological Commission, and the JQDC, but only one out of its seven voting members represented the Ministry of Religious Affairs and the city's Jewish orthodoxy.[70] More intriguing is the assumed professional "neutrality" of the local architectural establishment, which selected committee members "not of this or another strand," but "of the profession."[71] The chosen architects, like the overwhelming majority of their peers, were secular Ashkenazi men who identified with the *mamlachtiyut* project. Arieh Sharon, Avraham Yaski, and Yaakov Rechter were all from Tel Aviv. The first was *the* architect of Labor Zionism; the other two were leading architects of the Tel Aviv sabra circle and adherents to postwar architectural culture.[72] David Reznik, a well-known Jerusalemite architect, was also invited to take part in the committee, but his appointment was canceled shortly after he expressed his preference for greater restraint near the Wall.[73]

The committee interviewed a wide range of professionals, politicians, and public intellectuals. Among them were scholars of Jewish history and thought, who protested that among the decision makers "there is no . . . substantial representation of praying Jews from different ethnic communities, from different trends."[74] The Jerusalem branch of the Association of Architects, which was assembled away from the sabra architectural hegemony in Tel Aviv, urged the committee to foster greater representation. They demanded to form a conceptual program, to do a competition, and to revise the makeup of the evaluating team before any decision would be made.[75] Accustomed to his role as the spokesman for Israeli architects, Arieh Sharon ridiculed the demand for fair representation. With biting sarcasm, he hypothesized a scenario in which "the Head would add two or three wise men, one religious man, one archeologist and one Arab, and we, in half an hour, after we all get smarter, will make five guidelines."[76]

As with all transparent hegemonic discourse, the debate soon confronted objective universal professionalism with a claim for subjective sensitivities. The architects on the committee boasted of their unbiased professionalism, which surfaced during the deliberation of the program, or rather, the absence of elaborate design specification. Undermining the authoritative program of guidelines that typically precede architectural design, Sharon and the other members claimed a mandate of great national consequences. In Yaski's words, "In what we discuss here, we seek an attitude for how to design an essentially national monument. And I don't think there was ever a program for Piazza del Popolo, nor for San Marco, for Gothic cathedrals, or for the Etoile in Paris."[77] The secular architects of the Jerusalem branch refuted Sharon and Yaski's attitude. Their demand for unbiased representation extended the debate beyond the secular/religious divide. They demanded the establishment of "a position regarding the meaning of the Wall" before design is undertaken, because "What you expect from the Wall, is not if it is an enclosed or enlarged [space], what is the Wall for the Jewish people? What do we want from it?"[78]

Yaski kept insisting, in a manner similar to Safdie's, that, at times, "the presence of the work itself can become a means for examining that which you call a program . . . when you start analyzing [the project] you are actually touching the basic conception." With the conviction that architecture does not represent meaning external to it, but rather articulates meaning through its very own form and space and material, Yaski returned the argument back to its disciplinary frame.

For architect David Cassuto, who was a member of the Shimron Committee but also an Orthodox Jew, the entire premise of Yaski's speculation was erroneous: "I don't agree that this is a national monument," he contended. "What is it: a nature reserve, a zoo, a place to come watch?" He was appalled by the prospective sight of "the guys with the *peot* [the hairstyle of ultra-Orthodox Jews]" standing below as a spectacle for the secular men and women watching from above. He reminded the committee, "There are people for whom the Wall is not a monument but part of their lives . . . a living thing."[79]

Modernist and Jewish orthodoxies were uncompromisingly opposed to the *mamlachti* proposition of discussing a finite architectural design as a received embodiment of the ideas underlying a national monument. If the client is the Jewish people at large, then Jewish intellectuals should decide what these ideas should be. Thus, while debates were still unfolding, the minister

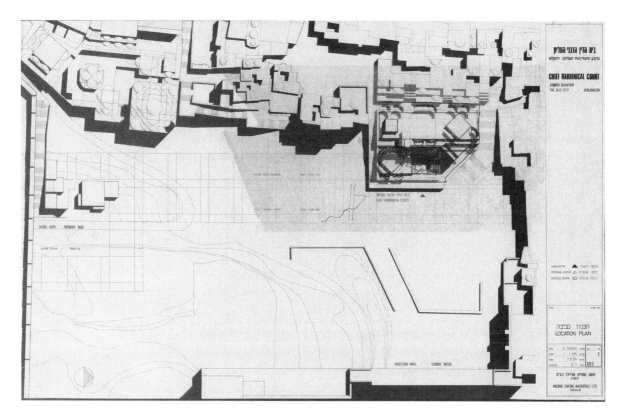

Figure 6.29. Moshe Safdie, preliminary design for the Supreme Rabbinical Court. Courtesy of Safdie Architects Archive.

of religious affairs formed the Conception Committee to counter what he considered a secular bias in deliberating the faith of the Western Wall Plaza. He asked David Cassuto, his representative in the Shimron Committee, to head the new forum,[80] whose 1976 interim report asserted: "The committee negatively sees any tendency and attitude to turn the Wall's plaza into an element or a monument that comes to emphasize only 'that which has passed.'"[81] In sharp opposition to the *mamlachti* desire to monumentalize the Wall, the Conception Committee preferred to emphasize everyday practices and human deed. Multiple everyday uses should shape the Wall rather than a top-down vision.

Concluding the debate, the new committee delivered a clear message: the conception of the Western Wall project must be decided outside the discipline of architecture. There was no point in judging whether Safdie's project was good or beautiful because those were qualities beyond its technical mandate. The beautification of the Wall's precinct, they insisted, would not enhance its virtues; it merely threatened to change them. The *mamlachti* notion of beauty stood for different virtues, which were neither modern nor Jewish. Safdie's project, they thought, beautified the *mamlachtiyut* rather than the Wall, whose virtues lay beyond any contemporary definition of urban aesthetics. Architecture, they exhorted, should humble itself in front of the Wall.

Like many debates in Jerusalem, this one had no end. The controversy hampered the Shimron Committee's work, which was halted for nearly two years until 1977, losing in the process Avraham Yaski, who could not tolerate the parallel Conception Committee. In the meantime Safdie continued to design the Supreme Rabbinical Court as part of his larger scheme (Figure 6.29). After Safdie exercised his Sephardi Aleppo charm on the Sephardi Chief Rabbi Ovadia Yoseph,[82] the authorized approval of the Orthodox Jewish community was at last secured. As a result, on May 5, 1977, the State of Israel officially approved Safdie's design.[83] When David Cassuto, the defeated head of the Conception Committee, asked his minister, "What shall we do?" the minister of religious affairs replied, "Nothing." Being in charge of the site, it was within his power to put the project to rest. All parties, fortified in their positions with sealed documents, would rest for a decade or two before embarking on more rounds in this endless battle.[84]

International Sabra

The position of different cultural actors is crucial not only for a deeper understanding of the events, but also for mapping the different postwar modernisms of these protagonists and their impact on Jerusalem. Safdie's position is the most remarkable. He negotiated a bicultural identity with great skill. On the one hand, he was recognized as an international master—an arbiter of the latest architectural expertise and beauty—and on the other, he labored to be accepted as an integral member of Israeli culture. In his book *Jerusalem: The Future of the Past,* for example, he is pictured in military uniform. This image helped him to fit into a society that considered obligatory military service a requirement for cultural legitimization (Figure 6.30).

Figure 6.30. Moshe Safdie during military service in 1972 (center, without hat). Source: Moshe Safdie, *Jerusalem: The Future of the Past* (Boston: Houghton Mifflin, 1989), 39.

One cannot overstate the importance of Safdie's mastery of identity politics. Consider, for example, how he deployed his family origin in Aleppo, Syria. Safdie was born and raised in Israel, in a country dominated by the cultural norms of its European elite, fostered by the Labor socialist Ashkenazi regime. During the first decades of statehood, the leaders of Eastern European origin notoriously marginalized the Arab Jews who immigrated to Israel en masse only after its independence. As a child, Safdie was the only Jew of Arab descent *(Mizrahi)* in his private school class. The Safdies left for Canada when he was fifteen years old,[85] unable to survive the economic restrictions of the Labor regime. At that time, Israelis saw such a departure as a betrayal of the Zionist cause.

In an intriguing twist, Safdie managed to use his Arab origin to assert his familiarity with Middle Eastern cultures and his command of the local vernacular: "The founders' generation has difficulties with the Middle East, which found expression in architecture. I think and believe that our generation has fewer problems with the region. My Middle Eastern origin provides me with an entirely different starting point than the cultural bedrock of Eastern Europe."[86] Safdie's origin helped him, as we have seen, gain the commission for the yeshiva, as well as the approval of the Western Wall project from the Sephardic chief rabbi. It was also useful in a country whose identity politics were undergoing a momentous shift; just a couple of years later, in 1977, the vote of Arab Jews would lead to the first fall of the Labor party. Scholars argue that his upbringing on the shores of the Mediterranean helped Safdie articulate his famous Habitat megastructure in Montreal. The open question is whether it gave him a different vantage point in devising a local modernism in Jerusalem.

Tension existed between the high modernists who formed the developmental coalitions of Israel's early master plans, including the one for Jerusalem. Their younger critics joined the situated coalitions that wished to concretize architecture in its local context. Among the latter were two in particular: the generational revolt of the sabra architectural circle and its search for a genuine Israeli "place"; and the Anglo circle's call to revise urban practices in order to address the spirit and character of the city and its residents. Although the two had a common enemy, developmental modernisms, Safdie's project for the Western Wall Plaza found them on two different ends of the dispute.

The sabra circle unequivocally supported Safdie's plan. The Anglo circle was similarly unified against Safdie's project. At the Van Leer symposium, Safdie and Karmi represented the first group, Aronson and Turner the other. This dichotomy reveals not only the propensity of different social and professional groups to practice distinct modernisms, but also the positions each modernism advances in relation to central issues such as nationalism, faith, Diaspora, and democracy.

Conspicuous differences between the two circles were formative. Safdie aligned with the sabra architects who were flattered by the young architectural celebrity's aspirations for an Israeli identity. When a petition to reject his project in favor of an open competition to design the Western Wall Plaza gained momentum, the outraged Karmi and Rechter interfered, insisting that no competition could yield better results.[87] Safdie's sabra allies were located primarily in Tel Aviv, where they grew up under the popular Labor Party leadership and were well integrated into its mechanisms of power. They were thoroughly secular and fully committed to the national cause—gathering the exiles and absorbing these new immigrants into the Israeli culture the sabra architects participated in shaping. Celebrated as the ultimate New Jews, the sabras sought refuge from diasporic uprootedness and strove instead to create a reality of certainties, of concrete and stable places, of obvious belonging. They wanted to crack the code of locality and harness its meaning as a new anchor of Israeli identity.

On the one hand, this group worked within the grand narratives of modernism: it was interwoven into the welfare state, adhered to its melting-pot ideology, and advanced a universal conception of Man. On the other hand, the sabras' quest for enduring national symbols contradicted the modernist notion of perpetual change, of modernity as a constantly shifting project to which any modernism must perpetually respond. When Bruno Zevi protested to Safdie that Jerusalem had spoiled him, that is, had damaged his modernism,[88] he summarized beautifully this sabra temptation to search in the ancient city for codes of eternal existence.

The Anglo group was different. Some of its members were new immigrants who came to an already established Israeli culture. Some were observant Jews. Almost all had been educated in leading English-speaking schools. Unlike their sabra colleagues, for whom the notion of the Diaspora was subjected to Zionist negation, the new immigrants lived overseas, experienced the modern mobility of migration, and worked in established urban contexts, unlike the sabras who, in most cases, tried to create urbanity from scratch.

While sabra architects were very ambivalent about what they called "Jerusalemism," most of the Anglo group lived in Jerusalem and some would dedicate their life careers to its planning, preservation, and documentation.[89] Unlike the sabras who held thriving private practices, the greatest influence of the Anglo group was within the public sector, a tradition inspired primarily by British planning agencies such as the Greater London Council. It accorded with their training at schools such as MIT, the University of California at Berkeley, and the Architectural Association, schools that put great emphasis on the process of creating a habitat—as opposed to creating finite neighborhoods—with and for the people who lived in these dynamic built environments.

The dispute between the two groups in relation to the Western Wall brought their different conceptions of both architecture and Judaism, and the possible ties between the two, to the surface. The highly modernist *1968 Jerusalem Masterplan* (rejected by both circles) asserted that the spirit of the Jewish religion inspired the plan's focus on the everyday life of people in the city, rather than the glorification of the city's monumental core. While the Anglo group wished to dispense with the developmental implications of this position, they endorsed its association between Judaism, people, and everyday practice. In their eyes the Wall's primary value lay in the sacred memories it stored. Since these memories move people differently, in different times and within different spatial configurations, members of the Anglo circle demanded that modern architects negotiate the striking new reality of the Western Wall's bulldozed plaza. It meant that they had to learn how people and institutions readjust to this new condition rather than dictating a top-down spatial configuration for the broader public. They argued for focusing on the ritual that would take place next to the Wall rather than on the embodied sanctity of its stones.

This concept contradicted the very project of sabra architects, because it perpetuated the diasporic condition that they wished to end. The Western Wall for them was not a site of yearning, but rather, of arrival and return. Accordingly, sabra archeologists knew their task—to scientifically establish the historical value of the Wall as a remnant of Herod's Temple. But how can such scientific data turn into "the emotional focal point of the Jewish people"?[90] Kollek, whose quote phrased this challenge, believed that only architects could achieve it. Their mandate was to transform archeological facts into a tangible, sensual experience that was no longer contingent on historical specificities but, rather, on a distracted everyday use of the urban space that rendered the monumental antiquity of the Western Wall as a matter of fact, an urban setting that sat comfortably and permanently in its place. According to Alois Rigel, this is exactly what distinguishes "the modern cult of monument" in the twentieth century. Its focus on the age value of a monument stresses the authenticity of its antiquity, where continuity and permanence reassure the modern subject in a world that has lost its transcendental truths. This position relies on the symbolic stability of the stones of the Wall, which are, in the words of a popular post-1967 song, "stones with human heart."[91]

Conclusions

Safdie's design for the Western Wall Plaza embodied the vision of the *mamlachtiyut,* the Israeli nation-building project, according to which modern Israel revives the Jewish sovereignty that existed in antiquity. As with most national projects, it addressed an imagined community of Jews emerging together from a distant biblical time, enduring ruptured history, and marching toward the unified future that was promised by the metaphor of United Jerusalem. The symbol of this unity was the Western Wall. The architect's task was therefore to cure the site's ruptured history in order to accommodate a seamless Jewish continuity. Safdie's healing formula fulfilled this call by integrating all the parameters pertinent to his design into a holistic matrix that meshed the past, present, and future of the Jewish people (Figure 6.31).

Safdie's plan for the Western Wall Plaza established the idea of the past through a descending architectural section, deep enough to reach the archeological seam between the stones of Herod's Wall and the ancient paving stones of the street underneath. It conveyed a holistic present by embracing both daily and monumental spaces and creating these in prefabricated concrete, following Herod's architectural precedents and the enduring models of the Palestinian vernacular. The plan's promising view toward the future harnessed the latest in the science of morphology in order to devise an ordering system that glued the fragments of the site, as if ingathering the Jewish Diaspora into a unified image of Jewish collectivity.

For Safdie, design was "a synthesizing process" striving for perfection.[92] From the passion of his early writing we can see his devotion to morphology: "I believe that as the man-made environment approaches the perfection of the form fulfillment of natural organisms, the separation between the man-made and the natural will disappear, that we as men will be equally fulfilled in either man-made or natural environments."[93] According to this credo the architectural task was to extract from the generic qualities of the environment the logic of space-makers that obey the deep structure of the city. This

	Architectural Device	Source of Inspiration	Material
Past	section	archaeology	stone
Present	space and volume	vernacular and Herodian	prefabricated concrete
Future	ordering system	morphology and technology	mobile fiberglass domes

Figure 6.31. A design matrix of Jewish continuity as it is articulated in Safdie's Western Wall Plaza project. Drawn by the author.

search for the inherent morphological logic of the place, the DNA of the city, has far-reaching consequences. It promises, Safdie argues, to simulate a natural organization of the urban fabric, to make the design of the Western Wall precinct feel as fulfilling and welcoming as natural phenomena.

This was arguably the ultimate purpose of the *mamlachti* agenda, to create in six years a Jewish setting that looked as if it was formed by nature, by the lasting spirit of Judaism. But this integrated, natural design was simultaneously made possible by what Zionists saw as a privileged, redemptive moment in history brought about by the military power of the state. Forceful, almost supernatural, this moment allowed a wholesale clearance of diasporic traces under which the true nature of the site could be found.

Jewish intellectuals were quick to remind Israeli authorities that such an approach was risky. They argued that the sacredness of the Wall, as a place of ritual and memory, was established during diasporic time. The critics stressed that the Wall is not only a historical remnant; its own importance emanates first and foremost from its being a praying place and a place to establish the past with hope and in the anticipation of what it encodes for the future.[94]

At issue is a fundamental distinction between different conceptions of the Jewish future. According to the *mamlachti* vision, the Diaspora expelled Jews from history; the founding of the State of Israel, and later Jewish victory in 1967, returned Jews both to history and to independent national life, which is the sole guarantee for a secure future. From the perspective of the religious opponents of the project, however, nationhood is just another moment in a very long Jewish history. Accordingly, the Jewish future primarily relies not on a very recent notion of nation, but on the far more abiding elements of Jewish faith, memory, and ritual.

The uneasy marriage between Judaism and nationalism delayed the work on the praying plaza but did not halt the archeologists. New and exciting archeological findings prompted Safdie to prepare an updated model for the Western Wall Plaza. "For a period of three months," he recalls, "model makers reconstructed the history of Jerusalem, layer by layers, all the way up from 1500 B.C. to the existing grade."[95] Safdie could not have simulated better the process that Kollek, the Archeological Commission, and the JQDC planned to complete in six years' time, the spatial reconstruction of Jewish history. According to Safdie, the model delivered a new message: "it was a transparent layering of past, present, and future."[96] The review of this integrated history is not only beyond the time period of this study, but also beyond the historical circumstances that allowed the secular *mamlachti* vision to override all others. Safdie packed the model "into three crates, each somewhat larger than a coffin." Too large for a regular delivery, they were "nestled among rockets and machine guns" on a Flying Tigers flight to the Holy Land. This airborne military funeral ended to the sound of Kollek's outcry: "I am not going to look at it. Send it back to the United States."[97] The flammable ground Kollek refused to incite already belonged to a different Jerusalem.

CONCLUSION

THE STRUGGLE OVER JERUSALEM—a sacred city to the three monotheistic religions and the symbolic and administrative capital of two contesting nations—has long been built upon extreme violence and extreme emotion. All this extremity of action and feeling has a subtle but significant side effect: it obscures the great nuances of historical processes. Our attention is quickly grabbed by the persistence of violence and the tragedy of innocent deaths, and we therefore focus enormous attention on its apparent cause: the official politics of war, the manipulations of territory, the logistics of legal treaties. As a result, we relegate to the margins of history the innumerable other processes by which women and men make life and create meaning. But the city of Jerusalem does not exist only in legal documents and on news broadcasts, or only in scholarly tomes and religious screeds. It is a concrete city, lived in and dreamed about in actual spaces and in real time. The cultural politics beneath these spaces—beneath Jerusalem's unprecedented post-1967 physical transformation—is so significant because our sensual perceptions of these storied streets indelibly affect the meaning we attribute to its edifices and the critical role they play in our lives.

This study has examined the cultural processes that shaped the image of contemporary Jerusalem; more precisely, it questions how the politics of architectural production affected the blueprint underlying contemporary Jerusalem. Although such politics have proven to be surprisingly efficient over the last half century, we have typically overlooked their meaning. Yet, in 1967 the Israeli government did not just triple Jerusalem's municipal size and double its population. They embarked on an industrious building and landscaping project that dramatically and irreversibly changed the way we experience and value a sacred city that people live and die for.

This staggering transformation was entrusted to a relatively small group of architects and planners, who competed to shape the unilaterally united Jerusalem. We have seen how, as individual architects working in contested sites, these professionals were always caught in a web of politics and rarely had the required power to freely execute their vision. It is therefore impossible to argue for the autonomy of architecture from politics. Quite the opposite. But it is similarly important to resist the temptation of reading architecture instrumentally as a direct result of political decisions, that is, as means toward a preconceived end. Instead, I argue that architecture acts as a mediator between the administrative maze of official politics and the physical city where actual life, everyday and ceremonial, is conducted. Such mediation, I maintain, is an active, and consequential, force.

According to Ann Swidler, we can understand such consequential force by studying the tool kit through which culture operates and produces meaning. In our case, we examined the architectural tool kit—the knowledge, debates, precedents, and procedures that architects work through and consider their own. It is necessary to analyze this tool kit in order to understand a player crucial to shaping Jerusalem's politics of space. Politicians, who were often helpless in translating their goals into praxis, entrusted the transformation of Jerusalem to architects. As a result, they found themselves dependent on this most unlikely source: the disciplinary processes of theory-obsessed, forward-thinking design professionals and the bodies of knowledge that informed their practice. But when these professionals articulated, in their obscure disciplinary languages, the ways they wanted to shape Jerusalem's built landscape, they were not merely executing an official political agenda. Rather, they were playing out a host of concerns currently roiling their professional field.

The more we explore the profession's enormous impact on the city, the more often we are brought back to the contemporary discourse on architectural modernisms and the tangled ways they shaped and reshaped Jerusalem. In this fashion, the post–World War II criticism of the modern movement in architecture, heard in various languages around the world, as well as ongoing debates about place and authenticity and the fate of urban renewal, became active players in Jerusalem's politics of space. By the same token, the embroilment of these concepts in the competition over Jerusalem helps us better understand the power of postwar modernism and the subtle distinctions between its different schools of architectural thought.

In order to reach this dual perspective—the intervention of postwar architectural knowledge in shaping Jerusalem and the reciprocal reflection of Jerusalem's politics on the meaning of postwar modernism—we began by theorizing the parallel modernisms of two vastly different cultures: architecture and Zionism. The former belongs to the visual arts, and its modernisms are well documented. The latter belongs to official politics, and by contrast, its various strands are rarely discussed from this cultural and aesthetic perspective. But this theoretical parallel is necessary to understand the productive encounter between the corresponding crises of the modern movement in architecture on the one hand, and of the Israeli nation-building project on the other.

The architectural transition from developmental modernism (driven toward progress and development) to situated modernism (committed to man, place, and disciplinary memory) can be seen as an attempt to salvage the autonomy and specificity of modern architecture. A similar ideological transition, from stressing progress and development to prioritizing the land and its biblically inspired culture, attempted to imbue the Israeli nation-building project, *mamlachtiyut* (kingdomism), with Jewish tradition and historical continuity.

When local architects tried resolving the inner contradiction between the actual and the generic Man of post–World War II architectural culture, they envisioned a coherent and identifiable Israeli home in East Jerusalem and drew on the ethics of New Brutalism and the nascent regionalism of Team 10. Their turn to the vernacular was a rebellious shift from the utopian aspects of the Zionist project to the real—and indeed, often brutal—existing world: the famed "as found" that was so effective in Britain during the 1950s. But the model of the native Jew that the sabra embodied was itself the result of an insecure possession of the actual place. Sabra architects defined themselves vis-à-vis a modernization project, which they thoroughly criticized, and a place for which they longed, but whose genetic code was undeniably Arab, especially when juxtaposed with the strict modernism of the Zionist project.

In this context our postcolonial analysis of the Israeli desire for the nativeness of the Palestinian has revealed the cultural formation of a dominant professional discourse. The ethnography of the colonizer rather than the colonized revealed the insecure desire of Israeli architects for the symbols of their constituent "other," the occupied Palestinians. The latter read the Israeli efforts to render the Palestinian vernacular as biblical, primitive, or Mediterranean as yet another form of occupation. Such claims to possess the authenticity of their native architectural forms turned into a major political tool against Israeli occupation. Hence, the Israeli architecture of place that became prevalent across the 1970s was deemed a colonial hijacking, a position that was also adopted by the Israeli Left despite the ambiguities of this architecture and its apparent social success. Like the architecture it studies, the architectural historiography of this period is similarly caught in a web of politics that this study labors to disentangle.

To bring our study to its inevitably inconclusive end, let's first explore how the essential threads of our narrative continue to braid (and tangle) together into our own day. We will first identify the political visions different competitors for Jerusalem held and the ways in which they articulated this vision through different postwar trends of architectural modernism. As we venture beyond the time frame of our study, we will further appreciate the impact of the postwar decade and the blueprint it continues to be for contemporary Jerusalem and its political tensions.

The Postwar Decade and Beyond

In many ways the decade we have studied was one of political suspense. As a result, and despite the seemingly unified Israeli efforts to reshape the city, opposing positions regarding the faith of Jerusalem could coexist: a state aspiring to shape in and through Jerusalem a collective identity for its citizens, a city aspiring to manage a mosaic of identities, and an international community aspiring to transcend national conflict for the benefit of all mankind. This elusive, and temporary, sense of coexisting Israeli agendas for Jerusalem was indebted to the city's vague political and legal status. As we have seen, in June 1967 Israel based its unilateral unification of the city on an amendment to a municipal law: an incredibly obscure evidentiary base, but important because it meant that the unification technically was not illegal expropriation of Jordanian land, nor a further violation of the 1947 UN decision to internationalize Jerusalem.

This vagueness allowed the national government to focus its monumental making of United Jerusalem on two primary goals: the demographic Judaization of Jerusalem and its territorial indivisibility. This firm mandate, as we have seen, was entrusted to the almighty Ministry of Housing, which not only centralized the building market in Israel, but also, and quite often, preempted the authority of the Ministry of Interior Affairs and of Jerusalem's municipal government. The post-1967 decade epitomized this dynamic: civic, municipal, and international objections to the rapid building of East Jerusalem did not restrain the demographic and territorial appetite of the ministry. Quite the opposite; contrary visions only accelerated the engine of this terribly efficient housing machine. The only territory the state relegated to local authorities—namely the Ministry of Interior Affairs and the Jerusalem Municipality—was the symbolic basin surrounding the Old City, where construction was limited, by definition, to the public gems that Mayor Teddy Kollek carefully selected and polished.

As the decade progressed, and particularly after the bitter 1973 war crushed whatever was left of Israelis' post-1967 euphoria, the firm leadership of the Labor government weakened. With the ascent of a new political party, the pacifying fog over Jerusalem's definition was mercilessly cleared. In 1980, Geula Cohen of the Likud—the right-wing party that in 1977 ended socialist rule in Israel—succeeded in passing the Jerusalem Law in the Israeli parliament, the Knesset. This "basic law," as it was defined, declared that "Je-

rusalem, complete and united, is the capital of Israel."[1] It is nearly impossible
to overstate the gravity of this decision, which was immediately considered a
violation of international law. Consequently, all national embassies left Jerusalem, and Israeli custodianship over Jerusalem, the pride of Mayor Kollek,
became a fierce contest. When the Likud assumed power in 1977, construction in Jerusalem was at its peak, but in the following years plans and budgets
started drifting to the outer ring of Jerusalem, cementing the settlements—
such as Ma'ale Edomim in the West Bank—that dominate so much of the
conversation about Jerusalem today.

The escalating conflict with Palestine intensified the tension between Israel's two simultaneous, and opposing, paths: advancing a national home that
would liberate Jewish refugees from centuries of vicious persecution, and by
the same token forcefully settling this home in the land by dispossessing the
Palestinian "other." Against the firm political borders of the 1950s and 1960s
besieged country, the *mamlachtiyut* could better mesh a modernist state and a
Jewish nation into a unified national form. But once the 1967 war territorially
unleashed the spirit of Israeli nationalism, the Israeli state could no longer
conceal the ambiguity of its intentions—its inflammatory blend of national
and colonial goals—even from its own citizens.

More recently, this predicament has become embroiled in the broader trajectory of globalization, which has challenged the unifying power of nation-
states all over the world, and in the case of Jerusalem, has challenged the
capacity of Israel to independently manage the conflict with Palestine. According to Uri Ram, the joined pressures of a privatized neoliberal market
and the bloody conflict with Palestine are weakening the ties that Israel's
socialist rule had forged with Jews and their Jewish traditions.[2] As the illu-
sion of unity fades away, a polarized society emerges. In Ram's analysis, one
end of this polarized society, which he identifies with the political left and
with a global economy, is "post-Zionist." Its adherents believe that Zionism
has already completed its historical mission—rescuing Jews from Fascism. It
should therefore be transcended by a democratic rule that equally distributes
the resources of the state to all its citizens. The other extreme, Ram argues, is
"neo-Zionist," belongs to the political right, and believes in the power of local
economies. Its advocates believe that the Land of Israel, that is, the former
territory of Mandate Palestine, is the birthright of the Jewish people, and it
should therefore be resettled by Jews and protected against Arab invasion.

A glimpse of two of today's powerful organizations helps us see these opposing poles and the vast gulf between them. The Bloc of the Faithful (Gush
Emunim), established in 1974 by right-wing religious Zionists in order to settle the Greater Land of Israel, considers itself the committed and true inheri-
tor of the Zionist mission. Peace Now, a left-wing activist group founded to
pursue the opportunities opened by Anwar Sadat's visit from Egypt in 1977,

argues for territorial compromise and for peace as a springboard to economic prosperity. As the distance between the two poles grows, so does their commitment to a common purpose. Both sides, it seems, have lost a crucial aspect of the early state: the belief, ambition, and ability to unify a coherent national body under a consensual national narrative and shared political goals.[3]

The architectural historiography of Israel in the last couple of decades reflects this political polarization. It is deeply engaged in the ensuing cultural war between neo- and post-Zionists, which colors the way Israelis see, experience, and interpret the built environment. Instead, this study sheds light on the multivocal competition over Jerusalem that precedes the contemporary extremes. Our focus has been limited to debates within Israeli society and has centered on a period during which Jordan was the contending Arab party for Jerusalem. By and large during the decade after the 1967 war, the Palestinians themselves, for whom the war was a second national disaster, were laboriously consolidating their institutional infrastructure and could not yet develop the means to forge their own competition over Al-Quds. But that would soon change.

Three Visions of Democracy: Beyond the National Cocoon

Even as we gain a better understanding of the sheer variety of modernisms that grew around the globe during the twentieth century, it is tempting to assume that the nationalism that accompanied each of these modernisms was itself a unified project. But as we have seen, the fierce competition that ensued over Jerusalem was not only between Israelis and Palestinians, but also between different facets within the Israeli national body. By considering not only the physical city but also the idea of the city, and by analyzing architecture as a form of political action, this book reveals an inherent paradox: the symbolic gravity of Jerusalem disturbs any attempt to surrender its meaning to a single national narrative or to subordinate its visual idea to a unified architectural form. As a result, rifts grew even between the political powers (and their attendant agencies) that shared nearly the same goal: to unify Jerusalem as a metaphor for the unity between the Jewish people and their promised territory—between, in other words, the Jewish nation and the Israeli state.

Looking back over not just the post-1967 decade, but across nearly the last half century, I suggest that the rifts we've explored—the competition between the planning agendas of the profession, the state, the city, and the international frontier—ultimately reveal a tension between at least three visions of political organization. Each offered different, and often incompatible, interpretations of what democracy means and how it should fit within the nation-state; as Liah Greenfeld insightfully remarks, democracies are contained within the nation-state "as a butterfly in a cocoon."[4] Yet the final, and evolving, form of that butterfly is nearly always fraught with tension. We can characterize these three visions as communitarian, liberal, and universal. By considering the development of Jerusalem through these three visions, we enhance our perspective not only on the post-1967 decade, but on the city today.

The Israeli state, as it absorbed a vast number of new immigrants and settled a contested land, followed a communitarian vision. Labor leaders forged for their increasingly diverse population the national narrative of the *mamlachtiyut*, a secularized Jewish tale of a return to the Promised Land, to the tangible territory of Jewish origin. This narrative emphasized the common denominator of the newcomers—though wildly varied, they were all Jewish—and succeeded, as a result, to structure the Israeli melting pot around the *mamlachti* interpretation of the New Jew. It consequently fostered bonds not only between various communities of new immigrants, but more significantly, between them and the land they settled. In political terms, this unifying narrative instilled in every citizen a collective drive toward a common good, yielding the desired result: "a 'constitutive' community, a community that would constitute the very identity of the individuals."[5]

The architecture of the place that sabra architects developed (the solution to their critique of developmental modernism), and its eventual practice by the Ministry of Housing throughout the 1970s, aimed to achieve exactly this goal: constituting, by means of architecture, and particularly through public housing, the *mamlachti* identity of Israeli residents. The built landscape, in other words, was to embody their affiliation to each other as a community and to the place as a unified people. Brutalism insinuated the roughness of the sabra and the directness of daily life, and regionalism endowed this architecture with the desired rootedness in a contested territory. Together they cohered a bold style that blurred an otherwise sharp line: the line dividing the poster that opened this study, the hyphen between nation and state.

Despite his formative years with David Ben Gurion, who authored the *mamlachtiyut*, Teddy Kollek was rather impartial to the communitarian performance of this nation-building project. I suggest that his cultural politics, and thus the vision offered by the city of Jerusalem, falls instead within the second vision, the liberal interpretation of democracy. Kollek ran the city as an organization that is instrumental to the different groups it contains without intervening in the way they define their identities or their own good. Because he considered Jerusalem a "sacred city of mankind,"[6] he did not labor to shape identities but, rather, to manage them; only a liberal rule, he believed, would convince the world that Israelis respect all the residents of the Holy City and is therefore entitled to assume the historical role of Jews as the forerunner of the monotheistic faiths. This position came closer to cultural Zionism than political Zionism, that is, the Zionism that believed Jews should shed a light onto all other nations rather than merely win a legal charter and become just another nation.

In order to overcome the gross asymmetry between Israeli Jews and occupied Palestinian residents—who refused to accept Israeli citizenship, and who refused to participate in the city's unification—Kollek developed his mosaic policy. In principle, members of every segment in Jerusalem's endless puzzle of ethnic groups could define their own essence, could use "their rights to promote their self-interest within certain constraints imposed by the exigency to respect the rights of others."[7] Kollek aimed to manage these (many) exigencies, and to find a common good agreed upon by all. Avoiding the obvious divisiveness of territorial possession, he promoted instead the flagship policy of urban beautification.

Since Jerusalem was by definition ensnared within the web of national politics, Kollek's vision more often than not failed the test of reality. Yet the architects Kollek employed and the bureaucratic coalition he created followed, by and large, this ambitious route. The Anglo circle of architects and planners he nurtured at 10 Shamai Street advanced the urban design of the city by authoring grand policies to regulate space. Landscape architects designed open spaces in between communities instead of shaping the intimate spaces of domestic life. Architectural commissions centered primarily on cultural institutions that were painstakingly located within the urban fabric. Kollek was similarly adamant about the overlap of finances between governmental and municipal enterprises. His coalition consisted of an agglomeration of companies; each ran with an independent budget, but all operated under his wide umbrella through shared assets or political allies. Moreover, the effective Jerusalem Foundation he established succeeded even in managing the flow of private money for institutional purposes.

By and large, the international community granted legitimacy to the liberal vision of Kollek's cultural politics. But the most respected elders of his Jerusalem Committee preferred to envision the city as a universal democracy, one that would allow the democratic butterfly to finally fly free from the national cocoon. Lewis Mumford bluntly asked both Jews and Arabs to halt their national aspirations from nearing Jerusalem, begging them to recognize the city as an idea much greater than their pitiful and outdated nationalisms. Louis Kahn sought in Jerusalem the authentic origin of human institutions, and for Buckminster Fuller, Jerusalem was still the center of the rotating earth. Younger architects from around the world, too, treated Jerusalem as a universal testing ground. In the ancient city they explored ways to redeem their own cities from the aggressive modernization they so despised back home. Despite their diverse positions toward Jerusalem, these international architects shared a common stance: the desire of two national groups for the city was either overlooked or intentionally undermined in the hope of transcending national conflict altogether.

Had the 1968 master plan been implemented, Jerusalem might have turned, like Tel Aviv, into a modernist city, with its Old City left as a reservoir of religiosity, a quaint destination for international tourists and pilgrims. However, as the Jerusalem Committee illustrated, the international community refused to relinquish its role in the spiritualizing of Jerusalem. Jerusalem became a test case, a site where the West could search for salvation from its own modernity. Concurrently, an alternative powerful program for Israeli national architecture emerged in agreement with the tenets of *mamlachtiyut*. This architecture of the place, however, has hardly been able to survive the tension between the conflicting pressures brought on by nation building, a settler society, and international politics.

Welfare or Occupation: The State and the Fate of the National Home

These three visions of democracy and their attendant depictions (or lack thereof) of nationhood in turn correspond with the different modernisms that were central to the Israeli making of United Jerusalem. The architecture of the place articulated the most powerful of these modernisms: the communitarian vision of democracy that substantiated the *mamlachti* project of the Israeli welfare state. This self-contradictory architectural culture flourished in the Ministry of Housing, which offered sabra architects a larger-than-life opportunity to construct massive residential settlements in East Jerusalem, the so-called ring or satellite neighborhoods. Architecturally their work was considered innovative and daring, but politically it was well anchored in the Israeli mainstream. Despite the outrage of many Jerusalemites by the ministry's quick and zealous construction in East Jerusalem, their criticism, by and large, failed to raise the most fundamental question of all: Why settle East Jerusalem? Instead, they were preoccupied with another question: How to settle?

The challenge politicians posed to the architectural profession addressed exactly this dilemma: how to turn a confiscated land into a reassuring home. But this mandate meshed together two contradictory agendas: one pertained to the social policy of a welfare state,[8] and the other to the territorial politics of a settler society.[9] In other words, the architectural testing ground the Israeli government entrusted to sabra architects had to implement a progressive policy for social housing that was also, and by the same architectural measures, geared toward the territorial occupation of Palestinian land and the demographic Judaization of East Jerusalem. Like modernity itself, this double-edged project of social liberation and political oppression charged the assessment of Israeli housing in East Jerusalem with a moral weight that often obscures the historical complexity and meaning of this turbulent decade. To put it bluntly, Israeli critics now deplore the very same architecture that their predecessors featured with pride in official and professional publications. This quandary merits further attention.

As a welfare state, Israel could best fulfill the promise of a national home in Jerusalem by addressing one of the most rudimentary needs of humanity: housing.[10] But Israelis and their leaders had already experienced the disappointing outcome of the first wave of social housing built in the 1950s in developing modernist towns. Critics of the ministry's earlier and entrenched developmental modernism demanded to revise the ministry's housing policy and to situate its housing blocks in the specifics of the place. Accordingly, the Israeli building of East Jerusalem had to be not only a functional and territorial, but also a social, cultural, and aesthetic project. Its performance on these grounds, critics argued, would determine if the land politicians confiscated would turn into solid middle-class Jerusalemite neighborhoods or into undesired slums.

A young generation of architects effectively addressed this call. By the end of the 1960s they already had at their disposal a decade of experiments with new forms of social housing inspired by post–World War II situated modernisms. Long before the occupation of East Jerusalem the aesthetics of concrete arches, buildings gathered in clusters, and residential cubes descending down the topography started appearing in the Israeli periphery.[11] After the war, these experimental architects started transforming Israel's centralized building machine. They turned the Ministry of Housing into an urban laboratory where numerous interdisciplinary teams formed think tanks for housing and urban design. In the initial designs we studied, first of Ma'alot Dafna, and later of the three residential settlements of Giloh, East Talpiot, and Ramot, they enacted diverse postwar modernisms, ranging from Team 10's definition of a residential cluster to Kevin Lynch's imageability; from the Smithsons' degrees of urban identification to MIT's development of public participation in the planning process. Team members of other disciplines augmented the planning process with sociological analysis, communal institutions, and financial policies.

By the 1980s the social success of these measures in Jerusalem's residential settlements had already been established. Professional publications and popular demand agreed: the new housing eclipsed the modernist residential block—the hated *shikunim*—and was better attuned to the needs of the people and their desire to be at home. Moreover, and despite critical predictions, the ring neighborhoods of East Jerusalem were far more successful than the modernist towns in bringing poor people and new immigrants into the warm embrace of the middle class. Against such powerful social mobility, and the consequential recovery of slums in West Jerusalem, we cannot but ponder: Why do critics of the last decade consistently praise the modernist residential block of early statehood as an authentic Israeli expression, while condemning the stone-clad housing of post-1967 East Jerusalem as denigrating Israeli modernism?[12]

The success of these ring neighborhoods, despite international outrage, proved that the Israeli welfare state, and its group of architects, had delivered to its Jewish citizens the promised national home in Jerusalem. But whether its citizens felt at home there or not, Jerusalem remained a contested city, and Israel's settlement machine was overturned by the job market it created. Between 1948 and 1967 East Jerusalem was under Jordanian rule. The many Palestinians who lived in Jordan gravitated toward Jerusalem, which was enough of a reason for Jordan to halt its development in order to strengthen Amman as a capital. But in 1967 that slow job market rapidly shifted. Thousands of Palestinians started working in the booming Israeli building industry, literally constructing the Jewish inhabitation of East Jerusalem.[13]

But their consequent migration to Jerusalem threatened to undo the demographic Judaization they were hired to make possible. Israeli authorities held back the inevitable growth of the Palestinian population by ensuring that the development of their neighborhoods would soon bump up against an invisible, yet solid, glass dome squelching further construction.[14] This policy created a steep shortage in housing (and by necessity, a steep rise in illegal construction). The result was a continual demolition of houses that Israel had denied building permits for. The violent destruction of these homes further fueled the rage underlying the Palestinian uprising that broke out in 1987 and would eventually be called the intifada.[15]

The Palestinian intifada gave a political charge to those already potent places that had, in the 1960s and 1970s, provided inspiration to architects looking for the authentic and the local. With the first intifada, it became difficult to regard Arab villages as mere landscapes of stone and light, of Mediterranean alleys and squares. They ceased to serve as architectural precedents for a generic Mediterranean and biblical localness. These stones were now thrown in protest, and these villages were now defiantly Palestinian, rather than generically Arab. Violence made the competition for ownership of the place plainly visible. Conflict spread to Jerusalem and the West Bank—the characteristic sites of authentic localness—making it even more difficult to find, anywhere in Jerusalem, the consensus necessary for casting a national heritage and for inspiring architecture that can metaphorically speak colloquial Hebrew.

Amid the violence, the architecture of the place quickly fell out of vogue. The historiographical impact was paradoxical. During these years of the intifada, the sabra architects who designed Jerusalem's housing during the 1970s turned to serve the free market—to design numerous shopping malls and office and residential towers for the ultrarich. At the same time, their state-commissioned public housing in Jerusalem—the architecture we have reviewed across this study—won the dubious title of postmodern, which critics paint with the colors of occupation and various other social ills. This criticism meshed architectural and ethical judgment by means of historical coincidence because the "spirits of the time have arrived in Israeli architecture together with the West Bank, East Jerusalem and the Old City."[16] The result, we are told, is a "mix of historicism, fundamentalism and camouflage," which "took place here a minute before similar phenomena spread through Europe and the United States under the general title 'post-modernism.'"[17]

But according to Charles Jencks, for example, who published the seminal *Language of Post-Modern Architecture* at the end of the postwar decade we reviewed, postmodernism cannot be so reductively categorized. It aimed— and, according to Jencks, succeeded—to liberate architects and their audiences from the Mythic Modern Man, the "3-M monster," that "of course does not exist, except as a historical fiction."[18] As we have seen, the Zionist version of this fiction was the New Jew, a modern man whose metaphoric return home—to Zion, that is, Jerusalem—secured his share in the grand narrative of modern nationalism. After 1967 Israel was able to consume this grand Zionist myth: to perform a centralized settlement of East Jerusalem. To call this building effort "postmodern" runs the risk of reducing what was an epic demonstration of state power, and a profound effort to control the symbolic meaning of the residential environment, into a mere formal school of thought—a set of aesthetic features rather than the spatial articulation of an ambivalent idea.

Divide and Rule: The Consequences of Kollek's Cultural Politics

The faith of the second vision of liberal democracy is inextricably linked to the continuing legacy of Teddy Kollek. Kollek's tenure as mayor lasted until 1993. Ever since, his legacy has been tied to the beautification of the ancient city. The sublime beauty of Jerusalem's ancient core turned, in Kollek's expert hands, into a prime political and civic tool. His brand of cultural politics was geared primarily toward the international community, from which he sought the legitimacy to rule Jerusalem on moral and aesthetic grounds.

Domestically, he negotiated his inferior share of the national budget through a coalition of mostly governmental organizations, which were under either his influence or his direct control. The power of Kollek's coalition has often gone under the radar of political and professional players, as well as scholars of Jerusalem. But Kollek's institutional network, and his skillful handling of its many components, made possible his enormous impact on Jerusalem.

Kollek's cultural politics have had long-lasting implications. Immediately after the war, critics argued that the numerous agencies working in parallel fashion to unite Jerusalem created an administrative mess. How could one governmental company develop the Jewish Quarter, another the national park, and yet another the city walls that separate the two? In practice, the common denominator of these agencies was their compliance with the charismatic mayor. By orchestrating the piecemeal work of these governmental agencies Kollek did more than just win control over their commissions. Also, and significantly so, by maneuvering their projects he succeeded in gaining considerable independence from the political machine of the national government, without losing access to its generous budget.

The outcome is plainly visible: almost every institution or park constructed after the 1967 war in the green belt surrounding the city walls was installed by a member of Kollek's coalition. That effort started with the initial declaration of this green belt as a national park. It is impossible to overestimate this remarkable feat: a weak agency succeeded in legalizing a park that was located at the heart of the sacred city and contained numerous possible land uses. Kollek's success is indebted to his own foresight, as he asked Prime Minister Levi Eshkol to entrust Jerusalem's open space to the National Park Authority, a logic based on the American precedent of designating Washington, D.C., as federally controlled land. After winning additional control over the southern slopes of the High Commissioner Hill, the design of which he entrusted to Louis Kahn, Kollek would institute a Cultural Mile that ran from the Sherover Promenade on top of that hill and threaded along its route a host of projects such as the Khan Theater, Mishkenot Sha'ananim, the Cinematheque, Wolfson Park, the Mamilla compound, and the city walls promenade. The different agencies responsible for them hold one thing in common—a distinguished place in Kollek's coalition.

Kollek's divide-and-rule heritage outlived his tenure, and indeed, it prevails to this day. Agencies have changed hands, and political convictions shifted, but multiple authorities still function next to each other. Each has a different degree of autonomy from the control of the national government, and some possess independent fund-raising mechanisms. In hindsight it seems that Kollek's clever strategy prepared the ground for a phenomenon nearly the opposite of his intentions. His particular interoperation of Zionist goals complemented the *mamlachti* legacy that he practiced since his days with Prime Minister David Ben Gurion. Eventually, however, his liberal policy, the degree of autonomy he had gained for his agencies from the state, and the flow of private money he encouraged into Jerusalem's public domain created an institutional framework that currently enables the distribution of the state's symbolic resources to private hands.

In Kollek's days there was a balance between a strong welfare state and various organizations with limited autonomy. Today, under the pressure of globalization, the state has weakened, and its capacity to mobilize capital for public projects is limited. The market, along with a number of nongovernmental organizations (NGOs) on both sides of the political divide, has identified this weakness and assumed the role of public benefactor.[19] In so doing, it also gains control over the meaning of the projects over which these organizations assume responsibility. But their message is different. These groups and NGOs, which either took over or replaced the governmental agencies and companies Kollek controlled, offer no pretense of addressing the Israeli public as a whole. They use the same shell of the *mamlachtiyut* but invest it with their own meaning.

The faith of these projects is also contingent on their architectural genealogies. After the death of Louis Kahn, "the Dean of all American architects,"[20] Kollek was primarily attuned to two strands of situated modernism. One was championed by Moshe Safdie and Lawrence Halprin, who promoted in Jerusalem their emerging vision of urban design. The other was promoted by the Anglo circle, which was absorbed into Kollek's municipal planning institutions. Safdie, Halprin, and their peers' advocacy of urban design was translated into the plans of many executed projects. The Anglo circle focused instead on the process of planning, on procedures and policies that could secure the civic values of the built environment. Although both belonged to the situated camp, they operated differently in Jerusalem.

The urban design that situated modernists advocated was attuned to the particularities of places and critical of modernist urban renewal. For Safdie, Halprin, and their ilk, the latter was aggressive because it was oblivious to existing patterns of human settlement—to the vernacular and to everyday life, to the value of sidewalks, to people's casual meetings, and to the ways that memories are embodied in particular places. This spirit was indeed instrumental in saving Jerusalem from the hated urban scars of modernist highways and housing blocks that irrevocably altered many global cities. But, and significantly so, the pacifying serenity they offered instead—the stripped ancient landscapes and the pseudo-vernacular purity of their megaprojects—also denied Jerusalem the dynamic, organic sense of conflict and community that comes from the chaotic meeting of people who hold diverse fates and opposing political affinities from the incongruities between their physical memories. Their version of United Jerusalem thus perfectly disguised and naturalized the power of the state apparatus and the insidious influence of global capitalism.

The Anglo circle was similarly dismissive of developmental modernism and shared the propensity for urban design, but it nevertheless objected to the project-oriented attitude of Safdie and his cohort. Instead, they understood urban design as a regulatory system that guides, negotiates, and monitors urban processes, that is, creates the rules of the game for planning procedures that put civic responsibility at the epicenter of all professional activity. To advance this approach, many Anglo-educated architects joined the municipal government of Jerusalem as professional public servants. In this capacity they guarded the image of Jerusalem, which they considered a public asset. They understood the city as designers—Arthur Kutcher's drawings are to this day a marvel of design analysis—but they often articulated their conclusions in policy documents. In so doing they succeeded in countering the market and the booming tourist industry, most famously with the triumphant reduction of Israel's first Hyatt Hotel Tower to a four-story structure.

The Anglo circle has gone under the radar of Israeli architectural historiography. But in hindsight, it offered a liberal version of situated modernism, one that demanded that urban, landscape, and architectural designers participate in the democratic management of the built environment. Quite a few of the members of the Anglo circle eventually left Israel, and others could not have reached the prominence of their famous peers. Nevertheless, they lay the foundations for a monumental project of documentation and preservation. David Kroyanker's volumes on the history of Jerusalem's architecture and the struggle for its image, and Michael Turner's public and academic contribution to the field of preservation and to the establishment of UNESCO's World Heritage Sites in Israel, are excellent examples.

Modernism and Democracy beyond Nationalism

The third vision of democracy is the call of Lewis Mumford and fellow elders of the Jerusalem Committee to eclipse all nationalisms. Their bold notion— that Jerusalem cannot be submitted to the dictates of national possession— relates to the responsibility for sites that transcend the upheavals of the present. These sites have belonged in the past and may belong in the future to communities that are not necessarily bound by the current divisions between nation-states and the violence that those divisions so often incite.

Although their vision is still looming in a distant future, the forces of globalization have already been weakening the grip of nationalism and empowering postnational forms of intervention. One such example is the field of preservation and the activation of preservation itself as a form of cultural politics. Paradoxically, the cultural politics that Kollek perfected—his assembly of an international jury as a means to legitimize his administration of Jerusalem—is a technique that not only has become commonplace, but has inspired his adversaries in competing international forums over the future of Jerusalem's historical sites.

UNESCO is a particularly good example. It declared the Walled City of Jerusalem a World Heritage Site, the only site—among 981 World Heritage Sites to date, spread across roughly 160 countries—that is listed independent of the country it is in. This is a striking exception: according to the UNESCO convention, only sovereign states can nominate sites. UNESCO nevertheless hurried to approve Jordan's nomination, and in 1981 added the Walled City to its prestigious list. The single vote against this declaration came from the United States, which "stressed that a property must be situated in the territories of the nominating State." In "the opinion of his government," the U.S. delegate stated, "Jordan had no standing to make such a nomination." And yet, only three years after the heritage list was founded, the Hashemite Kingdom of Jordan succeeded in passing a declaration for a city it did not control.[21]

At the time, it must be noted, the World Heritage Committee was conspicuously pro-Arab.[22] A year later the committee further alarmed and humiliated Israel, approving a description of Jerusalem as a site "in danger" due to "rapid urbanization," as well as "significant loss of historical authenticity" and "cultural significance."[23] Israel could not overrule these allegations because it did not sign the UNESCO convention until the year 2000. Nevertheless, these declarations are each pivotal, regardless of their validity and despite the bias of the committee that approved them. They are significant because they channeled Jordanian—and by extension Arab—resistance to Israeli occupation from official politics into the realm of cultural politics. Jordan's success in convincing UNESCO to accept its nomination severely challenged the heretofore successful agenda of Mayor Teddy Kollek, on the very grounds that he had used so ingeniously for the previous fourteen years. In other words, Jordan used the UN cultural agency in order to undermine the role that Kollek had claimed for Israelis: as the enlightened custodians of the Holy City.

Although this line of cultural activism has proven to be surprisingly efficient over the last half century, we have typically overlooked its political impact. Recently we have witnessed repeated failures by the Israeli government to implement adequate preservation procedures, most acutely in the City of David.[24] At the same time, heritage and preservation work has become a major line of action for Palestinians. In 1991, for example, Riwaq, an

NGO that combines preservation with social activism, was established. The Palestinian plan for the Old City and similar rehabilitation plans for Hebron have won the Aga Khan Award—the Pritzker of the Islamic world. The field of preservation has thus turned into a new arena of competition over the meaning of Jerusalem.

Today different groups—Palestinian and Israeli governmental agencies, as well as numerous NGOs loaded with public money, and an escalating number of private benefactors—continue to impose onto Jerusalem the narrative they consider to be the essence of the city. Against their vigorous truths, and their imposition of that truth onto both Jerusalem's corporeal landscape and virtual imagination, the possibilities opened during the post-1967 competition over the image of Jerusalem that we studied in this book are particularly telling and suggestive.

It is difficult to tell if globalization will change the rules of the game in Jerusalem. Although the state is weaker than it was during the heydays of nationalism, the urban layout that Israeli planners created since 1967 makes the reversal of Jerusalem's unification nearly impossible. Even if a two-state solution would be successfully negotiated, it is difficult to imagine a Palestinian capital emerging within East Jerusalem's geopolitical maze of former Palestinian villages and new Israeli settlements.[25] Moreover, after Israel's armed conflict with the Arab world shifted from the physical borders with Lebanon, Syria, Jordan, and Egypt to the inner and multifaceted urban borders between Israelis and Palestinians in Jerusalem, the Israeli government erected a Separation Wall around the city. But the long and winding gray concrete wall does not divide Israel from Palestine as much as it cuts through Palestinian neighborhoods and splits their residents into two geopolitical realities.[26]

The three hundred thousand Palestinians who live in illegal houses in East Jerusalem perform their right to the city despite the average destruction of seventy illegal houses per year. In doing so they persistently undermine the Israeli demographic war over Jerusalem, particularly in the visual basin around the Old City, which was so dear to the Jerusalem Committee that Kollek convened. The name of the sacred mosque, Al-Aqsa, is now bestowed on the entire area around al-Haram al-Sharif, and living at the foot of Temple Mount is thus conceived by Palestinians as an ethical duty based on a religious-national commitment. Jewish settlers take the same mandate to the opposite extreme. Similar sentiments drive Jewish NGOs to purchase and settle Palestinian houses under the protective umbrella of right-wing governments wishing to further Judaize the heart of the historic city.[27]

The escalating conflict sheds different light on Louis Kahn's search for the origin of human institutions in Jerusalem—for the foundational agreement that inspired people to form shared spaces of dwelling, learning, and worship. In Jerusalem we can certainly learn a great deal about the persistence of shared faith; but the city also forces us to reckon with the ineradicable antagonism existing in human societies. As this study reaches its inevitably open end, one wonders whether this antagonism can be transformed into agonistic reality, that is, whether we can accept that the genius loci of Jerusalem lies not only in its topography and sanctity, but in its divisions and borders and oppression.

If we take the predicament of competition and adversary as our premise, we can near Chantal Mouffe's advocacy for agonistic democracy: for democracy that does not try to resolve conflict, but to contain it, to manage it without compromising human rights and free access to the common good.[28] As official politics repeatedly fails to escape the zero-sum game of the conflict between Palestine and Israel, we may entertain the power of other bodies of knowledge, and of cultural politics, to fracture this stubborn formula and let the power of everyday life find alternative channels to rethink Jerusalem in a global age.

ACKNOWLEDGMENTS

I WOULD NEVER HAVE COME TO ASK how eruptions of strife shape cities and their architectural histories had I not experienced my first dislocation to Cambridge, Massachusetts, and the amazing group of people who challenged everything I previously took for granted. The encounter with the wisdom, depth, and emotions of their truths made me curious and humble about knowing my own. I am grateful for these people I was so fortunate to meet.

It started with heated lunch debates over Middle Eastern politics with the erudite Samer Madanat, Rabia Mishalani, Frannie Humplick, and Rina Schneur that despite many impasses fostered our lasting friendship even before I entered the History Theory Criticism kennel at the other end of MIT's infinite corridor. These formative years were ushered by a committee that I am happy and grateful to keep as close friends. I admire Mark Jarzombek's boundless intellectual curiosity. His incisive ventures into new frontiers of knowledge keep pushing my own. Sibel Bozdogan, the sincerest intellectual I have ever met, bared for me the visceral entanglement of life and inquiry that yielded her pioneering scholarship. Sadly, Stanford Anderson, to whom I owe my transition to scholarship, did not live to hold this book. I miss his joy with knowledge, his precision with words and ideas, and his radiant smile.

Funds for conducting and publishing this research were generously provided by MIT, the Israeli Science Foundation (ISF), the Azrieli Foundation, and the Graham Foundation for Advanced Studies in the Fine Arts. Particularly important were funds for residencies that provided the intellectual space and collegial brainstorms that kept this project alive. I thank Elizabeth Cropper, Therese O'Malley, and Peter Lukehart for making the Center for Advance Study in the Visual Arts (CASVA) at the National Gallery into a benevolent scholarly jumping board. I treasure the memory of the noble Irene Bireman, whose initiative to dedicate a UCLA/Getty summer school in Istanbul to question the vibrant presents of the past has cheerfully continued with Peg Olin and Khaldun Bshara. This book has taken its form during a fantastic year at the Frankel Center for Advanced Jewish Studies at the University of Michigan. Anita Norich and Deborah Dash-Moore were gracious hosts, Sarah Blair and Barbara Mann incisive critics, and Yael Shenker a wonderful intellectual teammate who graciously opens my interdisciplinary horizons. At my own disciplinary domain, I took great delight and important insights from brainstorming with Claire Zimmerman and Andrew Herscher our simmering manuscripts.

Several scholarly springboards provided excellent opportunities to advance this book. I am particularly grateful to Nezar AlSayyad and Barry Bergdoll for their gracious invitations and unfailing support. Gwendolyn Wright supported and inspired me throughout this journey, and Daniel Monk wittingly pacified the agonies of our excruciating subject matter. In Israel interdisciplinary research expanded my horizons. My greatest debt goes to Uri Ram, whose boundless intellectual generosity and drive for clarity shored up my spirit and this work. Liora Bilski and Ofra Rechter challenged the seams with law and philosophy, and David Neumann, Haim Yacobi, Oren Yiftachel, and the late Michael Feige offered geographical and sociological arenas and insights.

At the Technion I thank Rachel Kallus and Iris Aravot for much needed advice and encouragement. The sharp intellect and commitment Rachel extends to communities beyond academia, and Iris fosters within its bounds, inspired my own commitment to install a new curriculum as a department head, which might have delayed the publication of this book but earned me creative and vibrant colleagues. Gaby Schwartz, Oren Ben Avraham, and Ganit Mayslits Kassif in particular did not cease to remind me how closely knitted were practice and scholarship—creating yet another impetus for this book. The greatest reward of my academic life are the students I have been fortunate to advise. The seminar room turned into my favorite learning experience, and our conversations stimulated new venues of inquiry. Among them, Karen Lee Bracha, Oryan Shachar, Shira Wilkof, Inbal Pintzov, and Neta Feniger were not only invaluable research assistants for this book but also, with Fatina Abreek Zubiedat, Dan Handel, Shanee Shiloh, Irit Carmon-Popper, and Julia Gringruk, an incredible sounding board for its ideas.

My initial venture into municipal and state archives yielded mostly frustration. The lack of an architectural archive, the scant information in contemporary periodicals, and the surprising absence of secondary literature seemed unbridgeable. This picture completely changed once I started talking to the architects, planners, and politicians who built Jerusalem. I am grateful for the time they dedicated; the personal histories they shared with me kindly guided my way through the culture of their generation. Among them I would like to recognize particularly the time, commitment, and access to archival resources of members of the "Generation of the State": Shlomo Aronson, David Best, David Cassuto, Dan Eytan, Israel Kimhi, Sa'adia Mandel, Moshe Safdie, Yoseph Schweid, Mike Turner, Yaakov Yaar, and Shmulik Yavin. Younger and similarly helpful were architects David Guggenheim, Zeev Drukman, and the inspiring Elinoar Barzaki. I regret that Yehuda Drexler, Ram Karmi, Yaakov Rechter, David Reznik, Avraham Vachman, and Avraham Yaski did not live to see their contribution. I treat the wealth of knowledge that they generously entrusted with me as a precious will.

I am in great debt to Michaela Zonnenshein, Viki Davidov, and their team for their unfailing help and for turning our library and its collection of Israeli architecture into a scholarly oasis. I am similarly grateful to the archivists of the Jerusalem Foundation Archive, the Jerusalem Municipality Archive, the Moshe Safdie Archive at McGill University in Montreal, the Architectural Archive at the University of Pennsylvania, the Zionist Archive and the National Archives in Jerusalem, and the Israel Architecture Archive in Tel Aviv. I am grateful to Shanee Shiloh and Adi Zilberstein for reviving the archive and navigating through the collection of our Architectural Heritage Research Center at the Technion, and to Smadar and Arad Sharon, who provided generous access to their family archive before it found a home at the Azrieli Archive in the Tel Aviv Museum.

Without the careful reading, stimulating discussions, and culinary feasts with numerous friends, the ideas in this book and the spirit behind it would never have materialized. Full-hearted thanks go to Nnamdi Elleh, Juliana Maxim, Casey N. Blake, Sandy Isenstadt, Richard Ormond, Larry Silver, Ruth Fine, Peter Marshal, and Edward Eigen. Hadas Steiner and Juliet Koss cheered my spirit in many geographies, and with Pani Pyla I am delighted to embark on future projects. The European Architectural History Network that we founded a decade ago turned into a stimulating scholarly hub. Among many friends it was a pleasure to brainstorm historiography with Carmen Popescu, Belgin Turan Ozkaya, and Elvan Altan Ergut. The feminine intellectual force of Nancy Stieber, Hilde Heynen, and Maristella Cacciato constantly inspired me, as did their candid advice and insights.

Working with the masterful edits of David Lobenstine was simultaneously an intellectual and friendly experience that I cherish. I thank Ritu Bhatt for suggesting the Quadrant Fellowship that started my fruitful collaboration with the University of Minnesota Press, Pieter Martin for patiently guiding me through the intricacies of publishing, and Anne Carter for laboring with great care to make this book come true.

I returned to Israel for family and friends, and the rewards are immense. Michal Agmon-Gonen and Michal Youish secured for me necessary islands of joy and sanity. My beloved sisters, Marganit and Reuvat, are a source of

ACKNOWLEDGMENTS

300

ceaseless support and laughs. The anxiety we share for the future of our children fueled this intellectual labor. I am constantly inspired by the wit and insights of my sons Yuval and Itai—the best companions I could ever imagine. To their father, Yoram Shiftan, a precious man of lucid mind and boundless love, with whom I am so lucky to share my life, I owe more than words can tell. Together we decided to dedicate this book to Ruth and Yoav Nitzan, my parents, who instilled in me the desire for knowledge and the gripping curiosity that now inspire my sons. To Saba and Savta Nitzan, with love.

NOTES

Introduction

1. Architectural and place-making aspects have mainly gone under the radar of the otherwise rigorous scholarship on the Judaization of East Jerusalem. The overwhelming majority of studies focus on the territorial, political, and sociodemographic implications of this massive urban transformation. See, for example, the publications of the Jerusalem Institute for Israel Studies (JIIS), the International Peace and Cooperation Center (IPCC), Floresheimer Studies at the Hebrew University of Jerusalem, and the Institute for Palestine Studies (IPS) and its journal *Jerusalem Quarterly* (http://www.palestine-studies.org/jq). The Cambridge-based "Conflict in Cities and the Contested State," founded by Wendy Pullen with coinvestigator Mick Dumper, focuses also on the planning and architectural aspects of Jerusalem (http://www.conflictincities.org).

2. Terry Eagleton, *Ideology: An Introduction* (London: Verso, 1991), p. xiii.

3. David Kroyanker, *Jerusalem: Conflicts over the City's Physical and Visual Form* [in Hebrew] (Jerusalem: Zmora-Bitan, 1988).

4. Eyal Weizman and Rafi Segal, *A Civilian Occupation: The Politics of Israeli Architecture* (New York: Storefront for Art and Architecture, 2003); Eyal Weizman, *Hollow Land: Israel's Architecture of Occupation* (London: New Left Books, 2007).

5. Ann Swidler, "Culture in Action: Symbols and Strategies," *American Sociological Review* 51, no. 2 (1986): 277.

6. See Etienne Balibar, "The Nation Form: History and Ideology," in *Becoming National: A Reader,* ed. Geoff Eley and Ronald Grigor Suny (New York: Oxford University Press, 1996), 86–106. See also Ranabir Samaddar, *The Nation Form: Essays on Indian Nationalism* (Los Angeles: Sage Publications, 2012).

7. The term "developmental modernism" is related to the concept of development as it is articulated in Wolfgang Sachs, *The Development Dictionary: A Guide to Knowledge as Power* (London: Zed Books, 1992).

8. The choice of the term "situated modernism" is inspired by Sarah Williams Goldhagen, *Louis Kahn's Situated Modernism* (New Haven, Conn.: Yale University Press, 2001).

9. For scholarship on the dilemmas inherited in postwar architecture, see Sarah Williams Goldhagen and Réjean Legault, *Anxious Modernisms: Experimentation in Postwar Architectural Culture* (Cambridge, Mass.: MIT Press, 2000). See also Kenny Cupers, ed., *Use Matters: An Alternative History of Architecture* (London: Routledge, 2013); Panayiota Pyla, *Landscapes of Development: The Impact of Modernization Discourses on the Physical Environment of the Eastern Mediterranean* (Cambridge, Mass.: Harvard Graduate School of Design, 2013). For a theoretical reflection, see C. Greig Crysler, Stephen Cairns, and Hilde Heynen, eds., *The SAGE Handbook of Architectural Theory* (London: Sage, 2012).

10. For a comprehensive account on the modernization of Jerusalem under Ottoman

rule, see Yehoshua Ben-Arieh, *Jerusalem in the 19th Century: Emergence of the New City,* vol. 2 (Tel-Aviv: MOD Books, 1989).

11. On the Mandate period, see Yehoshua Ben-Arieh, *New Jewish Jerusalem in the Time of the British Mandate* [in Hebrew] (Jerusalem: Yad Izhak Ben-Zvi, 2011); Salim Tamari and Ihsan Salih Turjman, *Year of the Locust: A Soldier's Diary and the Erasure of Palestine's Ottoman Past* (Berkeley: University of California Press, 2011); Daniel Bertrand Monk, *An Aesthetic Occupation: The Immediacy of Architecture and the Palestine Conflict* (Durham, N.C.: Duke University Press, 2002).

12. For a comprehensive account of the profound impact of the British Mandate rule on the physical landscape in Palestine, see Roza El-Eini, *Mandated Landscape: British Imperial Rule in Palestine, 1929–1948* (London: Routledge, 2004). For the planning and development of Haifa as a strategic imperial harbor city, see Ziva Kolodney and Rachel Kallus, "The Politics of Landscape (Re)Production: Haifa between Colonialism and Nation Building," *Landscape Journal* 27, no. 2 (2008): 173–89.

13. On the work of Ashbee in Jerusalem, see Inbal Ben-Asher Gitler, "'Marrying Modern Progress with Treasured Antiquity': Jerusalem City Plans during the British Mandate, 1917–1948," *Traditional Dwellings and Settlements Review* 15, no. 1 (2003): 39–58; Noah Hysler-Rubin, "Arts & Crafts and the Great City: Charles Robert Ashbee in Jerusalem," *Planning Perspectives* 21, no. 4 (2006): 347–68; Benjamin Hyman, "British Planners in Palestine, 1918–1936" (PhD diss., London School of Economics and Political Science, 1994).

14. Aharon Ron Fuchs and Gilbert Herbert, "Representing Mandatory Palestine: Austen St. Barbe Harison and the Representational Buildings of the British Mandate in Palestine, 1922–37," *Architectural History* 43 (2000): 281–333.

15. Monk, *An Aesthetic Occupation.*

16. Henry Kendall, *Jerusalem, the City Plan: Preservation and Development during the British Mandate, 1918–1948* (London: His Majesty's Stationery Office, 1948).

17. See Salim Tamari, ed., *Jerusalem 1948: The Arab Neighborhoods and Their Fate in the War* (Jerusalem: Institute of Jerusalem Studies; Bethlehem: Badil, 2002).

18. See Meron Benvenisti, *Jerusalem: The Torn City* (Minneapolis: University of Minnesota Press, 1976), 43–44.

19. For an analysis of the status of Jerusalem under Jordanian rule and its competition with the Hashemite capital Amman, see Naim Sofer, "The Political Status of Jerusalem in the Hashemite Kingdom of Jordan, 1948–1967," *Middle Eastern Studies* 12, no. 1 (1976): 73–94.

20. See Benvenisti, *Jerusalem,* 46–47.

21. For background on the construction of the Israeli capital prior to 1967, see Avi Bareli, ed., *Divided Jerusalem, 1948–1967* [in Hebrew] (Jerusalem: Yad Izhak Ben-Zvi, 1994).

22. Sinai was returned to Egypt following the peace treaty of 1979. All other territories are to this day under Israeli rule.

23. For comprehensive accounts of the various aspects of the Israeli unification of Jerusalem, see Benvenisti, *Jerusalem;* Uzi Benziman, *Jerusalem: A City without a Wall* [in Hebrew] (Tel Aviv: Schocken, 1973); Asher Susser, ed., *Six Days—Thirty Years: A New Look at the Six Day War* [in Hebrew] (Tel Aviv: Am Oved, 1999).

24. In the metric system it is approximately 37 km² of Israeli West Jerusalem, 1 km² of the Old City, and 7 km² of Jordanian East Jerusalem.

25. See Israel Kimchi, "In Face of Change" [in Hebrew], in *Jerusalem, Here and Now,* ed. Ora Ahimeir (Tel Aviv: The Ministry of Defense, 2004), 9–26.

26. For a chronicle of political moves leading to the unilateral unification of Jerusalem, see Moshe 'Amirav, *Jerusalem Syndrome: The Palestinian–Israeli Battle for the Holy City* (Brighton: Sussex Academic Press, 2009).

27. Ibid., 50–58.

28. For the various aspects of unification, see Joel L. Kraemer, *Jerusalem: Problems and Prospects* (New York: Praeger, 1980); Yehoshua Prawer and Ora Ahimeir, eds., *Twenty Years in*

Jerusalem, 1967–1987 [in Hebrew] (Tel Aviv: Ministry of Defense, 1988); Michael Romman, "Jerusalem since 1967: A Profile of a Reunited City," *Geojournal* 2, no. 6 (1978): 499–506.

29. For a detailed analysis of these goals, see 'Amirav, *Jerusalem Syndrome,* x–xi.

30. Ibid.

31. See Shmuel Berkovitz, *The Battle for the Holy Places: The Struggle over Jerusalem and the Holy Sites in Israel* [in Hebrew] (Jerusalem: Jerusalem Institute for Israeli Studies, 2000), 61–62.

32. For primary resources chronicling the first years after the war, see Benvenisti, *Jerusalem*; Benziman, *Jerusalem*; Roger Friedland and Richard Hecht, *To Rule Jerusalem,* Cambridge Cultural Social Studies (Cambridge: Cambridge University Press, 1996). Also Abraham Rabinovich, *Jerusalem on Earth: People, Passions, and Politics in the Holy City* (London: Free Press, 1988).

33. For comprehensive accounts of the 1948 *Nakba* (disaster) and its aftermaths, see Benny Morris, *The Birth of the Palestinian Refugee Problem, 1947–1949* (Cambridge: Cambridge University Press, 1989); Ilan Pappé, *A History of Modern Palestine: One Land, Two Peoples* (Cambridge: Cambridge University Press, 2004); Rashid Khalidi, *Palestinian Identity: The Construction of Modern National Consciousness* (New York: Columbia University Press, 2010).

34. On the PLO, see Nigel Parsons, "The Palestine Liberation Organization (P.L.O.)," in *The Routledge Handbook on the Israeli–Palestinian Conflict,* ed. David Newman and Joel Peters (London: Routledge, 2013), 209–21. For a history of Palestinian politics in Jerusalem, see Hillel Cohen, *The Rise and Fall of Arab Jerusalem: Palestinian Politics and the City since 1967* (Abingdon: Routledge, 2011).

35. See Benvenisti, *Jerusalem,* 132. On the rise and fall of Jerusalem as the Palestinian capital, see Cohen, *Rise and Fall of Arab Jerusalem.*

36. See *Jerusalem: Heritage and Life,* The Old City Revitalization Plan, Welfare Association, http://ocjrp.welfare-association.org/en/media/get/20121203_englishjrevplanj.pdf. For a useful introduction to the post-1967 relations of the Jerusalemite Palestinian community and the Israeli municipality, see Anne Latendresse, *Jerusalem: Palestinian Dynamics of Resistance and Urban Change, 1967–94* (Jerusalem: PASSIA, 1995).

37. From the Hebrew song titled "Our feet shall stand within thy gates, O Jerusalem" (Psalm 122:2), written by Yossi Gamzu, composed by Yehezkel Brown. See also reference to Ezekiel 16:6.

38. For recent articulation of such ideas, see Aggregate (group), *Governing by Design: Architecture, Economy, and Politics in the Twentieth Century* (Pittsburgh: University of Pittsburgh Press, 2012).

39. Pierre Bourdieu, *Outline of a Theory of Practice,* 188, quoted in Kim Dovey, "The Silent Complicity of Architecture," in *Habitus: A Sense of Place,* ed. Emma Rooksby and Jean Hillier (London: Ashgate, 2005), 267.

40. Walter Benjamin, "The Work of Art in the Age of Mechanical Reproduction," in *Illuminations: Essays and Reflections,* ed. Hannah Arendt, trans. Harry Zohn (New York: Schocken, 1969), 217–52.

41. Kim Dovey, *Framing Places: Mediating Power in Built Form* (London: Routledge, 1999), 2.

42. See Arthur Kutcher, *The New Jerusalem: Planning and Politics,* revised ed. (London: Thames and Hudson, 1975).

1. Encounters

1. The first project was designed by David Anatol Brutzkus and was published in *Israel Builds* in 1964. The second project was designed by Salo Hershman, its few phases were built throughout the 1970s and the early 1980s, and it was published in *Israel Builds* in 1977 and 1988.

2. This definition is based on Raymond Williams, *Keywords,* rev. ed. (New York: Oxford University Press, 1983), 87–93.

3. Andrzej Piotrowski and Julia Williams Robinson, *Discipline of Architecture* (Minneapolis: University of Minnesota Press, 2001), ix.

4. Surveys of modern architecture include William J. R. Curtis, *Modern Architecture since 1900* (Englewood Cliffs, N.J.: Prentice-Hall, 1983); Manfredo Tafuri and Francesco Dal Co, *Modern Architecture* (New York: Electra/Rizzoli, 1986); Kenneth Frampton, *Modern Architecture: A Critical History,* World of Art (New York: Oxford University Press, 1980).

5. The forms, ideas, and movements that both of these cultures developed in order to counter, pacify, or accommodate the modern experience, aesthetically or politically, are considered here as their respective modernisms. The institutionalization of these movements, most notoriously by the Congrès Internationaux d'Architecture Moderne (CIAM) and the Zionist Congress facilitated the dissemination of these forms. In order to discuss these modernisms in between disciplines, the term "modernism" is qualified throughout this study according to its disciplinary practices. Thus, alongside the habitual description of "modern architecture" as a chronological, stylistic, or technological qualification of "architecture," I qualify this particular practice of modernism as architectural. Similarly, instead of describing "Zionism" as political, cultural, or pragmatic, I qualify the modernism that responded to the exclusion of Jews by modern nationalism as Zionist.

6. Consider the proximity of the following historical moments of international and Zionist modernism: at the time when Le Corbusier built his famous 1920s villas, when Walter Gropius, Hannes Meyer, and Mies van der Rohe were teaching successively at the Bauhaus, and when Ernst May was building his famous socialist housing estates in Frankfurt, Richard Kauffmann constructed numerous modernist settlements for European Jews in Mandate Palestine under the direction of the Land of Israel Office that Arthur Rupin ran for the Zionist Organization. In 1928, the year CIAM was formed, a modernist scheme won the momentous competition for the Zionist National Institutions Building. The winner, Yohanan Ratner, replaced, in 1930, the famed Orientalist architect Alexander Berwald as the head of the single architectural school at the Technion. In 1932, Henry-Russell Hitchcock and Philip Johnson exhibited European modernism at New York's Museum of Modern Art under the new umbrella of the "International Style." In the same year Zionist students of Le Corbusier, Erich Mendelsohn, and the Bauhaus formed the Tel Aviv circle, which contributed greatly to the very rapid establishment of the new architecture in Zionist circles.

7. See Gideon Shimoni, *The Zionist Ideology,* Tauber Institute for the Study of European Jewry Series 21 (Hanover: University Press of New England for Brandeis University Press, 1995).

8. For a history of the modern movement, see Giorgio Ciucci, "The Invention of the Modern Movement," *Oppositions* 24 (1981): 68–91; Eric Paul Mumford, *The CIAM Discourse on Urbanism, 1928–1960* (Cambridge, Mass.: MIT Press, 2000).

9. During the 1920s modern architecture was practiced by few, most notably Richard Kauffmann, the famed architect of the Zionist settlements at the time. Between 1928 and 1932 the changing deans at the Technion's school of architecture, the return of Zionists after European modern training, and changes in the course of the Jewish/Arab conflict in Mandate Palestine caused a massive change toward modern architecture as the official style of the Yishuv.

10. For a critical study on the official historiography of the Zionist movement, see, for example, Uri Ram, "Zionist Historiography and the Invention of Modern Jewish Nationhood: The Case of Ben Zion Dinur," *History and Memory* 7, no. 1 (1995): 91–124; for studies on the official historiography of the modern movement in architecture, see, for example, Sokratis Georgiadis, *Sigfried Giedion: An Intellectual Biography* (Edinburgh: Edinburgh University Press, 1993).

11. Recent studies shed new light on the concept of *mamlachtiyut,* focusing primarily on issues concerning state and religion, citizenship, democracy, and law but do not discuss the cultural politics that we examine. See Avi Bareli and Nir Kedar, *Israeli Republicanism* (Jerusalem: Israel Democracy Institute, 2011). In Hebrew: Nir Kedar, *Mamlakhtiyut: David Ben-Gurion's Civic Thought* (Beer Sheva: Ben-Gurion Research Institute for the Study of Israel and Zionism, Ben Gurion University of the Negev, 2009); and Arye Carmon, *Jewish Kingdomism* (Jerusalem: Israeli Democracy Institute, 1994).

12. This view is elaborated in the influential book Charles S. Liebman and Eliezer Don-Yehya, *Civil Religion in Israel: Traditional Judaism and Political Culture in the Jewish State* (Berkeley: University of California Press, 1983), 84. According to Liebman and Don-Yehya, first was statism, a civil religion sanctifying the "state." The new religion emerged only after, valuing primarily the Jewish "nation." They further explain: "In terms of symbols and style, statism reflects the effort to transform the state and its institutions into the central foci of loyalty and identification. Statism gives rise to values and symbols that point to the state, legitimate it, and mobilize the population to serve its goals. In its more extreme formulation statism cultivates an attitude of sanctity toward the state, affirming it as an ultimate value" (ibid.). I suggest, however, that the linguistic origin of *mamlachtiyut* as well as its cultural practices provoked a parallel rather than sequential emphasis on the prime values of a modern state and a Jewish nation.

13. David Lloyd and Paul Thomas, *Culture and the State* (London: Routledge, 2014).

14. For a comprehensive study of the Mandate period, early statehood, and the transition between the two, see Dan Horowitz and Moshe Lissak, *Origins of the Israeli Polity: Palestine under the Mandate* (Chicago: University of Chicago Press, 1978); Dan Horowitz and Moshe Lissak, *Trouble in Utopia: The Overburdened Polity of Israel* (Albany: State University of New York Press, 1989).

15. For the tension between "nation" and "state," see Clifford Geertz, "The Integrative Revolution: Primordial Sentiments and Civil Politics in the New States," in *Old Societies and New States: The Quest for Modernity in Asia and Africa,* ed. Clifford Geertz (New York: Free Press, 1963), 107–13; Walker Connor, "A Nation Is a Nation, Is a State, Is an Ethnic Group, Is a . . . ," *Ethnic and Racial Studies* 1, no. 4 (1978): 379–88.

16. Adriana Kemp, "Borders, Space and National Identity in Israel" [in Hebrew], *Teoria ve Bikoret* 16 (2000): 17.

17. Nezar AlSayyad, "The End of Tradition, or the Tradition of Ending?" in *The End of Tradition?,* ed. Nezar AlSayyad (London: Routledge, 2004), 7.

18. Lloyd and Thomas, *Culture and the State.*

19. Janet Abu-Lughod, "Disappearing Dichotomies: Firstworld–Thirdworld; Traditional–Modern," *Traditional Dwellings and Settlements Review* 3, no. 2 (1992): 7–12.

20. See Kim Dovey, *Framing Places: Mediating Power in Built Form* (London: Routledge, 1999).

21. W. J. Thomas Mitchell, *Landscape and Power* (Chicago: University of Chicago Press, 1994), 1.

22. Lauren Gail Berlant, *The Anatomy of National Fantasy: Hawthorne, Utopia, and Everyday Life* (Chicago: University of Chicago Press, 1991), 20, quoted in Eley and Suny, *Becoming National,* 493.

23. Etienne Balibar, "The Nation Form: History and Ideology," in Etienne Balibar and Immanuel Wallerstein, *Race, Nation, Class: Ambiguous Identities* (London: Verso, 1991), 86–106.

24. Sibel Bozdogan, *Modernism and Nation Building: Turkish Architectural Culture in the Early Republic,* Studies in Modernity and National Identity (Seattle: University of Washington Press, 2001); Talinn Grigor, *Building Iran: Modernism, Architecture, and National Heritage under the Pahlavi Monarchs* (New York: Periscope/Prestel, 2009).

25. Mia Fuller, *Moderns Abroad: Architecture, Cities and Italian Imperialism* (London:

Routledge, 2007); Brian Lloyd McLaren, *Architecture and Tourism in Italian Colonial Libya: An Ambivalent Modernism* (Seattle: University of Washington Press, 2006).

26. Gustavo Esteva, "Development," in Wolfgang Sachs, *The Development Dictionary: A Guide to Knowledge as Power* (London: Zed Books, 1992), 6–25.

27. Balibar, "The Nation Form," 94.

28. Liebman and Don-Yehya, *Civil Religion in Israel,* 84.

29. The transition from the Yishuv to the state was marked by the creation of a massive planning apparatus. Its blueprint was prepared by planners of the Circle for Settlement Reform, who joined Arieh Sharon after he was appointed by Ben Gurion. On the Circle for Settlement Reform, see Rachel Kallus and Hubert Law Yone, "National Home/Personal Home: Public Housing and the Shaping of National Space in Israel," *European Planning Studies* 10, no. 6 (2002): 765–79; Arieh Sharon, *Kibbutz + Bauhaus: An Architect's Way in a New Land* (Stuttgart: Kramer Verlag, 1976). For a primary source on this period, see Haim Darin-Drabkin, *Public Housing in Israel: Surveys and Evaluations of Activities in Israel's First Decade, 1948–1958* (Tel Aviv: Gadish Books, 1959).

30. See Zvi Efrat, *The Israeli Project: Building and Architecture, 1948–1973,* 2 vols. (Tel Aviv: Tel Aviv Art Museum, 2004); Miriam Tuvyah and Michael Boneh, eds., *Building the Country: Public Housing in the 1950s* (Tel Aviv: The Israel Museums Forum; HaKibbutz HaMeuhad, 1999); Kalus and Law Yone, "National Home/Personal Home." See also essays in S. Ilan Troen and Noah Lucas, eds., *Israel: The First Decade of Independence* (Albany: State University of New York Press, 1995). Additionally, in Hebrew, Smadar Sharon, "Planners, the State, and the Shaping of National Space in the 1950s," *Teoria ve Bikoret* 29 (2006): 31–57.

31. Julius Posener, "One Family Houses in Palestine" [in Hebrew], *Habinyan* 2 (1937): 1.

32. Le Corbusier, *The Radiant City: Elements of a Doctrine of Urbanism to Be Used as the Basis of Our Machine-Age Civilization* (New York: Orion Press, 1967).

33. Julius Posener, then a member of a modernist-socialist circle, clarified in 1937 that "the Jew wants to construct here, for the first time in his life, a house of his own, and moreover, this house should be the house of the country in which he is settling." This request did not merely express an ambition to shelter members of the emerging Zionist entity, but also expressed an aspiration to instill a new national consciousness in the inhabitants by means of modern dwelling. See Posener, "One Family Houses in Palestine," 1.

34. Arieh Sharon, *Physical Planning in Israel* (Jerusalem: Government Printer, 1951).

35. Niemeyer quoted in James Holston, *The Modernist City: An Anthropological Critique of Brasilia* (Chicago: University of Chicago Press, 1989), 20–21.

36. Devorah Cohen, "Immigration and Absorption" [in Hebrew], in *Trends in Israeli Society,* ed. Efraim Ya'ar and Ze'ev Shavit (Tel Aviv: Open University, 2001), 380–83. For further information, see Moshe Lissak, *The Mass Immigration in the Fifties: The Failure of the Melting Pot Policy* [in Hebrew] (Jerusalem: Bialik Institute, 1999), 3–5.

37. Aviah Hashimshoni, "Architecture" [in Hebrew], in *Israel Art,* ed. Benjamin Tammuz (Tel Aviv: Massada, 1963), 220; the quotes are my translations from the Hebrew publication. An English edition is Aviah Hashimshoni, "Architecture," in *Art in Israel,* ed. Benjamin Tammuz and Max Wykes-Joyce (Philadelphia: Chilton, 1965). The most significant difference between the original and translation is the definition of the term "'inyaniyut," which resembles the German term *sachlichkeit,* i.e., "matter-of-factness" (which usually appears in English translations as "the new objectivity"), a major trend promoting functional, stripped modernism that was advocated primarily by Hannes Meyer. Meyer taught at the Bauhaus from 1927 to 1930 and was the master and later employer of Arieh Sharon, Israel's most influential architect during early statehood. This connection is lost in the English text.

38. Hashimshoni, "Architecture" (1963), 221.

39. Ibid.

40. Consider, for example, Adolf Loos's immensely influential essay "Ornament and

Crime" (1908), in Adolf Loos and Adolf Opel, *Ornament and Crime: Selected Essays,* trans. Michael Mitchell (Riverside, Calif.: Ariadne Press, 1998).

41. Slavoj Žižek, "Formal Democracy and Its Discontents," in *Looking Awry: An Introduction to Jacques Lacan through Popular Culture,* ed. Slavoj Žižek (Cambridge, Mass.: MIT Press, 1991), 154–70.

42. Balibar, "The Nation Form," 94.

43. Žižek, "Formal Democracy and Its Discontents," 163. Žižek further explains: "It is because of this lack of identity that the concept of identification plays such a crucial role in psychoanalytic theory: the subject attempts to fill out its constitutive lack by means of identification, by identifying itself with some master signifier guaranteeing its place in the symbolic network" (ibid.). For Žižek, this unique content is "The Thing," which is the organization of enjoyment—the materialization, the embodiment of a lack. His compelling argument owes its force to his bold engagement with that which is absolute for the subject (rather than the familiar adjectives that characterize 1990s scholarship on identity: "transient," "shifting," "precarious," or "contingent"). In his words: "What confers on the other the dignity of a 'person' is not any universal symbolic feature but precisely what is 'absolutely particular' about him, his fantasy, that part of him that we can be sure we can never share" (156). In order to ethically protect this individual domain, Žižek argues for the ultimate enclosure of this private domain against the violating force of nationalism. Analytically, however, it is exactly the rules of the game of such "violation" that are at the center of our study.

44. Néstor García Canclini, *Hybrid Cultures: Strategies for Entering and Leaving Modernity,* trans. Christopher L. Chiappari and Silvia L. López (Minneapolis: University of Minnesota Press, 2005), 107.

45. For Ben Gurion's revival of the Bible, see Anita Shapira, "Ben Gurion and the Bible: Creating a Historical Narrative?" [in Hebrew], in *Old Jews, New Jews* (Tel Aviv: Am Oved, 1997), 217–47; Zeev Zahor, "Ben Gurion's Mythopoetics," in *The Shaping of Israeli Identity: Myth, Memory, and Trauma,* ed. Robert S. Wistrich and David Ohana (London: F. Cass, 1995), 61–84.

46. In contrast to Anderson, Richard Handler argues for the need of these societies to possess "culture" in order to secure binding national heritage. In the wake of postcolonial studies, Partha Chatterjee sheds new light on the issue of for and by whom traditions are appropriated, challenging the exclusivity of Western powers to imagine for their colonial subjects the parameters of their collective identities. The complementary question of how to imagine follows developments in cultural studies and the cultural turn in history. See Benedict Anderson, *Imagined Communities: Reflections on the Origin and Spread of Nationalism* (London: Verso, 1983); Richard Handler, " 'Having a Culture': The Preservation of Quebec's Patrimoine," in *Nationalism and the Politics of Culture in Quebec* (Madison: University of Wisconsin Press, 1988), 140–59; Partha Chatterjee, *The Nation and Its Fragments: Colonial and Postcolonial Histories,* Princeton Studies in Culture/Power/History (Princeton, N.J.: Princeton University Press, 1993).

47. Canclini, *Hybrid Cultures,* 110.

48. Mitchell Cohen, *Zion and State: Nation, Class, and the Shaping of Modern Israel* (Oxford: B. Blackwell, 1987).

49. A. B. Yehoshua, "The Literature of the Generation of the State," *Ariel* 107–8 (1998): 49.

50. Shlomo Avineri, "To the Image of the New Jew," paper presented at the "New Jews, Old Jews" conference, 1997.

51. "Alik was born out of the sea" is the opening line of Moshe Shamir, *Pirke Alik* [in Hebrew] (Tel Aviv: Sifriyat Hapoalim, 1966). It was originally written in 1951 in memory of the author's brother who was killed in the 1948 war.

52. Moshe Dayan, *Living with the Bible* (New York: W. Morrow, 1978).

53. Meron Benvenisti, "The Hebrew Map," in *Sacred Landscape: The Buried History of the Holy Land since 1948,* trans. Maxine Kaufman-Lacusta (Berkeley: University of California Press, 2000), 11–54; Maoz Azaryahu and Arnon Golan, "Renaming the Landscape: The Formation of the Hebrew Map of Israel, 1949–1960," *Journal of Historical Geography* 27, no. 4 (2001): 178–95.

54. Canclini, *Hybrid Cultures,* 109.

55. See David Ben Gurion, quoted in Anita Shapira, "Ben-Gurion and the Bible: The Forging of an Historical Narrative?" *Middle Eastern Studies* 33, no. 4 (1997): 653. For the cultural erasure this approach entailed, see, for example, Ella Shohat, *Forbidden Reminiscences: Collected Essays* [in Hebrew], Sidrat Keshet Ha-Mizrah 2 (Tel-Aviv: Bimat kedem le-sifrut, 2001).

56. Canclini, *Hybrid Cultures,* 111.

57. Ibid., 109.

58. The crisis of international and local modernism during the post–World War II period was closely related to the Israeli scene. For example, in 1956, during the tenth CIAM congress, a young generation of architects challenged architecturally and organizationally the premises of the organization. A year later, a young generation of Israeli-born architects confronted their modernist elders during the annual conference of Israeli architects near the Sea of Galilee. The dissolution of CIAM in 1959 by Team 10, which emerged as a leading architectural group, coincided with the rise of their slightly younger contemporaries in Israel into professional prominence.

59. Examples of writings of great influence are Rudolf Wittkower, *Architectural Principles in the Age of Humanism,* Studies of the Warburg Institute 19 (London: Warburg Institute, University of London, 1949); Bernard Rudofsky, *Architecture without Architects: A Short Introduction to Non-pedigreed Architecture* (New York: Museum of Modern Art, 1964); Sibyl Moholy-Nagy, *Native Genius in Anonymous Architecture* (New York: Horizon Press, 1957); D'Arcy Wentworth Thompson, *On Growth and Form,* abridged ed. (Cambridge: Cambridge University Press, 1961).

60. Aldo van Eyck, in Alison Margaret Smithson, ed., *Team 10 Primer* (Cambridge, Mass.: MIT Press, 1968), 15.

61. Lasdun in Jerusalem Committee, *Proceedings of the Third Plenary Session, December 16–19, 1975,* Archive of the Jerusalem Foundation, unsorted files.

62. Stanford Anderson, "Public Institutions: Louis I. Kahn's Reading of Volume Zero," *Journal of Architectural Education* 49, no. 1 (1995): 12.

63. Ibid., 10.

64. On the meeting that ended CIAM, see Oscar Newman, *New Frontiers in Architecture: CIAM 59 in Otterlo,* Documents of Modern Architecture 1 (New York: Universe Books, 1961). The influential manifesto of Team 10 is Smithson, *Team 10 Primer.* For a review of the group's work, see Dirk Van den Heuvel and Max Risselada, *Team 10: In Search of a Utopia of the Present, 1953–1981* (Rotterdam: NAi Publishers, 2005), and the site http://www.team10online .org/index.html. For writings by Team 10 members and some reflection on their work, see Alison Margaret Smithson and Peter Smithson, *Ordinariness and Light: Urban Theories 1952– 1960 and Their Application in a Building Project 1963–1970* (Cambridge, Mass.: MIT Press, 1970). Aldo van Eyck, "Steps toward a Configurative Discipline (From: Forum No. 3, August 1963)," in *Architecture Culture, 1943–1968: A Documentary Anthology,* ed. Joan Ockman and Edward Eigen (New York: Rizzoli, 1993), 347–60; Liane Lefaivre, Aldo van Eyck, and Alexander Tzonis, *Aldo Van Eyck, Humanist Rebel: Inbetweening in a Post-War World* (Rotterdam: 010 Publishers, 1999); Francis Strauven, *Aldo Van Eyck: The Shape of Relativity* (Amsterdam: Architectura & Natura, 1998); Shadrach Woods and Candilis-Josic-Woods, *A Decade of Architecture and Urban Design* (Stuttgart: Krèamer, 1968); Georges Candilis, Alexis Josic, and Shadrach Woods, *Toulouse le Mirail: Geburt Einer Neuen Stadt = La Naissance d'une ville nouvelle = Birth*

of a New Town (Stuttgart: K. Krèamer, 1975); Tom Avermaete, *Another Modern: The Post-War Architecture and Urbanism of Candilis-Josic-Woods* (Rotterdam: NAi Publishers, 2005).

65. On Louis Kahn, see Louis I. Kahn and Alessandra Latour, *Louis I. Kahn: Writings, Lectures, Interviews* (New York: Rizzoli, 1991); David Bruce Brownlee and David Gilson De Long, *Louis I. Kahn: In the Realm of Architecture* (Los Angeles: Museum of Contemporary Art; New York: Rizzoli, 1991); Sarah Williams Goldhagen, *Louis Kahn's Situated Modernism* (New Haven, Conn.: Yale University Press, 2001). On Le Corbusier, see Le Corbusier and Willy Boesiger, *Ouvre Complete 1952–1957: Le Corbusier et son atelier Rue de Sevres 35* (New York: G. Wittenborn, 1957); and for his Brutalist phase, see Reyner Banham, *The New Brutalism: Ethic or Aesthetic?*, Documents of Modern Architecture (London: Architectural Press, 1966).

66. On Lewis Mumford, see Lewis Mumford, *The City in History: Its Origins, Its Transformations, and Its Prospects,* 1st ed. (New York: Harcourt Brace & World, 1961); Casey Nelson Blake, *Beloved Community: The Cultural Criticism of Randolph Bourne Van Wyck Brooks, Waldo Frank and Lewis Mumford* (Chapel Hill: University of North Carolina Press, 1990); Kevin Lynch, *The Image of the City* (Cambridge, Mass.: MIT Press, 1960); Kevin Lynch, *What Time Is This Place?* (Cambridge, Mass.: MIT Press, 1972). On Jane Jacobs, see Jane Jacobs, *The Death and Life of Great American Cities* (New York: Random House, 1961). On Christopher Alexander, see Serge Chermayeff and Christopher Alexander, *Community and Privacy: Toward a New Architecture of Humanism* (Garden City, N.Y.: Doubleday, 1963); Christopher Alexander, *Notes on the Synthesis of Form* (Cambridge, Mass.: Harvard University Press, 1964); Christopher Alexander et al., *A Pattern Language: Towns, Building, Construction* (Oxford: Oxford University Press, 1977).

67. Lawrence Halprin, *Cities* (Cambridge, Mass.: MIT Press, 1963; rev. ed., 1978); Tim Cresswell and Peter Merriman, *Geographies of Mobilities: Practices, Spaces, Subjects* (Farnham: Ashgate, 2011); Rudofsky, *Architecture without Architects*; Felicity D. Scott, *Disorientation: Bernard Rudofsky in the Empire of Signs,* Critical Spatial Practice 7 (Berlin: Sternberg Press, 2016).

68. Posener, "One Family Houses in Palestine," 1–3.

2. Profession

1. See Knesset Proceedings (Divrey Ha'Knesset), Sixth Knesset, Meeting 252, February 12, 1968. Also Yehuda (Idel) Drexler, the Ministry of Housing employee in charge of the entire building activity in Jerusalem, interview with the author, Holon, September 2, 1998, and David Kroyanker, *Jerusalem Architecture—Periods and Styles: Modern Architecture Outside the Old City, 1948–1990* (Jerusalem: Keter, 1991), 41–42.

2. The Ministry of Housing was eager to build quickly on land confiscated immediately after the war in order to create a continuous built area between North Jerusalem and Mount Scopus. They therefore recruited completed housing plans that Yitzhak Perlstein had designed for another site and added to them prefabricated arches in order to provide Eshkol Heights with the appropriate Oriental look.

3. See Joseph Mali, ed., *Wars, Revolutions and Generational Identity* [in Hebrew] (Tel Aviv: 'Am 'oved; Merkaz Yitshak Rabin le-heker Yisra'el, 2001), particularly Menachem Brinker, "The Generation of the State: A Cultural or Political Concept?," 143–57.

4. Elinoar Barzaki, interview with the author, Tel Aviv, August 20, 1998. Barzaki studied in Europe during the 1968 events and was recruited by Ram Karmi upon her return to join his team at the Ministry of Housing. Later she became the city engineer of Jerusalem and, at the time of the interview, the head of the architectural school at Tel Aviv University.

5. Aviah Hashimshoni, "Architecture" [in Hebrew], in *Israel Art*, ed. Benjamin Tammuz (Jerusalem: Massada, 1963), 199–229. The English edition is "Architecture," in *Art in Israel,* ed. Benjamin Tammuz and Max Wykes-Joyce (Philadelphia: Chilton, 1965).

6. For the triple negation of the Jewish Diaspora, the bourgeoisie, and the Orient,

which preconditioned the adoption of modern architecture as a Zionist expression, see Alona Nitzan-Shiftan, "Contested Zionism—Alternative Modernism: Erich Mendelsohn and the Tel Aviv Chug in Mandate Palestine," *Architectural History* 39 (1996): 147–80.

7. Dan Eytan, interview with the author, Tel Aviv, July 29, 1998. Eytan pointed out that the founders of Labor Zionism did not entrust his sabra generation with political duties but assigned to them instead professional tasks. Indeed, one of the main questions facing scholars of this sabra generation is its members' political inefficacy in comparison to the founders of Labor Zionism. See Yonatan Shapira, *An Elite without Successors* (Tel-Aviv: Sifriyat Po'alim, 1984). Anita Shapira argues that this generation conformed to the activist message of Labor Zionism and saw in politics a field of verbal articulations rather than accomplishments. Following her comment that they turned instead to professional careers, this study questions the political efficacy of their action through "the profession"; see Anita Shapira, "'Dor Baaretz'" [in Hebrew], in *Old Jews, New Jews* (Tel Aviv: Am Oved, 1997), 122–54.

8. Not all the protagonists I study were actually born in Mandate Palestine. However, interviews have revealed that the great majority of the group under focus was indeed native-born. Others assimilated to the culture of the sabra at an early age, being young enough to study in the appropriate high schools and to participate in the activities of Zionist youth movements, which led to the required cultural path I describe below.

9. The analysis of the group's shared outlook and inclinations owes to Pierre Bourdieu's definition of the *habitus*. See Pierre Bourdieu, *Outline of a Theory of Practice* (Cambridge: Cambridge University Press, 1977); Pierre Bourdieu and Randal Johnson, *The Field of Cultural Production: Essays on Art and Literature* (New York: Columbia University Press, 1993).

10. The high schools were Tichon Hadash, Gimnasya Herzlia, and Bet Hinuch Tichon. Each of them was a hub for different youth movements.

11. Author interviews with Dan Eytan (July 29, 1998, Tel Aviv, and May 15, 2001, and June 6, 2001, Haifa) and with Avraham Vachman (August 8, 1998, Haifa, and ongoing personal communication).

12. This war started immediately after the UN resolution to divide Mandate Palestine between its Arab and Jewish populations. Israelis call it the War of Independence, the result of their national struggle for Jewish sovereignty. Palestinians call this war the *Nakba,* the disaster that dispossessed them of their homeland. The foundation of Israel was therefore based on a national project that was at the same time both liberating and oppressive.

13. In the group sent to Rosh HaNikrah were architects Saadia Mendel, Moshe Lofenfeld, Avraham Vachman, and Ram Karmi, as well as one who remains unidentified. Their commander was architect Dan Eytan. The training in such group was called *hachshara.* This particular *hachshara* was drafted to the Haganah, the mainstream Zionist military organization, and was sent to Kibbutz Rosh HaNikrah. After the declaration of independence they were drafted as a group to the newly formed Israel Defense Force, the Soldierly Pioneering Youth (*nahal*) of which was modeled after the combined military-settlement training of the *hachshara* (Vachman, interview).

14. Ratner was dean during the years 1932–41, 1943–51, and 1959–60. For his architectural career and writings, see Silvina Sosnovsky, ed., *Yohanan Ratner: The Man, the Architect, and His Work* (Haifa: President's Fund of the Technion, Faculty of Architecture and Town Planning, 1992).

15. Moti Sahar, phone interview with the author, July 1, 2001.

16. In interviews (for example, with Avraham Yaski, interview with the author, August 23, 1998, Tel Aviv; and Dan Eytan, July 29, 1998), the date of the conference was uncertain. In *Handasah ve-Adrichalut* (Engineering and Architecture), however, the 1957 conference in Ohalo is covered in detail as a typical modernist event, in which Ben Gurion tied national and architectural goals: "Addresses delivered at the Thirty-first General Conference at 'Ohalo,' March 8–9, 1958," *Handasah ve-Adrichalut,* March 1957.

17. Avraham Yaski, interview with the author, Tel Aviv, August 23, 1998.

18. The Mandate period is by far the most studied period in Israeli architectural historiography. For an analysis of this phenomenon, see Alona Nitzan-Shiftan, "Nationalism and the Politic of Israel Architectural Historiography" in "Israelizing Jerusalem: The Encounter between Architectural and National Ideologies, 1967–1977" (PhD diss., MIT, 2002), 35–47. For a primary source, see the journal published by the Tel Aviv circle of architects, *Habinyan* 1–3, Tel Aviv, 1937 and 1938. Examples of secondary sources are Michael Levin and Judith Turner, *White City: International Style Architecture in Israel* (Tel Aviv: Tel Aviv Museum, 1984); Jeannine Fiedler, ed., *Social Utopias of the Twenties: Bauhaus, Kibbutz, and the Dream of the New Man* (Wuppertal: Mèuller + Busmann Press, 1995); Gilbert Herbert and Silvina Sosnovsky, *Bauhaus on the Carmel and the Crossroads of Empire: Architecture and Planning in Haifa during the British Mandate* (Jerusalem: Yad Izhak Ben-Zvi, 1993); Gilbert Herbert, "On the Fringes of the International Style," *Architecture SA,* September–October 1987, 36–43; Irmel Kamp-Bandau et al., *Tel Aviv, Neues Bauen, 1930–1939* (Berlin: Tubingen, Wasmuth, 1993); Winfried Nerdinger and Peera Goldman, eds., *Tel Aviv, Modern Architecture, 1930–1939* (Berlin: Tubingen, Wasmuth, 1994); Jörg Stabenow and Ronny Schüler, eds., *Vermittlungswege der Moderne – Neues Bauen in Palästina, 1923–1948. The Transfer of Modernity – Architectural Modernism in Palestine, 1923–1948* (Berlin: Gebr. Mann Verlag, 2017).

19. Zvi Efrat, *The Israeli Project: Building and Architecture, 1948–1973* [in Hebrew], vol. 1 (Tel Aviv: Tel Aviv Museum of Art, 2004), the chapters "Size (Godel)," 249–304, "Emergency (Herum)," 513–64, and "Vernacular," 435–54; Miriam Tuvyah and Michael Boneh, eds., *Building the Country: Public Housing in the 1950s* (Tel-Aviv: Israel Museums Forum; HaKibbutz HaMeuhad, 1999). During the year of Israel's Jubilee, there were two art exhibitions that prepared the ground for the architectural interest in this period. See Galia Bar-Or, ed., *"Hebrew Work": The Disregarded Gaze in the Canon of Israeli Art* [in Hebrew], exhibition catalog (Ein Harod: Mishkan Le'Omanut, 1998); Gila Blas and Ilana Tatenbaum, *Social Realism in the 1950s, Political Art in the 1990s* [in Hebrew] (Haifa: The New Haifa Museum, 1998).

20. See, for example, Alexander Klein, "House Planning Principles and Methods for Plan Analysis," *Handasah ve-Adrichalut,* no. 4 (1942): 1–3; no. 5 (1942): 5–9.

21. Ram Karmi, interview with the author, Tel Aviv, July 7, 1998.

22. The circle's core consisted of Dan Eytan, Yizhak Yashar, Ram Karmi, Ora and Yaakov Yaar, Avraham Yaski, and Amnon Alexandroni. Moshe Zarhi and Yaakov Rechter also frequently participated. The circle also associated with other architects, whom they often invited to present their work, such as Eldar Sharon, Zvi Hecker, and David Best. Best together with David Reznik, who belonged to an earlier formation of this group (when he was working with Zeev Rechter in Tel Aviv), were the most influential nonsabras among Israeli architects.

23. *Handasah ve-Adrichalut,* the journal of Israel's Association of Engineers and Architects, was the single architectural periodical in Israel until the mid-1960s. At that time, Dan Eytan edited some special issues for the journal. The group of participants (who were usually associated with the circle) alternated according to the topic. They met to discuss issues such as new housing developments, institutes for higher education, and so forth—issues that preoccupied their generational group. The meetings were recorded and their transcriptions published in the journal in lieu of a manifesto.

24. Particularly important was the Model Housing Estate in Beer Sheva (1959–64), where a team experimented with different housing types, ranging from a quarter-kilometer-long housing block (Yaski and Alexandroni) to *casba*-inspired carpet housing (Havkin and Zolotov). The unrealized plans for the new town of Bsor (1961–64) generated new ideas that were strongly influenced by the British plans for Hook. Avraham Yaski headed both teams. Other examples of influential experiments are Eytan and Yashar's Victory Housing in Dimona of the mid-1960s (whose name was inspired by the Six Day War immediately

after which the housing complex was populated), Yaakov and Ora Yaar's housing and commercial center in Givat Hamoreh (1958–61), and David Best's plans for housing quarters in Arad (Yeelim, 1961, Avishur, 1965).

25. That two members of this very team headed two of three accredited architectural schools in Israel during the time interviews were conducted for this research is a powerful testimony to the ongoing influence of their agenda in Israeli architectural culture. Elinoar Barzaki headed the Tel Aviv University School of Architecture together with Avraham Yaski, a leading member of the 1960s Tel Aviv architectural circle. Zeev Drukman headed the School of Architecture at Bezalel Academy of Arts in Jerusalem.

26. Jacob Bakema, in Alison Margaret Smithson, ed., *Team 10 Primer* (Cambridge, Mass.: MIT Press, 1968), 24.

27. Stanford Anderson, "Memory without Monuments: Vernacular Architecture," *Traditional Dwellings and Settlements Review* 11, no. 1 (1999): 13–22.

28. Aldo van Eyck, "Is Architecture Going to Reconcile Basic Values?," in Oscar Newman, ed., *New Frontiers in Architecture: CIAM 59 in Otterlo* (New York: Universe Books, 1961), 28–29.

29. The authority was exercised mostly by members of CIAM whose Modern Movement is often capitalized in scholarly literature in order to emphasize its ideological underpinnings. See Giorgio Ciucci, "The Invention of the Modern Movement," *Oppositions* 24 (1981): 68–91. For the sake of ease I am using the more general phrase "modern architecture" in the text.

30. Bernard Rudofsky, *Architecture without Architects: A Short Introduction to Non-pedigreed Architecture* (New York: Museum of Modern Art, 1964), caption for illustration 1.

31. ATBAT-Afrique, "Statement of Principle," in Smithson, *Team 10 Primer*, 74.

32. Early New Brutalism stressed reverence to materials, affinity between building and man, and inspiration from peasant architecture (particularly from the Mediterranean vernacular). Aesthetically, the trend is known for its brute materials, especially its characteristic exposed concrete. The building that most inspired this trend is Unité d'Habitation in Marseilles, a monumental housing complex by Le Corbusier. The first history of this trend by a contemporary critic is Reyner Banham, *The New Brutalism: Ethic or Aesthetic?*, Documents of Modern Architecture (London: Architectural Press, 1966).

33. Ram Karmi, interview with the author, Tel Aviv, June 8, 2001.

34. See Zali Gurevitz and Gideon Aran, "Al Ha'makom (Israeli Anthropology)," *Alpayim* 4 (1991): 9–44.

35. Yoram Segal, "The Traditional House in the Arab Villages in the Galilee," *Tvai* 1 (1966): 20.

36. Yitzhak Danziger, interview in Moti Omer, *Yitzhak Danziger* (Tel Aviv: Tel Aviv Museum of Art, 1996). For Canaanites, see Yaacov Shavit, *The New Hebrew Nation: A Study in Israeli Heresy and Fantasy* (New York: Routledge, 1987).

37. Omer, *Yitzhak Danziger*, 160.

38. For texts by Danziger, see Omer, *Yitzhak Danziger*.

39. Ram Karmi, *Lyric Architecture* (Tel Aviv: Ministry of Defense Press, 2001), 13.

40. Ibid., 12.

41. Ram Karmi, "On the Architecture of Shadows," *Kav* 3 (1965): 55–56.

42. It is interesting to contrast it to the Israel Museum, built in 1965 by the European Israeli Al Mansfeld, which is also modeled on an Arab village. Mansfeld drew on the formal characteristics of the village, particularly on its morphological appearance of multiple cubical units, whose silhouette complements the landscape of Jerusalem. In contrast, Karmi's architecture hardly resembled the Arab vernacular in formal terms. Its interior spaces, however, emulated the spatial experience of shaded passages and enclosed courtyards that Karmi considered indigenous. Unlike the modernist Mansfeld, who sought in this vernacular a for-

mal architectural system, Karmi's turn to the Arab village precedent intended to evoke the homeness of the region.

43. In the wake of Said's *Orientalism* of 1978, many studies have demonstrated the Western/Oriental dichotomy in different contexts and locales. For the Israeli context, see Ella Shohat, *Israeli Cinema: East/West and the Politics of Representation* (Austin: University of Texas Press, 1989); Gil Eyal, *The Disenchantment of the Orient: Expertise in Arab Affairs and the Israeli State* (Stanford: Stanford University Press, 2006); and Yigal Zalmona and Tamar Manor-Fridman, *Kadima: The East in Israeli Art* (Jerusalem: Israel Museum, 1998). Particularly important in this context is Dan Rabinowitz, *Anthropology and the Palestinians* (Ra'ananah: ha-Merkaz le-heker ha-hevrah ha-'Arvit, 1998).

44. See, for example, Russell Ferguson et al., *Out There: Marginalization and Contemporary Cultures* (New York: New Museum of Contemporary Art; Cambridge, Mass.: MIT Press, 1990); Homi K. Bhabha, *The Location of Culture* (London: Routledge, 1994).

45. For critical discussions of the object of ethnography, see James Clifford and George E. Marcus, *Writing Culture: The Poetics and Politics of Ethnography* (Berkeley: University of California Press, 1986); Talal Asad, ed., *Anthropology and the Colonial Encounter* (London: Ithaca Press, 1973); George W. Stocking, *Observers Observed: Essays on Ethnographic Fieldwork* (Madison: University of Wisconsin Press, 1983).

46. David Resnik, interview with the author, September 8, 1999.

47. For the history of this project, see Diana Dolev, *The Planning and Building of the Hebrew University, 1919–1948: Facing the Temple Mount* (Lanham, Md.: Lexington Books, 2016); Ayala Levin, "The Mountain and the Fortress: The Location of the Hebrew University Campus on Mount Scopus in the Israeli Imagination of National Space" [in Hebrew], *Teoria ve Bikoret* 38–39 (2011): 11–34; Shaul Katz and Michael Heyd, eds., *The History of the Hebrew University of Jerusalem* [in Hebrew], vol. 1 (Jerusalem: Hebrew University Magnes Press, 1997); Hagit Lavsky, ed., *The History of the Hebrew University of Jerusalem* [in Hebrew], vols. 2 and 3 (Jerusalem: Hebrew University Magnes Press, 2005–9).

48. Architects of buildings in the university were Ram Karmi, Avraham Yaski, Dan Eytan, Shmuel Shaked, Haim Ketzef, David Reznik, and others.

49. This worldview and set of inclinations relates to Bourdieu's definition of the *habitus*. See Bourdieu, *Outline of a Theory of Practice*, 10.

50. David Cassuto, ed., *The Western Wall: A Collection of Essays Concerning the Design of the Western Wall Plaza and Its Surroundings* [in Hebrew] (Jerusalem: Jerusalem Post Press, 1975), 95.

51. Nadia Abu El-Haj, *Facts on the Ground: Archaeological Practice and Territorial Self-Fashioning in Israeli Society* (Chicago: University of Chicago Press, 2001).

52. Arye Dvir, "Overall Plan for the Jerusalem National Park," in Julian J. Landau, ed., *The Jerusalem Committee, Proceedings of the First Meeting, June 30 – July 4, 1969* (Jerusalem: The Committee, 1969), 24.

53. The publication of the Israel Defense Force, *BaMahane,* preached for the love of the country. It published stories and detachable centerpieces of images from "the Land of Israel." These posters became major visual stimuli in the military physical environment, service in which is obligatory. Many of these features were compiled in Irit Zaharoni, *Israel, Roots & Routes: A Nation Living in Its Landscape* (Tel Aviv: Ministry of Defense Publishing House, 1990). This edition is based on the Hebrew book: *Derech Eretz* (Tel Aviv: Bamahane, 1983).

54. The open-air model was reconstructed and largely imagined in the absence of accurate archeological data by the archeologist Professor Avi Yona. A recent appraisal of it in a publication dedicated to "knowing the country" is Gavriel Barkai and Eli Shiler, "A Tour in Second Temple Jerusalem in the Holyland Hotel Model," in *A Periodical for the Study of the Land of Israel* (Jerusalem: Ariel, 2001), 21–50.

55. Yoram Tzafrir, "Preface," in *The Eretz-Israeli Residential House in the Roman –*

Byzantine Period [in Hebrew], ed. Yizhar Hirschfeld (Jerusalem: Yad Ben Tzvi, 1987). See also the English edition: *The Palestinian Dwelling in the Roman-Byzantine Period* (Jerusalem: Franciscan Printing Press, 1995). Considering Palestine and *Eretz Israel* (the Land of Israel) as synonyms implies a teleology in which the Land of Israel is a constant that in spite of its many rulers, keeps its Jewish identity.

56. Hirschfeld, *The Eretz-Israeli Residential House,* 4.

57. Ibid.

58. Moshe Safdie, *Jerusalem: The Future of the Past* (Boston: Houghton Mifflin, 1989), 27.

59. Moshe Safdie, *Beyond Habitat* (Montreal: Tundra Books; Toronto: Collins Publishers, 1973), 146.

60. Ibid., 169.

61. Moshe Safdie, *Safdie in Jerusalem,* Slidcas no. 3, London, Pidgeon Audio Visual (extracted from a talk he gave to the Royal Institute of Architects in May 1979).

62. Safdie, *Jerusalem,* 29.

63. See Abraham Rabinovich, "Why a Fellah Has a Better Home Than a Professor," *Jerusalem Post,* August 8, 1975.

64. Safdie, *Beyond Habitat,* 216.

65. Safdie, *Jerusalem,* 28.

66. See Ita Heinze-Greenberg, "An Artistic European Utopia at the Abyss of Time: The Mediterranean Academy Project, 1931–34," *Architectural History* 45 (2002): 441–82.

67. Banham, *The New Brutalism,* 47.

68. Kenneth Frampton studied together with Karmi at the Architectural Association. They were married to two sisters, and Frampton started working in Israel as an architect. Later he would invest these British regionalist attitudes with critical theory. His eventual theorization of "Critical Regionalism" turned into one of the most influential concepts in late twentieth-century architectural culture worldwide: Kenneth Frampton, "Towards a Critical Regionalism: Six Points for an Architecture of Resistance," in *The Anti-aesthetic: Essays on Postmodern Culture,* ed. Hal Foster (Port Townsend, Wash.: Bay Press, 1983).

69. Ram Karmi, "Human Values in Urban Architecture," in *Israel Builds* (Tel Aviv: Ministry of Housing, 1977), 31–44.

70. For a succinct and illuminating account of the term in architectural culture, see Mia Fuller, "Mediterraneanism," *Environmental Design,* nos. 9/10 (1990): 8–9, and Mia Fuller, *Colonial Constructions: Architecture, Cities, and Italian Imperialism in the Mediterranean and East Africa* (New York: Routledge, 2003). For an in-depth study of this phenomenon and its remarkable influence on Italian modernism, see Brian Lloyd McLaren, *Architecture and Tourism in Italian Colonial Libya: An Ambivalent Modernism* (Seattle: University of Washington Press, 2006), and "Mediterraneita and Modernita: Architecture and Culture during the Period of Italian Colonization of North Africa (Lybia)" (PhD diss., MIT, 2001).

71. For Mediterraneanism in the Israeli context, see Yaakov Shavit, "The Mediterranean World and 'Mediterraneanism': The Origins, Meaning, and Application of a Geo-Cultural Notion in Israel," *Mediterranean Historical Review* 3, no. 2 (1998): 96–117, and Yaakov Shavit, "Culture Rising from the Sea (Tarbut Ola Min Hayam)" [in Hebrew], *zmanim* 34–35 (1990): 38–47.

72. Adam Mazor, interview with the author, Haifa, January 28, 2009.

73. Omer, *Yitzhak Danziger,* unpaginated.

74. Ibid.

75. For the bureaucratic management of national identity, see Michael Herzfeld, *The Social Production of Indifference: Exploring the Symbolic Roots of Western Bureaucracy* (Chicago: University of Chicago Press, 1993).

76. Karmi, "Human Values," 43.

77. Bar-Or, *"Hebrew Work,"* 157.

78. Karmi, "Human Values," 34.

79. Alison Margaret Smithson and Peter Smithson, *Ordinariness and Light: Urban Theories 1952–1960 and Their Application in a Building Project 1963–1970* (Cambridge, Mass.: MIT Press, 1970), 32.

80. Dan Eytan, interview with the author, Haifa, June 5, 2001.

81. Smithson, *Team 10 Primer,* 3.

82. Karmi, interview, 1998.

83. Ibid.

84. Karmi, "Human Values," 34.

85. Ibid., 44.

86. Ibid.

3. State

1. Amos Elon, "Building (Destroying!) Jerusalem: In the Fear that the Rogers Plan Would Be Accepted, Making Facts that Would Cause a Crying Shame for Years to Come," *Ha'aretz,* December 11, 1970.

2. During the first postwar decade the Jewish population grew from 200,000 to 270,000. In 1977 construction was at its peak and plans were already set for the following decade as well: Israel Kimhi, "Demographic, Economic and Metropolitan Development" [in Hebrew], in *Twenty Years in Jerusalem, 1967–1987,* ed. Yehoshua Prawer and Ora Ahimeir (Tel Aviv: Ministry of Defense, 1988), 70.

3. J. L. Sert, F. Léger, and S. Giedion, "Nine Points on Monumentality," in *Architecture Culture, 1943–1968: A Documentary Anthology,* ed. Joan Ockman and Edward Eigen (New York: Rizzoli, 1993), 370–78.

4. Ministry of Housing and Max Wolfsohn, *Planning the Residential Environment and Fulfilling of the Human Needs: Demonstrating New Neighborhoods in Jerusalem* (1976), author's collection.

5. The slogan that supported population dispersal was propagated by the state agencies. For posters carrying the slogan, see, for example, Batia Donner, *To Live with the Dream* [in Hebrew] (Tel Aviv: Tel Aviv Museum of Art, Dvir Publishers, 1989), 158.

6. A second, smaller confiscation occurred later that year, on April 18. Still along the boundaries of existing urban areas, Israel confiscated 765 dunams near the pre-1948 settlement of Neve Yaakov, and 116 dunams in the Jewish Quarter of the Old City (190 and 28 acres, respectively). For a detailed account of the 1968 confiscations, see Uzi Benziman, *Jerusalem: A City without a Wall* [in Hebrew] (Tel Aviv: Schocken, 1973), 244–65; Meron Benvenisti, *Jerusalem: The Torn City* [in Hebrew] (Jerusalem: Weidenfeld and Nicolson, 1973), 288–98.

7. I call these housing developments settlements because they followed the same pattern of conquering land for purposes of demographic Judaization. This was a consensual intention at the time. Today the term "settlement" is controversial and is used to describe Jewish villages and towns on occupied land that are not recognized by the international community. Israelis do not consider the housing developments within the extended municipal boundaries of Jerusalem "settlements." They are called ring or satellite neighborhoods, part and parcel of Jerusalem.

8. Minutes of a meeting on "building expansion in Jerusalem," May 5, 1970, Israel State Archive, GL/15555/12.

9. Ibid.

10. Minutes of a meeting on "Planning Guidelines for the Confiscated Lands in Jerusalem," September 4, 1970, Israel State Archive, GL/15555/12.

11. Elinoar Barzaki, interview with the author, Haifa, December 5, 2013.

12. Avraham Yaski, interview with the author, Ramat Gan, September 10, 1998.

13. On Israel's anxiety over the Rogers Plan and the government's firm decision to respond with mass construction, see Benvenisti, *Jerusalem,* 294–98, and Moshe 'Amirav, *Jerusalem Syndrome: How the Israeli Unification Policy Failed* [in Hebrew] (Jerusalem: Karmel, 2007), 159–65.

14. The plans were approved on December 1, and the press conference took place on December 8, 1970. Drexler, the single planner attending, was not allowed by the ministry's officials to present Ramot in order to avoid unbalanced presentation. See "The Housing Ministry Planners Didn't Show up at the Symposium on the Planning of Jerusalem," *Ha'aretz,* December 9, 1970.

15. Ha'Ezrahi is quoted in Abraham Rabinovitz, "The Ministry of Housing's Cloak of Secrecy Is a Target for Criticism," *Jerusalem Post,* December 9, 1970.

16. Elon, "Building (Destroying!) Jerusalem."

17. "Haste in Jerusalem," Editorial, *Ha'aretz,* January 7, 1971.

18. "Harsh Criticism in the Jerusalem City Council on Building Construction in Nebi Samuel and the High Commissioner Hill," *Ma'ariv,* January 7, 1971; "The Leadership of Teddy Kollek," Editorial, *Ha'aretz,* January 12, 1971.

19. "The Council for the Beautiful Land of Israel Attacks the Plans to Dismantle the Landscape of Jerusalem," *Al Hamishmar,* January 24, 1971.

20. Knesset Proceedings (Divrey Ha'Knesset), Sixth Knesset, Meeting 252, February 12, 1968.

21. Yehuda Drexler, interview with the author, Holon, September 2, 1998.

22. Yoseph Kolodny, phone interview with the author, October 8, 1998. Kolodny was the intellectual force behind the rebelling team whose members were eventually laid off from the Ministry of Housing. He refused to meet for a formal interview, claiming that any discussion about the architecture of Jerusalem is necessarily about official politics and not about architectural culture.

23. For the immensely popular texts setting this design trend, see Serge Chermayeff and Christopher Alexander, *Community and Privacy: Toward a New Architecture of Humanism* (Garden City, N.Y.: Doubleday, 1963); Serge Chermayeff and Alexander Tzonis, *Shape of Community: Realization of Human Potential* (Harmondsworth: Penguin, 1971).

24. Aldo van Eyck in Alison Margaret Smithson, ed., *Team 10 Primer* (Cambridge, Mass.: MIT Press, 1968), 27.

25. *Israel Builds, 1977* (Tel Aviv: Ministry of Housing, 1977), 188–89.

26. *Ramot, Jerusalem* (Tel Aviv: Ministry of Housing, 1976), 8, an internal publication prescribing the guidelines for planning the new settlement, private collection of architect Yehuda Drexler. See also *Israel Builds, 1977,* 174–90.

27. Yonathan Golani, interview with the author, Haifa, May 28, 1998.

28. Letter from A. Grostein, D. Sofer, Y. Fish, Y. Kolodny, A. Shwartz to Asher Olenik, head of physical planning in the Ministry of Housing, January 17, 1971, Israel State Archive, GL/15555/12.

29. Drexler, interview.

30. One handed me a large album filled with press releases; another refused to interview, claiming that no study of architecture is relevant for a city that is exclusively ruled by politics.

31. Minutes of a meeting of the National Planning Council's Subcommittee for Principle Planning Issues on "building expansion in Jerusalem," February 1, 1971, private collection of Yehuda Drexler.

32. Ibid.

33. Letter from Grostein, Sofer, Fish, Kolodny, and Shwartz to Olenik.

34. Ram Karmi, the newly appointed head architect of the ministry hired Yaakov and

Ora Yaar, prominent members of his Tel Aviv circle, to be the head planners of Ramot, a role that goes beyond our scope.

35. "Full Speed Ahead and Damn the Aesthetics," *Time,* March 1, 1971.

36. Uzi Benziman, "The Battle Was Lost—But Not the War over the Beauty of Jerusalem," *Ha'aretz,* February 22, 1971.

37. Yaski, interview.

38. Ibid. Later they added to the leading group architects Salo Hershman, Meir Levi, Giora Gamerman, and Moshe Lofenfeld.

39. Ibid.

40. Reyner Banham, *Megastructure: Urban Futures of the Recent Past* (New York: Harper and Row, 1976).

41. In 1968 the municipal government of Jerusalem declared a competition for the Western entry to the city. See interview with Moshe Zarhi [in Hebrew], *Alef Alef* 4 (April 1974): 12. These panels were found in Eldar Sharon's office, and its architecture is characteristic of his collaboration with Zvi Hecker.

42. Yaski, interview.

43. Ibid.

44. Ibid.

45. Alison Smithson and Peter Smithson, "Cluster City: A New Shape for the Community," *Architectural Review* 122 (1957): 336.

46. Alison Margaret Smithson and Peter Smithson, *Ordinariness and Light: Urban Theories 1952–1960 and Their Application in a Building Project 1963–1970* (Cambridge, Mass.: MIT Press, 1970), 108.

47. Hadas Steiner, "Life at the Threshold," *October* 136 (2011): 133–39.

48. Ibid.

49. *Israel Builds, 1977,* 209, indicates that planning for the first five stages of the decade we review consists of thirteen clusters and an additional five projects of public areas (schools, commerce, recreation).

50. Steiner, "Life at the Threshold," 154.

51. Sir Lancelot Law Whyte, Editorial Preface to the 1968 edition, in *Aspects of Form: A Symposium on Form in Nature and Art,* ed. Lancelot Law Whyte (London: Lund Humphries, 1968), xi.

52. Abraham Rabinovich, *Jerusalem on Earth: People, Passions, and Politics in the Holy City* (London: Free Press, 1988), 201.

53. Best was commissioned in May 1969, long before the confiscation was announced. Best was chosen as a city planner and the head of the team. Memorandum, "Team for the preparation of an outline scheme of south-east Jerusalem," meeting in Mr. Fabel's office, May 22, 1969, Israel State Archive, GL/5557/5.

54. Kahn, who designed the unbuilt Hurva Synagogue in the Old City, was Kollek's favorite architect. He officially commissioned Kahn in March 1971. See Kollek to Kahn, March 4, 1971, Architectural Archives, University of Pennsylvania, Louis Kahn Collection.

55. The most famous controversy was over the Hyatt Hotel on Mount Scopus.

56. Teddy Kollek, interview with the author, Jerusalem, March 24, 2000; David Best, *Architecture and Urban Planning: A Memoir,* unpublished professional autobiography, author's collection, 130–32; Rabinovich, *Jerusalem on Earth.* Apparently, Sharef accepted Best and Kollek's plea in the south after bitterly defeating Kollek in the north. Eventually, the ridge became a borderline between the two authorities: on the northern side Kahn envisioned a promenade along the ridge. It culminated into an unbuilt stepped hotel on the western end of the site, slightly hidden from the panoramic view of the Old City.

57. Rabinovich, *Jerusalem on Earth,* 202.

58. Best worked with Richard Kauffmann, the prime architect of the Zionist settlement project, and with Zeev Rechter, a member of the Mandate-era Tel Aviv circle, whose practice was a hub for a younger generation of architects.

59. Best, *Architecture and Urban Planning*; David Best, interview with the author, Givaatayim, May 25, 2001.

60. Best, who sought direct contact with Lynch's ideas, promised "to show him around the Old City of Jerusalem," which he told Lynch "was the built version of his own texts." Lynch passed away before making this pilgrimage. Best, *Architecture and Urban Planning*, 112.

61. Kevin Lynch, *The Image of the City* (Cambridge, Mass.: MIT Press, 1960), 2–3.

62. Ibid., 9.

63. Best, *Architecture and Urban Planning*, 127.

64. Ibid., 127–30.

65. Best, interview.

66. Best, *Architecture and Urban Planning*, 116. Best recalls lessons with Lisa Peattie and Don Schön; Rodwin bringing his European experience in housing policy to bear on the program; Albert Hirshman at Harvard advancing the "Hidden Hand" development theory and dissenting "from his home base of scientific economics for the comparative vagaries of sociology and psychology"; and Aaron Fleischer engaging the generational distaste with the car, figuring "how to continue to use the private car while mitigating some of its drawbacks" (115).

67. Kauffmann was a student of Theodor Fischer in Munich and the prime architect of the Zionist settlement since the early 1920s; Glikson was his mentor at the Ministry of Housing and a close ally of the American urban theorist Lewis Mumford, who was a fervent Garden City advocate.

68. Best, *Architecture and Urban Planning*, 128.

69. Ibid.

70. Arieh Sharon, in *Proceedings: Symposium on the Problems of National and Regional Planning, 13.12.1967,* the Supreme Planning Committee, Ministry of Housing, 16, Azrieli Architecture Archive at the Tel Aviv Museum Sharon Archives, Box 619.

71. Ministry of Housing and Wolfsohn, *Planning the Residential Environment.*

72. Abraham Harold Maslow, *Motivation and Personality* (New York: Harper & Row, 1954).

73. Ministry of Housing and Wolfsohn, *Planning the Residential Environment*, 3.

74. Aviah Hashimshoni, "Architecture" [in Hebrew], in *Israel Art,* ed. Benjamin Tammuz (Tel Aviv: Massada, 1963), 220.

75. Ministry of Housing and Wolfsohn, *Planning the Residential Environment*, 33.

76. Ibid., 17.

77. Ibid., 19.

78. Shlomo (Soli) Angel, phone interview with the author, October 26, 2013.

79. For prime examples, see Stanford Anderson, ed., *On Streets* (Cambridge, Mass.: MIT Press, 1978); Bernard Rudofsky, *Architecture without Architects: A Short Introduction to Non-pedigreed Architecture* (New York: Museum of Modern Art, 1964).

80. Ministry of Housing and Wolfsohn, *Planning the Residential Environment*, 26.

81. Ibid., 26–27.

82. Ibid.

83. For the English translation, see Henri Lefebvre, "The Right to the City," in *Writings on Cities,* trans. Eleonore Kofman and Elizabeth Lebas (Cambridge, Mass.: Blackwell Publishers, 1996), 147–59. The original French *Le Droit à la Ville* was published in 1968.

84. Ministry of Housing and Wolfsohn, *Planning the Residential Environment*, 42.

85. Charles Jencks, *The Language of Post-Modern Architecture* (London: Academy Editions, 1977), 24.

86. Ministry of Housing and Wolfsohn, *Planning the Residential Environment,* 42.

87. Ibid., 20.

88. Ibid.

89. Ibid., 43.

90. Barzaki, interview.

91. Łukasz Stanek, *Henri Lefebvre on Space: Architecture, Urban Research, and the Production of Theory* (Minneapolis: University of Minnesota Press, 2011), 118.

92. Ministry of Housing and Wolfsohn, *Planning the Residential Environment,* 43.

93. Minutes of a meeting of the National Planning Council's Subcommittee for Principle Planning Issues, Drexler collection.

94. Ministry of Housing and Wolfsohn, *Planning the Residential Environment,* 43.

95. Lefebvre quoted in Stanek, *Henri Lefebvre on Space,* 87.

4. City

1. The focus is on Dvir's early, systematic design for the NPA, which embraced the entire precinct around the city walls. Later, the NPA and Kollek commissioned the various smaller parks with which we are familiar today according to this initial plan.

2. Teddy Kollek, "Quotation of the Day," *New York Times,* June 30, 1967, 38.

3. Reuters, "Mayor Invites U.N. to Jerusalem," *Washington Post,* July 6, 1967.

4. Ibid.

5. Roger Friedland and Richard Hecht, *To Rule Jerusalem,* Cambridge Cultural Social Studies (New York: Cambridge University Press, 1996), 182.

6. David Ben Gurion, "Preface," in *The Story of Jerusalem: A Pictorial Report,* ed. Beno Rothenberg (Tel Aviv: Am Oved Publishers, 1967), unpaginated.

7. Ibid.

8. Teddy Kollek and Amos Kollek, *One Jerusalem* [in Hebrew] (Tel Aviv: Mariv Library Publishers, 1979), 118.

9. Ibid., 175.

10. Ibid., 138.

11. For the complex uses of tradition and heritage, see, for example, Nezar AlSayyad, ed., *Consuming Tradition, Manufacturing Heritage: Global Norms and Urban Forms in the Age of Tourism* (New York: Routledge, 2001).

12. In so doing he not only complemented Ben Gurion's agenda, but also excluded himself from the race to major political posts, pacifying as a result Ben Gurion's older colleagues, who were intimidated by the rise of some of "Ben Gurion's boys" such as Moshe Dayan and Shimon Peres to power.

13. Erik Cohen, *The City in the Zionist Ideology* (Jerusalem: Hebrew University Institute of Urban and Regional Studies, 1970).

14. The role assigned to the Engineering Force was limited to securing access for heavy machinery and putting in security fences. The force also committed to leading a tour of officials from the municipality to the Western Wall in the afternoon of the following day.

15. Protocol of a meeting between Jerusalem mayor and the commander of the Israeli Central Command, June 9, 1967; notes at the bottom confirming the completion of the task, July 18, 1967: Jerusalem Municipal Archives, file 2/22/6.

16. Amos Elon, "The Dispute over Planning Greater Jerusalem," *Ha'aretz,* July 1967.

17. Ibid.

18. Kollek and Kollek, *One Jerusalem,* 216.

19. David Kroyanker, "A Turnover in the Urban Image and Architectural Appearance of Jerusalem," in *40 Years in Jerusalem, 1967–2007,* ed. Ora Ahimeir and Yaacov Bar-Siman-Tov (Jerusalem: Jerusalem Institute for Israel Studies, 2007), 190.

20. "**Parti.** Choice, means, or method. *Parti pris* means a bias or a mind made up, so in architectural criticism the *parti* is the assumption made that informs a design as well as the choice of approach when realizing the scheme. *Prendre le parti* is to take a decision, or a certain course, as in architectural design." See "parti" from *A Dictionary of Architecture and Landscape Architecture,* at Encyclopedia.com, http://www.encyclopedia.com/education /dictionaries-thesauruses-pictures-and-press-releases/parti.

21. Ole Bouman, "The Architecture of Destruction (Editorial)," *Volume* 11 (2007): 4–5.

22. Kollek and Kollek, *One Jerusalem,* 216.

23. Andrew Herscher, *Violence Taking Place: The Architecture of the Kosovo Conflict* (Stanford, Calif.: Stanford University Press, 2010), 4.

24. Ibid., 7.

25. When answering an internal request to form a special authority that would be led by religious leaders and involve world Jewry, Brutzkus diverted the discussion from issues of sanctity and Jewish renaissance to those of history and landscape, arguing that the latter should be protected from "construction and population according to 'modern' guidelines." Eliezer Brutzkus, "The Planning Status Concerning the 'Historical' Part of Jerusalem," internal document, August 14, 1967, Israel State Archive, GL/2741/7.

26. Ibid.

27. Ibid. Having established the political momentum of his cultural claim, Brutzkus turned to the crucial question of how to translate these insights into legal and planning documents. First, Brutzkus turned to international precedents to explain why the Jerusalem Municipality, like any other municipality that is geared, by definition, toward immediate economic development and is subject to local pressure groups, cannot assume the long-term "historical and cultural perspective" that Jerusalem requires. If the preservation of Venice was taken by the central government of Italy, Jerusalem was unlikely to be different. Second was an argument against "big name" modern architects, who lacked the patience and technique to deal with projects of preservation and restoration. Italian experts, he suggested, should help conduct a thorough architectural research of the area. Finally, although he disqualified the municipality from leading the planning of the historical area, he proposed to legally involve municipal and professional representatives in a subcommittee for the special zone in his ministry that would consult experts from the situated coalition.

28. Dash, the head of the Planning Division in the Ministry of Interior Affairs, was superior to Brutzkus, the chief planner, yet the latter composed most of the written documents that pronounce the ministry agenda. From interviews, however, we learn that Dash was keen on design. Michael Turner, who sketched some of the drawings of the *Conceptual Plan,* for example, says that the "Outline Scheme for the Old City and Its Environs" was the dearest project to Dash and that no design decision there went without his close supervision. Michael Turner, interview with the author, Jerusalem, July 23, 2001.

29. In author interviews with Mike Turner (Jerusalem, July 23, 2001, and Jerusalem, February 23, 2010), he recalled trips to the Architectural Association to see the work of the Smithsons and others and cited the impact of the Greater London Council design for Hook.

30. In late September Dash, Kollek, and Arieh Sharon agreed that Sharon would lead a special team for planning the historical zone of East Jerusalem. By late October Sharon and landscape architects Zvi Miller and Moshe Blum were asked not only to commence with detailed plans, but also to evaluate every proposed plan in the area of the "Outline Scheme" that they prepared together with Brutzkus and Eldar Sharon. They were commissioned to prepare city and building plans together with an "Outline Scheme" in 1:10000 scale for the entire basin, and 1:1250 detailed developing plans for the Old City. See Arieh Sharon, David Anatol Brutzkus, and Eldar Sharon, *Old City of Jerusalem: Bazaars & Commercial Streets* (Jerusalem: Ministry of the Interior- Municipality of Jerusalem, 1970).

31. Arye Dvir, interview with the author and Shira Wilkof, Giv'atayim, June 17, 2009.

32. Ibid.

33. Ibid.

34. Letter from Teddy Kollek, Mayor of Jerusalem, to Levi Eshkol, Prime Minister, July 4, 1966, Israel State Archive, GL/3847/6.

35. September 21, 1967, Israel State Archive, GL/3847/5.

36. Inbal Ben-Asher Gitler, "'Marrying Modern Progress with Treasured Antiquity': Jerusalem City Plans during the British Mandate, 1917–1948," *Traditional Dwellings and Settlements Review* 15, no. 1 (2003): 39–58.

37. Kollek and Kollek, *One Jerusalem,* 216.

38. Quoted in Shahar Shapira, "Jerusalem's Planning—a Historical Review," in *Integrating the Old City in the New City,* ed. Council for the Beautiful Land of Israel (Tel Aviv, 1970), 7–15. General Edmund H. Alenbi called on William McLean, the city engineer of Alexandria, to prepare the first Jerusalem plan before the war was over. His famous decisions regarding the green belt around the Old City and the required stone cladding are regarded as the foundation of Jerusalem planning. Charles Robert Ashbee was recruited by Ronald Storrs to serve as Jerusalem city advisor and the secretary of the Pro-Jerusalem Society between 1918 and 1922.

39. For this pictorial practice, see Marshall J. Berger and Ora Ahimeir, eds., *Jerusalem: A City and Its Future,* 1st ed., Publication of the Jerusalem Institute for Israel Studies (Syracuse, N.Y.: Syracuse University Press, 2002). Julia Czerniak, "Challenging the Pictorial: Recent Landscape Practice," *Assemblage* 34 (1997): 110.

40. Aharon Ron Fuchs and Gilbert Herbert, "Representing Mandatory Palestine: Austen St. Barbe Harrison and the Representational Buildings of the British Mandate in Palestine 1922–37," *Architectural History* 43 (2000): 281–333.

41. Burke quoted in Forty, "Common Sense and the Picturesque," in *Architecture and the Sites of History: Interpretations of Buildings and Cities,* ed. Iain Borden and David Dunster (New York: Whitney Library of Design, 1996), 177.

42. The full text of the lecture can be found at https://archive.org/stream /englishnessofengoopevs/englishnessofengoopevs_djvu.txt.

43. Arthur Kutcher, *The New Jerusalem: Planning and Politics* (London: Thames & Hudson, 1973).

44. The CBD team under David Best also included David Fields, Colin Frank, and Dave Mitchell.

45. January 16, 1967, Israel State Archive, GL/3834/10. In similar fashion Yoffe shared responsibility with the Ministry of Transportation to oversee the architects working with Best on plans for the city's CBD. Before they became city employees members of this team also worked for the Ministry of Religious Affairs on the preliminary survey and design for the Western Wall Plaza.

46. The diverse and changing inspirations of this generation are currently being researched. A first product of this research is Nurit Lissovsky and Diana Dolev, eds., *Arcadia: The Gardens of Lipa Yahalom and Dan Zur* [in Hebrew] (Tel Aviv: Babel [Architecture], 2012).

47. Arthur Kutcher, "Recollections and Reminiscences," a video transcription of a tribute to Shlomo Aronson, 2010, courtesy of Nurit Lissovsky.

48. Peter Walker and Melanie Simo, *Invisible Gardens: The Search for Modernism in the American Landscape* (Cambridge, Mass.: MIT Press, 1994), 9.

49. See Anthony Alofsin, *The Struggle for Modernism: Architecture, Landscape Architecture, and City Planning at Harvard* (New York: W. W. Norton, 2002), for the history of the Graduate School of Design. After studies at Harvard, Halprin worked in the office of Thomas Church, who pioneered modernism in the region. Halprin opened his own practice in 1949.

50. Halprin's parents to Larry and Anna, November 11, 1955, Box 29, Architectural Archives, University of Pennsylvania, Lawrence Halprin Collection. I thank Susan Solomon for turning my attention to this list.

51. Arye Dvir, Paper regarding the transportation network, August 10, 1968, Israel State Archive, GL/3837/4.

52. Derek Gregory, "Emperors of the Gaze: Photographic Practices and Productions of Space in Egypt," in *Picturing Place: Photography and the Geographical Imagination,* ed. Joan M. Schwartz and James R. Ryan (London: I. B. Tauris, 2003), 195–225. AlSayyad, *Consuming Tradition, Manufacturing Heritage.*

53. P. Geddes [Director of the City and Town Planning Exhibition, Professor of Sociology and Civics, University of Bombay], "Jerusalem Actual and Possible: A Preliminary Report to the Chief Administrator of Palestine and the Military Governor of Jerusalem on Town Planning and City Improvements," November 1919, Central Zionist Archives, file Z4/10.202. Quoted in Noah Hysler-Rubin, "Arts & Crafts and the Great City: Charles Robert Ashbee in Jerusalem," *Planning Perspectives* 21, no. 4 (2006): 360.

54. Larry Halprin to Teddy Kollek, Tuesday, August 3, 1971, Jerusalem, in Halprin Sketchbooks, Architectural Archives, University of Pennsylvania, Lawrence Halprin Collection.

55. Arye Dvir, "National Park Plan," in *Jerusalem National Park: Preliminary Proposal by the National Park Authority* (Jerusalem: Israel's National Park Authority, 1969), 28.

56. Arye Dvir, "Arterial Road in the National Park of Jerusalem," October 8, 1968, Israel State Archive GL/3837/4.

57. Dvir, interview, 2009.

58. Elizabeth Meyer, "Site Citations: The Grounds of Modern Landscape Architecture," in *Site Matters: Design Concepts, Histories, and Strategies,* ed. C. J. Burns and A. Kahn (New York: Routledge, 2005), 93.

59. Ibid., 98.

60. Dvir, interview, 2009.

61. Dvir quotes McHarg, interview, 2009.

62. Ibid.

63. For his method, see his seminal book: Ian McHarg, *Design with Nature* (New York: Natural History Press, 1992).

64. McHarg quoted by Walker and Simo, *Invisible Gardens,* 279.

65. Arye Dvir, interview with the author and Shira Wilkof, Jerusalem, June 22, 2010.

66. Ariel Hirschfeld, "Between Symbols and Stones: Wolfson Park in the Hinnom Valley, Jerusalem," in Lissovsky and Dolev, *Arcadia,* 167.

67. James Feron, "World Panel on Jerusalem Supporting Plan for a Park," *New York Times,* July 6, 1969.

68. "Jerusalem Plan to Be Reexamined, Experts Reject Criticism," *Jerusalem Post,* December 24, 1970 (emphasis mine).

69. Ibid.

70. A letter sent to Teddy Kollek from Pierre Bugod, David Fields, Colin Frank, David Kroyanker, Arthur Kutcher, David Mitchell, and Michael Turner, "Observations on the Meeting of the Town Planning Sub-Committee of the Jerusalem Committee, held in Jerusalem, December 1970," Jerusalem, December 26, 1970, Architectural Archives, University of Pennsylvania, Louis Kahn Collection.

71. Nathaniel Lichfield, "Planning for the Spirit and Character of Jerusalem," paper sent to members of the Jerusalem Committee in preparation for the 2nd plenary meeting, June 7, 1973, 9, Architectural Archives, University of Pennsylvania, Louis Kahn Collection.

72. Mike Turner, interview with the author and Julia Grinkrug, Jerusalem, June 16, 2011. According to Turner this was the most intensive period in their professional life. He

describes early rises to measure the angles of the rising sun over the Old City basin, and the fierce struggle they led over public opinion.

73. Lichfield, "Planning for the Spirit and Character of Jerusalem."

74. Moti Shahar, phone interview with the author, July 1, 2001.

75. Lawrence Halprin to Teddy Kollek, Tuesday, August 3, Jerusalem (1971) [notebook + exchange with Safdie], Architectural Archives, University of Pennsylvania, Lawrence Halprin Collection.

76. Halprin was very close to Moshe Safdie, who was commissioned to design Mamilla, but it is uncertain if he had an official role beyond brainstorming the initial stages of the project (Mamilla model master plan, 1973–74, 014.box.38, Architectural Archives, University of Pennsylvania, Lawrence Halprin Collection).

77. Dvir, "National Park Plan," 27.

78. Shlomo Angel, Michael Turner, and Arthur Kutcher, *Building Height Policy for Jerusalem,* first draft (Jerusalem: Urban Planning Unit, Municipality of Jerusalem, 1972), 11.

79. Smith, "High-Rise Construction Stirs Jerusalem Debate."

80. Ibid.

81. Angel, Turner, and Kutcher, *Building Height Policy for Jerusalem,* 12.

82. Arthur Kutcher, "Recollections and Reminiscences," a video transcription of a tribute to Shlomo Aronson, 2010, courtesy of Nurit Lissovsky.

83. More on the Reznik design in the exhibition catalogue *David Reznik: A Retrospective,* ed. Sophia Dekel-Caspi (Tel Aviv: Genia Schreiber University Art Gallery, the Yolanda and David Katz Faculty of the Arts, Tel Aviv University, 2005).

84. Nathaniel Lichfield, "International Federation of Municipal Engineers 5th Congress," October 1974, 21, Private Archives of Israel Kimhi and Yoseph Schweid, Jerusalem Institute for Israel Studies.

85. Ibid., 17.

86. W. J. Thomas Mitchell, *Landscape and Power* (Chicago: University of Chicago Press, 1994), 1.

87. Ibid., 2.

88. W. J. Thomas Mitchell, "Holy Landscape: Israel, Palestine, and the American Wilderness," *Critical Inquiry* 26, no. 2 (2000): 2.

89. Teddy Kollek with J. Robert Moskin, "Introduction," in *Jerusalem: City of Mankind,* ed. Cornell Capa (New York: Grossman, 1974), 7.

90. Teddy Kollek, interview with Arnold Foster, 1971 (http://www.isracast.com/article.aspx?id=364).

91. Louis B. Fleming, "Jerusalem's Mayor, Kollek, May Retire," *Washington Post,* June 5, 1969.

92. Sahar, phone interview.

93. Meron Benvenisti, interview with the author, June 6, 2000.

5. Frontier

1. Lewis Mumford to Teddy Kollek, "Memorandum on the Plan for Jerusalem," November 22, 1970, 5, Architectural Archives, University of Pennsylvania, Louis Kahn Collection.

2. Ari Avrahami, "Jerusalem's Not So Golden Plan," *Architectural Design* 41 (1971): 209–16.

3. The analysis of Jerusalem's Oriental character is based on E. W. Said, *Orientalism* (New York: Pantheon Books, 1978); in the Israeli context, see Yigal Zalmona and Tamar Manor-Friedman, *Kadima: The East in Israeli Art* (Jerusalem: Israel Museum, 1998); Gil Eyal,

The Disenchantment of the Orient: Expertise in Arab Affairs and the Israeli State (Stanford, Calif.: Stanford University Press, 2006).

4. 030.II.box 47. 39.9, Architectural Archives, University of Pennsylvania, Louis Kahn Collection.

5. P. Johnson, "An Open Letter to Mayor Kollek," *New York Times,* February 26, 1971.

6. Mumford to Kollek, "Memorandum on the Plan for Jerusalem," 3.

7. Kollek in Julian J. Landau, *The Jerusalem Committee: Proceedings of the First Meeting, June 30 – July 4, 1969* (Jerusalem: The Committee, 1969), 13.

8. Abraham Rabinovich, "Leading World Architects Meet in Jerusalem," *Jerusalem Post,* December 18, 1970, 5. According to Kollek, only one guest, a Jew from Berlin, refused to visit Jerusalem as long as it was occupied.

9. Teddy Kollek to Golda Meir, June 23, 1969, Israel State Archive, Jerusalem General, Prime Minister Files on Jerusalem, 6500–18.

10. Letter from Golda Meir to Teddy Kollek, July 1, 1969, Israel State Archive, Jerusalem General, Prime Minister Files on Jerusalem, 6500–18.

11. The next meeting of the subcommittee, in a different format, followed the 1978 plenary session of the Jerusalem Committee. It was much more focused on specific projects, yet its content is beyond the temporal scope of this study.

12. The plenary meetings in 1978, 1982, and onward are beyond the scope of this study.

13. Teddy Kollek and Amos Kollek, *One Jerusalem* [in Hebrew] (Tel Aviv: Maariv Library Publishers, 1979), 237.

14. Fascist Italy and Kemalist Turkey are famous exceptions.

15. CIAM's secretary wrote the historiographical bible of the modern movement in architecture. See Sigfried Giedion, *Space, Time and Architecture: The Growth of a New Tradition,* Charles Eliot Norton Lectures for 1938–1939 (London: Cambridge University Press, 1941).

16. The group was photographed with "the coffin" of CIAM. On CIAM, see Eric Paul Mumford, *The CIAM Discourse on Urbanism, 1928–1960* (Cambridge, Mass.: MIT Press, 2000). On its last congress, see Alison Margaret Smithson, ed., *Team 10 Primer* (Cambridge, Mass.: MIT Press, 1968). On Team 10, see Joan Ockman, Edward Eigen, and Columbia University Graduate School of Architecture Planning and Preservation, *Architecture Culture, 1943–1968: A Documentary Anthology* (New York: Columbia University Graduate School of Architecture Planning and Preservation, 1993).

17. For excerpts from writings of leading protagonists of the period, see Aharon Ron Fuchs and Gilbert Herbert, "Representing Mandatory Palestine: Austen St. Barbe Harison and the Representational Buildings of the British Mandate in Palestine, 1922–37," *Architectural History* 43 (2000): 281–333.

18. See the recent publication of a manuscript of the period: Nikolaus Pevsner, *Visual Planning and the Picturesque* (Los Angeles: Getty Publications, 2010).

19. Fuller, quoted in Avrahami, "Jerusalem's Not So Golden Plan," 210. Abraham Rabinovich, "Idealized Jerusalem at Engineers Congress," *Jerusalem Post,* December 17, 1970, 8. On Fuller's ideas, see Richard Meier, "Planning for Jerusalem: An Eye-Witness Account of the Recent Conference, in Which an International Group Considered the Future of Sacred and Secular City," *Architectural Forum* 134, no. 3 (1971): 56.

20. Rabinovich, "Leading World Architects Meet in Jerusalem," 5.

21. Avrahami, "Jerusalem's Not So Golden Plan," 209.

22. The subcommittee analyzed the *1968 Jerusalem Masterplan,* the "Outline Scheme for the Old City and Its Environs," a plan for the Central Business District, and the Jerusalem Transportation Plan for 1985.

23. The thirty-one foreign reviewers were, in alphabetical order, such luminaries as Christopher Alexander, Max Bill, Etienne Boegner, Werner Düttmann, Buckminster Fuller, Luigi Gedda, Charles Haar, Lawrence Halprin, Britton Harris, Sir Philip Hendy, Philip

Johnson, Louis Kahn, Karl Katz, Denys Lasdun, Roslyn Lindheim, Harry Mayerovitch, Richard Meier, Samuel Moses, Isamu Noguchi, Paul Peters (editor, *Baumeister*), Sir Nikolaus Pevsner, Luigi Piccinato, Mrs. Monica Pidgeon (editor, *Architectural Design*), Ulrik Plesner, Mrs. Diana Rowntree, Moshe Safdie, Willem Sandberg, Goran Sidenbladh, Gilbert Weil, Bruno Zevi, and Robert Zion. Other, nonattending members among architects included Geoffrey Bawa (1969) from Sri Lanka and Jaap Bakema (1975).

24. Charles Haar to Teddy Kollek, August 1971, Architectural Archives, University of Pennsylvania, Louis Kahn Collection. Haar wrote these comments on behalf of "many members of the Committee, if not all."

25. "Town Planning Subcommittee of the Jerusalem Committee, a Brief Summery," a document from a package Kollek sent to the members on January 8, 1971, Architectural Archives, University of Pennsylvania, Louis Kahn Collection.

26. Lawrence Halprin notebook, p. 70, Jerusalem Committee, Saturday Eve, Architectural Archives, University of Pennsylvania, Lawrence Halprin Collection.

27. The planners opened an office employing a large multidisciplinary team of architects, planners, geographers, and economists, who ventured into an intensive four years of full-time work. Among many of the workers and consultants were graduates of planning schools in the United States, who had previously worked in Washington, D.C., on questions pertaining to social and ethnic conflicts. They enlivened local urban discourse with new methodologies. The team enjoyed the aura of a unique professional body, whose composite institutional structure prevented the rule of any single interest. The office regularly conducted two sets of meetings with representatives of the different agencies, corresponding to the two hierarchical tiers of ministerial officials. It produced numerous interim reports that testify to the consistency of their approach, which was finally presented in 1968 and was published in Hebrew as two impressive volumes in 1972 and 1974: Aviah Hashimshoni et al., *1968 Jerusalem Masterplan* (Jerusalem: Jerusalem Municipality, 1972–74). Those working on the plan still consider it one of Israel's most impressive planning documents ever. Many of the interim reports, which testify to the consistency of the team's approach, can be found in the library of the Ministry of Housing. The final document has a much greater degree of visual material, perhaps resulting from the Jerusalem Committee's criticism. The list of the team members is in David Kroyanker, *Jerusalem: Conflicts over the City's Physical and Visual Form* [in Hebrew] (Jerusalem: Zmora-Bitan, 1988).

28. Yoseph Schweid, interview with the author, June 12, 2000.

29. For the plan, see Arieh Sharon, *Physical Planning in Israel* (Jerusalem: Government Printer, 1951). For Sharon's English account on its making, see Arieh Sharon, "Planning a New Land," in *Kibbutz + Bauhaus: An Architect's Way in a New Land* (Stuttgart: Kramer Verlag, 1976), 76–95.

30. In early statehood the national campaign that privileged rural settlement was prevalent. A shift toward urbanity was greatly influenced by the presence of Jerusalem. For the role of the city in Zionist culture, see Erik Cohen, *The City in the Zionist Ideology*, Jerusalem Urban Studies 1 (Jerusalem: Hebrew University, Institute of Urban and Regional Studies, 1970).

31. See Hashimshoni et al., *1968 Jerusalem Masterplan*, 1:9–15.

32. Ibid.

33. Arthur Kutcher, *The New Jerusalem: Planning and Politics* (London: Thames & Hudson, 1973), 88.

34. All quotes in the paragraph are taken from Lawrence Halprin's sketchbook, in which he summarized in detail the Jerusalem Committee meetings he attended. See Halprin Sketchbooks, Architectural Archives, University of Pennsylvania, Lawrence Halprin Collection.

35. Abraham Rabinovich, "Planners under Fire," *Jerusalem Post*, December 25, 1970, 20.

36. Louis Kahn, quoted in Rabinovich, "Planners under Fire," 20.

37. Wolf Von Eckardt, "Jerusalem the Golden," *Planning,* February 1987, 25.

38. Amos Elon, "Jerusalem as a Gas Station Sacred to the Three Religions," *Ha'aretz,* December 14, 1970, 8. This was a response to the release of the Jerusalem Transportation Plan by the Ministry of Transportation that was prepared in collaboration with the Jerusalem Masterplan Office.

39. Ari Avrahami, "Planning for Change," in Avrahami, "Jerusalem's Not So Golden Plan," 215.

40. Yoseph Schweid, one of the master plan authors, had already protested, in the 1968 Symposium on the Image of Jerusalem, against this attitude. He decided, "with all due respect to the noble sentiments of the large part of the civilized world who sees in this country a possession that needs to be treated as a preserve—we do not see ourselves as living on a preserve. There are landscapes in this country which require museal guard. But our first consideration must be the actual needs of life in this country." Michael Avi-Yona et al., "A Symposium on the Image of Jerusalem," *Adrichalut,* no. 6 (1968): 36–41.

41. Kollek, quoted in Meier, "Planning for Jerusalem," 57.

42. For writings on Zionist/Israeli planning, see S. Ilan Troen and Noah Lucas, eds., *Israel: The First Decade of Independence* (Albany: State University of New York Press, 1995); Haim Yacobi, ed., *Constructing a Sense of Place: Architecture and the Zionist Discourse* (Aldershot: Ashgate, 2004). In Hebrew, Zvi Efrat, *The Israeli Project: Building and Architecture, 1948–1973,* 2 vols. (Tel Aviv: Tel Aviv Art Museum, 2004); and Yehuda Shenhav, ed., *Space, Land, Home,* special issue, *Theory and Criticism* 16 (2000).

43. For post–World War II architectural culture, see Ockman, Eigen, and Columbia, *Architecture Culture;* and Sarah Williams Goldhagen and Réjean Legault, *Anxious Modernisms: Experimentation in Postwar Architectural Culture* (Cambridge, Mass.: MIT Press, 2000).

44. The term "developmental" refers to studies of high modernism such as James C. Scott, *Seeing Like a State: How Certain Schemes to Improve the Human Condition Have Failed* (New Haven, Conn.: Yale University Press, 1998); and Wolfgang Sachs, *The Development Dictionary: A Guide to Knowledge as Power* (London: Zed Books, 1992). The term "situated" is borrowed from Goldhagen's account of Louis Kahn, who was the most influential architect of the Jerusalem Committee; see Sarah Williams Goldhagen, *Louis Kahn's Situated Modernism* (New Haven, Conn.: Yale University Press, 2001).

45. Lewis Mumford, letter to Kollek, cited in Avrahami, "Jerusalem's Not So Golden Plan," 210.

46. Examples of writings of great influence are Rudolf Wittkower, *Architectural Principles in the Age of Humanism,* Studies of the Warburg Institute 19 (London: Warburg Institute, University of London, 1949); Bernard Rudofsky, *Architecture without Architects: A Short Introduction to Non-pedigreed Architecture* (New York: Museum of Modern Art, 1964); Sibyl Moholy-Nagy, *Native Genius in Anonymous Architecture* (New York: Horizon Press, 1957); D'Arcy Wentworth Thompson, *On Growth and Form,* abridged ed. (Cambridge: Cambridge University Press, 1961).

47. See Stanford Anderson's account on disciplinary memory in connection to the work of Louis Kahn, "Memory in Architecture (Erinnerung in der Architektur)," *Diadalos* 58 (1995): 35.

48. See Sibyl Moholy-Nagy, *Native Genius in Anonymous Architecture* (New York: Horizon Press, 1957); Rudofsky, *Architecture without Architects;* Smithson, *Team 10 Primer.*

49. Christopher Alexander, "A City Is Not a Tree," *Ekistics* 23 (1967): 344–48.

50. Wolf von Eckardt, "Summing Up a Period," in Kroyanker, *Jerusalem,* 452.

51. The full proceedings of the 1970 subcommittee meeting did not survive. The notes taken in preparation for it were found in the special collection of Tamar Eshel, who was the Ministry of Foreign Affairs liaison for the committee. I thank Menachem Levin, the

legendary archivist of the Jerusalem Municipal Archive, for his resourcefulness in finding these notes.

52. "Town Planning Subcommittee of the Jerusalem Committee, a Brief Summery."

53. Khan in Rabinovich, "Planners under Fire," 20.

54. For further reading on religious Zionism, see Aviezer Ravitzky, *Messianism, Zionism, and Jewish Religious Radicalism* (Chicago: University of Chicago Press, 1996). Also see Michael Feige, *Settling in the Hearts: Jewish Fundamentalism in the Occupied Territories* (Detroit: Wayne State University Press, 2009); Akiva Eldar and Idit Zartal, *The Lords of the Land: The Settlers and the State of Israel, 1967–2004* [in Hebrew] (Tel Aviv: Kinneret, 2005).

55. Bernard Lewis introduced "Dr. Wilson, who teaches Arabic literature at the Hebrew University and who is the author of a number of writings on the subject" (see Jerusalem Committee, *Proceedings of Third Plenary Session, December 16–19, 1975,* 13, Archive of the Jerusalem Foundation, unsorted files).

56. For the debate between Lewis and Said, see Said, *Orientalism.* For a response, see "The Question of Orientalism," in Bernard Lewis, *Islam and the West* (New York: Oxford University Press, 1993), 99–118.

57. Charles Robert Ashbee quoted in Shahar Shapira, "Jerusalem's Planning—a Historical Review," in *Integrating the Old City in the New City,* ed. Council for the Beautiful Land of Israel (Tel Aviv: Council for the Beautiful Land of Israel, 1970), 7–15.

58. Daniel Monk, "An Aesthetic Occupation: Architecture, Politics, and the Menace of Monuments in Mandate-era Palestine, 1917–1929" (PhD diss., Princeton University, 1995), passim.

59. Fuchs and Herbert, "Representing Mandatory Palestine." See Avi-Yona et al., "A Symposium on the Image of Jerusalem."

60. Although some of the British planning principles were kept, such as the required stone cladding in Jerusalem and the maintenance of open green valleys, the British underpinning of Orientalism and the design approach it inspired were strictly rejected. The overwhelming opposition to the British colonal regionalism existed even within Zionism's own contextualized modernism that was best exemplified in the work of Erich Mendelsohn. Mendelsohn's architectural achievement was largely recognized as a masterpiece. Nevertheless, its local cultural context created a dead end for Israeli followers. Aviah Hashimshoni, the author of the 1968 master plan, clarified this point in his principle architectural history of Israel of 1963. See Aviah Hashimshoni, "Architecture" [in Hebrew], in *Israel Art,* ed. Benjamin Tammuz (Tel Aviv: Massada, 1963), 226–27.

61. Hashimshoni et al., *1968 Jerusalem Masterplan,* 1:49.

62. For the British fascination with the Orient, see Fuchs and Herbert, "Representing Mandatory Palestine."

63. The team did not mention Christianity in particular. However, the notion of "heavenly Jerusalem" is a clear and erroneous reference to Christian tradition, for which heavenly Jerusalem is an abstract notion devoid of corporeal expression. For the notion of heavenly Jerusalem in Christian culture, see Yehoshua Prawer, "Christianity between Heavenly and Earthly Jerusalem" [in Hebrew], in *Jerusalem through the Ages: The Twenty-fifth Archaeological Convention, October 1967* (Jerusalem: Israel Exploration Society, 1968), 179–92.

64. Ibid.

65. Hashimshoni et al., *1968 Jerusalem Masterplan,* 1:48.

66. W. J. Thomas Mitchell, "Holy Landscape: Israel, Palestine, and the American Wilderness," *Critical Inquiry* 26, no. 2 (2000): 5.

67. Daniel Bertrand Monk, *An Aesthetic Occupation: The Immediacy of Architecture and the Palestine Conflict* (Durham, N.C.: Duke University Press, 2002).

68. Yoseph Schweid in Michael Dumper, *The Politics of Jerusalem since 1967* (New York: Columbia University Press, 1997).

69. Tamar Eshel, private archive.

70. Abraham Rabinovich, "Jerusalem Committee Repudiates Masterplan," *Jerusalem Post,* December 22, 1970, 8.

71. Ibid.

72. Mumford to Kollek, "Memorandum on the Plan for Jerusalem," 4.

73. Another example is in the first plenary session of the Jerusalem Committee, when Judge Hayim Cohen confessed his admiration for the prophet who celebrated the city as one would celebrate a lover. Hayim Cohen, "Eternal Jerusalem," in Landau, *The Jerusalem Committee, Proceedings of the First Meeting,* 9–12.

74. Resolution of the first meeting of the Subcommittee for Town Planning of the Jerusalem Committee, which appears in all the preparatory documents of the following Jerusalem Committee meetings.

75. Nathaniel Lichfield, "International Federation of Municipal Engineers 5th Congress," October 1974, 17, Private Archives of Israel Kimhi and Yoseph Schweid, Jerusalem Institute for Israel Studies.

76. Nathaniel Lichfield, "Planning for the Spirit and Character of Jerusalem," paper sent to members of the Jerusalem Committee in preparation for the second plenary meeting, June 7, 1973, 9, Architectural Archives, University of Pennsylvania, Louis Kahn Collection.

77. Ibid.

78. Ibid., 10.

79. Ibid.

80. Nikolaus Pevsner, "The Reith Lectures: The Englishness of English Art (1955)," http://www.youtube.com/watch?v=7KoX6Zb_E24.

81. Lichfield, "International Federation of Municipal Engineers 5th Congress," 30–31.

82. Alona Nitzan-Shiftan, "Modernisms in Conflict: Architecture and Cultural Politics in Post-'67 Jerusalem," in *Modernism and the Middle East,* ed. Sandy Isenstadt and Kishwar Rizvi (Seattle: University of Washington Press, 2008), 161–82. The term "developmental modernism" is based on definitions such as those found in Sachs, *Development Dictionary.* The term "situated modernism" is drawn from Sarah Goldhagen's analysis of Louis Kahn's postwar architectural thought, which was extremely influential in Jerusalem. See Sarah Williams Goldhagen, *Louis Kahn's Situated Modernism* (New Haven, Conn.: Yale University Press, 2001).

83. Kutcher, *New Jerusalem,* 9.

84. Christine Boyer traces the situated/developmental dichotomy back to two nineteenth-century concepts for improving cities: one "normal" and the other "pathological." In the first, architects seek to recover the form of the city by consolidating and adding sensitively to its existing fabric. They identify the city's innate formal logic and attempt to recover it in order to realize its potential for evoking collective memories and civic sentiments. In the second concept of architecture, the modern city is viewed as pathological. Developmental architecture is the cure, and its acute interventions can correct the city's aberrations. Scientific analysis and professional charts help planners open arteries, revitalize the heart of the city, and remove sites of abnormal growth. See M. Christine Boyer, *The City of Collective Memory: Its Historical Imagery and Architectural Entertainments* (Cambridge, Mass.: MIT Press, 1994), 17–18.

85. See Jane Jacobs, *The Death and Life of Great American Cities* (New York: Random House, 1961); Smithson, *Team 10 Primer.* For the history of the tension between architecture and urban planning, see David Gosling and Barry Maitland, *Concepts of Urban Design* (London: St. Martin's Press, 1984).

86. For the conference proceedings, see "Urban Design," *Progressive Architecture,* August 1956, 97–112. At this conference, interdisciplinarity was defined as a collaboration between architects, urban planners, and landscape architects, a concept that was later expanded to include other professions dealing with the built environment.

87. Paul Rudolph, "Alumni Day Speech: Yale School of Architecture" (1958), reprinted in *Oppositions* 4 (1974): 143.

88. For the GSD trajectory of urban design, see *The Origins and Evolution of "Urban Design," 1956–2006,* special issue, *Harvard Design Magazine* 24 (2006). See also Gosling and Maitland, *Concepts of Urban Design*; and Anthony Alofsin, *The Struggle for Modernism: Architecture, Landscape Architecture, and City Planning at Harvard* (New York: W. W. Norton, 2002).

89. Kevin Lynch, "The Form of Cities," *Scientific American* 190 (1954): 54–63.

90. Denys Lasdun, "An Architect's Approach to Architecture," *RIBA Journal* 72, no. 4 (1965): 190.

91. Moshe Safdie, Rudy Barton, and Uri Shetrit, *The Harvard Jerusalem Studio: Urban Designs for the Holy City* (Cambridge, Mass.: MIT Press, 1986), 16.

92. Gosling and Maitland, *Concepts of Urban Design,* 7.

93. Moshe Safdie, *The Harvard Jerusalem Studio: Urban Designs for the Holy City* (Cambridge, Mass.: MIT Press, 1986), 13.

94. See 18 C/RESOLUTION in UNESCO report: http://unesdoc.unesco.org/images /0002/000228/022874eb.pdf.

95. Lichfield, "Planning for the Spirit," 11–12.

96. Jerusalem Committee, *Proceedings of the Third Plenary Session.*

97. Ibid., December 18, 1975, 54. Ballén was the mayor of Quito (1970–78) and the president of Ecuador (1992–96). His position in the meeting is characteristic of a politician and leader from the developing world.

98. Ibid., 12, my emphasis, based on the tone of a similar discussion during a Benvenisti interview with the author, June 6, 2000.

99. Ibid., 20–21.

100. The demand for such a model appeared in the resolution of the 1973 and 1975 plenary meetings, and the result is the Jerusalem Model that is now installed in the municipality in order to test every new project.

101. Lawrence Halprin, "The Use and Misuse of Plans," *Design and Environment* 6, no. 3 (1975): 45.

102. Bakema stated in the proceedings: "You need to know how the in between has to be . . . you can only discuss the connectors if the pieces of the mosaic can be seen in a total model. And a total model is not only a superficial thing, it is also the appearance to make clear the social backgrounds, of what should be for what, when this neighborhood comes to life now. Because you have now the neighborhoods and in the neighborhoods are people . . . how do you prepare them so that these neighborhoods can make clear how their lives can be developed over time?" Jerusalem Committee, *Proceedings of the Third Plenary Meeting,* 28–29.

103. Lasdum in Jerusalem Committee, *Proceedings of the Third Plenary Meeting,* 39.

104. Ibid.

105. Larry Halprin to Teddy Kollek, December 27, 1975, Jerusalem, in Halprin Sketchbooks, Architectural Archives, University of Pennsylvania, Lawrence Halprin Collection.

106. Amnon Niv, lecture in the "Architecture and Politics" conference of the Israel United Architect annual conference, 2005.

107. Dumper, *Politics of Jerusalem since 1967,* 103.

108. Similar title was given to a lectures series at MIT, "Cities against Nationalism: Urbanism as Visionary Politics"; the collected papers were published as Diane Davis and Nora Libertun de Duren, eds., *Cities and Sovereignty* (Bloomington: Indiana University Press, 2011).

109. Mumford to Kollek, "Memorandum on the Plan for Jerusalem," 2.

110. Ibid., 6.

111. Ibid., 4.

112. Ibid., 5.

113. Ibid., 8.

114. See Alona Nitzan-Shiftan, "Contested Zionism—Alternative Modernism: Erich Mendelshon and the Tel Aviv Chug in Mandate Palestine," *Architectural History* 39 (1996): 147–80.

115. For possessive nationalism, see Richard Handler, "'Having a Culture': The Preservation of Quebec's Patrimoine," in *Nationalism and the Politics of Culture in Quebec* (Madison: University of Wisconsin Press, 1988), 152–58.

116. Ulrik Plesner, Chief Architect, City of Jerusalem, to Monica Pidgeon, Editor of *Architectural Design* magazine, in response to the letter Arthur Kutcher circulated to the Jerusalem Committee's architecture and town-planning members, October 19, 1976, Architectural Archives, University of Pennsylvania, Louis Kahn Collection. Ulrik Plesner graduated from the Royal Academy Architecture School in Copenhagen, Denmark, and established an office in Sri Lanka with Geoffrey Bawa. Together they designed schools, private houses, hotels—as well as large-scale projects for the World Bank. Returning to Europe, Plesner worked as a group leader in Ove Arup. Eventually, he moved to Israel in 1972 and started his own firm; during this period he was also Jerusalem's city architect from 1974 to 1976.

117. Teddy Kollek, interview with the author, Jerusalem, March 24, 2000.

118. Mumford to Kollek, "Memorandum on the Plan for Jerusalem," 5.

119. Ibid., 7.

120. Ibid.

121. Dr. George Appleton, Anglican Archbishop, in "Jerusalem and the Middle East," in Jerusalem Committee, *Proceedings of the Second Plenary Session, June 18–21, 1973* (Jerusalem: The Committee, 1973), 26.

6. Project

1. See Teddy Kollek and Amos Kollek, *One Jerusalem* [in Hebrew] (Tel Aviv: Mariv Library Publishers, 1979), 212–23; Uzi Benziman, *Jerusalem: A City without a Wall* [in Hebrew] (Tel Aviv: Schocken, 1973), 3, 7–44, 155–71; and Meron Benvenisti, "The Western Wall and the Jewish Quarter," in *Jerusalem: The Torn City* (Minneapolis: University of Minnesota Press, 1976), 305–22.

2. Sharon's original sketched map, signed on June 10, 1967, is reproduced in Benziman, *Jerusalem,* 39.

3. Yehudah Ha'ezrahi and Shelomoh Rozner, *A New Chapter in the History of the Western Wall* [in Hebrew] (Jerusalem: Ministry of Religious Affairs, 1972), unpaginated.

4. Nadav Shragai, "The Spirit of Safdie Hovers over the Western Wall," *Ha'aretz,* September 15, 1985, 13.

5. "Whoever Changes Gets the Lower Hand," *Hamodi'a,* June 29, 2001.

6. For a comprehensive bibliography of the Western Wall, see Ruth P. Goldschmit-Lahmanen, "Bibliography: The Western Wall," in *Jerusalem: From "Shivat Zion" to the Expansion out of the City Walls* (Jerusalem: Yad Itzhak Ben Zvi, 1980), 269–82.

7. For the Muslim perspective, see Abdul Latif Tibawi, *Jerusalem: Its Place in Islam and Arab History* (Beirut: Institute for Palestine Studies, 1969).

8. Daniel Bertrand Monk, *An Aesthetic Occupation: The Immediacy of Architecture and the Palestine Conflict* (Durham, N.C.: Duke University Press, 2002).

9. Yitzhak Rabin on the occasion of receiving an honorary doctorate from the Hebrew University during a ceremony on the Mount Scopus Campus immediately after the 1967 war, June 28, 1967. See http://zionism-israel.com/hdoc/Rabin_Doctorate_Acceptance.htm.

10. Yoseph Schonenberg et al., *Planning Research for the Western Wall Precinct* (Jerusalem: Ministry of Religious Affairs, 1972), unpaginated.

11. Ariel Hirschfeld, *Essays on Place* [in Hebrew] (Tel Aviv: Am oved, 2000), 13–20.

12. Benvenisti, *Jerusalem* (1976).

13. Charles S. Liebman and Eliezer Don-Yehya, *Civil Religion in Israel: Traditional Judaism and Political Culture in the Jewish State* (Berkeley: University of California Press, 1983).

14. Meron Benvenisti, *Jerusalem: The Torn City* [in Hebrew] (Jerusalem: Weidenfeld and Nicolson, 1973), 256. Mazar started digging on February 28, 1968.

15. Benziman, *Jerusalem,* 38.

16. On June 7, following the conquest of the Old City, Eshkol promised that sacred sites of the different religions will be managed by their own authorities. The most sacred Jewish site was allocated to the Ministry of Religious Affairs. See Benziman, *Jerusalem,* 155–71; Benvenisti, *Jerusalem* (1973), 119–208.

17. The team included Kutcher and Aronson and consultants Yoseph Schweid, Michael Turner, Ehud Menchel, and supervisor Schonenberg. See Schonenberg et al., *Planning Research for the Western Wall Precinct.*

18. Moshe Safdie, *Beyond Habitat* (Montreal: Tundra Books; Toronto: Collins Publishers, 1973), 59.

19. Ibid., 145.

20. Ibid., 155.

21. Bernard Rudofsky, *Architecture without Architects: A Short Introduction to Nonpedigreed Architecture* (New York: Museum of Modern Art, 1964).

22. Stanford Anderson, "Memory without Monuments: Vernacular Architecture," *Traditional Dwellings and Settlements Review* 11, no. 1 (1999): 13–22.

23. Safdie, *Beyond Habitat,* 169.

24. Ibid., 169, emphasis mine.

25. Ibid., 148.

26. Ibid., 149.

27. Ibid., 148.

28. Ibid., 155. In their discussion Alexander and Safdie found an affinity between Alexander's term "patterns" and Safdie's term "structures." Safdie quotes particularly from Alexander's book *Notes on a Synthesis of Form* (Cambridge, Mass.: Harvard University Press, 1964), where Alexander defines patterns as "a system of generating principles, which can be richly transformed according to local circumstances but which never fail to convey their essentials." See Safdie, *Beyond Habitat,* 155.

29. Safdie, *Beyond Habitat,* 165.

30. Ibid., 164–65.

31. Ibid., 166.

32. See, for example, Rachel Kallus and Hubert Law Yone, "National Home/Personal Home: Public Housing and the Shaping of National Space in Israel," *European Planning Studies* 10, no. 6 (2002): 765–79. Yael Allweil, *Homeland: Zionism as Housing Regime, 1860–2011* (London: Routledge, 2016).

33. Safdie, *Beyond Habitat,* 151.

34. See ibid.

35. Ibid., 216.

36. Moshe Safdie, *Jerusalem: The Future of the Past* (Boston: Houghton Mifflin, 1989), 28.

37. Ibid., 115.

38. Safdie's design removed the bridge ramp to the Mughrabee Gate, thus connecting the traditionally exposed section of the Wall with the southern segment that was dug by the commission. The two were combined into this long stretch.

39. Yitzhak Leibland, interview with the author, November 8, 2011.

40. Quoted in Bernard Leupen et al., *Design and Analysis* (Rotterdam: 010 publishers, 1997), 120.

41. See "space frame," *The Free Dictionary,* http://encyclopedia2.thefreedictionary.com/space+frame.

42. Safdie's sketchbook, January 4, 1972, Safdie Architects Archive.

43. Safdie, *Beyond Habitat,* 146. Safdie refers to D'Arcy Wentworth Thompson, *On Growth and Form,* abridged ed. (Cambridge: Cambridge University Press, 1961).

44. Thompson, *On Growth and Form,* 179. This quote was highlighted in Safdie's original copy of Thompson's book: Moshe Safdie, interview with the author, Montreal, March 24, 2008.

45. See the Shimron Committee Proceedings, Sharon's Office Archive, Box 737. The Sharon collection was later moved to the Azrieli Architecture Archive at the Tel Aviv Museum.

46. Ibid.

47. The Jerusalem Committee, *Proceedings of the Second Plenary Session, June 18–21, 1973* (Jerusalem: The Committee, 1973), 69.

48. Ibid., 70.

49. For a virtual reconstruction of the different phases of the Hurva design, see Kent Larson and Louis I. Kahn, *Louis I. Kahn: Unbuilt Masterworks* (New York: Monacelli Press, 2000). For a scholarly study of it, see Yasir Mohammed Sakr, "The Subversive Utopia: Louis Kahn and the Question of the National Jewish Style in Jerusalem (Israel)" (PhD diss., University of Pennsylvania, 1996).

50. Ram Karmi, "'The Hurva': A Story with No End" [in Hebrew], *Studio* 91 (1998): 66–69.

51. Sakr, "The Subversive Utopia."

52. The Jerusalem Committee, *Proceedings of the Second Plenary Session,* 70.

53. The description is based on Schonenberg et al., *Planning Research for the Western Wall Precinct* (unpaginated) as well as on Shlomo Aronson's report to the Shimron Committee. Aronson said that Noguchi worked in his office, and he therefore had firsthand knowledge of his project, which influenced him greatly. Consequently, he preferred looking first for a conceptual direction rather than concrete, final design. See Shimron Committee, *Proceedings of the Shimron Committee,* February 10, 1975, particularly 39, 49, and 57, the Sharon Archive.

54. This interpretation related to its construction as a memorial for the Jewish people.

55. Safdie, *Jerusalem,* 135–36.

56. I have not encountered any evidence that attributed to Noguchi any of the interpretations that I have mentioned above (besides the metaphor of Jewish endurance throughout the ages). The archeologist Meir Ben-Dov, who worked closely with Moshe Safdie and actively supported his design, reported in his book on the Western Wall that Noguchi intended to memorialize the Holocaust in this prime site of Jewish revival. See M. Ben-Dov et al., *The Western Wall* [in Hebrew], Mahad, 2nd ed. (Tel Aviv: Ministry of Defense, 1981), 172–74.

57. Teddy Kollek in the *Proceedings of the Shimron Committee,* September 3, 1975, 65.

58. Letter from Yosheph Schonenberg to Moshe Safdie, June 24, 1973, Jerusalem Archive.

59. Kollek wrote to Schonenberg on June 28, 1973: "Regardless of what plan would eventually be implemented on site, it is clear to us that international criticism is expected, along with arguments in the Security Council and so forth. Therefore, I thought that if we succeed in gaining support for the plan in this forum [i.e., the Jerusalem Committee], it might help us in all future arguments. I am convinced that all parties related to the plaza issue would be as interested in it as I am." Safdie had written Schonenberg a day earlier, portraying the presentation as a last-minute decision and lamenting the presence of journalists of which, he wrote, he did not know in advance. Jerusalem Archive.

60. A letter from Zerakh Verhaftig, Minister of Religious Affairs, to Teddy Kollek, June 28, 1973, copied to the minister of justice, the head of the Ministerial Committee for Jerusalem Affairs, private archive of David Cassuto. Verhaftig refused to accept a plan that was prepared without his architectural consultant. The agreement between the Jerusalem

mayor, the minister of religious affairs, and the JQDC was based on meetings on August 10, 1971, and May 15, 1972. It was accepted by all parties but was never signed in full. The agreement joined Safdie and Schonenberg as planners for the precinct and indicated that no plan could be presented in public before all parties had approved it.

61. Teddy Kollek, "Advancing the Planning and Construction of the Western Wall Plaza," Jerusalem, August 22, 1974, Israel State Archive, A/7341/3.

62. The appointment was made by the Ministerial Committee for Jerusalem Affairs, headed by the minister of justice, Haim Tzadok. The committee was headed by Erwin Shimron, a lawyer, and consisted of the following voting architect members: Meron Benvenisti, the deputy mayor for Jerusalem planning, representing the Jerusalem Municipality; the archeologist Meir Ben-Dov, who participated in excavations with Professor Mazar at the southern part of the Wall, representing the Archeological Commission; architect David Cassuto, the architectural consultant to the minister of religious affairs, representing that ministry; and architects Arieh Sharon, Avraham Yaski, and Yaakov Rechter, representing the Israel Association of Engineers and Architects. Yehuda Tamir, the former head of the JQDC, was a permanent observer, and David Tzifroni was the administrator.

63. The program was part of the weekly news *(yoman)*, featured on Friday night prime-time television. In it, Safdie explained his project with the aid of his impressive model. The program also featured Minister of Justice Haim Tzadok, who commissioned the committee, and supporters and critics of the project. The favorable coverage did not obscure the bitter controversy surrounding the project. See Ester Dar, "The Western Wall Plaza," in *Yoman Hashavuah,* 1974, Israeli Television Archive, Jerusalem.

64. Ram Karmi in "The Design of the Western Wall Plaza and Its Surroundings: An Open Debate" [in Hebrew], in *The Western Wall: A Collection of Essays Concerning the Design of the Western Wall Plaza and Its Surroundings,* ed. David Cassuto (Jerusalem: Jerusalem Post Press, 1975), 95.

65. Michael Turner in "The Design of the Western Wall Plaza and Its Surroundings," 104.

66. For examples of instances in which history has been essentialized to serve national purposes, see, for Greece, Michael Herzfeld, *A Place in History: Social and Monumental Time in a Cretan Town* (Princeton, N.J.: Princeton University Press, 1991); for Italy, Henry Millon, "The Role of History of Architecture in Fascist Italy," *American Society of Architectural Historians* 24, no. 1 (1965): 53–59; and Peter Gathercole and David Lowenthal, *The Politics of the Past* (London: Routledge, 1994).

67. David Cassuto, interview with the author, Jerusalem, November 21, 1996 (when he was the deputy mayor of Ehud Ulmart).

68. Letter from Mordechai Shoshani, Head Architect of the Department of Public Works, to David Glass, General Manager of the Ministry of Religious Affairs, April 20, 1975, private archive of David Cassuto.

69. Ibid.

70. The Shimron Committee was assigned to review Safdie's project during a short period in which the religious party was not part of the coalition. At that unusual occasion, the minister of justice was also the minister of religious affairs, a ministry that is the stronghold of the Mafdal (the Zionist religious party). The religious community thought that the Labor movement exploited this window of opportunity to compose a committee that would stress secular national values, in which archeology had a privileged status (see above). From comments made throughout the committee's deliberation, it is clear how incompatible the views of the archeologist Meir Ben-Dov and the representative of the minister of religious affairs, David Cassuto, were. Small details inflamed arguments, often petty, between the two. In the committee's final statements, Cassuto wrote the single minority opinion objecting to the project.

71. See Shimron's answer to the question of who chose the appointed members. *Proceedings of the Shimron Committee,* July 8, 1975. The head of the Israel Association of Engineers and Architects was Elhanan Peles.

72. Alona Nitzan-Shiftan, "Israelizing Jerusalem: The Encounter between Architectural and National Ideologies, 1967–1977" (PhD diss., MIT, 2002), ch. 5.

73. Reznik had a special status: a Jerusalemite and a Zionist immigrant from Brazil, he took part in the formation of the Tel Aviv sabra circles in the 1950s. He apprenticed with Zeev Rechter (whose son, Yaakov Rechter, was a member of the Shimron Committee) from whose practice many architects of the sabra generation entered into the profession. Reznik's own firm became a hub for a younger generation of Jerusalemite architects who were drawn to Jerusalem after the 1967 war. He began his testimony in front of the Shimron Committee with a protest against the reversal of his appointment as a committee member, which he took as a sign of the partiality of this committee.

74. Professor Shmuel Safrai, *Proceedings of the Shimron Committee,* September 3, 1975, 2.

75. Letter from Gidon Yeger and Izhak Blat to Erwin Shimron, Sharon Archive. The letter followed the testimony of Gidon Yeger, the head of the Jerusalem branch of the Association of Architects, in front of the Shimron Committee. It further articulated the same position, emphasizing that it "justly represents the majority of our members."

76. Arieh Sharon in *Proceedings of the Shimron Committee,* July 8, 1975, D 11.

77. Yaski, ibid., July 8, 1975, D 7.

78. Yeger, ibid., July 8, 1975, D 8.

79. Yaski and Cassuto, ibid., D 12.

80. This was the Conception Committee that was headed by Cassuto, the architectural consultant to the minister of religious affairs. It consisted of the Rabbis Tzimerman, Israeli, Druk, and Edri; Professors S. Safrai and David Flusser, who specialized in Jewish history and thought; the archeologist and professor Trude Dothan; and architects David Reznik and Yisha'ayahu Ilan (both of whom appeared in the proceedings as professors). Cassuto's membership in the Shimron Committee was interpreted by Avraham Yaski as a conflict of interest and was the reason he resigned from the Shimron Committee halfway through. Cassuto, for his part, insisted that the Conception Committee did not undermine the Shimron Committee. Its mandate, he said, was to help the minister of religious affairs decide whether the project accorded with Jewish law and thought.

81. *Interim Report of the Conception Committee,* Ministry of Religious Affairs, March 8, 1976, private archive of David Cassuto.

82. Safdie met Rabbi Ovadia Yoseph and the Chief Rabbinical Council during the period in which the committee's work was halted in the absence of collaboration from religious authorities. He sent a report of the meeting to the authorities involved on August 30, 1976. In *Jerusalem: The Future of the Past,* he explains the dynamics of the encounter with the rabbi, who became a central figure in Israeli culture and politics in the 1990s. See Safdie, "The Council of the Torah Sages," in *Jerusalem,* 183–94.

83. See the Shimron Committee Proceedings, Sharon Archive, Box 737, n. 3.

84. For the differences between the 1970s and 1990s battles over the Wall, see Alona Nitzan-Shiftan, "'Yesh Avanim im lev adam': On Monuments, Modernism, and Conservation in the Western Wall" [in Hebrew], *Teoria ve-Bikoret* 38–39 (2011): 65–100.

85. Autobiographical notes by Safdie in *Beyond Habitat,* 50.

86. Moshe Safdie, "Prof. Zeev Naveh, Moshe Safdie, Prof Yeshaihu Leibovitz, Dan Ben-Amoz, and Nisim Alony Discussed Architecture with Adina Koren, Amos Gitai and Bemi Fishbein" [in Hebrew], *Alef Alef* 11 (October 1975): 16.

87. Ram Karmi, letter to the Supreme Council for Architecture and Town Planning, August 1, 1973, Jerusalem Archive. Safdie, who got the letter as a council member, quickly delivered it to Yehuda Tamir, Roni Gloskinos, and Teddy Kollek. Yaakov Rechter, a future

member of the Shimron Committee, adopted Karmi's opinion (letter to the Council, August 13, 1973, Jerusalem Archive), followed by Aba Elhanani (letter to the Council, August 16, 1973, Jerusalem Archive).

88. Safdie, interview.

89. For example, David Kroyanker, a graduate of the Architectural Association in London, started his career as the chronicler of Jerusalem's architecture with the municipal reports he prepared for the Jerusalem Committee.

90. Teddy Kollek, "Advancing the Planning and Construction of the Western Wall Plaza," Jerusalem, August 22, 1974, Israel State Archive, A/7341/3.

91. "The Kotel," words: Yossi Gamzu, music: Dubi Zeltzer.

92. Safdie, *Beyond Habitat,* 143.

93. Ibid., 147.

94. *Interim Report of the Conception Committee,* private archive of David Cassuto.

95. Safdie, *Jerusalem,* 217.

96. Ibid., 218.

97. Ibid., 220.

Conclusion

1. For the full version of the law, see Basic Law: Jerusalem, Capital of Israel, https://www.knesset.gov.il/laws/special/eng/basic10_eng.htm.

2. Uri Ram, "The State of the Nation: Contemporary Challenges to Zionism in Israel," *Constellations* 6, no. 3 (1999): 325–38. For a compressive elaboration of this thesis, see Uri Ram, *The Globalization of Israel: McWorld in Tel Aviv, Jihad in Jerusalem* (London: Routledge, 2008).

3. Michael Feige, *One Space, Two Places: Gush Emunim, Peace Now and the Construction of Israeli Place* [in Hebrew], Sifriyat Eshkolot (Jerusalem: Hebrew University Magnes Press, 2003). For a detailed elaboration on Gush Emunim, see Michael Feige, *Settling in the Hearts: Jewish Fundamentalism in the Occupied Territories* (Detroit: Wayne State University Press, 2009).

4. Liah Greenfeld, *Nationalism: Five Roads to Modernity* (Cambridge, Mass.: Harvard University Press, 1993), 10.

5. Chantal Mouffe, *Dimensions of Radical Democracy: Pluralism, Citizenship, Community* (London: Verso, 1992), 226.

6. Teddy Kollek, *Sacred City of Mankind: A History of Forty Centuries* [in Hebrew] (Jerusalem: Steimatzky, 1985).

7. Mouffe, *Dimensions of Radical Democracy,* 226.

8. For architecture that is geared toward the goals of a welfare state, see Mark Swenarton, Tom Avermaete, and Dirk van den Heuvel, eds., *Architecture and the Welfare State* (London: Routledge, 2015).

9. For Israel as a settler society, see Lorenzo Veracini, *Israel and Settler Society* (London: Pluto Press, 2004); and for a more general definition of the concept, see Lorenzo Veracini, "Introducing Settler Colonial Studies," *Settler Colonial Studies* 1, no. 1 (2011): 1–12.

10. On the notion of housing in Israeli culture, see Rachel Kallus and Hubert Law Yone, "National Home/Personal Home: Public Housing and the Shaping of National Space in Israel," *European Planning Studies* 10, no. 6 (2002): 765–79; Yael Allweil, *Homeland: Zionism as Housing Regime, 1860–2011* (London: Routledge, 2016). For the history of the Ministry of Housing, see Hadas Shadar, *The Building Stone of the Public Housing: Six Decades of Urban Building of Public Initiative in Israel* [in Hebrew] (Jerusalem: Ministry of Housing, 2014).

11. See, for example, in Hadas Shadar, *Sunstrike: Brutalist Building in Beer Sheva, a Reconsideration of Mamlachti Architecture* [in Hebrew] (Jerusalem: Yad Ben Zvi, 2016).

12. For a fuller critique of this historiographical dichotomy, see Alona Nitzan-Shiftan,

"On Concrete and Stone: Shifts and Conflicts in Israeli Architecture," *Traditional Dwellings and Settlements Review* 21, no. 1 (2009): 51–65.

13. For figures on this demographic trend (analyzed from a typical Israeli vantage point), see Ori Shtendal, "Changes in the Palestinian Population" [in Hebrew], in *Twenty Years in Jerusalem, 1967–1987,* ed. Yehoshua Prawer and Ora Ahimeir (Tel Aviv: Ministry of Defense, 1988), 95–120.

14. In 1997, during the first conference in which Israeli planners refused to enlist their own professional labor to prepare a plan for "green areas" that they deemed unnecessary and politically motivated, Elinoar Barzaki, the former head of the Jerusalem Division in the Ministry of Housing and former city engineer of Jerusalem, asked the audience to acknowledge this prevalent practice.

15. For background on the Israeli demolition policy, see Nathan Marom and BIMKOM, *The Planning Deadlock—Planning Policy, Land Regularization, Building Permits and House Demolitions in East Jerusalem* (Jerusalem: BIMKOM, 2004).

16. Sharon Rotbard, *Avraham Yaski, Concrete Architecture* [in Hebrew] (Tel Aviv: Bavel, 2007), 721.

17. Zvi Efrat, *The Israeli Project: Building and Architecture, 1948–1973,* vol. 2 (Tel Aviv: Tel Aviv Art Museum, 2004), 936; quoted in Rotbard, *Avraham Yaski,* 719.

18. Charles Jencks, *The Language of Post-Modern Architecture* (London: Academy Editions, 1977), 24.

19. For a useful introduction to the neoliberalization of the Israeli welfare state and the rise of the public-service NGOs, see Joseph Katan and Ariela Lowenstein, "Privatization Trends in Welfare Services and Their Impact upon Israel as a Welfare State," in *The Welfare State in Post-Industrial Society* (New York: Springer, 2009), 311–32.

20. Teddy Kollek, interview with the author, Jerusalem, March 24, 2000.

21. For the UNESCO documentation regarding the "Old City of Jerusalem and Its Walls" listing, see http://whc.unesco.org/en/list/148/documents. For the minutes of the 1981 vote, see Report of the First Extraordinary Session of the World Heritage Committee, http://whc.unesco.org/archive/repext81.htm.

22. Seven of the twenty voting delegates at the 1981 meeting were members from Egypt, Iraq, Jordan, Libyan Arab Jamahiriya, Pakistan, and Tunisia.

23. UNESCO, Proceedings of World Heritage Committee, December 1982, 10, http://unesdoc.unesco.org/images/0005/000546/054656eb.pdf.

24. For the award winning website of the City of David see http://www.cityofdavid.org.il/en. For the urban analysis of the site, see Wendy Pullan and Maximilian Gwiazda, "'City of David': Urban Design and Frontier Heritage," *Jerusalem Quarterly* 39, no. 2 (2009); for archeological critique, see the site of the NGO Emek Shaveh: http://alt-arch.org/en/.

25. Oren Yiftachel and Haim Yacobi, "Planning a Bi-National Capital: Should Jerusalem Remain United?" *Geoforum* 33 (2002): 137–45; Jonathan Rokem, ed., "Special Feature: Learning from Jerusalem: Rethinking Urban Conflicts in the 21st Century," *City* 20, no. 3 (2016).

26. For assessments of Jerusalem's contemporary geopolitics, see Michael Dumper, *Jerusalem Unbound: Geography, History, and the Future of the Holy City* (New York: Columbia University Press, 2014); Wendy Pullan et al., *The Struggle for Jerusalem's Holy Places: Radicalisation and Conflict* (London: Routledge, 2013); Haim Yacobi, "Jerusalem: From a 'Divided' to a 'Contested' City—and Next to a Neo-apartheid City? Review Article," *City* 19 (2015): 579–84; Philipp Misselwitz and Tim Rieniets, eds., *City of Collision: Jerusalem and the Principles of Conflict Urbanism* (Berlin: Walter de Gruyter, 2006); Eyal Weizman, *Hollow Land: Israel's Architecture of Occupation* (London: New Left Books, 2007).

27. For an architectural, ethnographic, and philosophical analysis of the settlers NGOs' activity in East Jerusalem, see Yehotal Shapira, "Non-Structural Knowledge and Practice:

Architectural Testimony in East Jerusalem" (PhD diss., Technion – Israel Institute of Technology, 2016).

28. See Chantal Mouffe, *Agonistics: Thinking the World Politically* (London: Verso Books, 2013). For her encounters with the disciplines of architecture and planning, see Chantal Mouffe, "Democratic Politics and Agonistic Public Spaces," https://www.youtube.com /watch?v=4Wpwwc25JRU; "The Architecture Exchange—How Is Architecture Political? Mouffe in Conversation with Aureli, Martin, Weizman and Whiting," December 2014, http:// www.aaschool.ac.uk/VIDEO/lecture.php?ID=2702.

INDEX

Alona Nitzan-Shiftan is associate professor at the Technion, Israel Institute of Technology.